BESSARABIA
DISPUTED LAND BETWEEN EAST AND WEST

Coperta de VASILE OLAC

© Copyright 1985 by George Ciorănescu – Munich

Editura Fundaţiei Culturale Române
Aleea Alexandru nr. 38
Sector 1, Bucureşti 71273
România

ISBN 973–9155–17–0

GEORGE CIORĂNESCU

BESSARABIA

DISPUTED LAND BETWEEN EAST AND WEST

EDITURA FUNDAȚIEI CULTURALE ROMÂNE
Bucureşti, 1993

The British Empire, France, Italy, Japan, principal Allied Powers, and Romania:

Considering that in the interest of general European peace it is of importance to ensure from now on over Bessarabia a sovereignty corresponding to the aspirations of the inhabitants, and guaranteeing to the racial, religious and linguistic minorities there, the protection which is due them;

Considering that from the geographical, ethnographic, historic and economic viewpoints, the union of Bessarabia to Roumania is fully justified;

Considering that the inhabitants of Bessarabia have manifested their desire to see Bessarabia united to Roumania;

Considering finally that Roumania has expressed of her own free will the desire to give sure guarantees of liberty and justice, without distinction of race, religion or language, in conformity with the Treaty signed at Paris, December 9, 1919, to the inhabitants of the former kingdom of Roumania, as well as to those of the territories newly transferred;

Have resolved to conclude the present treaty...:

Article 1. The High Contracting Parties declare that they recognize the sovereignty of Roumania over the territory of Bessarabia, comprised within the present Roumanian frontier, the Black Sea, the course of the Dniester from its mouth to the point where it is cut by the former line between the Bucovina and Bessarabia, and this former line.

Excerpt from the Treaty of Paris of October 28, 1920.

CONTENTS

A Word of Explanation 9

I. A polemicist Rewrites the History of Moldavia 14

II. The Origin of the Bessarabian Problem: the Diplomatic Talks Regarding Moldavia, Bessarabia and Wallachia (1805-1812) 22

III. Romanian Historians on Russo-Romanian Relations 34

IV. Moldavian and Western Interpretations of Modern Romanian History 40

V. Romanian-Russian Co-operation in the Context of the Independence Centenary 52

VI. Bessarabia again on the Tapis 73

VII. Romanian-Russian Relations during World War I 82

VIII. Octavian Goga's Views on the Russian Revolution and Bessarabia 94

IX. Bessarabia's Place in Nicolae Titulescu's Foreign Policy 100

X. 40th Anniversary of Annexation of Bessarabia and Northern Bucovina 108

XI.	The Problem of Bessarabia and Northern Bucovina during World War II	127
XII.	Romania's 35th Anniversary of 23 August 1944: The Role of National Forces and Soviet Army in Romania's "Liberation War"	181
XIII.	The Policy of Russification	196
XIV.	The New Constitution of the Moldavian Soviet Socialist Republic	238
XV.	Walew's Plan Raised Again the Bessarabian Issue	246
XVI.	A Political Shifting of One's Ground	255

A WORD OF EXPLANATION

This volume comprises 16 articles, which, with the exception of the one entitled: "The Origin of the Bessarabian Problem, " were published in various periodicals or in the context of collective works between the years 1965 and 1982. Most of the articles appeared as a spontaneous reaction to certain Soviet historians' interpretations distorting the history of the Romanian people with the view of facilitating, in this way, the achievement of some Soviet political objectives, headed by the expansion of the Soviet Empire toward South-Eastern Europe. Such is the case, for instance, with the article written in answer to historian A.M. Lazarev's assertion of the existence of a Moldavian nation, as distinct from the Romanian nation. Or with the commentary addressed to Professor L.B. Walew, who suggests a new division of Romania. Or with the critical examination of the self-serving affirmations of some Soviet historians regarding Romanian–Russian–Turkish war of 1877 and the first and second world wars, when, as ally or enemy, Moscow always aimed at the dismantling of the unitary Romanian state and the annexation of Romanian territories in its expansion toward the Straits, the warm--water seas, and the Middle East.

The above-mentioned articles were not written from a purely polemical position, nor were they written as a reply in an academic dispute whose objective is the historical truth and nothing more. The author aimed implicitly at provoking thoughts regarding the global political objectives of the Soviet Union, which are identical with the aims pursued in the smaller sector of the contacts between the Romanians and the Russians. These aims are called "expansion through the conquest of neighboring nations."

The studies comprised in this volume are not designed to repeat known facts. They try to throw a new light upon certain less known aspects of the Bessarabian problem. Thus, while it is generally considered that the Bessarabian problem begins with the year 1812, when the province was annexed by Russia by means of the Treaty of Bucharest, this book endeavors to go further into the past, demon-

strating that, in fact, this problem had its origins in the beginning of the last century, when the two great European autocrats, Emperor Napoleon I and Tzar Alexander I, indulged in all sorts of projects for the division of the world. In certain instructions sent to French ambassadors at St. Petersburg, as well as in the letters of the latter to Napoleon, we find many signs pointing to bargaining over the regions which the emperor of France and the tzar of Russia claimed from, or offered, each other, without wasting any thought over the wishes of the populations whose destinies were involved. In the end, Bessarabia fell victim to this bargaining, which originally included – through the secret treaty of Erfurt (1808) – the cession not only of the territory between the Pruth and Dniester Rivers, but of the whole of Moldavia and of the territory of Wallachia.

Other information regarding the way in which the Bessarabian problem was raised and temporarily solved in our own days comes to us from the collections of documents on international relations before and during the second world war, published recently in the United States, Great Britain, and the Federal Republic of Germany. In the light of these documents, we can better understand the drama of the Soviet ultimatum to Romania in the summer of 1940, when Bessarabia was again snatched from Romania, this time with the Herţa region and with Northern Bucovina, which had never belonged to Russia. The secret Treaty of Erfurt (1808), which ceded the Romanian Principalities to Russia, is paralleled by the secret protocol of the Soviet-German nonaggression treaty of August 23, 1939 which, in Article 3, left Bessarabia within the Soviet sphere.

The same newly published documents help us understand the unsuccessful, though tenacious, attempts made during the last world war by Marshal Ion Antonescu and by the leader of the democratic opposition, Iuliu Maniu, to keep Bessarabia and Northern Bucovina within the borders of postwar Romania.

Despite the fact that there were fundamental differences of opinion between the two political figures, regarding the type of order to be installed in Romania, as well as the system of alliances which the country was to belong to (Antonescu, as head of state, imposed an authoritarian system and the adherence to the Tripartite Pact, while Maniu favored a Western-type democracy and alliance with the great Western democracies) the two men met on common ground as regards the Bessarabian problem, aiming to save the province from renewed Soviet annexation.

The process of Russification and Sovietization of Romanian Bessarabia, which became, in the context of the USSR, " The Soviet Socialist Republic of Moldavia," is also described in the present volume, which lists all the methods – classical and modern – employed for the purpose of denationalizing the Romanians. These, after being "promoted" to the "autonomous Moldavian Nation," are now earmarked for amalgamation with the Russian masses.

Particularly tragic are, in this respect, the deportations which took thousands upon thousands of Moldavian-Romanians from their homes in order to transplant them to the remote, bare, inhospitable lands of the immense Soviet Empire, as well as the colonization of populations like the Chuvaks, Bashkirs, and other Turkmens, transplanted from the Upper Volga, Urals, etc., to Bessarabia, with the aim of giving this province as Asian an aspect as possible. Finally, the articles in this book also touch upon a more recent, though not well-known problem: the reappearance, in a new way, on an international level, of the Bessarabian question.

In principle, Communist Romania has no legal foundations for raising the problem of Bessarabia, because it recognized the retrocession of the province in the Treaty of Paris (1947). Nor does it have moral arguments, since the Romanian Socialist Republic is, in fact, a creation of the USSR, without whose support it would never have appeared upon the map of Europe. In fact, however, Romanian historians have found certain subtle ways in which to bring up the various aspects of the Romanian-Russian dispute for public discussion and implicitly the problem of Bessarabia.

It goes without saying that these activities of Romanian historians, of the old, but also of the "new" schools, who even invoked Karl Marx in order to prove Romanian rights to Bessarabia, attracted the anger of their Soviet colleagues, beginning with A.M Lazarev. Reading through and trying to decipher the Romanian-Russian polemics over Bessarabia — we include here Northern Bucovina — is interesting and encouraging, for it brings proof that national sentiment supersedes the obligation to serve proletarian internationalist solidarity, even in a state with a communist regime.

Although the articles in this volume are not interconnected, they are somehow brought together by the undeniable existence of Romanian-Russian-Soviet litigation which has not been solved and has not even been alleviated since the settling of the Russians on the Dniester by the Treaty of Iaşi of 1792. To this permanent factor, one must add another – the perennial Russian and Soviet expansionist objective.

In the light of these facts, the role given Romania in the last century, of a "Bastion of Europe at the Mouth of the Danube", acquires a new meaning and becomes actual, while the cession of Bessarabia through the Treaty of Paris of 1947 begins to be seen not only as a simple loss of territory by Romania at the hand of a very powerful neighbor, but as the loss of an important strategic position of Europe in its millenary confrontation with Asia. As a matter of fact, whenever Bessarabia's fate was decided, through the Bucharest (1812), Paris (1856), Berlin (1878) and Paris (1947) treaties, this Romanian-Russian-Soviet territorial dispute was not discussed as a bilateral Soviet-Romanian problem, but in its European context because Bessarabia has always been disputed between East and West, and its annexation by Russia has occurred at moments of political decline in a Western

Europe weakened by the human and material sacrifice brought upon it first by Napoleon, then by Hitler.

Of course, the recuperation of Bessarabia and Northern Bucovina by the Romanians through direct confrontation with the Soviets is out of question, for obvious reasons. Consequently, the return of Bessarabia can only be envisaged in the framework of an alliance with another superpower, in the framework of an anti-Soviet coalition unforeseeable at the present, with Europe not yet consolidated as an independent political-economic entity and the United States unwilling to get involved in an adventure with unpredictable implications, as long as such action is not demanded by its own security interests.

This does not mean, however, that the cause of Bessarabia and Northern Bucovina is irretrievably lost. It is not inconceivable for the "Moldavians" to reach self-determination and autonomy, in the first place within the USSR, and then independence at a later stage. It is certain that the national vigor of the Romanian peasant is considerably slowing down the Russification of Socialist Moldavia, despite heavy population losses incurred as a result of the war, deportations, and the changing of the demographic composition through local colonization. The 1979 census (the latest) showed the number of "Moldavians in the Moldavian Republic to be 2,526,000, representing a growth of 9.63% as compared to the results of the 1970 census. Calculating for a period of 35 years, i.e., from the moment of the most recent annexation of Bessarabia until around 1980, it appears that the number of inhabitants of the region called "Socialist Moldavia" has doubled, reaching the figure of 4,000,000. The Soviet news agency Tass considers this "an unheard-of population growth" and adds that Socialist Moldavia now has 122 inhabitants per square kilometer, the highest population density in the Soviet Union (Tass, Chişinău, September 30, 1981).

True, the number of Byelorussians and Russians in Socialist Moldavia grew faster than that of the Romanians (due to colonization), but the Romanian population remains by far in the majority. It represents 63.9% of the total population of the republic. If one takes into account the demographic situation in the Soviet Union as a whole, one arrives at the conclusion that the position of the Russians, as the dominant nation, deteriorates in time. In 1979 the Russians represented 82.6% of the total Soviet population, as compared to 82.8% in 1970. In eleven of the Soviet republics the local populations constitute the dominant nations (in Ukraine the figure is 73.6%, in Byelorussia 79.4%, in Uzbekistan 68.4%, in Tadzhikistan 58.8%, in Turkmenistan 68.4%, in Azerbaijan 78.1%, in Armenia 89.7%, in Georgia 68.8%, in Lithuania 80%, in Latvia 53.7%, and in Estonia 64.7%), while in eight of these republics — Uzbekistan, Kazakhstan, Tadzhikistan, Turkmenistan, Kirgizia, Azerbaijan, Armenia, and Georgia – the demographic growth of the local populations is higher than that of the Great Russians. An alliance of the Moldavians with the other oppressed nationalities cohabiting the vast prison of nations called the USSR could exert sufficient pressure upon the Kremlin leaders to remind them of the fact that the principle of self-determination and the right of secession were granted to the minorities by Lenin himself.

On the other hand, the dissident movement in the Soviet Union, which militates for a fairer deal for all Soviet citizens, regards with sympathy the nationalities' aspirations to autonomy, while the vast Soviet colonial empire is fated, in the view of Andrei Amalrik and Andrei Sakharov, to disintegrate if it does not eventually take the road of democratization. Moreover, other Soviet dissidents, such as Leonid Plyushch, believe in the necessity of the Ukraine's separation from Russia (Le Monde, February 4, 1976), while Solzhenitsyn appealed to the Soviet authorities to renounce ideological control of society, in order to promote a more open and more pragmatic regime. Solzhenitsyn realizes that "a switch of this kind would oblige us, sooner or later, to withdraw our protective surveillance of Eastern Europe" and that there can be "no question of any peripheral nation being forcibly kept within the bounds of our country" (Sunday Times, March 3, 1974).

Finally, on the international level, the Soviet Union could enmesh itself more and more in various Asian complications, with China obviously unhappy with the situation created by the unfair treaties signed with the tzars, and Japan refusing to sign a peace treaty with Moscow as long as the Soviets do not agree to return the Kurile Islands.

In our century, which seems to be the era of the dismantling of the great empires and of the universal triumph of democratic order, the Soviet Union's position is not at all as solid as it looks at first. This is so because this superpower, with feet of clay, is faced internally with the difficult problem of the awakening of the nationalities who aspire to independence, and internationally with the rise, in Asia, of two great powers – China and Japan – who compete for supremacy on that continent. In Europe, Moscow has failed to solve the German problem; 38 years after the war, no peace treaty has been signed with Germany.

Bessarabia, the strategic beachhead for tzarist and Soviet imperialism on its way toward the domination of Europe and the world, is at the same time the barrier of Western Europe against Eurasian expansion. Bessarabia, this land contested between East and West for more than 170 years, could become an integral part of the European Continent at the moment when internal evolution in the Soviet Union and the international situation would favor the achievement, by stages, of self-determination, independence, and finally union with a Romania belonging to a European Democratic Federation.

I

A POLEMICIST REWRITES THE HISTORY OF MOLDAVIA

A book has been published, with much ado, in Chişinău (Kishinev) dedicated to the history of Moldavia under Soviet rule. This voluminous work by A.M. Lazarev (1) is presented by the critics as one of great significance from a scholarly and socio-political point of view (2). It is, however, nothing more than a mere plea *pro domo sua* in favor of Great-Russian imperialism, trying to justify the Soviet seizure of Bessarabia. In an aggressive, often abusive style, Lazarev, whose claim to being a Moldavian historian is a double imposture, seeks to demonstrate, by way of invectives, the fundamentally false theory that Moldavians are different from Romanians and that their language is also different.

His method (for demonstrating the nondemonstrable) does not suffer from scholarly restraint. He simply attaches epithets to the names of scholars who have delved into the Bessarabian problem, such as "bourgeois", "occidental", "nationalist", "fascist" historian, or even – the ultimate insult – that of «*deviationist communist*». And in doing so, the Soviet historian finds himself alone, with the delusion that the Moldavians are not Romanians and that their most fundamental wish is to remain part of the Soviet motherland!

Lazarev is aware of the weakness of his thesis, which substitutes a tendentious and distorted presentation of events for a search for truth, and, in order to give credence to his untruths, he cites the Moscow Academy «which helped him edit his text with good advice after having examined the manuscript» (3). Thus, he admits, by implication, that his book represents the official Soviet point of view regarding the Bessarabian problem.

Lazarev and his scholarly and political patrons considered it necessary to take a stand on the Bessarabian problem – albeit without valid arguments – because «of its intense acuteness and immediacy», of the manifest interest which it arouses in international political circles and because it is being utilized in order to exert political pressure (4).

The urgency of the task causes him, however, to make a fatal tactical error: he simultaneously attacks all historians and opens up a front far too large to defend, if his thesis can be defended at all.

The first ones to be taken to task are the so-called bourgeois historians, allegedly representing Romanian great-nation chauvinism (5): Nicolae Iorga, Onisifor Ghibu, Ion Nistor, Alexandru Boldur, Ştefan Ciobanu, P. Cazacu, etc. ... are supposed to have mystified the whole world (with the exception of Lazarev) by applying the name «Romanian» to the inhabitants of Bessarabia, Bucovina and Dobrogea (Dobruja) (6). To maintain that the Moldavians of Bessarabia and Bucovina are not Romanian is as ludicrous as saying that the natives of Touraine are not French, the Piedmontese or the Sicilians not Italian, or the Prussians not German. The Soviet historian seems to have forgotten that, in the Middle Ages, it was in Bucovina, where one of the first Romanian ethnic (Etantiques) entities appeared and latterly played a determining role in the formation of the modern Romanian nation and state. He seems to ignore the fact that it was a Moldavian, the chronicler Grigore Ureche, who for the first time asserted in Romanian historiography the Latin origin of Romanians and first advanced the idea of the unity of all Romanians who called themselves Romanians of Wallachia, Moldavians or Romanians of Moldavia or Romanians of Transylvania. And, whether Lazarev likes it or not, it was another Moldavian, Prince Ion Alexandru Cuza, who accomplished the union of Moldavians and Wallachs into the modern Romanian state (1859-1862). Because of the linguistic and spiritual community of the Moldavians and Wallachs and the contiguity of their lands, this union proved, in a sense, easier to achieve than that of Sardinia and Piedmont. Again, it was a Moldavian, Mihail Kogălniceanu, who, as foreign minister, demanded, before and during the Congress of Berlin (1878), that Bessarabia remain part of Romania, and yet another Moldavian (or Bessarabian), Constantin Stere, an escapee from the Siberian camps of the tzars, who militated, with singular purposed fullness, before the First World War, for the union of his native province with Romania.

The absurdity of Lazarev's attempt to divide the Romanian nation by inventing a separate Moldavian nation emerges clearly from the fact that five of the six «bourgeois» historians who represent, according to him, Romanian great-nation chauvinism, are Moldavian: Nicolae Iorga, born in Botoşani; Ion Nistor, born in Vicovul de Sus, Suceava, Bucovina, Alexandru Boldur, born in Chişinău, Bessarabia; Ştefan Ciobanu, born in Talmaz, Tighina – Bessarabia and P. Cazacu, born in Chişinău, Bessarabia. Is there no significance in the fact that Bucovina and Bessarabia produced four of the six historians accused by Lazarev of Romanian chauvinism, and not a single one to write the history of

Soviet Moldavia, which had to be undertaken by Lazarev? The remote Chinese know that the inhabitants of Moldavia are Romanian. Citing Marx and Engels, highly respected in the communist camp, Radio Peking said recently that in 1853, «the Wallachs or the Daco-Romanians represented the most important population in the regions situated between the lower Danube and the Dniester» (7). Have the Peking communists become bourgeois because they maintain that the Moldavians are Romanian?

Along with the Romanian «bourgeois» historians, Lazarev quotes several Western historians and philologists, whom he profoundly despises, accusing them of complete lack of originality, of blindly following the sense and direction of Romanian publications of the 1920s and 1930s (8).

Here, we come across names of historians such as Seton-Watson Jr., Richard Burks, Henri Prost, etc. ... and of the philologists Carlo Tagliavini, Klaus Heitmann and A. Klees. All these authors, together with Alexandru Șuga and A. Popovici, two Romanian authors who wrote their doctoral theses on Bessarabia, are accused of anti-Soviet feelings and of supporting «Romanian historic, geographical, economic and ethnic rights over Bessarabia out of pure ignorance or simply for personal reasons». There is no need to defend these great scholars, against such insinuations and insults. It is worth mentioning though, that Lazarev abjectly suggests that a scholar as prestigious as Professor Carlo Tagliavini could have sunk so low as to uphold the tenet that the Moldavian language is identical with the Romanian, just because this brought him the title of «doctor honoris causa» of Bucharest University !

Another group of scholars criticized by Lazarev is that of the «fascist» historians of the 1940-1944 period who are supposed to have argued in favor of the annexation by Romania of the Soviet Socialist Republic of Moldavia, Northern Bucovina, and the Southern Ukraine, as well as for an extension of Romania's eastern border to the river Bug. To start with, it should be noted that what Lazarev designates under three different names – The Moldavian Republic, Northern Bucovina and the Southern Ukraine – is, in fact, the Romanian territory snatched by the USSR following the ultimatum of June 26, 1940. Claims to this area were not raised by any more or less «fascist» historians and statesmen, but by Romanian public opinion in the spirit of the principle of national self-determination. So far the idea of Romania's territorial extension to the Bug, nobody politically or otherwise responsible ever formulated such a claim. In fact, Lazarev cannot quote a single author, a single work supporting the idea of Romania's trespassing its ethnic boundaries to the detriment of the Soviet Union. And it was not the Romanians who created an autonomous Moldavian Republic on the left bank of the Dniester in 1924; it was the Soviets who set it up, as a lure to the Moldavians living on the right bank of the river. But they awakened instead the national feelings of the Moldavians on the

Soviet side of the Dniester, who began to feel more attracted to Iași and Bucharest than to Balta and Moscow.

The Soviet historian shows more understanding for his Marxist colleagues, Petre Constantinescu-Iași, Mihai Bujor, and Vasile Liveanu, who reconsidered the bourgeois concepts and studied the Bessarabian problem in «its Marxist framework». (10) These historians speak of an agreement reached on June 27, 1940 between the USSR and Romania on the cession of Bessarabia, and maintain that this accord «liquidated» the territorial conflict that had existed between the two states. (11) In fact, it was not an agreement between the USSR and Romania, but a Soviet ultimatum to which the Romanian government had to submit, in order to avoid war and the complete dismemberment of the Romanian state and nation resulting from an agreement between the Soviets and the Nazis. That ultimatum by no means «liquidated» the Soviet-Romanian territorial issue; Lazarev himself admits that 34 years after the so-called «liquidation» of the Bessarabian problem, the issue is very much alive and still current. (12)

As for the «Marxist» positions of the above-mentioned historians, it should be noted that they do not even quote Marx on Bessarabia. Should a Marxist blindly support the imperialistic interests of the Soviet Union, ignoring Marx and Engels? Should a Marxist practice «marxless» Marxism? Otherwise, why do the so-called Marxist historians ignore Marx's most significant text on Bessarabia: «(Dniester) or Bessarabia surrendered (and this by the Treaty of Bucharest). Turkey could not surrender (something that did not belong to her) for she was only a suzerain power over the Romanian lands. Turkey actually confessed that when she was pressed by the Austrians, at Karlowitz, to surrender the Moldavian-Wallach principalities, she declared that she did not consider herself to have the right to surrender any territories, since the capitulations only entitled her to suzerainty». (13) By recognizing that the Turks had no right to alienate Romanian territory in 1812, Marx destroys the paramount argument by which ulterior «Marxist» historians justify the possession of Bessarabia by the Russians, because this territorial alienation was «ab initio» void.

To this it should be added that the more or less Marxist historians cited by Lazarev do not espouse the Soviet thesis on Bessarabia unconditionally. Constantinescu-Iași, who, according to Lazarev, supports the Soviet annexation of Bessarabia, congratulated the vice-chairman of the Bessarabian Parliament – Sfatul Țării – in 1918 on the proclamation of the Union of Bessarabia with Romania or, in his own words, «on the realization of the ideal to which you dedicated your life: a democratic Bessarabia united with the mother country». (14)

As a matter of fact, Lazarev is not quite happy with the attitude adopted by «Marxist» historians. He reproaches them «for not having criticised murderously enough the false concepts of Romanian bourgeois historiography about the problems under discussion, not to have condemned them to the point of categorically rejecting them». He reproaches them for contenting themselves with simply presenting the facts and avoiding all comment. (15)

Even more surprising is the criticism which Lazarev has for the so-called Romanian national-Communist historians who have expressed their views on the Bessarabian problem during the past 10 years. This time, his objection is that his Romanian colleagues ignore the class position and, instead of developing new theories on Moldavian-Romanian relations, «they return to the old bourgeois theories». (16) By such behavior, they «justify the actions of the ruling classes of monarchist Romania regarding the annexation of Bessarabia; the annexation of this territory by the Romanian oligarchy is considered by them to be a righteous act». (17)

The Soviet historian does not hide his anger at the fact that the ruins of Soroca are mentioned in the *History of the Rornanian People*, in the chapter on «*The Formation of the Romanian States*» (X-XIV centuries) by Ștefan Ștefănescu. (18) Also, he objects to the presence, in The History of Romania, edited by Miron Constantinesciu, Constantin Daicoviciu and Ștefan Pascu (19), of a map representing «Romania after 1918». Lazarev complains that this map represents Romania within the frontiers of «Greater Romania», its territory extending in the east to the Dniester, while Soviet territory stops on the left bank of that river. (20)

Finally, Lazarev is appalled at the choice of language of the so-called «national-Communist» historians who, instead of speaking of the annexation and occupation of Bessarabia by the Romanians in 1918 and 1941, refer to the union of this province with Romania and reserve the words «occupation» and «annexation» for the surrender of the territory to Russia in 1812 and to the Soviet Union in 1940.

We do not propose to come to the defense of the accused historians – they can, and they should, defend themselves. We wish to underline though, that historical maps must, by definition, show the borders in existence at whatever time they illustrate and not the present borders. With no regard for Lazarev's wishes, medieval Moldavia stretched to the Dniester, and Romania of the 1918-1940 period contained Bessarabia within its borders.

The Romanian Communist historians have often erred in their interpretation of historical events and one may justly criticize them. But one cannot reproach them mystification when they reproduce a map of their country with the frontiers in existence at the particular time under discussion.

As for the choice of language, what else could one call a note defining the irreversible conditions which Molotov presented on June 26, 1940 to the Romanian ambassador to Moscow, ordering the Romanian government to surrender Bessarabia and Northern Bucovina within 24 hours, other than an ultimatum? In diplomatic language, an ultimatum is a precise and peremptory proposal by one power to another, refusal of which would result in certain war. The Soviet note was an ultimatum, even though Lazarev wishes it to be called a plebiscite.

Finally, it seems that the «national-Communist» historians took the hint from Lazarev's objection that they ignored the class position in their analysis of events regarding Bessarabia, for they are now trying to accommodate him on this point. The latest studies on the subject demonstrate, with powerful arguments, that the Union of Bessarabia and Bucovina with Romania was «an essential claim of the popular masses», (21) a claim supported by the Romanian Socialist Party. (22) It is added that this «struggle for the social liberation of the Romanian People» was preceded, before the First World War, by «a struggle of the popular masses». (23)

The Romanian «national-Communist» historians' attitude to Bessarabia annoys Lazarev more than the positions of other historians, simply because he cannot as easily accuse them of obtuse thinking as he has the bourgeois historians. This time, he is forced to confess, clearly and candidly, that he cannot find a valid reply. «The Moldovian historians – says Lazarev – take into account the interests of friendship and fraternal collaboration (editor's note: with the Romanian historians) and tread delicately (if one can say so here) into polemics with their Romanian colleagues, often even abstaining from criticizing erroneous opinions».

But this noble attitude has proved to be unwarranted. In the beginning, the benign attitude of the Moldavian historians was mistaken by certain Romanian historians «for a sign of agreement with their own conceptions, as a lack of convincing arguments». (24)

It seems that the work of Soviet historian Lazarev marks the abandonment of «Moldavian» historians' «benign caution» and the first result of this is his polemic «The History of Moldavia» which led to an exacerbation of the Bessarabian problem.

One last group of historians is taken to task by Lazarev, the Romanian researchers living in the free world. These are, alphabetically: George Ciorănescu, Grigore Filiti, Radu Florescu, Dionisie Ghermani, Alexandru Gorj, Mihai Korne and Nicoară Neculce, coauthors of a book on Russian-Romanian relations. (25) Lazarev bestows upon them the collective epithet of «renegade historians who slander their fatherland and people,» (26) and accuses them of having resumed the «notorious» chauvinistic thesis of the division of the Romanian nation in 1940, affirming – in order to be in agreement with the revanchist circles of the Federal Republic of Germany– that «this division of the Romanian nation reminds one of the division of Germany» (27). And the pseudohistorian of the pseudo-republic of Moldavia continues his tirade, mixing bad faith with bad words: «In their anti-Soviet book, *Aspects of Russian-Romanian relations*, Ciorănescu & Co. grossly calumniate the people of Moldavia. They insolently declare, for instance, that the Soviet Union «created the fiction of a Moldavian people» and «of a Moldavian language» as distinct entities from the Romanian people and language» ... with the sole aim of justifying its (Romania's) claims to Bessarabia». (28)

According to the Soviet historian, the «renegade historians» simply revive the chauvinistic theses of Alexandru D. Xenopol, Alexandru Philippide, Nicolae Iorga, Onisifor Ghibu, Ion Nistor, Alexandru Boldur, etc., the difference being that «the demagogy and pseudoscientific procedures are more refined, the revanchist spirit and anti-Sovietism have a new dressing.» (29) By similar erroneous reasoning, Lazarev, who writes under the orders of the Soviet Communist Party, supposes that the «renegade historians» are themselves in the pay of a powerful «protector», to be found in China. (30)

All in all, the Soviet historian seems to be implying that the «renegade historians,» whom he acrimoniously criticizes, were molded at the best Romanian school of history, represented by Xenopol and Iorga, and that they have brought to fruition the teaching of their great masters by placing the Bessarabian problem in its contemporary political context. As for the presumed patron of the «renegade historians,» it is clear that Lazarev is alluding to Mao Tse-tung, who declared in 1964 that the Soviet Union «annexed part of Romania.» (31) Fortunately we are in a position to set Lazarev's mind at rest by assuring him that the work of the «renegade historians» who gave him such headaches was not inspired by Mao, but by their own national conscience and the respect they have for the historical truth, which the Soviet historian so thoroughly tramples underfoot in his book. For he who does not respect the fundamental laws of historiography – *primam esse historiae legem ne quid falsi dicere audeat* – robs himself of the noble privilege of serving Clio and remains but a dishonest polemicist.

Apoziția, No. 4-5,
Munich, 1976-1977

BIBLIOGRAPHY:

1) A. M. Lazarev: *Moldovskaya Sovetskaya Gosudarstvennost i Bessarabskiy Vopros. /The Organization of the Soviet Moldavian State and the Bessarabian Problem/*, (Chișinău: Cartea Moldovenească, 1974)
2) N. Mokhov and Muntyan: «In the Interest of Truth» (in Russian), *Sovietskaya Moldavia*, Chișinău, March 5, 1975.
3) Lazarev, *op. cit.*, p. 16.
4) *Op. cit.*, p. 14.

5) *Op. cit.*, p. 40.
6) *Ibid.*
7) Radio Peking in Romanian, February 4 and 20, and March 21, 1976.
8) Lazarev, *op. cit.*, p. 57.
9) *Op. cit.*, p. 59.
10) *Op. cit.*, p. 43.
11) *Ibid.*
12) *Op. cit.*, p. 14.
13) Karl Marx: *Însemnări despre români. Texte Manuscrise Inedite cu un Comentariu / Notes on Romanians. Unpublished Manuscripts with a Commentary/*, (Madrid: Carpaţii, 1965), p. 84.
14) Ion Ardeleanu and Mircea Muşat, 1918: «The Romanian Socialists and the head of the Struggle of the Masses for the Completion of the Process of Forming the National State», *Anale de Istorie*, XXI, 1975, 6, p. 50.
15) Lazarev, *op. cit.*, p. 44.
16) *Op. cit.*, p. 45.
17) *Ibid.*
18) Andrei Oţetea: *Istoria Poporului Român / History of the Romanian People/*, (Bucharest: Editura Ştiinţifică, 1970), Plate no. 24, between pages 128 and 129.
19) Miron Constantinescu, Constantin Daicoviciu and Ştefan Pascu: *Istoria României /History of Romania/*, (Bucharest: Editura Didactică şi Pedagogică, 1971), Compendiu, Plate no.13.
20) Lazarev, *op. cit.*, p. 46.
21) Ştefan Pascu, «Moments in the Struggle of the Romanian People for the Formation of the National State», Magazin Istoric, X, 2 p. 6.
22) Ardeleanu and Muşat, *op. cit.*, p. 46-50.
23) *Op. cit.*, p. 56.
24) Lazarev, *op. cit.*, p. 54.
25) G. Ciorănescu, G. Filiti, R. Florescu, D. Ghermani, A. Gorj, M. Korne and N. Neculce: *Aspects des Relations Russo-Roumaines. Retrospectives et Orientations*, (Paris: Minard, 1967) p. 267.
26) Lazarev, *op. cit.*, p. 44.
27) *Op. cit.*, p. 45.
28) *Ibid.*
29) *Op. cit.*, p. 64.
30) *Op. cit.*, p. 856.
31) «Mao's Statement to the Japanese Socialist Delegation», Dannis J. Doolin, *Territorial Claims in the Sino-Soviet Conflict, Documents and Analysis*, (Stanford University: 1965), p. 43.

II

THE ORIGIN OF THE BESSARABIAN PROBLEM: THE DIPLOMATIC TALKS REGARDING MOLDAVIA, BESSARABIA AND WALLACHIA
(1805-1812)

Among the inaccuracies which abound in the «treatise» on the History of Moldavia written by Lazarev, a particularly flagrant one surprises even the forewarned reader. It is not concerned with either ancient or medieval history (where sources of information are sometimes lacking or are open to more than one interpretation). Nor is it concerned with very recent history, where interests at stake can turn certain exegets into historians with a preconceived thesis or even into downright political partisans. It is concerned with contemporary history, an epoch rich in reliable sources of information that lend themselves to being evaluated with modern scholarly methods. According to Lazarev, the Bessarabian problem did not originate in 1812, when Russia occupied the region situated between the Dniester and Pruth Rivers, but in 1918, when the «Sfatul Țării – the Bessarabian National Assembly – voted in Chișinău for the union of Bessarabia with Romania. In other words, the point is being made that it was Romania, not Russia, which occupied Bessarabia. This historical inaccuracy deserves to be singled out and refuted, because it lies at the very foundation of the Romanian-Russian dispute.

At the beginning of the last century, the name «Bessarabia» was used to describe Southern Moldavia, the region situated between the Dniester and Pruth Rivers and the Black Sea, corresponding geographically to the Steppe of the Bugeac – or, roughly, one third of the region annexed by Russia in 1812. It is in this narrow sense of the word that the name «Bessarabia» appears in the documents of the epoch (instructions and diplomatic notes, memoirs and letters which we are going to quote), and until 1812 when the Russians extended its meaning to include the north of Moldavia, that portion between the Rivers Dniester and Pruth. Since at that time one ignored the right of peoples to self-determination, the destiny of peoples and of nations was decided either by diplomatic negotiations or by the force of arms. It is not surprising, therefore, that, in the general state of division in Europe, caused by the Napoleonic wars, many studies assign Moldavia, Wallachia and little Bessarabia to the great neighboring empires: Russian, Austrian and Ottoman. In fact, the Romanian regions were, and remain to date, one of the routes of access to Constantinople, (Istanbul) and the Mediterranean. The Russian dream of domination of the Orient could not be achieved in the 19th century, because the Western political leaders of the period had halted the advance of the colossus from the North, at the Pruth. Bessarabia was the price paid by Europe for saving the south-east of the continent from the Russian Empire. Tzar Alexander I, who had accepted the title of Great King of Macedonia in the hope that he would re-enact the great feat of the conquest of the Orient, had to content himself with this small scrap of Moldavian soil, even though he continued to look beyond the Pruth valley.

The orientalist ambitions of Alexander I were on a collision course with the Western projects of Napoleon I. After the Battle of Trafalgar (October 21, 1805), which meant for France the closing of the sea routes to the Orient, Napoleon sought to open a continental road to Constantinople. An astute strategist, he realized the political and military importance of Moldavia, Bessarabia, and Wallachia for the domination of the Eastern Mediterranean. To start with, Talleyrand, his foreign minister, had already the idea to offer Moldavia, Bessarabia and Wallachia, the Danube, and some of the Black Sea shore, to Austria, in exchange for positions that the Hapsburgs were relinquishing in Germany and Italy. In his note dated Strasbourg, October 17, 1805, the subtle exbishop suggested to the Emperor that the Austrians should be pushed in the direction of Eastern Europe, so that they would block the Russian route to Constantinople.

After the battle of Austerlitz (December 2, 1805), thanks to the treaty of Pressbourg, (Bratislava) (December 26, 1805), France acquired better positions on the way toward the East. Russia reacted to the French advance by means of the so-called Adam Czartoryski plan, drafted in 1805. This project gave Moldavia, Bessarabia and Wallachia to Russia, which was at the same time offered suzerainty over several Christian states in the Balkans. Russia was determined to start implementing the Czartoryski Project. In 1805 General Ivan Ivanovich Michelson, who commanded the Russian forces posted on the Dniester, was ordered to be ready to invade Moldavia the instant Napoleon attacked the Ottoman Empire. On July 7, 1806, Talleyrand told state counsellor Oubril, the envoy of Czartoryski, that "Moldavia and Wallachia are already *de facto* Russian provinces", a state of affairs which France was not ready to accept.

A few days later (July 18), General Henri-Jacques-Guillaume Clarke, the French plenipotentiary charged with continuing the talks begun with Ourbil, tabled a counterproposal based on notes dictated by Napoleon himself. France called upon Russia to renounce all its privileges in Moldavia and Wallachia, a suggestion which alluded to the rights acquired by the Russians through the Treaty of Kuchuk-Kainarji.

In fact, in the instructions given to General Clarke, Napoleon was simply repeating in a new form, the idea which he had expressed a month before in his instructions to Horace Sebastiani, (June 20), France's new ambassador to Constantinople. According to these instructions, the Sublime Porte was to retain its absolute rights over Moldavia and Wallachia. The 24th of June saw the «hospodar» of Moldavia, Alexandru Morouzi, and that of Wallachia, Constantin Ypsilanti, both protégés of Russia, removed from office. They were both reinstated on the 15th of October however, following the forcible intervention of Andrei Yakovlevich Italinsky, the Russian ambassador in Constantinople, who had threatened with an immediate break if not given satisfaction. Sultan Selim III gave in to Russian pressure, because the news of the victory over the Russians, won by the French the day before, at Jena, had not arrived yet in Constantinople. This diplomatic success of the Russian ambassador so infuriated Napoleon that, as he dictated his peace conditions to the Prussians, he asked them not only to guarantee the integrity of the Ottoman Empire, but also to join the French forces in case Russia invaded Moldavia and Wallachia.

As for Talleyrand, he also referred directly to the reinstatement of the two pro-Russian «hospodars» in a declaration to the Prussian envoys, in which he deplored the fact that «Wallachia and Moldavia, governed by men whom Turkey had rightly dismissed but had to reinstate in the face of Russian threats, had become a veritable Russian conquest.» In conclusion, Talleyrand asked «that the Sublime Porte reassert its full rights in Moldavia and Wallachia.»

Napoleon went even further, considering an intervention necessary at the first sign of alarm: an energetic counterstroke was planned in case the Russians crossed the Dniester. In this context, he wrote to Alexandre La Rochefoucauld: «Do not fail to keep an eye on Moldavia and Wallachia, so that you can forewarn me of the movements of the Russians against the Ottoman Empire» (October 30, 1806). The moment had come, for on October 16, General Michelson was ordered to cross into Moldavia.

In order to contain the Russian advance on Europe, Napoleon had kept Poland at the ready. He was thinking of eventually reinforcing the Polish bastion by adding to it Moldavia and Wallachia. This had been proposed by Alexandre-Maurice Comte D'Hauterive, the head of the foreign ministry, in a memorandum to Talleyrand (October 23, 1806). To give yet more weight to the importance France attached to the Danubian Principalities, a rumor was started that Marshal André Masséna was to be sent to Moldavia at the head of an army of 30,000.

At the same time, Napoleon applied himself to strengthening the fighting spirit of the Turks and promised aid to Selim III, in order to save the Ottoman

Empire (November 11, 1806). Talleyrand, on the other hand, informed Sebastiani that the imperial government was determined not to relinquish Warsaw and Berlin until the Sublime Porte recovered its authority in Moldavia and Wallachia through the installation of «hospodars» faithful to the Sultan. The policy proved fruitful. On the 5th of January 1807, the Porte declared war on Russia, pushed back the English before Constantinople, and started a campaign on the Danube. Napoleon wrote to Sebastiani that the Turks could easily force the Russians to withdraw from the Danubian Principalities, where they only had 35,000 men and advised the Grand Vizier to cross the Danube and reconquer Wallachia and Moldavia while the Turkish fleet landed troops in the Crimea. Moreover, Napoleon intended to send help to his allies in the form of the army of Illyria commanded by Marshal Auguste-Frédéric-Louis Viesse de Marmont with the task of joining the Turkish troops on the lower Danube. Finally, he invited the Turks to march in order to meet the French forces in the region of Kamiensc. These plans seemed too daring, however, to the Turkish army, which had lost its fighting spirit and subsequently put up a poor show in Wallachia. On their part, the French had inflicted a new defeat upon the Russians (Eylau, February 8, 1807); Talleyrand exploited it in order to reiterate his request that Moldavia and Wallachia «be no longer dependent on Russia».

The complications which the Turkish alliance implied for France and the problems that arose in Constantinople where Selim III had been overthrown (May 31, 1807) determined Napoleon to revise his eastern policy. During their meeting at the Niemen (June 24, 1807), he gave tzar Alexander to understand that there was a possibility of dividing Turkey. He continued, however, to demand the withdrawal of the Russian troops from the Danubian Principalities. This French wish, so often expressed, was stipulated in Article 22 of the Treaty of Tilsit (July 7, 1807). Yet the treaty contained the implicit threat of the division of the Ottoman Empire, in case the Turks did not accept France as mediator for the conclusion of peace with Russia, Sebastiani convinced the Sublime Porte that it was in its interest to settle for an agreement which would leave it in possession of Moldavia and Wallachia, lands which the Turkish forces had been unable either to defend or reconquer. The Armistice of Slobozia (August 24, 1807), an achievement of French mediation, comprised the stipulation, demanded by Napoleon, that the Russians had to withdraw from the two Danubian Principalities. Tzar Alexander refused, however, to ratify the armistice and the Russian troops, which had already begun slowly to retreat northward, halted and dug in at certain points along the Danube.

Jean-Baptiste de Nompère de Champagny, who had replaced Talleyrand as Foreign Minister, continued to demand of Count Piotr Tolstoy, the new Russian ambassador in Paris, the withdrawal of the Russian troops from Moldavia and Wallachia emphasizing that such a move would be interpreted as a gesture of good will. Champagny added that in the meantime, it was to be desired that the evacuation of Wallachia and Moldavia should proceed according to the Treaty of Tilsit and to the Armistice of Slobozia, and «that one was surprised to learn that the evacuation process begun by the Russians had been suspended.»

This request was answered by Piotr Aleksandrovich Tolstoy with the counterproposal that the French evacuate Prussia. Tolstoy was following the instructions of the new Russian Chancellor, Count Nicolai Petrovich Rumyantzev, an advocate of Russian expansion in the Orient. Napoleon saw certain advantages in the new Russian proposal and declared himself ready to accept the Russian occupation of the Danubian Principalities, provided that the Russians accept the French occupation of Prussia. He considered this arrangement advantageous, because the strategic position of Prussia was more important to him than that of Moldavia-Wallachia. Alexander, however, did not fall for this. He declared to General Anne-Jean-Marie-René Savary, French Ambassador to Saint Petersburg, that he saw no connection between the occupation of Prussia and the «Wallachian and Moldavian affair» (December 1, 1807). Savary replied that Napoleon simply demanded compensation for the acquisition by Russia of Moldavia and Wallachia. This was totally untrue. In fact, Napoleon wished to keep Prussia without surrendering anything at all to Russia, while Alexander wished to keep the Danubian Principalities and at the same time dislodging the French form Prussia.

The situation, already complicated, grew even more tangled with the intervention of England which, wishing to keep Russia's good will, offered Alexander the same unfortunate Danubian Principalities, still unaware that they were being auctioned off in Europe. Moscow rejected the offer, which London was not in a position to guarantee in any case (November 7, 1807), but asked France to ratify the occupation of Moldavia and Wallachia, in exchange for Russia's turning down the English offer and its break with England (November 18, 1807). N.P. Rumyantzev told Savary that the acquiescence by Napoleon to the Russian occupation of the Danubian Principalities would popularize the alliance with France in Russia, thus gaining a lot for France at little expense. The French Emperor rejected the suggestion, telling Tolstoy that Russia was formally committed to leaving Moldavia by the Treaty of Tilsit, which did not provide for any obligation on France's part to leave Prussia.

The Marquis Armand de Caulaincourt, France's new ambassador to St. Petersburg, continued the negotiations. On November 12, 1807, he informed the tzar that Napoleon would like to see Russia withdraw from Moldavia and Wallachia, but that he would consider negotiating the surrender of the two principalities to Russia for adequate compensation. De Caulaincourt outright rejected Albania as an object of exchange, considering it to be too far away from France, and named as his choice Silesia, whose value to France supposedly equalled the significance of Moldavia-Wallachia for Russia. The price demanded by Napoleon was deliberately high, in order to make Alexander understand that he should renounce the idea of keeping the Danubian Principalities.

Pressure on Russia to relinquish its Danubian quarry also came from Prince William of Prussia. While in St. Petersburg, he asked the Russians to abandon Moldavia, in order to set the French an example to follow in Prussia.

At the beginning of 1808, Napoleon seemed ready to accept the proposal of Rumyantzev – the evacuation of Prussia in exchange for the evacuation of Moldavia–Wallachia. "I would be the lowest of the low, said he to Piotr Tolstoy, if I did not scrupulously honor what I undertook at Tilsit, were I not to evacuate Prussia and the Duchy of Warsaw, while you withdrew your troops from Moldavia and Wallachia! How could you possibly doubt it?" (February 2, 1808).

However, since the names of Moldavia and Wallachia appeared so often in diplomatic projects for territorial exchanges, Napoleon wanted to know more exactly the value of this object which he wished to deny Russia. He therefore ordered Captain Aubert, Chief-of-Staff Adjunct of the Grande Armée, to visit Moldavia and Wallachia and establish the value of the two regions and the possibilities of their development. In his report, Aubert noted that «Moldavia could become one of the most affluent provinces of Europe, provided the population could be increased and the country governed.»

As he merely crossed these countries, he is sometimes wrong in his estimates, writing, for instance, that the distance between Bucharest and Focşani is only 39 Km instead of 199 Km. It is true that he uses a local unit, the «hour» and that he defines this unit as «the distance covered in one hour on camel back». Unfortunately, there were no camels around there and it was partly on such reports that Napoleon had to base his oriental policy!

Napoleon, who wished to find out more about the nature of Russian interests, authorized de Caulaincourt to discuss not only an eventual exchange of Moldavia–Wallachia for Prussia, but also the division of the whole Ottoman Empire (March 2-12, 1808). N.P. Rumyantzev, who was aware of the strategic importance of the Danubian Principalities, insisted on their being allotted to Russia and offered Albania as compensation. De Caulaincourt turned down this offer, remarking that Russia already occupied the two countries, while France would have to mount a campaign in order to occupy Albania, which implied risks. In reality, Napoleon, Champagny and de Caulaincourt had no intention whatsoever of dividing the Ottoman Empire with Russia and did not plan the surrender of the Danubian Principalities either, because they were aware that the big winner in such a division would be Russia. Champagny found a pretext for formally opposing the surrender of Moldavia and Wallachia, and maintained that the abandonment of the two territories would revive Moslem fanaticism and light the torch of a new war between the Sublime Porte and Russia.

Napoleon's position regarding Moldavia and Wallachia changed abruptly after the French defeat in Spain (Baylen, July 23, 1808), when the emperor was forced to withdraw his troops from Prussia and send them to Spain. In order to save face, he chose to give this withdrawal the appearance of a one-sided gesture of good will toward Russia. Champagny wrote de Caulaincourt: «One should be aware of the extreme deference for the Russian emperor that made Napoleon evacuate the Prussian state without demanding in exchange the evacuation of Moldavia and Wallachia» (August 16, 1808).

These were the circumstances under which Napoleon, in consenting to a meeting with Alexander, did not commit himself formally to the division of the Ottoman Empire, which was being shaken by new internal convulsions. On the eve of the Erfurt meeting, he asked Talleyrand to prepare a draft for a convention with Russia. Talleyrand, who opposed Napoleon's project of a conquest of the East, wished that France would content itself with Western Europe and worked behind the scenes to sabotage the policy of his master. Article 6 of his convention draft provided that Napoleon would not oppose at all the union of Moldavia and Wallachia with the Russian Empire. Reading this text. Napoleon exclaimed: «I do not want that article, it is too positive!» Unfortunately, this paragraph, which became Article 8 of the Convention of Erfurt, was modified in such way as to commit France to an even greater extent; the words «will not oppose at all» were replaced by the words «will recognize.» The article emerging from Talleyrand's project provided for negotiations to take place, either at Constantinople or on an island on the Danube, through the mediation of France, on the problem of the cession of the Danubian Principalities. It added that the negotiations were to commence when the talks with Germany had reached some conclusion. «This article is good» – commented Napoleon – «thanks to my mediation, I remain master of the situation, while the preceding article should unsettle Austria, my real enemy.»

At the Franco-Russian negotiations (September-October 1808), however Rumyantzev rejected Talleyrand's formula, which made Russia's acquisition of Moldavia-Wallachia dependent upon the issue of the negotiations with England. Moreover, France was forced to renounce its mediating role, depriving Paris of the possibility of opposing the annexation of the Danubian Principalities by Russia. The result of all this, partly due to Talleyrand's treason, who counseled intransigence to Alexander, was that Napoleon had to surrender Moldavia, Wallachia, and Finland to Russia at Erfurt and to undertake, moreover, to convince England to recognize this cession (Art.11). Napoleon conceded all this in order to obtain the respite he needed to regain control in Spain.

Summing up the situation, Champagny wrote de Caulaincourt, on instructions from Napoleon, that Russia has derived «great advantages from the alliance with France, because she acquired and incorporated Wallachia, Moldavia and Finland, and a population of 1,000,000 in Galicia, while France has not gained a single village and has acquired no advantage other than that of having acquitted debts of gratitude» (August 12, 1809). Napoleon continued to hope that he would be compensated somehow for the cession of Moldavia and Wallachia. He now thought of Illyria, whose occupation would bring him nearer Byzantium and would cancel the advantage achieved by the Russians through the annexation of the Danubian Principalities.

Publicly, Napoleon hid his anger at the cession of Erfurt: «My ally and friend, the Emperor of Russia», said Napoleon in his State-of-the-Empire message to the Legislative Assembly, «has added to his vast empire Finland, Moldavia, Wallachia and a district of Galicia. I am never displeased when anything good happens to this emperor». (December 3, 1809). Later though, Napoleon making a balance sheet of the Franco-Russian alliance, drew the following, more sincere conclusions: «Was it not Russia who gathered all the fruit of the alliance? Finland, the object of so many wishes, of so many battles, is it not now, in its entirety, a Russian province? Without the alliance, would Moldavia and Wallachia continue to belong to Russia? What good was the alliance to me?» (June 30, 1810). The Emperor was furious every time he remembered the occupation of Moldavia and Wallachia, but accepted responsibility for the abandonment of the two territories. It came to Napoleon's attention that the Russian rulers maintained that they had obtained Moldavia and Wallachia without having really expected it, and only because France had incited Turkey to wage war against Russia. Champagny wrote to de Caulaincourt explaining what the Emperor expected of him: «The Emperor wishes that you react energetically, answering that, had it not fitted his policy and had it not been his will that Wallachia and Moldavia be part of the Russian Empire, he would not have opposed the events with mere intrigues, but with an army of 400.000 soldiers capable of changing the destiny of the two provinces» (July 20, 1810). It appears that Napoleon did not want to unleash full-scale war against Russia to dislodge it from Moldavia and Wallachia, but that he could not quite swallow the pill of the Erfurt Treaty either, a treaty which he had decided to accept because of the momentarily unfavorable military and political conjuncture of circumstances.

A military genius, Napoleon had understood that, through the annexation of Moldavia and Wallachia, Russia had acquired a better starting position for the conquest of the Balkans and of the Eastern Mediterranean. Consequently, he moved his line of resistance to Russia from the Dniester to the Danube. Champagny spelled out the Emperor's new, post-Erfurt policy when he informed de Caulaincourt that the Emperor did not wish to change «the order consolidated at Erfurt», but that he would not tolerate, at any price, that the Danube cease being the barrier between the Ottoman Empire and Russia. His

Majesty would oppose by all means any treaty, any transaction giving the Russians possession of even one single point on the right bank of the Danube...» (July 20, 1810). Should the Russians attempt to cross the Danube, Napoleon was determined to reach an understanding with Austria, in order to stop them at this new barrier. «The Emperor regards the Danube» – wrote Champagny in the same letter to de Caulaincourt – as the only barrier that could guarantee the existence of the Ottoman Empire, and he takes as much interest in the perpetuation of this empire as does Austria» (July 20, 1810).

We are approaching the moment in history when Russia had to choose between the alliance with France, which could no longer offer the possibility of new territorial conquests, and a rapprochement with England, which could offer conquest possibilities in Eastern Europe, where London had no immediate interests. In view of the approaching Franco-Russian war, Alexander ordered an end to the continental embargo and accepted English merchandise transported by ships (December 31, 1810). He sought, at the same time, Austria's friendship, by promising Saint-Julien, Austria's ambassador to Moscow, that in case of success in a war with France, he intended to make up to Vienna her territorial losses suffered in Germany and Italy, following the Treaty of Pressburg (December 26, 1805). He would make good these losses by surrendering to Austria Wallachia and that portion of Moldavia situated between the Siret River and the Carpathians, as well as all that Austria wished to take of Serbia (January 23, 1811). This offer was renewed in a letter addressed by the tzar to Emperor Francis I. The tzar added that, in view of the complications that could arise because of Turkey, Russia would be ready to occupy the Danubian Principalities on behalf of Austria (February 8, 1811). Francis I replied that he could not enter into negotiations regarding the dividing of Ottoman spoils, since he entertained good relations with Turkey (March 2, 1811). In his instructions to Saint-Julien, Metternich remarked that the tzar reserved for Russia the Duchy of Warsaw and Galicia and offered Austria in exchange Wallachia, part of Moldavia, and Serbia. «We are being offered, in other words» – said Metternich – «to exchange what we possess for what Russia does not possess.» The Chanchellor requested his ambassador to explain to the Russian rulers the absurdity of this proposition (March 29, 1811).

Austria's friendship was also being solicited at the same time by France, which would have liked to win Vienna over to its new anti-Russian policy. Champagny, on behalf of Napoleon, requested the French ambassador in Vienna to sound out Metternich regarding Austria's attitude in case of war between France and Russia. «Moldavia and Wallachia are of secondary interest to France, while they are of prime importance to Austria. It would be useful to know how far Austria would be prepared to go and what it could do in order to prevent their reunion.» Furthermore, Champagny asked himself, in the letter to his ambassador Louis-Guillaume Otto: «The displeasure caused to M. de Metternich by the occupation of Moldavia and Wallachia, is it sufficiently important to allay his fear of a war with Russia?» (February 25, 1811). In other words, the French Foreign Minister was asking if a Russian occupation of Moldavia and Wallachia did not constitute sufficient reason for Austria to go to war with Russia, side by side with France. In the same letter, Jean-Baptiste Nompère, comte de Champagny, asked Louis-Guillaume Otto to inform him of the «names and force of the Russian regiments stationed in the two provinces» and also if the Sublime Porte would be able to defend them should the need arise.

The storm was approaching. The Franco-Russian confrontation loomed on the horizon. The instructions to Jacques Law, Count de Lauriston, for his embassy in St. Petersburg, mention the attitude to be adopted on the problem of Moldavia and Wallachia. «One must keep silent on these two provinces and abstain from all declarations regarding them. For it is probable that, in case of a war with us, Russia will not have them.» New Foreign Minister Hugues Maret indicated the reason why Russia would have to surrender all she had taken by force and by astute maneuvering some years before. He demonstrated that the balance of power had been disturbed by the latest Russian annexations to the point that the whole of Europe was in danger of being invaded by Russia; «This increase in power» – said Maret, and what he said applies perfectly to the present situation – «will bring the Russian frontiers to the Oder and to the limits of Silesia. This power, which Europe has tried in vain for a century to contain in the north and which through invasion after invasion has already extended itself far from its natural limits, will become a power south of Germany; will establish with the rest of Europe relations which no wise statesman can contemplate and will obtain, at the same time, extremely dangerous advantages through its new geographical position. It will have acquired in a few years, by the possession of Finland, of Moldavia, of Wallachia and of the Duchy of Warsaw, an increase in its population of 7,000,000 to 8,000,000 and an increase in force beyond all proportion between itself and the other powers. We are witnessing the making of a revolution which will threaten all the southern states, which the whole of Europe always contemplated with dread and which will be completed perhaps in the next generation» (August 16, 1811). Among the practical measures advocated in this memorandum, so impressive in its lucidity, one finds the proposal «to reconsider the concession which gave Russia Wallachia and Moldavia.» In fact, Maret believed that it would have been possible for France to force Russia to return the Danubian Principalities to the Sublime Porte, either by negotiating a revision of the stipulations of the Treaty of Tilsit or by pressure exerted more directly on Moscow through French military preparations /*Résultat du travail fait à Sa Majesté*, le 16 Août 1811/. At any rate, the evacuation of Moldavia and

Wallachia by the Russians seemed to the French Foreign Minister to be a condition «essential to obtain».

In the end, Napoleon returned, therefore, to his old policy regarding Moldavia and Wallachia. A policy from which he had departed at Erfurt, where he was forced to bow to unfavorable and constraining circumstances. This policy consisted of not recognizing the occupation of the Danubian Principalities by Russia and, after the occupation became a *fait accompli* of trying to recover the two territories by negotiation or by force of arms. He wanted to rally Turkey to join in this policy and had sent there as chargé d'affaires Just-Pons-Florimond de Fay, marquis de Latour-Maubourg, whose mission was to conclude a formal French-Turkish alliance by which Moldavia and Wallachia would be returned to the Sultan. In exchange, the Sultan was to lead an army of 100,000 to the Danube. Having reached Iași, the Sultan was to send to the Dniester 40,000 cavalry with orders to join the right wing of the Grande Armée in a battle against the Cossacks. In the instructions given to General Antoine-François comte d'Andréossi, dispatched to Constantinople to reinforce Latour-Maubourg's mission, the Emperor showed that «it was in the interest of the Porte that Russia be weakened, that she lose the shores of the Black Sea, the provinces (Moldavia and Wallachia) which belong to the Ottoman Empire» (April 18, 1812).

The danger of war with France resulted in a moderation of the Russian claims in the negotiations with Turkey which followed. In order to prevent a Franco-Turkish alliance and to insure peace on its southern border, Russia no longer claimed all of Moldavia and Wallachia, declaring itself satisfied with the annexation of the region comprising land between the Dniester and the Pruth, which was named Bessarabia. The Turks, surprised by the modesty of the Russian claims, accepted the compromise by which Wallachia and a good portion of Moldavia was returned to them. The Russo-Turkish peace treaty, signed in Bucharest on May 28,1812, formalized this shameful snatching of Bessarabia by Tzarist Russia and is the basis of the present Soviet claims to the province. It is said that the Turkish envoys to Bucharest, Galib effendy and Dimitrie Morouzi, had received a message from Napoleon counseling them not to conclude peace with Russia, because of the imminent Franco-Russian war, but that they disregarded this advice. Bessarabia was lost, because Andréossi only arrived in Constantinople with the instructions which were meant to reinforce the Turkish stance on July 25, 1812, i.e., after the signing of the Treaty of Bucharest. It is true that Andréossi asked the Sultan not to ratify the treaty providing for the cession of Bessarabia to Russia, but his intervention came too late. Nevertheless, it is a fact that, when the Sultan learned that war had broken out between Napoleon and Alexander, he executed the two envoys who had been over eager to sign away Bessarabia.

Lazarev seems to ignore all these details and gives no explanation whatsoever for the annexation of Bessarabia in 1812. He thus avoids discussing the background of the problem, the fundamental fact that rape cannot be considered today to represent right of possession and that the only owner of Bessarabia is and remains the Moldavian people – i.e., the Romanian people – who have inhabited the land for almost two millenniums.

Avoiding a discussion of the origins of the Bessarabian problem presents another advantage, and a capital one at that, for Lazarev and Russia – the obligation of unveiling the real political motives for Russia's occupation of this Romanian province is thus bypassed. It is evident that the occupation of Bessarabia is no ordinary territorial conflict with a foregone conclusion between a big and a small power, it is a major dispute between Great-Russian imperialism, hungry for *Lebensraum* and aspiring to world domination on the one hand, and the Western countries on the other, who must stop the Russian advance at defendable geopolitical and military frontiers, in order to defend their own way of life. The Russians began by claiming the Bugeac, i.e., only the south of Bessarabia, but increased their claims, in 1812, to include the whole of Bessarabia, from Hotin to the Black Sea, and extended this bridgehead even further in 1940, by also annexing Northern Bucovina and the region of Herţa. The only reason they did not occupy the whole of Romania was because they came up against the opposition of powers interested in defending the gateway to the Orient, but plans for the division of the Romanian state were in existence in Moscow. One cannot say too often that the occupation of Bessarabia is but a single stage in the Russian march to the Mediterranean, which it has now reached, by infiltration, by means of the Moscow-provoked Middle East conflict. Our contemporaries must understand what Napoleon understood at the beginning of the last century: the defense of Istanbul and of The Straits, of Israel and Lebanon should be organized on the Dniester, which was and remains the first barrier in the way of the Russian march to conquest in the Orient, "the seat of world empire".

BIBLIOGRAPHY:

1) Archives Nationales, AF IV, 1697 Russie 1807-1808, Correspondances de Savary et de Caulaincourt; 1699 Repports de Caulaincourt.
2) Edouard Driault, *Napoléon et l'Europe,* 5 vol. (Paris: 1910 – 1927).
3) Marcel Emerit, "L'Enquête de Napoléon I-er sur les Principautés Roumaines", *Revue Historique du Sud-Est Européen,* No. 4-6, 1936, pp. 188–196.
4) Germaine Lebel, *La France et les Principautés Danubiennes (du XVIe Siècle à la Chute de Napoléon),* (Alger: 1955).

III

ROMANIAN HISTORIANS ON RUSSO–ROMANIAN RELATIONS

When Ceauşescu was asked about Romania's relations with the Soviet Union at his June 12, 1981 Vienna press conference, he pointed out that «We have been neighbours from the remotest times. Hence, we are very close to each other and will keep on being close and neighborly». (1) This rather blithe formulation does not, however, go very far in indicating the true nature of Romania's relations with its big Eastern neighbour, about which Romanian historians are more specific in a series of recent works that recall Bessarabian and other themes, such as Russian disregard for Romanian sovereignty. Dan Teodor of the A.D. Xenopol Institute of History and Archaeology in Iaşi, for example, said that since the second half of the sixth century especially, more or less compact groups of Slavs (the Russians' forefathers) penetrated into and settled in the Eastern Carpathian areas and on the eastern Danubian plain. The relations between the Romanians' forefathers and the Protoslavs do not seem to have been particularly friendly from the very beginning, because their penetration into and settlement in the areas of present-day Moldavia and Bessarabia – called jointly and nonpolitically «the East Carpathian areas» – were not – as is quite understandable – of a peaceful nature». (2) As a matter of fact, the description of the civilization of the present-day Russians' forefathers is not very flattering either, for, compared to the civilization of the Dacian-Roman population, «the culture brought by the Slavs who, at that time /the sixth and seventh centuries A.D./ had come into the extra-Carpathian areas, was at a lower stage, containing some archaic elements.» (3)

Beside having a culture superior to the Slavs, the Dacian-Romans also allegedly had the merit of being indigenous to the territory of Moldavia. As far back as the fourth to third centuries B.C., there were numerous Getae-Dacian settlements in central and northern Moldavia. Historians claim that there have allegedly been two Getae-Dacian political-military groups: «One in the northern area (Galicia-Bucovina-Upper Moldavia) and a second one in central

Moldavia, east of the River Pruth; the Cucuteni-Băiceni treasure, dating back to the first half of the fourth century B.C., represents the main discovery of relics of this second group.» (4)

Quotations from Soviet and Hungarian historians, (a favorite device of Romanian political scholarship), such as N.S. Derzhavin and András Huszti, are presented to lend more authority to the claim that Dacians occupied the entire territory nowadays inhabited by Romanians, including Bessarabia. Derzhavin, for instance, said: «for many decades, the territory of Transylvania, Wallachia, Moldavia, and Bessarabia down to the Black Sea and the Dniester River, put up a particularly fierce resistance to the Roman conquerors ...» (5). In his turn, Huszti wrote in his work *O es ujj Dacia* (1791) that «the Getae-Dacians were the oldest inhabitants of Transylvania, Moldavia, and Wallachia, and were very brave, indeed peerless in battle» (6). Finally, historians added that, in fact, the name Bessarabia stems from the ruling dynasty of Wallachia which, under Basarab I, had extended its dominion «in the east as far as southern Moldavia, north of the Danube Delta, between the Pruth and the Dniester Rivers, and the Black Sea – the future counties of Cahul, Ismail, and Cetatea Albă, territory called at that time Bessarabia, a name deriving from Basarab I». (7)

As a matter of fact, one cannot speak of any direct contact between Romanians and Russians during the Middle Ages. Some strictly scholarly articles trace the history of some commercial cities, such as Chilia, which is now located in the Ukraine, and in the past had been ruled in turn by the Byzantines, the Hungarians, the Genoese, the voivodes of Wallachia and Moldavia, and finally by the Turks, (8) but never by the Russians in the Middle Ages.

Since Russia was continually extending its rule, drawing closer to the borders of Moldavia, the Romanians tried to conclude an anti-Turkish alliance with the tzars. In 1656, for example, the Moldavian voivode Gheorghe Ștefan concluded a political treaty with tzar Alexei Mikhailovich of Russia. In its very first article the treaty stipulated that «Russia pledges that it will respect the integrity and traditions of Moldavia, as they had been earlier, before the country was a vassal of the Turks, that is, without any interference in its policy and administration.» (9) Similarly, the treaty concluded between Dimitrie Cantemir and Peter the Great on 13 April 1711 is a treaty between two sovereign states, by which Russia pledged (Article 11) to observe Moldavia's historical borders, set down as follows: «In accordance with its ancient rights, the borders of the Principality of Moldavia are circumscribed by the Dniester River, Camenet, Bender (Tighina), the entire territory of Bugeac, the Danube, Wallachia, the Grand Duchy of Transylvania, and the entire territory of Poland, as per the present agreement.» (10)

In 1787 the tzarist empire first extended as far as the Dniester River, on the border of Moldavia, after it had conquered and annexed the territory between the Bug and Dniester Rivers. Russia did not, however, stop long at the new frontier, for in September 1808 «at the Erfurt Congress Napoleon gave tzar Alexander I his consent for the latter to annex Moldavia and Wallachia, as soon as peace was concluded». Karl Marx is quoted as saying about this agreement: «At Tilsit and Erfurt Napoleon promised Moldavia and Wallachia to the tzar of Russia and gave him to understand that Turkey, except for Constantinople, would be divided .» (11) Therefore, in lieu of commentary, an appeal was made to the authority of Karl Marx who, when writing about the Bucharest peace of 28 May 1812, under which Bessarabia was surrendered to Russia, denounced its character as follows: «The Sublime Porte surrendered Bessarabia. Turkey cannot surrender something that does not belong to it, for the Porte has never had full sovereignty over the Romanian Principalities.» The Porte itself admitted this at Karlowitz /Sremski Karlovci/, when pressed by the Austrians to surrender Moldavia and Wallachia to them, it answered that it had no right to make any territorial concessions, for the Capitulations conferred upon it the right to homage and allegiance only.» (12) Nevertheless, according to the terms of an act of surrender signed at Palmuta, on the Dniester, in 1775, an act later included in the Treaty of Sistova /Svistov/ in 1791, the Porte surrendered the northern part of Moldavia, which was called Bucovina, to Austria. «In this way, a densely populated area which had formed the core of the Moldavian state and where testimonies of a glorious past, in the form of monuments and works of considerable value abounded, was cut off from the body of Moldavia.» (13) «The protests of the Romanian masses, boyars, and clergy, headed by the voivode Grigore Ghica, against the violation of the country's territory, did not evoke any response. In October 1777 the voivode was vilely murdered by the Turks in Iaşi» . (14)

As a result of the shaky suzerainty exerted by the Turkish Empire and of their closeness to the Russian and Austro-Hungarian Empires, the Romanian Principalities became an area where interests clashed, and this led not only to the seizure of Bessarabia and Bucovina, but also to that of Banat and Oltenia, annexed by Austria in 1718. A number of misfortunes, due to the frequent Russian and Austrian military occupations, were reported, on top of the territorial losses mentioned by the Romanian historians. Constantin Căzănişteanu writes of four anti-Turkish wars in which Russia was involved in the 18th century: the 1711 Russian-Turkish War, the 1735-1739 Russian-Austrian-Turkish War, the 1768-1774 Russian-Turkish War, and the 1787-1792 Russian--Austrian-Turkish War, with the successive occupations of Moldavia (1735-1739; 1769-1774, and 1788-1792) and of Wallachia (1769-1774, and

1788-1792). (15) During these occupations, extraordinary corvées and obligations deriving from the state of war or occupation, such as catering for the fighting forces whenever they were on Romanian territory, and the payment of tribute, constituted the duties demanded of the Romanian Principalities. During the 1735-1739 Russian occupation, for example, under the pretense of granting Moldavia a semblance of autonomy, General Münich tried to impose on it the obligation to pay the upkeep of an army of 20,000, supply 3,000 men to work on the fortifications, pay 90 bags of ducats as a gift to the Russian commander, on top of the 100 bags due as an annual tribute, and so on. The Moldavian boyars who had accepted these conditions only under the threat that the city of Iaşi would otherwise be burned down, wondered whether this was the promised autonomy and «began more thoroughly thinking over the true goals of tzarist policy in the Principalities». (16)

According to the historian Căzănişteanu, the introduction of pathogenic agents causing epidemics, which destroyed the population of Moldavia and Wallachia in the 18th century, represented another baleful consequence of the presence of the Russian and Austrian armies on Romanian territory. Căzănişteanu writes that during the 1769-1774 occupation the Russian troops carried the plague to Moldavia, to which half of the population of the city of Iaşi and two thirds of the population of Botoşani fell victim. The same occupation armies carried and spread typhus and venereal diseases. Finally, the privations and the epidemics, which swept through Moldavia because of the frequent Russian occupations, caused the birhrate in the areas most exposed to Russian invasion to fall. These areas include Orhei county in Bessarabia and the Moldavian counties located on the Pruth River, such as Iaşi, Fălciu, and Covurlui counties. (17)

It was not only the human population that had to suffer from Russian occupation, but so also did the livestock. The first epizootic outbreak to affect Moldavia was caused by Russian occupation troops in 1740. (18)

The situation did not change in the 19th century, for the 1828 war and the resulting Russian occupation brought in their train robberies, destruction, and a ravaging of the country's wealth, as well as a loss of spiritual values. Karl Marx is quoted to lend more weight to this assessment. On that occasion, Marx admitted that «terible excesses had taken place. All kinds of contributions in fodder, cattle, and corvées; robberies, murders, etc.». It is estimated that the Russian military occupation of 1829-1834 cost 37,101,297 lei, to which must be added supplies in kind amounting to 35,861,849 lei. (19) It has been calculated that the obligations in money and kind extracted from Moldavia and Wallachia in the 1789-1854 period, for the periods during which they were occupied by the tsarist armies, totaled 200,000,000 lei in gold, that is 64,516 kg. of gold. To this one should add the incorporation of the territory between the Pruth and Dniester Rivers. (20)

Present-day historians are willing to describe in objective terms more recent events, such as the union of the provinces annexed to Romania and their reannexation by Russia. The problem of the union of Bessarabia is presented within the general frame work of the movement of peoples for national self-determination:

These acts were based on Lenin's principles, who in the booklet published in September 1917, under the title The Tasks of the Proletariat in Our Revolution, *wrote: «On the national issue, the proletarian party should first support the proclamation and immediate implementation of the full freedom to separate from Russia of all nations and peoples oppressed by tzarism, included by force or kept by force within the state frontiers, that is, annexed.» Starting from the abovementioned statement and within the given historical context, on 27 March 1918, by the people's will, Bessarabia was united with Romania.* (21)

Historians speak openly about the episode of the union of Bessarabia with Romania, praising some of the protagonists who fought for the implementation of this union, such as the writer and politician Constantin Stere. Some of these statements are now being reproduced, such as that in which Stere reminisces about the historical role he played:

The true sanction for my political stand was given by my country /Bessarabia/ when I was unanimously elected chairman of its council, at that solemn moment when, disregarded and forgotten by all, it stretched out its arms toward the Fatherland, as the latter was being humiliated and trampled upon. (22)

The 1940 Soviet annexation of Bessarabia and Northern Bucovina is explained as being made easier by the difficult situation of isolation in which Romania found itself after France capitulated and the British Army was driven off the continent:

On 26 June 1940 the Soviet government sent an ultimatum to the Romanian government concerning the territory between the Pruth and Dniester Rivers (Bessarabia), which was going to be incorporated into the Soviet Union. In that ultimatum Bucovina was claimed as damage for the 22 years during which Bessarabia had been a part of Romania. As a result, the territory between the Pruth and Dniester Rivers as well as Northern Bucovina were incorporated into the Soviet Union. (23)

In conclusion, it is worth mentioning that in its relations with its big imperialist neighbors Romania's national lot was at stake, for, as historian Adăniloaiei said, «the Romanian nation, located at the crossroads where the interests of three big absolutist empires – the Turkish, the Austrian, and the Russian – clashed, had to struggle not only to protect its fatherland and its independence, but also to preserve its national existence, jeopardized by its powerful neighbors ». (24) Since Secretary General Ceauşescu also considers himself to be an expert on history, and gives directives to professional historians, he is supposedly acquainted with the facts related by the historians subordinate to him and with the true nature of Russian-Romanian relations. That could be the explanation why he gave a diplomatic retort at the press conference in Vienna, one that concealed more than it expressed.

Romanian Background Report No. 193,
Munich, 8 July 1981,
Radio Free Europe Research.

BIBLIOGRAPHY:

1) Agerpres, 12 June 1981.
2) Dan Teodor, «The Roman World in the Second Half of the First Millennium», *Era Socialistă* No. 11, 5 June 1981.
3) *Ibid.*
4) George Trohani and Larisa Nemoianu, «The Political History of GetaeDacians in the Sixth-Seventh Centuries B.C.», *Revista de Istorie* No. 2, 1981, pp. 277-278.
5) Mircea Muşat, «Considerations Concerning the Consequence of the Domination and Foreign Interferences on Romanian People's Historical Evolution», *Anale de Istorie,* No. 2, 1981, p. 77.
6) *Ibid.*, p. 76.
7) *Ibid.*, p. 81.
8) Silvia Baraschi, «Written Sources on Dobrogean Settlement on the Banks of the Danube in the 11th to 14th Centuries», *Revista de Istorie* No. 2, 1981, pp. 311-347.
9) Mircea Muşat, *op. cit.*, p. 85.
10) *Ibid.*, p.85.
11) *Ibid.*, p. 87.
12) *Ibid.*, p. 87.
13) Constantin Căzănişteanu, «Consequences of the Russian-Austrian- Turkish Wars in the 18th Century on the Romanian Principalities», *Revista de Istorie* No. 2, 1981, p. 267.
14) Mircea Muşat, *op. cit.*, p. 86.
15) C. Căzănişteanu, *op. cit.*, p. 262.
16) Nichita Adăniloaiei, «Economic Implications of Turkish Domination in the Romanian Principalities (1750-1859)» *Revista de Istorie* No. 3, 1981, p. 452.
17) Căzănişteanu, *op. cit.*, p. 265
18) *Ibid.*, p. 264.
19) Adăniloaiei, *op. cit.*, p. 459.
20) M. Muşat, *op. cit.*, p. 88.
21) *Ibid.*, p. 91.
22) L. Kalustian, «Constantin Stere – The Man of Storm», *Flacăra* No. 18, 30 April 1981.
23) M. Muşat, *op. cit.*, p. 97.
24) Adăniloaiei, *op. cit.*, p. 451.

IV

MOLDAVIAN AND WESTERN INTERPRETATIONS OF MODERN ROMANIAN HISTORY

The Soviet Moldavian Party journal *Comunistul Moldovei* published an essay by E. Certan, a candidate of historical sciences in the Soviet Socialist Moldavian Republic, which reviews Russia's attitude towards the liberation movement among Balkan peoples in the 1774-1879 period, and emphasizes the «progressive, unselfish» role played by Russia, as compared to that of the major Western powers of the time, which were allegedly pursuing their own self-interests.

Although Certan professes to introduce new archival materials, his article (1) boils down to little more than a simple chronological review of the major events in Balkan history of the past two centuries. These events are interpreted in an apologetical light, turning Russia into a constantly unselfish and progressive factor in South-East European developments. It is, however, worth noting that the Moldavian Certan lays particular emphasis on the Moldavian–Wallachian issue in the Balkan context, considering it correct to criticize various Western historians who, in his opinion, have allegedly distorted their picture of Balkan events of that era, playing down Russia's role in the liberation of the South-East European countries from the Turkish yoke and overstating that of the Western powers. Here are the «bourgeois» historians, in the order listed by him: Hugh Seton-Watson, W.E. Mosse, Barbara Jelavich, Leften Stavros Stavrianos, Denise Basdevant, Evangelos Kofos, Uta Bindreiter and M. Rüttner. Certan also mentions the titles of the works which, in his opinion, distort the historical truth. These are fundamental works, books as well as articles, some based on original documents published between 1952 and 1977, so that it is not difficult to identify the excerpts which have annoyed Certan by comparing his text with those of the authors criticized.

Kuchuk Kainarji and all that

Certan begins by analyzing the 1774 Treaty of Kuchuk Kainarji (Cainargea-Mică in Romanian, now Kainardzha in north eastern Bulgaria), the most significant treaty in modern Balkan history negotiated between Russia and Turkey. He confines himself to mentioning the advantages it conferred upon the Romanian (Danubian) Principalities, such as: limiting the tribute they had to pay, giving them the right to maintain authorized agents in Constantinople, and releasing some Wallachian, Moldavian, Greek and Slav citizens from prison. Nevertheless, he passes over in silence the fact that the treaty recognized Russia's right to «protect» the Christians in the Balkan countries, which in the 19th century served as a pretext for numerous Russian incursions into the area.

On the other hand, Professor Leften Stavros Stavrianos of Northwestern University, one of those criticized by Certan, write that Russia obtained great advantage through the above-mentioned clause. He quotes Baron Johann Thugut, Austria's representative to Constantinople, as saying that the Kuchuk Kainarji Treaty was «a rare example of the imbecility on the part of the Turkish negotiators», for it turned «the Ottoman Empire henceforth into a kind of Russian province». (2)

Discussing the Bucharest Treaty of 1812, under which Russia annexed Bessarabia, Certan says that, «in this way, the population of that province was liberated from the yoke of the Porte, a fact which had an enormous progressive significance, for it speeded up the development of the province's economy and culture.» According to Certan, the population enjoyed such privileges as «participating in the revolutionary movement (then stirring) all over Russia». Professor Stavrianos provides a different version of the annexation of Bessarabia. He says that, as part of the process of dividing Europe into zones of influence, Napoleon, when meeting tsar Alexander I in 1808 at Erfurt, agreed to transfer the whole of Moldavia and Wallachia to Russia. But then, when Russia formally requested Turkey to turn over the Romanian Principalities, the Sublime Porte indignantly rejected the demand, a move that launched the Russian-Turkish war of 1806–1812. Therefore, the wish to annex Moldavia and Wallachia was the root cause of that war. Since Franco-Russian relations had taken a turn for the worse in the meantime, Napoleon reversed himself, trying to encourage Turkish resistance to Russia, promising Sultan Mahmut II that, were he to continue the struggle, he would be allowed to retain not only Moldavia and Wallachia but also to get back the Crimea. Faced with the threat of a Franco-Turkish *rapprochement,* Russia was compelled to make its claims more modest, giving up hope of annexing the whole of Moldavia and Wallachia and contenting itself only with Bessarabia. When, later on, the sultan tried to retrieve Bessarabia, using the good offices of Austria, Russia retorted that such a return was entirely out of the question. Moreover, tsar Alexander I declared that he did not consider the provisions of the Bucharest Treaty final, for they had been accepted under pressure of Napoleon's campaign in Russia, which meant that the tsar still wished to annex the whole of Moldavia and Wallachia.

Certan's views on the Treaty of Adrianople (1829) also differ from those of Western historians. While the Moldavian historian claims that this treaty «granted autonomy to Moldavia, Wallachia, and Serbia», the American historian Barbara Jelavich (who has also been criticized by Certan) considers that the treaty strengthened Russian control over the Romanian Principalities to such an extent that «from 1829 to 1856, Russia had been in virtually complete control of the Principalities, and only the balance of forces existing between Russia and Austria prevented Russia from annexing them outright. As a matter of fact, Russia's approach to the Romanian Principalities was not clearly mapped out. Count Pavel Kiselev, chairman of the Moldavian and Wallachian governing councils (divans) under Russian occupation (1829–1834), favored an indefinite prolongation of the Russian occupation, which terminated in 1834, and perhaps, an eventual annexation». (3) Count Karl Robert Vasilievich Nesselrode, the Russian chancellor, «had given the opinion that a protectorate was preferable to annexion or emancipation of the Balkan states, because no prior agreement was necessary with Austria». (4)

Certan does not mention the 1848 revolution, during which Russia played what Marx and Engels considered a negative role, thwarting the success of the revo- lution in the Romanian Principalities. He merely mentioned that, after the revo- lution had been suppressed in several European countries, the interest of the big powers in «the Eastern question» grew. British historian Hugh Seton-Watson writes that «the result was that the unsuccessful (Romanian) revolution had, in fact, led to another Russian occupation of Romania.» (5) Russia's adverse role in the suppression of the 1848 revolution has even been admitted by Romanian historians, (6) as well as by Nicolae Ceauşescu himself, who said:

At the same time, the suppression of the revolution was the direct result of the military intervention of the absolutist Tsarist, Turkish, and Habsburg empires which, in the face of the revolutionary wave, joined hands in supporting the reactionary forces of the three Romanian Principalities, repressing the bourgeois-democratic revolution by force of arms. (7)

In Certan's opinion, the Crimean War (1853-1856) merely «reflected the aggravation of the Eastern question,» for at that time Russia's goal was «to fight for the establishment of a number of independent states which were placed under its protection.» The historical truth, as seen by the Western historians criticized by Certan, is that the Crimean War, too, broke out because of Russia's refusal to withdraw its occupation army from the Romanian Principalities, which they had entered in July 1853, in order to force Turkey to sign a convention guaranteeing the old privileges of the Orthodox population in the Balkans. When France and Great Britain declared war on Russia, the latter immediately withdrew its troops from the Principalities, in order to remove any reason to prolong the war. Nevertheless, once the war had started, it continued, resulting in considerable loss of prestige for Russia, for under the terms of the Paris Peace Treaty (1856), Russia had to give up many of the privileges it had won for itself in the Balkans under the Treaty of Kuchuk Kainarji. Not only did it lose Southern Bessarabia, which was returned to Moldavia, but it also lost the right to act as protector of the Romanian Principalities, which opened the way for the latter to union, to political and national organization. «The period of Russian domination of Romania was thus ended for nearly a century,» Seton-Watson concludes, emphasizing that, from then on, «the Romanians tended to place their hopes on France ...» (8)

Romanian Unification and Its Problems

Certan also reiterates the classical claim that Russia supported the union of Moldavia with Wallachia as far back as 1858. He maintains that this union was possible «mainly due to the support provided by Russia, France, and Sardinia.» This opinion was upheld by Vladimir Ilin, political commentator on Radio Moscow's Romanian language service when discussing the 120th anniversary of the Union of the Principalities, (9) as well as by V. Vinogradov, Doctor of Sciences, in a speech delivered at the Institute for Balkan and Slavonic Studies of the Soviet Academy of Sciences. (10)

In this respect too, however, Western experts have reached conclusions that differ from Certan's in nuance. They maintain that Russia supported the union of the Romanians for reasons of political expediency. Russia helped the Romanian Principalities to unite, not because it was concerned about the welfare of the Romanians, but rather because it was anxious to please France from which it hoped to obtain various political concessions. «In the crisis which followed the Romanian elections, Russia stood with France but made it clear that she would undertake no independent action and that she was acting in support of a friend and not because she favored Romanian unification». (11) According to the same author, the fledgling Romanian state's relations with Russia lacked sincerity, for, during his reign, Principe Alexander Ioan Cuza, united Romania's first ruler, avoided frank discussions about his current plans and future intentions with Russian representatives and, more often than not, refused to accept Russian advice when it was given. He succeeded in withstanding «Russian pressure in almost all matters by avoiding making a direct challenge on any issue – by promising everything and doing nothing.» (12)

Instead of recognizing the leading role played by France and Napoleon III in the Union of the Principalities and in the period immediately following it, Certan accuses the French emperor of having pursued an adventurer's policy and denounces the back–stairs schemes of the time, whereby France twice suggested that Romania be placed under Austrian rule – the first time in 1864, in exchange for Austria's surrendering of Venice to Italy, and the second time in 1867, when Napoleon III met the Emperor Franz Josef in Salzburg. These schemes, which have never been precisely aid out, allegedly show that France considered Romania «as petty currency in its big diplomatic game.» In response to this haggling, which «would have resulted in the total disappearance of the Romanian state,» St. Petersburg gave a resolute reply: «This is inadmissible. It could even lead to war.»

It is true that tsar Alexander II had written on the margin of a confidential document: *«inadmissible jusqu'à la guerre.»* The impulse that prompted him to take the risk of a new war, however, was the fear lest Austria become too strong as a result of the annexation of the Romanian Principalities, not the desire to defend the existence of the freshly hatched and still weak Romanian state. In reality, the tsar thought that the Romanian Principalities were *"une oeuvre batarde"* and that under Cuza, Bucharest would turn into a hotbed of Polish conspirators and revolutionary agitators. Under these conditions, Russia hoped that, if the union were abolished and the two Principalities separated, it could once again exert its preponderant influence, as it had done in the past, if not in both Principalities, then at least in Moldavia alone. (13) It is the French istorian Denise Basdevant who indicates where the truth lies – that only thanks to France could the issue raised by the reforming zeal of Cuza be satisfactorily settled. (14) Just as it is true that Romania's policy of seeking France's support yielded satisfactory results. (15)

Certan's theory is that the stance of the Russian revolutionary movement, which, through the agency of some of its representatives, such as Nikolai Gavrilovich Chernyshevski, Alexander Ivanovich Herzen, Nikolai Alexandrovich Dobrolyubov, supported the idea of creating sovereign national states in Southeastern Europe, would have helped to improve Russia's (the state's as well as the movement's) relations with the Balkan countries. This is not in any event applicable to Romania, for the Russian revolutionaries had few partisans among the Romanians, since the Romanian radicals were directly linked with the French ideological movement, rather than with their Eastern neighbors. (16) On the other hand, official Russian policy failed to win partisans or to create a Russophile current or party in Romania, (17) because « Russia ... financed separatist policy movement in Moldavia,» (18) which caused the Romanian intellectuals to believe that Russia, not the Ottoman Empire, was the true enemy of Romania.

San Stefano and Berlin

In his evaluation of Russian policy in the Balkans, Certan also mentions the suggestions made around 1876 by Prince Alexander Mikhailovich Gorchakov, Russia's Minister of Foreign Affairs, at the Berlin meeting of foreign ministers of Russia, Germany, and Austria–Hungary to grant national autonomy to Turkey's Balkan provinces, which had risen in arms. These suggestions were rejected by both Germany and Austria, for Russia's obvious goal was to create Balkan states that it hoped to make vassals. The plan to set up a large Slavic state in the Balkans under Russian influence also worried Romania for, were it to be caught in a Russian vice – between Russia in the west and a Russian–influenced state in the south – it, too, would have been reduced «to the status of a vassal of St. Petersburg,» as the historian Evangelos Kofos put it. On the basis of original documents, Kofos demonstrates that Romania turned to Greece, suggesting a joint front against the creation of a major Slavic Russian–guided state in the Balkans. It even went so far as to suggest that a Romanian-Greek alliance be concluded, to prevent the Eastern questions from being settled in an exclusively Slavic manner. (19) These probes and diplomatic discussions at the foreign ministry level failed, however, to produce any concrete result.

In Certan's opinion, the 1877 war was «a natural response to the Slavs' requests for help.» So far as Romanian-Russian relations were concerned, the war started when the former agreed to let Russian troops pass through Romanian territory. The Moldavian historian avoids mentioning the Reichstadt Agreement of 8 July 1876 between Gorchakov and Count Gyula Andrássy, under which it was decided that Russia should regain control over Southern Bessarabia. This agreement was made final on 15 January 1877 in Budapest under the terms of the military convention signed between Russia and Austria, providing that, in the case of Turkey's collapse, Russia would move into Bulgaria, while Austria would annex Bosnia.

Commenting on the Russo-Romanian military agreement signed on 16 April 1877, Seton-Watson writes:

The convention provided for passage of Russian troops through Romania in exchange for a payment in gold, and also engaged the tsar to "maintain and defend the existing integrity of Romania". This last provision was in direct conflict with Russia's intention, already stated to the Austrians and agreed to by them, of annexing Southern Bessarabia. (20)

According to Certan, the Treaty of San Stefano, which was signed at the end of the 1877 war, «played a significant role in the liberation of the southeast European peoples,» without, however, specifying that:

This treaty was insufferable to Britain, as it brought a state which was expected to be a vassal of Russia down to the Aegean, and to Austria because it created the «large compact Slav state,» which the Budapest convention had precluded and failed to grant Austria's claim for Bosnia and Hercegovina. (21)

On the other hand, the annexation of Southern Bessarabia and the implementation of Russia's plans, which jeopardized Romania's security, had also aroused considerable discontent in Romania:

Romania's animosity against Russia had reached such proportions that, were a war with Russia to break out, it offered to place 50,000 soldiers at the disposal of [the Austro-Hungarian Monarchy] and to allow Vidin to be occupied by Austrian troops. (22)

According to the historian Uta Bindreiter, in a bid to curb Russian expansion, Andrássy expressed his readiness to support he cause of the Romanians at any future European congress, but made no promise regarding Southern Bessarabia, whose annexation by Russia he had accepted under the Reichstadt Agreement. He told the Romanian representative in Vienna that:

*Were the congress to lead to peace and ... were all other powers to agree to this Russian claim [for three counties in Southern Bessarabia], we alone would not make the Bessarabian issue a **casus belli**... On the other hand, were the congress to result in a war, which is quite possible, we would surely add the Bessarabian issue to all our grievances against Russia. (23)*

Andrássy was unwilling to give Romania any false hope for he was well aware that Bessarabia was lost, but at the same time he did not miss the opportunity to emphasize that the Bessarabian issue had a European significance and, as such, should be discussed by a European congress. In any case, Romania was carefully observing the aggravation of Russo-Austrian relations, in the hope that, were a new war to break out, this would give it a chance to claim Bessarabia. (24)

Although the Treaty of San Stefano did not last long, being replaced by the Treaty of Berlin in 1878, nevertheless, the discussion about it has continued down to the present day. No later than last year, on the occasion of the 100th anniversary of its signing, the Bulgarian historian Khristo Khristov characterized it as «a progressive treaty [that could serve as a model] for other enslaved peoples of the Ottoman Empire,» (25) while Mihajlo Apostolski, Chairman of the Academy of

Sciences and the Arts of the Yugoslav Republic of Macedonia, said that it had merely been an attempt to create a greater Bulgaria, incorporating the whole of Macedonia, parts of southern Serbia, Kosovo, and northern Greece. This was «an attempt by tsarist Russia to achieve its long-standing goal of gaining access to the Mediterranean ...» (26) At that time, the Greeks viewed the Treaty of San Stefano as a national disaster on a par with the fall of Constantinople in 1453. (27)

Certan criticizes the Treaty of Berlin, which he feels «prevented the southeast European peoples from being fully liberated,» mentioning the territorial annexations of Austria and Great Britain, but not those of Russia. Regarding the annexation of the three counties in Southern Bessarabia and the negotiations of this issue both before and during the Congress of Berlin, Western historians criticized by Certan provide extensive and interesting information, which could not be to the liking of the Moldavian historian. Uta Bindreiter, for example, says that the fate of Southern Bessarabia had been decided even before the congress, during the diplomatic negotiations among the chancelleries, with Russia basing its claims on the argument that it had taken this territory in 1812 not from the Romanian state, which was not founded until 1859, but from Moldavia, at that time under Turkish domination:

The Russian government justified its claim by maintaining that, at that time, the Moldavian Principality, not Romania, had surrendered Southern Bessarabia; no other provision of the Treaty of Paris [30 March 1856, ending the Crimean War] under which Russia had taken it, save for this one, was any longer valid. It would, therefore, be unjust for Russia alone to be made to continue observing that treaty; besides, regaining this part of Bessarabia was a matter of national honor for Russia. When reminded of Article 2 of the Russo–Romanian Convention of 16 April 1877, Gorchakov imperturbably retorted that Russia had merely pledged itself to guarantee Romanian possessions vis-à-vis Turkey; under no circumstances did that article concern Russia's relations with Romania. This was, therefore, the reward for Romania's placing its army at the disposal of Russia at a decisive moment and allowing Russian troops to cross its country on their way to the Balkans! The disappointment and bitterness were boundless, the more so since the hope placed in support from the big powers at the forthcoming peace conference gradually evaporated in the spring of 1878....

Romania [decided] not to take the initiative, particularly since the big powers seemed to have agreed on the surrender of Bessarabia; besides, according to Prince Bernhard von Bülow, then serving in the Secretariat of the Congress of Berlin, the surrender of the three counties did not influence the freedom of navigation on the Danube. France was not at all concerned about the Bessarabian issue and had decided to let itself be governed by Austria's stand. (28)

The discussions which had taken place at the Congress of Berlin have been reproduced in detail by Denise Basdevant, who emphasized the opposition of Great Britain to this backing-down and the decisive say here of Germany, which favored Russian annexation:

Lord Beaconsfield (Disraeli), the British delegate, was very strongly opposed to Russia's claims, recalling that these territories had been assigned to the Principalities by the Treaty of 1856 «to better insure the freedom of navigation on the Danube.» That was a commitment «made to Europe». So it was fitting to adhere to the agreements made by the Treaty of Paris.

Prince Gortchakov, representative of the tsar, replied adroitly hat he could not see what influence the ceding of Bessarabia could have over free navigation on the Danube which depended on the implementation of the work accomplished by the European Danube Commission. He added that Southern Bessarabia had been annexed, in 1856, to Moldavia alone. Since then, the union of the two Principalities had created a new situation. «My government,» he anounced, «cannot give in on this question..»

Bismarck threw the weight of his authority on the side of the Russian thesis. «The work of this Congress would, in the future, give the Russian nation painful memories while Romanian interests do not appear to be contrary to the proposed exchange.»

Ultimately the Conference backed the return of Bessarabia to Russia and the annexation of the Dobrogea (Dobruja) by Romania. The French delegate, Waddington, had demanded on behalf of the Principality of Romania, «which had been treated rather harshly and to which insufficient compensation had been offered,» an extension of territory, in southern Dobrogea which included Silistra and Mangalia. To this the British delegate had succeded in obtaining the addition of the Isle of Serpents to the territory conceded to Romania. (29)

Uta Bindreiter describes the stand taken at the Berlin Congress by the Romanian delegates, Ion Brătianu and Mihai Kogălniceanu. She describes the dignified defense submitted by the two Romanian representatives, the decision made by the congress with no discussion about Russia's right to take Southern Bessarabia, and the negative response of Romania, which was even ready to «renounce» an independence obtained under such humiliating conditions. In any case, Romania insisted that the acquisition of Dobrogea could not be considered compensation for the surrender of Bessarabia, which meant that it was not willing to renounce forever its claim. Uta Bindreiter adds that:

Rising to speak after Kogălniceanu, Brătianu said:

«Romania will trust the sense of justice and good will of the congress; the dispossession of a part of its national heritage would grieve the Romanians

deeply and would make them lose all confidence in the efficacity of the agreements. »

Unfortunately, the speeches, which were elaborate, but delivered with tact and moderation, were not very impressive, because of the explicable reserve displayed by the delegates.....

The above-mentioned conditions produced considerable anger in Romania; some people even suggested that, under such circumstances, it would be better to give up independence. Dobrogea was not viewed as real reparation for Bessarabia, but rather as war damage, and this acquisition, whose southern border ran along the Mangalia-Silistra line, turned out bigger than Russia had foreseen, thanks to the intercession of Andrássy, who combined his efforts with those of the French delegate, Waddington. (30)

Turning to the 1877 war and the Berlin Congress, Certan mentions Bessarabia only in connection with the fact that, on 12 (24) April 1877, the manifesto proclaiming the launching of the Russo-Turkish war had been issued at Chişinău and that 8,000 soldiers, natives of Bessarabia, that is, of the north of the province, which was under Russian occupation, had been drafted into the Russian army. He left it to Western historians to comment on Romania's treatment under the Berlin Treaty. On this point, Seton-Watson confines himself to stating that Russia «obtained her own minimum territorial aims. She recovered the mouth of the Danube by taking Southern Bessarabia from her loyal ally Romania,...» (31) while Uta Bindreiter defends small states which, more often than not, are victims of the cupidity of the big powers, saying:

The Berlin Congress provides a classical example of how easily a small state can fall victim to the interests of the big powers. Romania had won its independence through active military aid in the Russo-Turkish war; however, Europe was going to recognize this independence only under conditions that were the equivalent of interference in Romanian domestic affairs; besides, all this was connected with the backing down regarding a province that had been given to Romania 12 years earlier, at the Paris Congress, a fertile area, inhabited mostly by Romanians, the possession of which was a matter of national honor to the Romanians. The anger aroused by the perfidy of Russia, which had so shamelessly disregarded the agreement with Romania and had not hesitated to give it an entirely different interpretation when the war was over, naturally resulted in a change in Romanian foreign policy (leading to Romania's alliance with the Central Powers). (32)

Russia's Role

In concluding his article, Certan comes to the political conclusion that the Soviet Union is continuing Russia's policy of «disinterested help in defending the independence and sovereignty» of the Balkan states. In fact, the Soviet Union *is* continuing the classical policy of tsarist Russia, which was not, however, the «selfless» one Certan describes.

It is worth noting that the stand adopted by some modern Romanian researchers regarding Russia's help to the Romanians in their efforts to win liberation from the Ottoman yoke is miles away from that maintained by Certan. Ion Papuc, for example, cites the political last wills and testaments of Prince Mircea the Old and Stephen the Great, who had come to the conclusion that the Turks were more trustworthy than the Romanians' other neighbors. Stephen even said: «You should trust no one except the Turk.» National poet Mihai Eminescu is also quoted as siding with the Turks when he says: «Never, in the course of the centuries, did the Turks threaten the Romanian language and nationality.» And, continuing this game of expressing truths of present-day applicability through quotations from the classics, Papuc adds, citing the Bessarabian writer Constantin Stere:

Owing to its very form of state, tsarist Russia appeared in history as a reservoir of universal reaction, which continually threatens normal political and social development in Europe. (33)

Background Report No. 198,
Munich, 19 September 1979,
Radio Free Europe Research.

BIBLIOGRAPHY:

1) E. Certan, "Russia's Progressive Role in the Liberation of the Southeast European Peoples from Under the Turkish Yoke," *Comunistul Moldovei* No. 12, 1978, pp. 26-30.
2) Leften Stavros Stavrianos, *The Balkans Since 1453* (New York: Holt, Rinehart, and Winston, 1958), p. 192.
3) Barbara Jelavich, *Russia and the Romanian National Cause, 1858-1859* (Bloomington: Indiana University Publications, 1959) p. 2.
4) *Ibid.*, p. 11.
5) Hugh Seton-Watson, *The Russian Empire 1801 – 1917* (Oxford: Clarendon Press, 1967), p. 313.
6) "The Formation and Consolidation of the Capitalist Order (1848 – 1878)," *Istoria României /The History of Romania/*, Vol. IV (Bucharest: The Academy Publishing House, 1964), pp. 103 and 174; Dumitru Almăşan,

"Our 1848 Revolution Within the European Context," *România Liberă,* 9 June 1978, Dan Berindei; "From the 1848 Revolution to Union and Independence," *România Liberă,* 27 May 1978.
7) Nicolae Ceaușescu, "Speech at the Popular Meeting in Bucharest," *Scînteia,* 11 June 1978.
8) Seton-Watson, *op. cit.*, p. 330.
9) Radio Moscow in Romanian, 24 January 1979.
10) *Ibid.,* 27 January 1979.
11) Barbara Jelavich, *op. cit.*, p. 16.
12) *Ibid.,* p. 132.
13) W.E. Mosse, *The Rise and Fall of the Crimean System 1857-1871* (London: Macmillan, 1963), p. 134.
14) Denise Basdevant, *Against Tide and Tempest: The Story of Romania* (New York: Robert Speller and Son, 1965), pp. 61–62.
15) Barbara Jelavich, *op. cit.,* p. 132.
16) Cyril E. Black, "Russia and the Modernization of the Balkans," in Charles and Barbara Jelavich, eds., *The Balkans in Transition* (Berkeley and Los Angeles: University of California Press, 1963), p. 155.
17) Barbara Jelavich, *op. cit.,* p. 3.
18) Denise Basdevant, *op. cit.,* p. 62.
19) Evangelos Kofos, *Greece and the Eastern Crisis 1875-1878* (Salonica: 1975), p. 69.
20) Hugh Seton-Watson, *The Decline of Imperial Russia 1855-1914* (New York: Frederick A. Praeger: 1952), p. 103.
21) *Ibid.,* p. 105.
22) Uta Bindreiter, *Die Diplomatischen und Wirtschaftlichen Beziehungen Zwischen Oesterreich-Ungarn und Rumänien in den Jahren 1875-1888, /Diplomatic and Economic Relations Between the Austro-Hungarian Empire and Romania in 1875-1888,/* (Vienna, Köln: Böhlan, 1976), p. 143.
23) *Ibid.,* p. 144.
24) *Ibid.,* p. 147.
25) Tanjug, Sofia, 20 February 1978.
26) Tanjug, 18 March 1978.
27) Evangelos Kofos, *op. cit.,* p. 191.
28) Uta Bindreiter, *op. cit.,* pp. 142-143, 148.
29) Denise Basdevant, *op. cit.,* pp. 70-71.
30) Uta Bindreiter, *op. cit.,* pp. 150-151.
31) Hugh Seton-Watson, *The Russian Empire...,* *op. cit.,* p. 458.
32) Uta Bindreiter, *op. cit.,* p. 151.
33) Ion Papuc, "Constantin Stere Today (II)," *Luceafărul* No. 27, 7 July 1979, p. 6.

V

ROMANIAN–RUSSIAN CO–OPERATION IN CONTEXT OF THE INDEPENDENCE CENTENARY

Originally, the celebration of the centenary of Romania's independence was planned as a massive spectacle that would surpass all previous events of the kind – no small task in a country that prides itself on such displays. A huge national festival was planned between October 1976 and June 1977 that would mobilize and stimulate the populace to artistic creation and enjoyment in all their various forms. The scale of the festivities was cut down to normal size, however, after the March 4 earthquake had turned public attention toward more immediate and pressing concerns.

Nevertheless, the centenary has preserved an unusual significance owing to its political background, for the principle of independence and national sovereignty is the cornerstone of socialist Romania's foreign policy. Although this principle has already been generally acknowledged, the question of its relationship to proletarian internationalism has not been resolved.

Telling the Truth in Quotations

Both political dailies and the specialized press abound in articles appropriate to the occasion, all of them written in a lyrical patriotic style. At the first sight these studies and articles seem unobjectionable: they do not contain any adverse comments on Russia – Romania's ally in the 1877 war – and lack of the cryptic hints which Romanian historians have often resorted to in the past as a means of putting across unorthodox political opinions. (l) Although Romanian-Russian political and military collaboration a hundred years ago was far from being a model of friendly co-operation, contemporary politics require that this fact should be glossed over. This moderation may be a consequence of the improvement in the Romanian-Soviet relationship that occurred after the Crimea meeting of August 1976 between Ceauşescu and Brezhnev, and the September gathering of Roma-nian and Soviet historians in Moscow (2) to discuss Romanian-Russian links in the 1877-1878 period.

This does not mean, however, that Romania's historians have confined themselves to writing an objective history of Romania's independence struggle, or have ignored the contemporary political parallels. Noteworthy is the unambiguous manner in which Ion Popescu-Puțuri, director of the party historical institute and member of the State Council, expressed his dissatisfaction with Russian violation of Romanian independence in the 1877-1878 period. (3)

Besides this significant exception, there are several specialized studies that have turned up numerous details – some previously unknown – on Romanian-Russian friction. In these studies, Romanian historians avoid expressing their own opinions and evaluations, but let the documents of the time speak for themselves. This explains the publication and republication of specific texts concerning Romania's struggle for independence. In the ticklish instances when Russia and its diplomats and army are criticized, documents and participants are quoted. Preference is usually given to quotations from Russian political and military personalities – tsar Alexander II and the Grand Duke Nicholas – who cannot be suspected of overestimating Romanian virtues and rights; from the contemporary Hungarian press, which as a rule was hostile to Romania and is therefore to be believed when it praises Romanian military exploits; and even from Bismarck, who was acquainted with the European political realities of the day and spoke freely about Russian expansionist ambitions.

The Question of Romanian Neutrality

Before the outbreak of the Russian-Turkish conflict of 1877 Romanian diplomats sought to obtain the country's independence through peaceful means and requested the major powers of the time (Austria-Hungary, France, Great Britain, Italy, Prussia, Russia, and Turkey) to guarantee its neutrality and territorial integrity. These diplomatic efforts to achieve a Belgian- or Swiss-type neutrality have attracted the attention of the present Foreign Minister George Macovescu, who is a talented historian and a university professor. (4) In the appendix to his study, Macovescu published a diplomatic note sent on 25 November 1876 by General Ghica, the Romanian representative in Constantinople, to Savfet Pasha, the Turkish Foreign Minister, on Romania's role in the confrontation of the two major powers of the time:

Two are about to come to blows; the others /i.e., the other major powers – author's note/ are deserting their positions for more or less plausible reasons. Who is to stand firm among those who were called to defend the outlet in question

[Russia's outlet to the West] Romania! The weakest state, the abandoned child of Europe! And what is this small country asked to do? To resist, to become the champion of Europe's honor, to turn itself into a field of slaughter and destruction, to maintain its devotion up to the point of sacrificing its own interests, and to hazard its future and fate on a single card. This is an impossible demand. I maintain that the remedy is not to be found along the lines indicated by your Excellency, for Romania's resistance would not change anything, I repeat: the remedy lies in neutralizing Romania and in a special guarantee which – were it to be granted on the first days of the conference [a conference of the ambassadors of the big powers which was to open in Constantinople on 11 December 1876 – author's note] would cause all the contingencies I have mentioned above to disappear. (5)

Macovescu discussed the difficulties that Nicolae Ionescu, who was then Romanian Foreign Minister, found in trying to persuade the great powers that Romania's strategic location should be used to block Russian access to the Balkans by neutralizing Romanian territory. That the current Foreign Minister should have raised such issues, even in a historical article, raises questions about current policy goals, including Romania's Balkan policy and its approach to the nonaligned world.

Macovescu cited Lord Salisbury's statement that no guarantee granted to Romania could be regarded as a *casus belli*, for, unlike Switzerland and Belgium, Romania was geographically distant from the guaranteeing powers: «It is Romania's misfortune to be located on the most direct road to Turkey,» the British statesman said. «Even the most ingenious diplomatic arrangements to ensure the closing of this road would be worthless as soon as any power thought it in its interest to violate them.» The advice given to the Romanians by Salisbury is interesting in the light of contemporary policy:

Make efforts to increase your resources. Derive as much benefit as you can from the sacrifices you are imposing on yourselves. Strengthen your country, be capable of opposing an enemy with your own forces, not by erecting an impassable barrier, for Romania cannot aspire to this, but by creating a serious obstacle to the dangers you fear. Europe will then show an interest in your cause proportional to your efforts. (6)

Russian Hostility to Neutrality

Romania's attempt of a century ago to secure its neutrality through diplomatic channels is sympathetically treated by the current Foreign Minister, but Soviet historians have taken a different line. One of the latest issues of the journal *Novaya i Noveishaya Istoriia* contains an article by Mikhail Zaliskin, a candidate of historical sciences, on «Foreign Policy Aspects of the Proclamation of Romania's Independence in 1877» in which he said that Romania planned to proclaim its neutrality «under direct pressure exerted by the Western powers, who were interested in maintaining the **status quo** in the Balkans.» He went on to say:

Although Great Britain, France, Italy, and the Austro-Hungarian Empire pursued different goals and resorted to various methods of influencing the Romanian Principalities, they were nevertheless agreed that Romania's neutrality should thwart the development of the liberation movement among the Southern Slavs. The foreign policy considerations relative to the struggle for Romania's independence were of such a nature that liberation could be obtained only through **rapprochement** *with Russia.*

Zaliskin claimed that the policy of neutrality "still represented the official line of all the governments, which succeeded up to the spring of 1877.» He was particularly annoyed that even after the Romanian-Russian agreement of Livadia (1876), «Romanian official circles continued to seek increased autonomy of the Principalities from the Western powers as the price of neutrality in the Russian-Turkish war.» He concluded, with restrained satisfaction, that Romania «was unable to obtain anything more than encouraging promises» that the question of its neutrality would be taken up at the Constantinople ambassadors' conference. Plans to achieve independence through neutrality proved unrealistic and, as a result, the movement in Romania toward immediate **rapprochement** with Russia grew rapidly. (7)

Supplies of American and German Arms

Although Romania was planning to achieve independence mainly through diplomatic channels, this did not preclude strengthening its military capacity with an eye on a possible resort to arms. Lacking its own heavy industry, Romania depended on foreign sources of armament, and particularly on sophisticated American weapons. Despite the difficulties of transporting weapons through the Bosporus, Romania signed contracts with American firms and also with Prussia. When military circles around Gheorghe Adrian, the War Minister, decided to place an order for advanced Peabody-type cartridge guns in the US, however, the Turks became upset. The historian Radu Vasile has said:

Romania's policy of equipping itself with modern arms gradually attracted the attention of the European governments, which did not hesitate to express their disapproval in various forms. But the Romanian government did not let itself be bullied and proceeded to modernize its weaponry. On 13 September 1868 the daily **Românul** opened a subscription list for the purchase of 10.000 Peabody guns in addition to the 15.000 previously ordered from the US, which were by then on their way to Bucharest; the list was to prove successful. (8)

Contemporary Romanian historians approve the 19th century Romanian governments' arms policy: «It is worth emphasizing that the efforts made by the governments to secure first-rate armaments yielded results and in 1877 the Romanian army was in some respects better armed than that of its ally» – that is better than Russians. The Romanian historian concluded:

As far as power range and rapidity go, the Peabody guns were better than the Kruka or Prussian needle guns with which most of the Russian troops were equipped, and as good as the Berdan (American) guns which only certain elite Russian troops possessed. (9)

Diplomacy and Espionage

The months preceding the war saw Romanian diplomacy striving to make the other European governments aware of Romania's right to national independence and sovereignty. (10) Under the new Constitution of the Turkish Empire, proclaimed by the sultan in December 1876, Romania, along with Serbia, Montenegro, and Egypt, was denied independence and merely declared a privileged province. This provoked a vehement protest from Romanian Prime Minister Ion Brătianu who declared that «Bayazid's and Mehmet Ali's long swords could never penetrate into the Romanian mountains where Midhat Pasha dares to go through with his Constitution.» Macovescu cited this declaration as an expression of «the profound indignation that pervaded the country.» (11)

Since diplomatic channels were proving less and less effective, and hope of achieving independence through voluntary Turkish concessions and recognition by the major powers was vanishing, the Romanian government increasingly contemplated the option of war. With this in mind, it collected valuable information on the plans and intentions of the big powers. An article dealing with some aspects of the secret struggle waged by Romania on the eve of the independence war concluded that:

Although Romania did not have a specialized espionage service, the government received a constant flow of interesting and often accurate information. The patriotism and intelligence of those who had been charged with collecting information helped overcome the deficiencies attributable to lack of training in such a difficult profession. (12)

The Problem of Transit for Russian Troops

The Russian government believed that in the event of a conflict with Turkey, Romania would allow its troops to cross Romanian territory into the Balkans, in exchange for recognition of Romania's in dependence. From the talks which the Romanian Prime Minister had in Livadia on 29 September 1876 with Russian Chancellor Gorchakov, and later with tsar Alexander II, «it was clear that Ion Brătianu considered himself the representative of a country which considered itself absolute master of its territory and fate». (13) Reporting to Prince Carol I on his meetings with Gorchakov, Brătianu said that the Russian Chancellor had requested unconditional permission for Russian troops to cross Romanian territory: «If this is not forthcoming, they will advance without any restraint, treating Moldavia and Wallachia as provinces of the Turkish Empire. In this respect the tsar was more reserved, for he did not directly raise the issue of the Russian army crossing Romania by force.» (14)

During the Livadia negotiations, the Romanian delegation was said to have insisted that Romania join in the talks as a fully independent state, and demanded that the talks and the convention should correspond to international political and judicial forms. This was reflected in Article 2 of the convention concluded between 4 and 16 April 1877:

In order to prevent any disadvantage or danger to Romania resulting from the crossing of its territory by Russian troops, the government of His Majesty the Emperor of All the Russians **pledges itself to maintain and observe the political rights of the Romanian state, according to internal laws and existing treaties, and to maintain and defend the present integrity of Romania** *(15) (emphasis in original).*

Neither of the two partners was particularly happy about a collaboration imposed more by geographical conditions than by common interests and feelings. Contemporary historians allowed this truth to be told through the medium of progressive Hungarian publications of the time which «considered that a possible alliance with Russia would not be salutary; on the contrary, it could even be dangerous to Romania.» Such a diplomatic act, with its political and especially military ramifications, «would have grave consequences for Romania». (16)

Besides lacking respect for a tiny country deprived of international legal standing, Russia had reservations regarding collaboration deriving from fear of the liberal Bucharest regime's potential influence on the autocratic Russian state. In this regard, Romanian historians of today cite the opinions expressed in a recent work by Soviet historian Zaliskin: "Russian government circles were indeed ready to co-operate with Romania, but they were afraid of a liberal government and of the growth of revolutionary trends in our country.» (17)

Finally, on 14 April 1877 the legislative bodies, the Chamber of Deputies and the Senate, met in Bucharest to sanction the convention of April 4. After justifying the conclusion of the convention, despite the failure of attempts to obtain recognition of the country's neutrality, the opening message of the session declared that «it was not its intention... to affect Romania's rights and institutions.» (18) On April 28, after lengthy and fiery discussions that lasted until 03.00 hours, the Chamber of Deputies approved 69 to 25 the Romanian-Russian convention. (19)

While the legislative bodies were still discussing whether to permit the passage of Russian troops through the country's territory, the latter had already entered Romania and occupied several strategic points. Only four days later did the tsar's adjutant send Prince Carol an explanatory letter from Alexander II. (20)

Foreign Minister Mihail Kogalniceanu immediately sought assurances other than the precarious ones given by Russia about the future of his country. On 14 May 1877 he belatedly justified the signing of the convention to the guaranteeing powers: «No matter how insignificant Romania is, it has the right to be concerned about its preservation, for, because of its geographical position, it is in the center of a war that is becoming inevitable.» He demonstrated to the great powers that Romania had gained «respect for its individuality and institutions, along with a formal guarantee of its territorial integrity.» (21)

Romanians Insist on Retaining Independent Command

Romanian-Russian military co-operation was implemented by stages and not without difficulties: «In the early period of the fighting tsarist Russia intended that the Romanian army be controlled by the Russian high command, a situation which the Romanian command did not accept.» (22) On 2 May 1977 at a meeting in Ploeşti, Grand Duke Nicholas, commander of the Russian army in the Balkans, suggested to Prince Carol that the Romanian army join directly in the incipient war. The Romanian prince answered that the Romanian army «is all afire to start fighting,» but the conditions of co-operation with the Russian army must permit the Romanians to have their own command. (23) According to the Hungarian daily *Kelet,* which appeared in Transylvania, «right from the start Prince Carol and the Romanian government accepted military collaboration only on condition that the Romanian army be allowed to act independently and that no Russian troops be inserted among the Romanian ones.» The daily expressed its understanding and sympathy for the Romanian position when it reported that «the Romanian government has denied rumors that the Romanian army has been integrated into the Russian one. The Romanian troops will fight independently, under their legitimate command.» (24)

On 8 July 1877, the Romanians crossed the Danube and entered the battle in the Balkans after the first defeat of the Russians at Pleven. According to a recent article, «on the insistence of the Russian general staff, supported by Grand Duke Nicholas and the tsar, the command of the Romanian army occupied positions opposite Nikopol.» (25)

On 19 July 1877, the day following the second Russian defeat at Pleven, a very alarmed Grand Duke Nicholas telegraphed Prince Carol to beg for help. The text of this telegram – reproduced in many of the recent studies – reads as follows:

The Turks who have concentrated most of their troops opposite Pleven are crushing us. Please merge, stage a demonstration and, if possible, cross the Danube with the army, according to your wishes. This demonstration is indispensable between the River Jiu and Corabia to facilitate my movements. Nicholas. (26)

In his recently discovered memoirs, General Alexandru Cernat, Romania's Minister of War, recorded that the Grand Duke was particularly emotional when he received him immediately after issuing a request for Romanian help. He embraced Cernat and exclaimed: *«Vous tombez comme la Providence...* We accept all your conditions, only come as quickly as you can. Tell your prince that he shouldn't worry about supplies: we shall take care of all your needs. Only cross the Danube this very day, if possible.» (27) Under pressure of the situation the Russian leaders accepted a policy in line with Romanian conditions. Following the August 16 talks with Alexander II and Nicholas in Gorni Dubniak, Prince Carol took over command of «all Romanian-Russian forces around Pleven (the Western Army), with General Pavel Zotov as head of the general staff.» (28)

On August 30, the Romanian-Russian units, now concentrated around Pleven, launched a general attack against the Turks who had strongly fortified their positions and were fighting fiercely under the command of a capable general, Osman Pasha. This attack is criticized at the present time by Romanian historians as having been planned «without a thorough analysis of the battle preparations and weather conditions.» (29) In his memoirs, General Cernat wrote of being informed by a Greek captured at Pleven that Osman Pasha was expecting an attack on August 30, the tsar's name day. Consequently, the Turks were not going to be taken by surprise and the risk of heavy losses would be great. Cernat considered it his duty to suggest to Grand Duke Nicholas that the planned offensive be put off, but the answer was: «Since it is the anniversary of the Emperor of All the Russians, either the entire imperial army will die or it will take Pleven.» Describing this episode, the Romanian commentator wrote that the third attack on Pleven resulted in 18,000 Russian and 2,200 Romanian casualties, dead or wounded – all within the space of a few hours.

Present-day Romanian historians have avoided direct criticism of the Russian failure at Pleven, but quote a host of foreign military experts. The Austrian Colonel Anton Springer was quoted as saying: «Had the Romanian help not been available at short notice, very likely the Russians would have been obliged to abandon Bulgaria, withdrawing across the Danube»; and the British General V. Baker stated: «It is quite clear to any impartial military historian that, had it not been for the aid given by the Romanian forces, the entire Russian army that was fighting north of the Balkans would inevitably have been thrown into the Danube.» Even the Turkish historian T. Yilmaz admitted that, «without the Romanian army, the enemy could not have won the battle of Pleven.» (31) Perhaps the most impressive testimony was the citation for valor awarded to the Romanians by Friedrich Engels, who wrote in a letter: «Without the Romanians, the Russians would have been helpless at Pleven.» (32)

Eulogy of the Romanian Forces and Criticism of the Russian Army

Participation in the 1877–1878 war represented a considerable effort on the part of Romania: 100,000 men were mobilized, of whom 60,000 were combat troops; there were 10,000 casualties on the battlefield, and the cost of the fighting was around 100,000,000 gold lei. (33) Present-day Romanian historians, caught up by socialist patriotism, praise the independence army in terms that have a remarkably topical ring. Colonel General Ion Coman, the present Minister of National Defense, has said that the achievements of the Romanian army were due to its organization and «recruitment of the masses as participants.» (34) The 1877 war was won «because the entire nation mobilized all its resources to support the front,» (35) in a kind of dress rehearsal for total war.

Regarding the conduct of the army in the field, Romanian military experts claim that while it was thought at first that the lack of experience of the Romanian army was a handicap, historical perspective points to a contrary conclusion: «The Romanian army proved to be less bound by routine procedures which were more to the disadvantage than to the advantage of the troops. It could adjust itself to new requirements in the tactical field.» (36) In contrast, to highlight the deficiencies of the Russian army, Romanian historians quote the negative opinions expressed in a Soviet work published after World War II (N.I. Belzhaev, *The Russian-Turkish War 1877-1878*, p. 43). According to this account, Russia failed to make full use of its huge military potential:

The supreme commanders of the Russian army, who were reactionary stick-inthe-muds, thwarted most of the army's war preparations and created extremely unfavorable conditions for the Russian troops in their struggle against the enemy.

The author continues:

More often than not, the leadership of the troops during offensives was confused regarding both the goals of the original mission and the directions to subordinates. Sometimes the troops were left without any guidance at all during the offensives... . The Russian army's experience of defensive engagements was far superior to its knowledge of the offensive. (37)

Reluctance of the Great Powers to Accept Romanian Independence

Romania's independence, proclaimed on 9 May 1877 and subsequently affirmed on the battlefield, was not recognized immediately by the European powers, despite Romanian Foreign Minister Mihail Kogalniceanu's statement: «I am convinced that, far from being a threat to the peace of Europe and of the neighboring states, Romania's independence will satisfy not only our national requirements but those of Europe as well.» (38)

Great Britain viewed Romania's independence with «obvious disapproval», considering it «an act contrary to its treaties and interests». France, «which no longer set the fashion in international politics,» adopted «an excessive reserved attitude.» Russian diplomatic circles told the Romanian representative in Saint Petersburg that the Romanian declaration of independence had been «hasty», and Ignatiev, former Russian ambassador in Constantinople, told Prince Carol that «the Romanians are being unjust if they do not have full confidence in Russia.» (39)

The Romanian leadership was «profoundly dissatisfied» with the attitude of the big powers. Romanian diplomatic activity in the summer of 1877 to secure recognition of independence had yet another significance:

It clearly showed those who faced reality and were prepared to learn from experience that the path to establishment of the country's independence through international regulations remained very long and difficult. In realizing our century-old dream of independence we had to rely mainly on the work, ability, and capacity for abnegation of our people, on national unity and solidarity, on clear awareness of our rights; in sum, on our own means. (40)

The similarity between such sentiments and current policy statements is most likely intentional.

Romania hoped to be represented at the peace negotiations at San Stefano and, with this in mind, sent Colonel Eraclie Arion to present to Grand Duke Nicholas letters of accreditation from Prince Carol. Grand Duke Nicholas, however, had already answered Carol directly: «Regarding the details of the peace terms set by the Romanian government and the forthcoming negotiations, please refer to Petersburg; I do not know them.» (41) These details were given to Romania's diplomatic representative in Russia by Alexander II, who commented: «Since Romania's independence has not been recognized by Europe, it would be inappropriate for it to participate in the negotiations and become a contracting party.» Kogălniceanu directed his agent to tell the tsar: «It is impossible for the Romanian government to accept this situation. The tsar has already recognized Romania's independence and it is impossible to deny the Romanian government the right to participate in the peace negotiations and in the congress». (42)

Despite these protests, the Russian-Turkish protocol of Adrianopole which set the terms of peace, was worked out in Romania's absence. This led the Romanian Council of Ministers to send Grand Duke Nicholas a letter expressing regret that Russia had refused to approve Romanian participation in the negotiations. The Hungarian dailies *Kelet* and *Magyar Polgar,* published in Transylvania, criticized Russia's acceptance of the Peace of San Stefano without Romanian participation, emphasizing that «it would have been right for a battlefield ally to be treated with equal respect in the diplomatic arena.» (43)

Romania and the Berlin Congress

Romania did, however, have representatives at the Berlin Congress, although their status was ambiguous: they were «heard» by the Congress but not «listened to». (44) According to *Kelet,* «the Romanian political leaders Ion Brătianu and Mihail Kogălniceanu, went to Berlin to guard the country's territorial integrity and to persuade the Congress to recognize Romania's independence and neutrality". (45) The Romanian representatives reported that «during the talks with prominent Congress personalities the Romanian delegates received declarations of sympathy from everyone; however, these assurances reflected only an academic – that is, sterile – good will.» (46) Eventually, they presented a memorandum to the Congress in which they asked that: «No territory should be detached from the Romanian state; Romania should not serve as a corridor for the Russian armies»; and «Romania's independence should be formally recognized and its territory declared neutral.»(47)

According to a modern scholar, «despite the merits of its case, Romania suffered from its treatment at the Berlin Congress; the great powers imposed their will, diminishing the rights of peoples such as the Romanians and the Bulgarians who had made so many sacrifices for the war.» (48) In a chronology of events prepared by Ilie Ceauşescu, the decision of the Congress on Romania's independence was described as follows: «Article 43 of the Berlin peace treaty recognized Romania's independence, linking it with the terms set in Articles 44 and 45 under which Southern Bessarabia was incorporated into tsarist Russia.» (49) The present-day Foreign Minister, Macovescu, has also mentioned this theme, but in more veiled terms.(50) When the Romanian delegates to the Berlin Congress remarked that the great powers had responded with ingratitude to the sacrifices of the Romanian people, Lord Beaconsfield (Disraeli), the British delegate, replied: «You speak of ingratitude? Well, in politics ingratitude is often the reward for outstanding service.» (51)

Romanian Disappointments – Old and New

Dissatisfaction with the Berlin decision is clearly indicated by the republication of documents dealing with events of the period, including the reluctant compliance of the two houses of the Romanian parliament with the decision of the Congress to give up Southern Bessarabia. (52)

In a letter to Prince Carol, Bismarck expressed regret that:

The results following the conclusion of peace were not commensurate with the gallantry of the army of Your Royal Highness. Bearing in mind the strength of the powers surrounding Romania, however, and the difficulty of ensuring a modus vivendi *among them to guarantee peace, I could not find any way out of the situation that would have served Romania's interests better.*

Bismarck went on to add that since Romania was caught between two great empires, its policy must be «to have one of these empires as an ally.» (53)

The contemporary historian Popescu-Puţuri summarized this disappointment:

Although Romania made considerable contribution to the conduct and short duration of the war... because of the practice of disregarding the rights of small countries to participate in the settlement of international issues, the major European powers did not approve of our country's attending the negotiations for the signing of the armistice – something that Romania will again be faced with in the course of its tormented history. (54)

Another Romanian historian wrote: «Romania had trouble in obtaining its legitimate rights, especially in connection with its efforts to have the cobelligerent status of our country recognized, which had political, moral, and economic repercussions.» (55) Both statements recall, in terminology as well as sentiment, the problems faced by Romania at the Paris Peace Conference in 1946.

Russians Abuse of the Right of Passage for their Troops

The original Romanian reluctance to cooperate with Russia in the war waged south of the Danube was in part justified by the differences that had arisen during the Romanian-Russian military collaboration and by the humiliating refusal to allow Romania to attend the peace negotiations in San Stefano. Romanian--Russian relations deteriorated so that on 25 February 1878, when the Russian government suggested a new agreement granting Russia passage through Romanian territory for two years to maintain a direct land link with Bulgaria, the proposal was turned down for many reasons. (56) On February 25, however, the Romanian agent in St. Petersburg met Chancellor Gorchakov and drew his attention to Article 2 of the April 4 convention under which the Russian government «pledged itself to maintain and respect the political rights of the Romanian state, according to its domestic laws, and to defend the territorial integrity of present-day Romania.» On March 12, the Romanian Premier and Foreign Minister issued a protest against Article 8 of the San Stefano treaty which stipulated that the Russian occupation troops in Bulgaria could maintain their links with Russia via Romania, «where they are permitted to organize depots for the duration of the occupation.» (57)

The situation worsened to such an extent that on March 26 Foreign Minister Kogălniceanu suggested to Prince Carol that the entire army, ammunition depots, supplies and drugs be concentrated in Oltenia, the westernmost region of Romania, to which the Russian troops had no access. The 1878 contingent was called to arms and Prince Carol went to visit the area where the troops were concentrated «in order to become acquainted with the situation, the condition of the troops, and their preparedness to implement possible missions.» (58) At the same time, Kogălniceanu handed over a note to the Russian Consul-General in Bucharest alleging that «some actions of the Russian army are going beyond the agreement to make use of Romania's territory only for passage to Russia,» and urged that privileges granted to the imperial troops «be reduced to simple passage by stages on their way back to Russia.» (59) A parallel may well have been intended here by contemporary authors regarding similar questions in more recent Soviet-Romanian relations.

Independence and Unity

Romanian historians have also been anxious to use the independence anniversary as an occasion to reaffirm national unity. Thus, particular emphasis is laid on the solidarity of the Transylvanian Romanians with the independence war, expressed in the participation of numerous volunteers, and in the money, medicines, clothes, and other aid provided by the rescue committees organized in various towns and communes of Transylvania. (60) This pan-Romanian solidarity is said not only to demonstrate the organic unity of the Romanian nation but also to foreshadow the union of Transylvania with Romania in 1918.

Romanian historians have repeatedly made clear that, unlike the other Balkan peoples, the Romanians have never lost their independence. A certain degree of economic dependence undoubtedly existed when both Wallachia and Moldavia were obliged to pay tribute to the Porte, but the Romanian voivodes possessed considerable political autonomy. Those voivodes who defended the country's independence, opposing Turkish dominion with arms, have been preserved as legendary in popular Romanian lore. (61)

The Turks accepted the legitimacy of Romanian principalities having their own voivodes, administration, institutions, laws, and ways of life: «These areas constituted the only exceptions they made in their relations with the peoples of South-Eastern Europe in the era of conquest,» (62) which otherwise entailed simple capitulation.

The concept of independence did not disappear from Romanian political thinking in the centuries that followed. On the contrary, the Romanian humanists Dimitrie Cantemir and Constantin Cantacuzino (63) conferred on it a European significance. (64)

The Ideological Slant to Independence

In keeping with the present ideological climate, the Marxist interpretation is prominent in the historical writings associated with the independence centenary. Although a century ago the socialist movement in Romania was only in its initial stage, it is said to have strongly supported the cause of independence and the independence war. The workers joined in the fighting south of the Danube and made collections for the struggle and for the wounded while the socialist press embraced the cause of independence. (65)

True independence, however, corresponding to the century-old aspirations of the Romanian people, could be implemented only after 23 August 1944 when «Romania again appeared on the world map as an independent state.» (66) Communist historians maintain that Romania was not really independent in the period between the two world wars, since it was subject to «foreign capital» which often violated the prerogatives of national sovereignty. Even in the period between 23 August 1944 and the conclusion of the Paris peace treaty Romania was not a fully sovereign state, for the Allied Control Commission, a body with comprehensive powers, «set up a new framework for the exercising of the prerogatives of the Romanian state, thus inevitably limiting its freedom of action and its independence, especially on the foreign scene.» (67)

The independence of socialist Romania cannot be conceived without its material base: industrial development. Industrialization is not only «necessary to ensure and strengthen Romania's independence, it is also vital to the defense of our national existence as an independent people.» (68) Socialist Romania ensures its independence by maintaining diplomatic relations with 129 countries and economic links with 149 states, all based on the new norms of interstate relations. These principles and norms represent Romania's contribution to the development of international law and they are enshrined in almost 5,000 treaties, agreements, conventions, and other bilateral official acts concluded in the postwar period. (69)

Romania's Rapprochement with Bulgaria and the Balkan Countries

The independence war and the proclaiming of Romania's state independence also had consequences on the international level. First, the links between the Romanian and Bulgarian peoples were strengthened, since many revolutionary organizations of Bulgarian emigrants found shelter on Romanian territory. There they issued publications calling for Bulgaria's independence and organized armed raids south of the Danube, such as the expedition mounted by the poet Hristo Botev's group. (70) A mausoleum for the Romanian soldiers who had fallen on the battlefield was built in Grivitsa between 1892 and 1897 by public subscription, and a museum was opened in 1907 and modernized in 1974. (71) Romania's interests extended from Bulgaria to the entire Balkan area and have been maintained to this day, when «inter-Balkan collaboration is enjoying the sovereign support of all the peoples of the area.» (72)

The Russian Problem

The newly independent Romania was located at the «crossroads of expansion by the major powers toward the Balkans and the Black Sea straits.» (73) Therefore, Romania was faced with a political choice of the kind adumbrated by Bismarck – an alliance either with Russia or with the Austro-Hungarian Empire.

Through their recognized leader Dobrogeanu-Gherea, Romanian socialists opposed the alliance with Russia:

Will a triumphant Russia, having the command of the Balkans and perhaps part of Austria, allow us to escape from its clutches? And does anyone believe it will spare us because we were formerly its allies? It could not do so even if it wished to, for how could it rule over the Balkan Peninsula with an independent Romania blocking the bridge connecting the peninsula to Russia? Further, are the Romanians persuaded that Moscow is grateful to them? Were we not Russia's allies in 1877, when it grabbed Bessarabia stealthily as a reward for the blood we spilled in the war? To conclude an alliance with Russia means putting the yoke around our own necks and handing over our corpses to Russian tsarism. (74)

The recollection of Romanian-Russian differences in the independence war still weighs heavily on the Moscow-Bucharest relationship. In a recently published book, historian C.C. Giurescu wrote that in 1915, when he was received by Prime Minister Ionel Brătianu – the son of the prime minister during the independence war – the latter «began talking to me about the independence war, especially about relations with tsarist Russia and Bessarabia. Obviously these relations greatly worried him; he had inherited from his father his suspicion of the policy of our eastern neighbor, a suspicion increased by the attitude of the tsarist General Headquarters to our army in 1916 and 1918.» (75)

Independence – a Continuous Struggle

In 1877 Romania's ultimate political goal was to obtain not only independence from the Turkish Empire, but also absolute independence through liberation from Ottoman suzerainty, elimination of the threat of reassertion of the Russian Protectorate, and liberation from the control of the seven guaranteeing powers. (76) Owing to its rapid evolution and its self-assertion on domestic and international levels, modern Romania succeeded in obtaining this four-fold independence.

Nevertheless, at peace conferences such as those held in Paris in 1919 and 1946, Romania did not receive any better treatment than in Berlin in 1878, when its dignity and aspirations to independence were offended. In 1919 the major powers either did not consult the Romanian delegation on matters that concerned it, or else presented it with draft treaties at the last moment, behavior often amounting to direct interference in Romanian domestic affairs – e.g., on the minorities question. It was generally recognized, however, that «in the delegation sent to Paris, Romania had a consistent defender of its sovereignty and territorial integrity» (Ionel Brătianu) who finally walked out of the conference in protest. (77)

At the 1946 conference the states were divided into two categories: those with «general interests» and those with «limited interests.» Despite its active participation in the anti-Hitlerite war, Romania was not given cobelligerent status and was excluded from the first of these groups. The researcher Gh. Buzatu has concluded that, bearing in mind the special conditions imposed on Romania and Poland, the 1946 peace was «even more unjust than the imperialist peace of 1919». (78)

Communist historians consider that Romania's independence and the formation of the Romanian national state which followed were not an accidental outcome of the peace treaties, but an achievement won by the entire people as a result of its century-long struggles. This battle of the Romanian people for freedom and national independence «laid its stamp on the entire social evolution of Romania, on ways of living and thinking, and on the country's historical destiny. Characterized by a resolute struggle, marked by many sacrifices, the Romanian people's fight was for freedom and unity, for the right to be master of their country». (79) Earlier and contemporary historians alike are unanimous in emphasizing Romania's «vocation for independence»; the struggle is one of the constants of Romanian history. (80)

The Romanian appreciation of the principle of national independence is strengthened by continued attempts to impose it as a fundamental policy in international relations. This is considered an essential contribution by the RCP to the enrichment of the historical, sociological, and political sciences, and even of Marxism-Leninism in general. (81)

Many of these themes, developed in special studies by Romanian historians of the independence war, were reflected in party leader Nicolae Ceauşescu's May 9 speech in connection with the centenary celebrations. (82)

Background Report No. 163
Munich, 11 August 1977,
Radio Free Europe Research.

BIBLIOGRAPHY:

1) See, for example, George Cioránescu, "Michael the Brave – Evaluations and Revaluations of the Wallachian Prince", RAD Background Report/191 (Romania), *Radio Free Europe Research,* 1 September 1976; and the same author's "Vlad the Impaler – Current Parallels with a Medieval Romanian Prince," RAD BR/23 (Romania), *RFER,* 31 January 1977.
2) See Romanian Situation Report/37, *RFER,* 22 October 1976, Item 4.
3) Ion Popescu-Puţuri, "The RCP Program on Romania's National Independence, *Anale de Istorie* No. 1, 1977, p. 24.
4) George Macovescu, "All the Prerogatives of a Sovereign State," *Magazin Istoric* No. 2, 1977, p. 7.
5) General Ion Ghica, "Note to N. Ionescu; Constantinople, 25 November – 7 December 1876," in Macovescu, *op. cit.*, p. 7.
6) Ghica, "Note to N. Ionescu; Constantinople, 6/18 December 1876," in Macovescu, *op. cit.,* p. 8.
7) Radio Moscow in Romanian, 4 May 1977.
8) Radu Vasile, "Strengthening the Country's Defense Capacity in the 1866–1877 Period with a View to Independence," *Revista de Istorie* No . 2, 1977, pp. 278–273.
9) *Ibid.,* p. 274.
10) Nicolae Ciachir, "Romanian Diplomacy – An Active Factor on the European Political Arena on the Eve of the Independence War," Part III, *Lumea* No. 9, 24 February 1977, p. 20; and Constantin Căzănişteanu and Mihail E. Ionescu, "1876 – A Romanian Diplomatic Mission to Constantinople," *Magazin Istoric* No. 2, 1977, pp. 911.
11) George Macovescu, "The Feeling of National Dignity," *Magazin Istoric* No. I, 1977, p. 7.
12) "Facts from the Shadow. Romania in the 1876–1877 Period," Part I, *Lumea* No. 5, 3 February 1977, p. 25.
13) Vasile Betea, "A Romanian Diplomatic Mission to the Crimea," *Magazin Istoric* No. 4, 1977, p. 18.
14) Ilie Ceauşescu, "Pages from the Chronicle of the Romanian People's Struggle for Independence," *Anale de Istorie* No. 1, 1977, p.59.
15) Netea, *op. cit.,* p. 19.
16) Ştefan Csucsuja, "The Independence War as Seen by the Hungarian Progressive Public Opinion of the Time," *Revista de Istorie* No. 4, 1977, pp. 625–626.
17) Ciachir, *op. cit.,* Part II, *Lumea* No. 8, 17 February 1977, p. 21.
18) Ceauşescu, *op. cit.,* p. 62.
19) Beatrice Marinescu and Şerban Rădulescu-Zoner, "We Shall Rely on the Patriotism of All Romanians," *Magazin Istoric* No. 4, 1977, p. 22.
20) *Ibid.,* p. 42.
21) George Macovescu, "Strong Through Our Right and the Justice of Our Cause", *Magazin Istoric* No. 4, 1977, p. 11.
22) Popescu-Puţuri, *op. cit.,* p. 23.
23) Ceauşescu, *op. cit.,* p. 63.

24) Csucsuja, *op. cit.*, p. 66
25) Constantin Corbu, "The Operations of the Romanian Army in the First Stage of the Independence War (April-August 1877)," *Revista de Istorie* No. 4, 1977, p. 608.
26) Ceauşescu, *op. cit.*, p. 65; Corbu, *op. cit.*, p. 609; Popescu-Puţuri, *op. cit.*, p. 23; Marian Ştefan and Vasile Mocanu, "Plevna", *Magazin Istoric* No. 5, 1977, p. 6.
27) Stan Valeriu, «*Report on Alexandru Cernat, Memoirs. The 1877–1878 Period*», Bucharest: Ed. Militară, 1976 in *Revista de Istorie* No. 4, 1977, pp. 777–778; Corbu, *op. cit.*, p. 610.
28) Ceauşescu, *op. cit.*, p. 71.
29) Corbu, *op. cit.*, p. 616.
30) "Facts from the Shadow", Part II, *Lumea* No. 7, 10 February, 1977, p. 26.
31) Vasile Alexandrescu and Constantin Căzănişteanu, "Foreign Opinions on the Romanian Army in the Independence War of 1877–1878", *Revista de Istorie* No. 4, 1977, pp. 697 and 703.
32) *Ibid.*, p. 701.
33) Major-General Constantin Antip, "A Premiere in Romanian Historiography", *Viaţa Militară* No. 3, 1977, p. 20.
34) Ion Coman, "The Command of the Romanian Army in the Independence War of 1877–1878", *Anale de Istorie* No. 1, 1977, p. 407.
35) Căzănişteanu and Ionescu, "The Historical Victory of Independence Was Gained Through the Heroic Struggle of the Romanian People", *Scînteia*, 23 April 1977.
36) Major General Eugen Bantea, "The Experience of the Independence War and the Development of the Armed Forces of Romania Before World War I", *Revista de Istorie* No. 3, 1977 p. 392.
37) *Loc. cit.*
38) G. Chiriţă, "The Attitude of the European Powers to the Proclamation of Romania's Independence", *Revista de Istorie* No. 4, 1977, p. 676.
39) *Ibid.*, pp. 678–687.
40) *Ibid.*, pp. 688–690.
41) Ceauşescu, *op. cit.*, p.73.
42) *Ibid.*, p. 74.
43) Csucsuja, *op. cit.*, pp. 670-671.
44) *Istoria României /The History of Romania/*, IV (Bucharest: Romanian Academy Publishing House, 1964), p. 637; Macovescu, "The Governments", *Magazin Istoric* No. 5, 1977, p. 56.
45) Csucsuja, *op. cit.*, p. 671.
46) Macovescu, "The Governments", p. 55.
47) Ceauşescu, *op. cit.*, p. 77.
48) Alexandru Porţeanu, "1877–1977: Significance of the Achievement of Romania's Independence in the Testimonies of the Time", *Lumea* No. 18, 28 April 1977, p. 14.
49) Ceauşescu, *op. cit.*, p. 77.
50) Macovescu, "The Governments", p. 56.
51) Nicolae Ciachir, *România în Sud-Estul Europei, 1848–1886/Romania in Southeastern Europe, 1848–1886/* (Bucharest: Ed. Politică, 1968), p. 179.

52) "From the Historical Archives of Romania", I, *Anale de Istorie* No. 1, 1976, pp. 105–107.
53) *Ibid.,* pp. 112–113.
54) Popescu-Puțuri, *op. cit.,* p. 24.
55) Aron Petric, "The Consolidation of National Independence: A Basic Factor in Romania's Development", *Revista de Istorie* No. 4, 1977, p. 744.
56) Ceaușescu, *op. cit.,* p. 75.
57) *Ibid.,* p. 76.
58) *Ibid.*
59) *Ibid.*
60) Paul Abrudan, "The Monetary and Material Aid Given by the Transylvanians to Support the War for Romania's State Independence", I and II, *Revista de Istorie,* Nos. 1 and 2, 1977, pp. 23–46 and 279-300; Nichita Adăniloaie, "The Achievement of National Independence – Crowning the Romanian People's Century – Old Aspirations toward Freedom", *Revista de Istorie* No. 4, 1977, pp. 569-597; Gh. Anghel, "The Mobilization of the Entire Country in a Just, Popular, and National War", I and II, *Revista Economică* No. 6 and 7, 11 and 18 February 1977, pp. 9 and 24–25; Toader Ionescu, "The Contribution of Transylvanian Romanians to the Independence War", *Revista Economică* No. 16, 22 April 1977, pp. 17-18, Vasile Netea, "Century–Old Testimonies to the National Solidarity of the Romanians", *Lumea* No. 16, 14 April 1977, pp. 22-23; Alexandru Porțeanu, 1877–1977 – State Independence –The Cause of the Entire Romanian Nation", *Lumea* No. 17, 21 April 1977, pp. 18–19; I.D. Suciu, "The Banat Romanians' Solid Support for the Independence War", *Revista de Istorie* No. 3, 1977, pp. 397–412.
61) Ion Pavelescu, "The Centenary of the Achievement of Independence", Interview with Professor Dumitru Almaș, *România Liberă* 21 February 1977.
62) Virgil Cândea, "Romania's Concept of Independence", *Magazin Istoric* No. 4, 1977, p. 7.
63) Dimitrie Cantemir, (1673-1723) Prince of Moldavia (1693 and 1710– 1711) and Constantin Cantacuzino (1650–1716), influent Wallachian boyar, are responsable for the anti-Turkish-minded foreign policy of their countries.
64) Cândea, *op. cit.,* p. 8.
65) Alexandru Porțeanu, "The Socialist Movement and the Problems of Independence, Sovereignty, and National Unity", I, *Revista de Istorie* No. 4, 1977, pp. 634–635; Georgeta Tudoran, "The Centenary of Independence", *România Liberă* 25 April 1977.
66) Alexandru Bolintineanu, "The Concept of National Independence in the Foreign Policy of Socialist Romania", *Revista de Istorie* No. 4, 1977, p. 749.
67) Petric, *op. cit.,* p. 741.
68) Dan Popescu, "National Independence – The Fiery Goal of the Thinking of Our Predecessors, the Promoters of the Country's Industrialization", I and II, *Revista Economică* No. 12 and 13: 1977, p. 24 and 12, respectively.
69) Lieutenant Colonel Vasile Iosipescu, "Romania, Unflinching Promoter of the Principles of Independence and National Sovereignty", *Viața Militară* No. 4, 1977, p. 25.

70) Şerban Rădulescu–Zoner, "Romania and the Struggle for Liberation of the Balkan Peoples (1875-1877)", *Era Socialistă* No. 4, 1977, p. 44.
71) I. Cioară, "Griviţa, Pleven, Smîrdan, Rahova – An Itinerary of Heroic Struggle", *Lumea* No. 18, 28 April 1977, p. 15.
72) George Serafim, "Independence and National Sovereignty – An Objective Law of Social Development, a Basic Imperative of History", *Lumea* No. 20, 12 May 1977, p. 4.
73) Bantea, *op. cit.*, p. 383.
74) "From Romania's Historical Archives", I, *Anale de Istorie* No.1,1976, p. 125.
75) Constantin C. Giurescu, *Amintiri* /Recollections I/ (Bucharest: Editura Sport-Turism, 1976), p. 208.
76) Popescu–Puţuri, *op. cit.,* pp. 21–22.
77) Nicolae Dascălu, "Romania and the Versailles Peace Treaties", *Revista de Istorie* No. 2, 1977, p. 335 (on Eliza Campus, "The Problem of Noninterference in Domestic Affairs at the Paris Peace Conference", report presented to the Cuza University of Iaşi on 26 November 1976).
78) Dascălu, *op. cit.,* p. 337 (on Gh. Buzatu, "Romania at the Paris Peace Conference, 1919 and 1946").
79) *Programul Partidului Comunist Român de Făurire a Societăţii Socialiste Multilaterale Dezvoltate şi Înaintarea României spre Comunism*/The RCP Program for the Creation of a Multilaterally Developed Socialist Society and Romania's Advance Toward Communism/(Bucharest: 1975), p. 29.
80) Leonid Boicu, "The Conquest of State Independence – An Expression of the Assertion of the Will to Freedom of the Romanian People", *Era Socialistă* No. 1, 1977, p. 25.
81) Victor Cuculescu, "Independence and Sovereignty – Requirements of the New World Economic and Political Order", *Revista Economică* No. 19, 13 May 1977, pp. 5–6 and 32; Mircea Moarcăş, "Independence and National Sovereignty – Basic Ideas of the Foreign Policy of Socialist Romania", *România Liberă*, 9 May 1977; Serafim, *op. cit.,* pp. 2-5; N.S. Stănescu, "Observing States' Sovereign Rights – A Prerequisite for the Construction of a New International Order", *Lumea,* No. 20, 12 May 1977, pp. 19–20.
82) *Scînteia* 10 May 1977; Romanian SR/16, *RFER,* 12 May 1977, Item 1.

VI

BESSARABIA AGAIN ON THE TAPIS*

Issue No. 4 (1978) of the bimonthly *Anale de Istorie,* published by the Institute for Historical and Political Sciences of the RCP CC, featured an article signed by Vasile Maciu dealing once again with the Bessarabian problem. After more than an one year lull in Soviet-Romanian polemics over Bessarabia, this sensitive subject reappeared in the Romanian press in December 1977, when Mircea Muşat wrote an article with many references to Bessarabia for *Anale de Istorie*. The difference between these two articles is that Muşat views the Bessarabian problem in the larger historical context of the 1918 union of Romanian provinces, while Maciu analyzes only the 1878 events, when the Bessarabian question was discussed by European chancelleries and the Congress of Berlin. The intention of Maciu's article is obvious: to demonstrate that at the Congress of Berlin Romania did not renounce Bessarabia in exchange for Dobrogea, united with Romania by decision of the Congress. The Romanian historian argues that Romania never accepted the bargain offered by Russia, i.e., an exchange of territories, for the simple reason that Dobrogea was not «annexed» by Romania but «reunited» with it – union considered by Maciu to be just and lawful.

Vasile Maciu is a Professor of Modern Romanian History at Bucharest University and a Corresponding Member of the Romanian Academy; he was a member of the National Council of Socialist Unity Front from 1968 to 1974. As an historian he adheres to the school of thought which maintains that historical writing should always demonstrate a precise thesis, that the demonstration must be rigorous, using only correct and verified data *(Viaţa Studenţească* No. 30, 20 September 1978). His study on «Romania and the Congress of Berlin» is largely based on recently published primary materials and successfully complements earlier studies on the same subject by the historians Nicolae Iorga, Gheorghe Brătianu, and R.W. Seton-Watson. Maciu's article underlines the unfriendly

---

* As in the Romanian original, dates are given according to both the old and new calendars.

attitude adopted by Russia toward Romania during the diplomatic negotiations preceding the Congress, as well as during the Congress itself. First of all Russia did not agree on *de jure* recognition of Romania's independence, but only *de facto;* furthermore the Russian military command refused to receive a Romanian delegate at the armistice and peace negotiations, and even more than that, the tsar and Chancellor Gorchakov formally demanded annexation of Southern Bessarabia, which had been united with Moldavia at the Paris Peace Conference in 1856. Russia continued its anti-Romanian political line by annexing Southern Bessarabia in the 1878 Treaty of San Stefano, by opposing Romanian participation at the Congress of Berlin, and finally by putting strong military pressure on Romania which almost led to hostilities between the two former allies.

* * *

Romania and the Congress of Berlin (1878)
By Vasile Maciu

«On the eve of the 1877-1878 war, Romania was a state with full autonomy guaranteed by the seven powers which signed the Paris treaty in 1856, but at the same time under the sovereignty of the Ottoman Empire to which it paid tribute. Romania's attempts in the summer of 1876 to obtain, with the assent of the majority of major European powers, absolute political independence were not successful. Both England, the defender of the integrity of the Ottoman Empire, and tsarist Russia, which intended to annex from Romania Southwest Bessarabia which had been reattached to Moldavia by the Paris Congress of 1856, were in opposition. Romania's petition to the seven European powers at the Constantinople Conference from December 1876 to January 1877 to grant it absolute political autonomy «through a special guarantee of its perpetual neutrality» and, in case of war between one of the great powers and the Sublime Porte, to grant it «a special guarantee respecting its rights, neutrality, and integrity,» was not accepted for discussion at the conference.

* * *

Ion C. Brătianu, President of the (Romanian) Council of Ministers, declared: «We must first of all find the guarantee of independence in ourselves.» As a result of the motion voted on 9/21 May 1877 the legislative bodies passed a new motion in which they proclaimed Romania's absolute independence.

* * *

None of the guarantor powers hastened to approve Romania's decision to become an independent state. Russia recognized Romania's independence **de facto,** *but not* **de jure***; as Chancellor [Prince Aleksandr] Gorchakov declared to*

Lord Loftus, British ambassador to St. Petersburg, on May 19/31: «It is a problem, which need not be discussed until later by the assembled European powers.»

The Romanian delegate was not received by the command of the Russian army at the armistice and peace negotiations. A. I. Nelidov, director of the diplomatic Office of the Great Headquarters of the Imperial Army, telegraphed the Romanian Prime Minister that he should convey to St. Petersburg his views concerning the peace terms.

Shortly after, on 14/26 January 1878, [Emi] Ghica, the Romanian diplomatic agent in Petersburg, relaled that the tsar and the chancellor formally informed him about «their intentions to regain the part of Bessarabia extending up to Chilia.» General Ghica stated further that the arguments referred to the fact that this part of Bessarabia was reunited with Moldavia and not with Romania, through the decision of a treaty «from which nothing more remains...» General Ghica replied that the territory in question «is a part of our body» and the act of 1856 was made without stipulation, but the tsar and the chancellor stood their grounds.

* * *

On January 19/31 General [Count Nikolai Pavlovich] Ignatiev, who had arrived in Bucharest the previous day, had a meeting with Ion C. Brătianu and /Mihail/ Kogălniceanu. He openly claimed Southwest Bessarabia: «Prince Carol I, and the government – as Kogălniceanu informed General Ghica – answered that since this territory was returned to us by Europe and since our territorial integrity has been guaranteed by the convention of 4 April 1877, we could not agree with the demand to cede [this land] and that the great powers have the right to give their opinions on this problem.» The confidence in «Europe» was based on the assumption that England and Austria-Hungary would oppose Russian demands to the end.

* * *

Knowledge of the tsarist government's pretentions caused strong anxiety in Romania. At the Deputies Assembly session on 26 January/ 7 February 1878, historian [Vasile Alexandrescu] Urechia, professor at Bucharest University, asked whether the government would «be willing to tell us how much credibility we should give the threatening rumors being spread in the national and foreign newspapers.» Ion Brătianu, President of the Council of Ministers, answered by saying that Russia did not «formally» inform the Romanian government «about the cession of Bessarabia,» but did categorically tell Romania – «albeit, only informally» – of its intention «to take back our part of Bessarabia. Our answer

/to this/ was that the Romanian nation will never agree, either to return or to exchange any of its territory, even if we get the most advantageous compensation (applause).» Deputy Gheorghe Vernescu then proposed a motion which, recalling the great powers' guarantee and article two of the Romanian-Russian Convention of 4/16 April 1877, stressed the great material and human sacrifices made by the country in the war «in order to preserve its integrity and to consolidate its independence»; it concluded with the declaration that the Assembly «resolved to preserve the integrity of the country's territory, and not to allow any annexation of its land, under any pretext and for no territorial compensation or indemnification.»

A vote was taken and the motion was approved unanimously. The Senate passed a similar motion. The vote of the legislative bodies was made known through a circular cable to Romanian diplomatic agents abroad.

* * *

Inasmuch as Romania's admission at the conference as an independent state entitled to speak and to vote would have hindered Russia's pretentions, on February 14/26 Nikolai de Giers, Gorchakov's deputy, informed the Romanian diplomatic agent, General Ghica, that Romania's independence «will be recognized by the conference»; the prince chancellor had no objection to Romania's sending a delegation to the conference with only advisory voting power, but «concerning admission of our country with a full vote,» General Ghica reported, «the prince can neither take initiative, nor support us, bearing in mind that a similar proposal has no chance of being received favorably by the powers....»

After five days, on 19 February/3 March 1878, the peace preliminaries between Russia and the Ottoman Empire were signed at San Stefano. Article five of the preliminaries anticipated that the Sublime Porte would «recognize Romania's independence,» while article eighteen stipulated that Russia would agree to repay «a great amount from the sums mentioned in the paragraph through the assignment of the following territories: the Sanjak of Tulcea, that is, the districts of Chilia, Sulina, Mahmudia, Isaccea, Tulcea, Măcin, Babadag, Hîrşova, Küstendge (Constanţa), and Medgidia; together with the islands of the Danube Delta and the Island of Serpents – territories for which «Russia reserves an option to exchange that part of Bessarabia detached in 1856 and restricted in the south by the river bed of a branch of Chilia River and by Gura Stara-Stambul". Article eight, indirectly referring to Romania, foresaw that «the Russian occupation troops in Bulgaria will keep their ways of communication through Romania, but also through the ports of the Black Sea...»

Knowledge of the provisions of the Peace preliminaries of San Stefano caused dissatisfaction in Romania, as they required it to relinquish a part of its territory in exchange for a former Romanian territory wich had been usurped from Wallachia in the second decade of the fifteenth century by the Ottoman Empire. The Romanian government tried on this occasion to enlist Germany's support, but, on February 26/March 10, the Romanian diplomatic agent in Berlin related that German Secretary of Foreign Affairs /Ernst von/ Bülow made known to him that «he thinks it would be difficult for Germany to oppose the wish of such a great state as Russia, especially since the other powers agreed on Bessarabia's return, which to him seems almost certain.» Romania's protests against the territorial clause of the San Stefano Preliminaries greatly angered Gorchakov because «they tend to submit the tsar to Europe's open criticism... " He said he would not put this problem before the Congress and, if necessary, he would forcibly occupy the requested territory.

* * *

In view of an eventual alliance with Romania /Austro-Hungarian Foreign Minister Count Gyula/ Andrássy declared to Ioan Bălăceanu that he did not share Gorchakov's opinion concerning Bessarabia, though he had agreed, as far back as 1876 at Reichstadt, that this Romanian territory would be given to Russia. He maintained that this problem was «among those which Europe was called to discuss,» and he «openly» agreed to Romania's admittance in the Congress and thought "that the other powers will not make any objection".

* * *

In the last 10 days of March, Ion C. Brătianu went to Vienna and Berlin in order to find out to what extent Romania would be supported by Austria-Hungary and Germany. On March 23/ April 4 he was received by Emperor Franz-Joseph and had, of course, meetings with Andrássy who «firmly urged him to resist. »

* * *

On March 27/ April 8 I.C. Brătianu was received by Chancellor Otto von Bismarck in Berlin. However, the German government «showed caution concerning the Bessarabian problem,» Bismarck urged Brătianu to show good will toward the Russian proposals, in order that «he could ask and get much more from them – one hundred million and even greater territorial compensations. » On April 3/15 the President of the Council of Ministers returned to Bucharest from Berlin at a time when relations with Russia had worsened and a powerful military pressure was being exerted by the tsarist government. Relating to the Russian military actions, on April 5 and 17 an interpellation was made in the Deputies Assembly, which Ion C. Brătianu was obliged to answer. The legislative bodies wanted to move the government to Craiova; The President of the Council of Ministers, fearing aggression, agreed to withdraw the government to Oltenia; but King Carol I and /Mihail/ Kogălniceanu opposed the move. Yet, on April 20/May 2 the Council of Ministers decided that «the army take the defense position at the Carpathian Mountains, between Piteşti, Cîmpulung and Tîrgovişte.» On April 29/May 11 Carol himself left for Oltenia, returning to Bucharest in the second part of May.

* * *

Nevertheless, as the Congress meeting approached the anxiety caused by these military actions started to lessen as well as the hope of Romania's admittance as a full participant in the Congress. The opening to participation was made by the British government, as the Romanian diplomatic agent in Paris (on mission in London) reported on May 26/June 7, noting that marques of Salisbury, the British Minister of Foreign Affairs, had sent him a letter in which he informed him that his government did not object to the presence in Berlin of «representatives or delegates who could explain to the Congress, as consultants, Romania's views and wishes....» Salisbury added, however, that concerning Bessarabia «he cannot indicate the policy he will follow until he knows precisely what the other powers intend to do» (he had already agreed on it with /Count Piotr Andreievich/ Shuvalov, the Russian ambassador to London).

* * *

The attitude of the rest of the British plenipotentiaries could be explained – as Kogălniceanu was loath to do – by their embarrassment to talk to the Romanian delegates after The Globe revealed the agreements England had already made with Russia. «Everywhere,» as /Mihail/ Kogălniceanu noticed, «I receive assurances of sympathy, but they are merely academic, and they only show a theoretical or sterile good will.» Only /William Henry/ Waddington took a «more realistic stand,» in order not to incite them to hope for too much. «Bessarabia must be considered as lost....» he told them.

Within a few days, on June 12/24 the Romanian plenipotentiaries presented the Romanian Memorandum to Bismarck, president of the Congress, expressing again "the hope to be consulted before the decision concerning Romania is taken." The signers of the Memorandum indicated that it «summarized the points which Romania requests be adopted by Europe.» The Memorandum contained five requests:

1. No part of its actual territory should be taken from Romania;

2. Russian armies should not have a right of way over Romania's territory;

3. The principality, by virtue of its secular titles, should regain possession of the islands and the Danube mouths, including the Island of Serpents;

4. Romania should receive, proportional to the military forces it had deployed, damages in the most useful form;

5. Romania's independence should become definitive and its territory should be declared as neutral.

The Congress debated the Romanian problem in two sessions. In the first, on June 17/29, after having listened to the Greek delegates, Lord Salisbury proposed to decide whether or not the Romanian representatives should be heard by Congress. Salisbury argued that the Congress «after having listened to the delegation of a nation which claims foreign provinces, should also listen to the representative of a country which asks to keep regions which belong to it.» The Italian representative, /Lodovico/ Corti, agreed at once with his British colleague. Bismarck admitted his inclination was against admitting the Romanian delegates, whose claims «do not seem to be of a nature to facilitate a good understanding.» He agreed, however, to submit the question to a vote. Salisbury's proposal was accepted by Andrássy and Waddington – the votes of the English and Italian representatives had been given before. Gorchakov felt «the presence of the Romanian representatives is liable to cause lively discussions,» but he did not vote against their admission. Bismarck, asking the Russian representatives for a precise vote, was told by Count Shuvalov that «the remarks of the Romanian delegates cannot but increase the difficulties of discussion, as Russia certainly will not allow itself to be accused without being able to defend itself.» Yet, he added, since the majority of the Congress favored admission, the Russian did not want to be alone in sending the opponents away and would not oppose Lord Salisbury's proposals. Andrássy, with the approval of the whole assembly, then proposed that the Romanian delegates «should be heard under the same conditions as the Greek ministers.» The president of the Congress announced he would invite the Romanian representatives to the next session.

They went on to discuss the articles of the Treaty of San Stefano which concerned Romania.

* * *

Lord Beaconsfield /Benjamin Disraeli/ declared that he regretfully considered the stipulations concerning Bessarabia of Article XIX of the Treaty of San Stefano as being against the 1856 Treaty of Paris. He added, however, that since the other signatories of the Treaty had not intervened in this problem, he «would not be in a position to advise the government of the Queen / Victoria / to use force in enforcing the stipulations of the Treaty of Paris»; but he protested the move.

Gorchakov supported the stipulations of the Treaty of San Stefano concerning the territorial exchange imposed on Romania, asserting that in 1856 Bessarabia was only given to Moldavia when the Principalities were separated. He hoped, he went on to say, that Lord Beaconsfield «will not persist in his objections when His Excellency recognizes that the liberty of the Danube will not be affected by Bessarabia's retrocession.» Shuvalov, considering the Chancellor's argument weak, completed it by saying that the Bessarabian problem was for Russia «a mere point of honor.» Taking the floor again, Gorchakov insisted on «the advantage» which Romania would obtain in exchange for the yielded territory. Bismarck, interrupting the discussion, said that concerning the assurance of free navigation on the Danube, he «agrees with the British representatives, but he does not find any connection between the Danube's liberty and Bessarabia's retrocession.» He then proposed «to postpone the continuation of the discussion until next month's session when the Romanian representatives will be listened to.»

On the morning of the day the Romanian delegates were received at the Congress, Kogălniceanu was received by Bülow, with whom «he had a long conversation.» Of course, the German minister strove to convince his Romanian colleague of the necessity to accept the eventual decisions of the Congress. After that, both Romanian delegates were received by Lord Beaconsfield who confined himself to listening to them attentively, after which he told them, «that in politics ingratitude is often the reward for outstanding service».

* * *

On 19 June/1 July 1878, at 14.30 hours, the Romanian delegates were received at the Congress session, in the same manner as the Greek representatives.

* * *

Ion C. Brătianu made a short speech, emphasizing that «our loss of a part of our patrimony would not only cause a deep grief for the Romanian nation, it would shatter in her heart any trust in the strength of the treaties and their sanctity, both in the principles of absolute right and in the written rights.» The president replied that "the Congress will conscientiously examine the observations made by the Romanian delegates", and Brătianu withdrew.

* * *

Nevertheless, Shuvalov also made Romania's independence conditional on the carrying out of the Russian government's territorial claims. Agreeing to comply with these terms, Waddington asserted that the French delegates considered «the Romanians were treated in a rather strict way....» Waddington,

Andrássy, and Corti agreed with the return of Dobrogea to Romania, which in the end made Shuvalov accept a frontier from Rasova toward Silistra, with the Black Sea border not going beyond Mangalia; this proposal was accepted by the Congress. Salisbury added, with agreement of the Russians, the Island of Serpents. Further details were left to the editing panel. Three days after his appearance at the Congress, Kogălniceanu wrote to Bucharest that the Romanian delegates had been asked to state whether they would submit to the Congress's verdict; they refused. They did «not commit themselves at all», leaving it to the country to express its own opinion. They were told the term «exchange or compensation /had been / carefully removed from the text.»

* * *

Under Article XIV of the treaty, Russia annexed Southern Bessarabia from Romania, the territory bordered «on the western side by the bed of the Pruth and on the south by the river bed of the arm of the Chilia and the Stara-Stambul mouth». The same article promised the reunification with Romania of the islands of Danube Delta and the Island of Serpents, the Sanjak of Tulcea with the districts of Chilia, Sulina, Mahmudia, Isaccea, Tulcea, Măcin, Babadag, Hîrşova, Constanţa (Küstendge), Medgidia, together with «the territory at the south of Dobrogea as far as a line streching from Silistra to the south of Mangalia on the Black Sea.» It was decided that the border be established on the spot «by the European commission in charge of establishing the frontiers of Bulgaria.» It should be noted that concerning the territorial problem, the treaty did not foresee any change; the territories forming Dobrogea – part of the ancient Dacia – were reunited to the motherland.

* * *

Without waiting for the end of the Congress, Brătianu and Kogălniceanu returned to Bucharest, bringing with them Romania's independence and the Dobrogea region, though in exchange for the loss of important territory and the imposition of a modification of the constitution.

Defending the national territorial integrity, supported by the entire Romanian people, they adopted a firm and principled position, which they did not give up despite all the pressures put upon them. They rejected the territorial exchange asked of them, considering the Congress's reunification of Dobrogea with the motherland, as just and legitimate.»

Background Report No. 224,
Munich, 11 October 1978,
Radio Free Europe Research.

VII

ROMANIAN–RUSSIAN RELATIONS DURING WORLD WAR I

The echoes of the centenary of Romania's state independence which gave Romanian historians an opportunity to recall the political-military divisions created by the 1877 Russian-Romanian-Turkish war and by the ensuing Treaty of Berlin –had hardly died (1), when a new national celebration – the 69th anniversary of the formation of the «unitary Romanian state» arose to prompt discussion on Romanian-Russian co-operation during World War I. In six months, 1 December 1978 will mark 60 years since the adoption of the Alba Iulia Declaration, which served officially to unite Transylvania, the Banat, Crişana, and Maramureş with the Kingdom of Romania. In keeping with traditional Romanian communist practice, however, this celebration will be dragged out over a lengthy period of time for propaganda purposes.

As usual, the guidelines were set down by the party secretary-general, who said that «the implementation of the union in 1918 should be interpreted within the context of the entire development of the Romanian people, whose history (2) began thousands of years ago.» In commemorative articles, meetings, and ceremonies particular significance will most likely be paid to the minorities which had been included in Romania's borders as a result of the 1918 union. Official historiography has stressed both that they joined the Romanian national state voluntarily, and the idea that the nationalities issue has been democratically settled. (3)

The first commemorative articles to appear were signed by Ion Popescu-Puţuri (b. 1906), a member of the State Council and director since 1966 of the Bucharest Institute for Historical and Sociopolitical Studies, and Lieutenant-General Gheorghe Zaharia, deputy director of the above-mentioned institute. (4)

The discussion of Romanian history, from the Thracian-Dacian-Getae of over 2,500 years ago and up to World War I, follows the well-known patterns of

Romanian historiography: the historians try to prove that the idea of state unity and political independence constitutes a permanent factor in the thinking and acting of the Romanian people, present in all generations and social strata of the population, and in all prominent personalities of Romanian political and cultural life. Things become more complicated, however, when the need arises to explain the exact nature of Romanian-Russian relations before and after Romania actively entered World War I. According to Popescu-Puțuri, tsarist Russia's tactics were to draw closer to Romania politically in order to subjugate it. «This method was not new. As a matter of fact, the entire policy of tsarist Russia is characterized by similar methods. It was first aimed at drawing Romania near to tsarist Russia, so that having acquired it as an ally, in exchange for fictitious promises to recognize its independence and territorial integrity, it could deal with Romania's adversaries alone and, more often than not, decide on matters affecting the vital interests of our country.» (5) Karl Marx, quoted in the footnotes, supports this denunciation of Russian diplomatic perfidy when he states that, "before Russia incorporated Crimea, it proclaimed the latter's independence,» while addressing the Poles, whose country he sought to reannex, tsar Alexander I said: «Arm yourself to defend your fatherland and preserve your **political independence**» (emphasis in original). Speaking about the solicitude over the Romanians displayed by Russia, Karl Marx added: «What shall we say about the Danubian Principalities? Since Peter the Great first entered them, Russia has taken care of their **independence**» (in quotation marks and emphasized in original).

Popescu-Puțuri also cites Engels who, in a letter to the Romanian socialist Ion Nădejde, writes that the problem of the Romanians and of the other oppressed peoples cannot be settled as long as the two major absolutist powers – tsarist Russia and the Habsburg monarchy – exist. Engels adds that a victory of one of these powers and a defeat of the other represents a constant danger to the very existence of the Romanian state and that, «in such a struggle, we could not side with either of the combatants; on the contrary, we would wish them both to be defeated, if this were possible» (6). Consequently, according to Popescu-Puțuri, the Romanians preferred to remain neutral in the first years of the war between the two neighboring imperialist powers and decided to enter it only in order to attain national unity, and only upon receiving the Entente's ultimatum.

Romania had been bargaining with both sides for the best terms for entering the war since early in the conflict, and the Romanian leadership contained both pro-allied and pro-German parties. The Allies generally had the upper hand in these complex negotiations, since they alone could offer the plum of all Romanianinhabited Habsburg provinces, although some German and Austrian circles tried to persuade Hungarian Prime Minister Count Istvan Tisza to make concessions in Transylvania.

In a typical oversimplification of intricate developments, a Soviet historian writes that «the rulers in Romania were cynically awaiting a favorable moment to cast their country's working people into a massacre, so that their plans for conquering neighboring territories could be realized.» (7) Furthermore, Gheorghe Zaharia claims that Lenin wrote that the national wars waged by small states against the imperialist power were just, (8) therefore implicitly acknowledging that Romania's war efforts were just. Bucharest had requested that the Entente not only recognize Romania's right to achieve national unity through self-determination, but also observe conditions of belligerency, i.e.: at least 300 tons of war material – including ammunition – to be shipped daily, routed through the Russian harbors of Arkhangelsk and Vladivostok; military support, particularly by Russia, of the Romanian offensive against the Austro-Hungarian Empire; guarding the Romanian rear in Bucovina and Dobrogea by the Russian Army, which was to send two infantry divisions and one cavalry division to Dobrogea. But Zaharia goes on to note Russia's «disloyalty» to Romania, for Russia not only failed to honor its obligations, but also went so far as «almost to come to an understanding with the enemy, intending to divide Romanian territory.» (9)

Such charges are not new, and British historian R.W. Seton-Watson, dismissed them as "fairy tales". (10)

Russia's failure to observe the commitments it had formally assumed in the military convention of 4-17 August 1916 is clearly documented. (11) *Anale de Istorie* prints the minutes of the secret meeting of the French Chamber of Deputies of 28-30 November 1916, (12) particularly concerned with the conditions under which Romania had entered World War I, and the reasons for its defeat in 1916. The embarrassment of French Premier Aristide Briand is evident in this document. Obliged to relate how France sought to rescue the Romanian armed forces, which were under pressure from German-Bulgarian forces, Briand said: «We first turned to Russia and pleaded with it to rush to Romania's help. We said to it: «The war is there! It is there that one should seek a success which might spur a rapid development toward victory...» Russian brigades are ready to come to France; they are at Arkhangelsk. Send them to rescue the Romanians; you would save them the long voyage to France or to Salonica. Now there is only one front: the threatened front is the one in Romania. Send the men assigned to us there, but send them at once, as quickly as you can, to rescue our allies.» (13) But the plaintive appeal of the French premier evoked no response, and no Russian aid was forthcoming... because of transport difficulties, prompting French Deputy André Lebey to remark that Russian aid would arrive *post factum*, like the colorfully clad soldiers in French musical comedies, that is, after Bucharest had been occupied by the Germans, or in 100 years, as another French deputy, Brizon, put it.

Georges Leygues emphasized that Romania had to defend frontiers as long as the entire Russsian front – 600 kilometers (372 miles) along the Carpathians, 500 kilometers (310 miles) along the Danube, and 150 kilometers (93 miles) between the Danube and the Black Sea – and this constituted a military assignment that could hardly be undertaken by an army of only 500,000 Romanians. Emile Constant asked the French government bluntly: «What? Do you imagine that with 50,000 Russians you will succeed in hingering such a vast plan and such a tremendous organization as the German?» (14) There was uproar in the French Chamber of Deputies when Victor Dalbiez cried: «Russia must rescue Romania!» He was followed immediately by J. Longuet who asked: «What concessions did Russia make? Did it offer Bessarabia?» (15) After listening to the explanations provided by Minister of War General Pierre-Auguste Roques, F. Merlin concluded that the Romanian army would have been doomed to defeat under any circumstances, «unless it was supported and aided by a Russian Army of 200,000 or 300,000, whitout which the Romanian offensive was foolhardy, mad. And then, I wonder whether the government's efforts should not have been mainly concentrated on maintaining Romania's neutrality and not on throwing it into an offensive which merely served the purposes of our enemies.» (16) When pressed hard, Aristide Briand was obliged to admit that, together with Lloyd George, he had asked Russia to help the Romanian war effort by sending 200,000 men. However, «Russia could not do it. We are extremely sorry for it. ...From the French point of view we did what we could.» But Briand, who used considerable diplomatic tact to avoid offending France's Russian ally, was interrupted from the benches of the Socialist Party with the question: «What about Russia?» (17)

In his article, supported by documentary evidence of the debate in the French Chamber of Deputies, Popescu-Puțuri deals at length with the question of Russia's disloyalty to Romania. He argues that General Aleksey Alekseyevich Brusilov's offensive was not launched to support the Romanian offensive, and that the tsarist Foreign Minister Boris Vladimirovich Stuermer had planned to conclude an agreement with German Kaiser Wilhelm II to divide Romania – a project which Lenin has also mentioned. Quoting a text by Russian Minister of Education L.A. Kasso in footnotes to the first part of his article, Popescu-Puțuri emphasizes that, right from the beginning, Russia's annexationist plans went far beyond occupying a province: they sought to occupy all of Moldavia and Wallachia. «Certainly, our initial plans were far more comprehensive. In 1805 we thought we would be able to conquer the two principalities without any struggle and to carve four Russian provinces out of them. Eventually, circumstances obliged us to be satisfied with a far more modest gain. From what we got, we made up the province of Bessarabia.» (18)

Furthermore, unlike the other texts analyzed here, Popescu-Puţuri's article elaborates on the decision of the Moldavians living between the Pruth and Dniester Rivers «concerning the future of the Romanian province of Bessarabia, which must be resolved in the spirit of Lenin's ideas.» He shows that the National Assembly (Sfatul Ţării) that voted for union with Romania was truly representative of all nationalities in Bessarabia and not just of Romanians. It is worth noting that Popescu-Puţuri talks about «the Romanians of Moldavia beyond the Pruth," (19) while Soviet historians always refer to a Moldavian people allegedly distinct from the Romanians. Popescu-Puţuri also makes use of the expression of «the union of the Moldavian Republic with the mother country,» (20) instead of the expression «the occupation of Bessarabia,» to be found in such works as the *Romanian Encyclopaedic Dictionary* (1962): « In January 1918, the Romanian bourgeois-landowners' government occupied Bessarabia. » (21)

Popescu-Puţuri concludes that, 60 years ago, the Romanians had seen «their strongest, 1,000-year-old wish» of re-establishing ancient Dacia come true, a dream that, through the agency of yesterday's Romanian socialists, is indirectly attributed to present-day Romanian communists as well.

Below is a translation of excerpts from Part II of Ion Popescu-Puţuri's «For a Just Cause – How Romania Entered World War I in August 1916», which appeared in *Anale de Istorie* No. 2, 1978.

«According to the plan of operations approved by the leaders of the Romanian state, the strategic targets of the Romanian Armed Forces included crushing the Austro-Hungarian forces of resistance in Transylvania and rapidly advancing into the Hungarian Plain, which would have resulted in a considerable shortening of the Romanian front, initially running along the entire Carpathian range. This would have helped the Romanian Army to join up with the Russian, a move that would have had the gravest effects upon the state of Hungarian counts and barons, and the armies of the Central Powers in the Balkan Peninsula.

Romania's declaration of war, which took the Central Powers by surprise, and the swift advance of its army into Transylvania constituted valuable assistance to the French, since the German Army had already launched a major offensive at Verdun. Almost 40 powerful German divisions, taken from the Western Front, were sent to strengthen the Austro-Hungarian units on the Transylvanian front, which were not able to hold back the Romanian troops alone.

However, the victorious offensive of the Romanian Army was stopped because Romania's allies, the Great Powers – Russia, France, Great Britain, and Italy –

failed to honor the obligations they had assumed in August 1916, when they concluded a military convention with the Romanian government. It is worth mentioning that despite those obligations, also signed by Chief of Staff of the Imperial Russian Armies Mikhail Vasilyevich Alekseyev, the tsarist offensive on the Eastern Front, led by General Aleksey Brusilov, did not proceed vigorously, which produced the most adverse repercussions. Many of the military units of the Central Powers made available on that front were sent to the Romanian sector. The second reason why the Romanian offensive failed was that the Western Allies did not honor the commitments they had assumed in the military convention to start a major offensive of the combined French-British forces, led by General Maurice Sarrail, at Salonica in the Balkans **one week before Romania joined the war** *(emphasis in original). The purpose would have been to hold back the armies of the Central Powers under Field Marshal August von Mackensen, who had been sent to Bulgaria, and who had prepared a major offensive against the Romanians from the south. Since they were not held back in the Balkans by any offensive by the armies of the* **Entente,** *the armies of the Central Powers – especially the Bulgarians – suddenly pitted their entire 120,000 – man strength against Romania, which had sent the bulk of its armed forces to the Transylvanian front. Besides, the tsarist government had failed to honor the obligations it assumed by signing the military convention:* **after Romania mobilized** *(emphasis in original) it was supposed to send one cavalry division and two infantry divisions to co-operate with the Romanian Army on Romania's southern front against any possible offensive from the south by the armies of the Central Powers. The Russian units, led by General Andrey Medardovich Zaionchkovsky, turned up belatedly and did not start a decisive offensive, thus contributing to the defeat of the Romanian Army at Turtucaia in Northeastern Bulgaria. The fourth reason explaining the failure of Romania's offensive concerned the state of preparedness of its army, for neither the tsarist government, nor France, nor England, nor Italy honored any of the obligations assumed under the military convention signed with Romania regarding the average daily supply* **on schedule** *(emphasis in original) of 300 tons of ammunition and other war material. These obligations were honored only at the outset. Later, however, supplies arrived quite sporadically, for the majority of this war material earmarked by the Western Allies for Romania was delayed at railway stations in tsarist Russia (the only possible transit route at the time) or sent erroneously by the tsarist rail authorities elsewhere, but not to Romania. Its eastern neighbor is responsible for the fifth reason for its failure. This did not directly result from the concrete stipulations contained in the military convention concluded between the major* **Entente** *powers and Romania, but nevertheless directly derived from the general* **political treaty** *under which Romania was considered an* **ally** *(emphasis in original) of the* **Entente** *powers. When our country found itself in a particularly* *grave situation, and despite considerable loss of life and many heroic deeds, the Romanian military units were obliged to yield, step by step, important territories in Transylvania, Oltenia, Wallachia and Dobrogea, with the enemy even occupying Bucharest, the country's capital, on 6 December 1916. Under these critical circumstances the insistent appeals of the Romanian General Headquarters and Romanian government to their ally in Petrograd to rush to their help in order to halt the offensive of the armies of the Central Powers did not produce any response. What is more, despite the gravity of the situation, General Alekseyev cynically replied that conditions on the Romanian front were not as tragic as the Romanians claimed. When the front was consolidated along the Focșani-Nămoloasa line, the tsarist troops crossed the Pruth River, overran the Siret front, and consolidated their position there. This aroused considerable concern among the Romanians, for there was a rumor afloat that «so far as the tsarist troops were concerned, this constituted the possible frontier of a greater Russia.» (22)*

Romania had entered the war following the ultimatum it had been given by the Great Powers of the **Entente** in order to rescue them from the precarious condition in which they found themselves on both the Western and Eastern Fronts. Romania was defeated as a result of the imperialist plans of the great powers of both camps and of the agreements concluded between them prior to Romania's entry into the war. «The Romanian defeat had been foreseen and planned by Russia's Foreign Minister Boris Stuermer, who was one of the Germanophile group in the Petrograd cabinet that hoped to put an end to the war,» General Dumitru Iliescu remarked...

The Russian diplomat Aleksey Andreyevich Polivanov emphasized at that time:

Romania's failure will not arouse displeasure in Russia for Romania would have been capable of barring Russia's push to Constantinople, especially as it (Romania) would have grown stronger, and Russia was aware of the fact that Romania's claims would only diminish with the failure of the army of the Romanian king.

Had the situation developed in such way as to allow for the 1916 political and military agreement with Romania to be fully implemented a very strong state – made up of Moldavia, Wallachia and Dobrogea (pre-war Romania), and of Transylvania, the Banat, and Bucovina (obtained following the 1916 treaty) with a population of almost 13,000,000 inhabitants – would have been established in the Balkans. The same diplomat remarked: «In future, this state would hardly have entertained friendly feelings toward Russia and would have been ambitious enough to make its national dreams in Bessarabia and the Balkans come true.»(23)

Russia's pro-German Foreign Minister Stuermer contemplated concluding a separate peace with the Central Powers as a direct result of the failure of the Romanian Army, and not of a Russian defeat, which would have diminished his and the tsar's powers. After all, the sacrificing of Romania was to crown a long-standing plan drawn up among the Great Powers. In January 1917, V. Lenin himself said that «the German imperialist press is now dealing with the plan of dividing Romania between Russia and the Quadruple Alliance (that is, the allies of Germany, the Austro-Hungarian Empire and Bulgaria).» (24) In fact, in his book **Le mystère roumain et la défection russe,** published in Paris in 1918, C. Steinon mentions that Russian Foreign Minister Stuermer «had allegedly concluded an agreement with German Emperor Wilhelm II to divide up Romania: Wallachia going to the (German) Empire, and Moldavia to the tsar, thus explaining why the enemy had halted at the Siret River line.» The French author adds that:

> M. Stuermer managed once more to bring up his project of a separate peace following the dismemberment of Romania, on which an agreement with Mr. Zhagov had been reached as far back as the spring of 1916. And, according to the Romanian deputy (Nicolae Basilescu), here is proof of it: crossing the Siret River, Baron von dem Busche, the German minister to Bucharest, said to the American secretary, Mr. Andrews, who was accompanying him as far as Iaşi: «This is the Siret, the frontier with Russia.»

It is worth emphasizing that during the negotiations conducted in Brest-Litovsk to conclude a truce with Romania, the representatives of the Central Powers made use of their influence over the Russians to request that they exert pressure on the Romanians, whose army, left isolated, continued to fight the troops of the Central Powers on the Romanian-Russian front in Romania, and to persuade them to conclude a truce as well. This would have permitted the Central Powers to transfer their not inconsiderable military units from the Romanian front to strengthen their attacks in the West.

In this respect, the representatives of the Central Powers indicated the means by which the Romanian command and the Iaşi government could have been forced to agree to the conclusion of a truce with the Central Powers. Later, on 31 December 1917, Adolf Abramovich Ioffe, a member of the Soviet commission at the peace negotiations in Brest-Litovsk, sent guidelines «to the national commissars,» including the concrete indication given by Foreign Minister Leon Trotsky along this line. Ioffe wrote: «When Comrade Trotsky declared that the council had no way in which to exert influence upon the Romanian Headquarters,

General Max Hoffmann (head of the delegation of the Central Powers at the Brest-Litovsk negotiations) emphasized the necessity and possibility of sending trustworthy agents to the Romanian Army, of arresting the Romanian mission in Petrograd, and of taking steps **to get rid of the Romanian king and the command posts of the Romanian army»** *(emphasis in original) (25) ....*

Shortly after it was victoriously established, the Soviet government published «The Declaration of the Rights of the Peoples of Russia» their right to self-determination – including their separation and formation of independent states – the abolition of all privileges and national or national-religious restrictions, the right to free development of all oppressed and exploited peoples and of the national minorities.

At the time when the two Russian revolutions occurred, Romanians living in all their ancestral provinces were fighting their country's invaders, resolute in their determination to liberate their national territory at any cost, and to unite in a single, strong Romanian national state. This determination accorded with the revolutionary policy laid down by V.I. Lenin as far back as September 1917 in the pamphlet **The Tasks of the Proletariat in Our Revolution.** Lenin wrote:

On the nationality issue, the proletarian party should first support the immediate proclamation and implementation of the full freedom to part from Russia of all nations and peoples suppressed by tsarism, incorporated (in the Russian Empire) by force and kept within the Russian state frontiers by force, that is, annexed.... (26)

The struggle of the Romanian people in the several historical provinces they inhabited intensified under these domestic and international circumstances, and triumphed in 1918, culminating in the inclusion of those provinces in a unified, national, and independent state. The Romanians of Moldavia living beyond the Pruth River, for example, were among the peoples oppressed by tsarism who resolutely rose to fight for their national and social liberation. It is worth noting that, as far back as the bourgeois-democratic revolution of February 1917 that overthrew the tsarist government, the Moldavian Romanians had organized national committees both in Bessarabia and in many other localities of Greater Russia, where they found themselves as a result of the war.

In his projects, Lenin was contemplating co-operation with all revolutionary forces in all areas invaded by tsarism. And the Moldavian soldiers successfully made use of Lenin's guidelines. The storming of the provisional government in Petrograd found the Moldavian soldiers right in the middle of a national congress, making decisions on the future of the Romanian province of Bessarabia in the spirit of Lenin's ideas.

On 20 October – 2 November 1917, basing themselves on «The Declaration of the Rights of the Peoples of Russia,» the representatives of the Romanian province located between the Pruth and Dniester Rivers (which had been included in Tsarist Russia in 1812), assembled in the National Soldiers' Congress, proclaimed «the territorial and political autonomy of Bessarabia, and decided to establish a representative body to rule Bessarabia.»

On 2-15 December 1917, the representative body of this province proclaimed the Moldavian Democratic Republic as a member with full rights within the Russian Democratic Federative Republic. On 24 January 1918, «in accordance with the will of the people,» the Moldavian Democratic Republic proclaimed itself «the free, independent, and national Moldavian Republic,» with the sole right to decide upon its own future.

On 27 March-9 April 1918, the representative body – the National Assembly (Sfatul Țării) composed of delegates sent by the entire population, irrespective of nationality or political orientation – voiced the wishes of the broad masses by adopting, by overwhelming majority (86 votes to 3, with 36 abstentions, and 13 absentees), the Decision of the Moldavian Republic to unite with the mother country. (27)

On 14-27 October 1918, the union of Bucovina with the mother country was proclaimed at a meeting held in Cernăuți, and on 15-28 November 1918 a congress was convened there, attended by representatives of the entire population of Bucovina – thousands of Romanians who made up the majority of the population of that province, as well as people from the national minorities, belonging to all classes and social strata.

The congress sessions were presided over by the Romanian patriot Iancu Flondor, formerly a Romanian deputy to the Vienna Parliament. He proposed a motion declaring «the eternal, unconditioned union of Bucovina, within its historic borders... with the Kingdom of Romania.» This motion was supported by the representatives of the Council of National Minorities of the province. The Bucovinan congress **unanimously** (emphasis in original) approved the union of this Romanian province with the mother country. In the final months of 1918, the more than 3,000,000 Romanians of Transylvania, the Banat, Crișana and Maramureș, led by the Romanian National Central Council, decided to hold a large national assembly, for the purpose of preparing a plebiscite, in Alba Iulia, on 1 December 1918....

The historic Alba Iulia Declaration, a remarkable document proclaiming the union of the Romanians of Transylvania, the Banat, Crişana, and Maramureş with the mother country, was adopted at that assembly. Later, this declaration was signed by representatives of the national minorities of those historical provinces – the Saxons, Swabians, etc. – who met in their own national assemblies to agree unanimously to the historic decisions reached at Alba Iulia on 1 December 1918....

The Peace Treaty with Hungary, signed at the Grand Trianon on 4 June 1920, stated that the Western territories, now included in the Romanian state, were Romanian.

On 28 October 1920, the representatives of the Great Powers – Great Britain, France, Italy, and Japan – on the one hand, and Romania, on the other, signed a treaty in which Romania's sovereignty over the territory between the Pruth, Dniester, and the Black Sea was recognized.

The union of these historic Romanian provinces, under the above-mentioned domestic and international conditions, in a single, unified, national state was the outcome of the struggle of the Romanian people, of the masses all over the country...

The strong, 1,000-year powerful, 1,000-year-old wish,– which fiery patriots and socialist revolutionaries grouped around the magazine **Dacia Viitoare** *in 1883 kept constantly alive – to rebuild ancient Dacia as it used to be, was fulfilled as a result of the resolute struggle of the entire Romanian people on both slopes of the Carpathians, and of the left bank of the Pruth, for history and law, the 20-century-old land in which our ancestors have been buried, entitle the Romanians to aspire to a Romanian Dacia.»*

Background Report No. 129,
Munich, 16 June 1978,
Radio Free Europe Reserch.

BIBLIOGRAPHY:

1) See George Cioranescu, "Romanian-Russian Co-operation in the Context of the Independence Centenary", *supra* pp. 52-72.
2) Nicolae Ceauşescu, Interview with the Mexican daily *El Nacional,* printed in *Scînteia* 10 May 1978.
3) *Ibid.*

4) Ion Popescu-Puţuri, "For a Just Cause – How Romania Entered World War I in August 1916", *Anale de Istorie,* Nos. 6 and 2, 1977 and 1978, respectively; and Gheorghe Zaharia, "The Making of the Unified National State – the Century-old Dream of the Romanian People", *Magazin Istoric* Nos. 4 and 6, 1978.
5) Ion Popescu-Puţuri, *op. cit.,* p. 15.
6) Ion Popescu-Puţuri, *op. cit.,* p. 16.
7) A.M. Lazarev, *Moldavskaya Sovetskaya Gosudarstvennost i Bessarabskiy Vopros,* /The Organization of the Soviet Moldavian State and the Bessarabian Problem/ (Chişinău: Cartea moldovenească, 1974), p. 70.
8) Gheorghe Zaharia, "The Making of the Unified National State – the Century-old Dream of the Romanian People", *Magazin Istoric* No. 5, 1978, p. 20.
9) *Ibid.,* p. 21.
10) R.W. Seton-Watson, *History of the Romanians,* (Cambridge, England: Cambridge University Press, 1934), p. 494.
11) *Anale de istorie* No. 2,1977.
12) Published in *Journal Officiel,* 10 November 1920.
13) Viorica Moisiuc, "From Romania's Historical Archives" *(X), Anale de Istorie* No. 2, 1978, p. 135.
14) *Ibid.,* p.146.
15) *Ibid.,* p. 148.
16) *Ibid.,* p. 160.
17) *Ibid.,* p. 162.
18) Ion Popescu-Puţuri, *op. cit.,* p. 18.
19) *Ibid.,* Part II, p. 11.
20) *Ibid.,* p. 12.
21) *Ibid.,* p. 308.
22) Michel Prevost, *Românii şi Ruşii* /Romanians and Russians/, (Bucharest: 1925), pp. 221-222.
23) C. Stienon, *Le mystère roumain et la défection russe* (Paris: Plon, 1918), pp. 221-222.
24) V.I. Lenin, *Opere complete /Complete Works/,* Vol. 30, (Bucharest: Political Publishing House, 1965), p. 342.
25) RCP CC Archives, Collection No. 50, File 477, pp. 51-52.
26) V.I. Lenin, *Despre Problema Naţională şi Naţional-Colonială /On the National and National-Colonial Issue/,* (Bucharest: Publishing House for Political Literature, 1958), p. 465.
27) The Royal Decree for the Union of Bessarabia with Romania is dated 9 April 1918 in Iaşi, where the government resided during the German occupation of Bucharest.

VIII

OCTAVIAN GOGA'S VIEWS ON THE RUSSIAN REVOLUTION AND BESSARABIA

When in April 1981 the Romanian literary magazines celebrated the centennial of Octavian Goga's birth, emphasis was placed, as was to be expected, on his significance as a lyric poet and bard of the national and social aspirations of the Transylvanian Romanians prior to World War I, while his right-wing political activities, as a leader of the National Christian Party and prime minister under Carol II, were deplored. (1) Indeed, some reports preferred not to mention Goga's political activities at all, since, according to one literary critic, «the rest /i.e., his political activity/ should be silence, to use Shakespeare's profound expression.» (2) A new discussion has emerged, however, centering on Goga's possible sympathies with one or both of the Russian Revolutions of 1917, with interesting Bessarabian implications.

Recollections on Goga by Onisifor Ghibu, the organizer of Romanian education in Transylvania as well as a close friend of Goga, were published in 1943 and in 1974, and still more have now appeared in *Viața Românească*. (3) These deal in particular with Goga's pre- and postrevolutionary Russia, as well as his campaign to reconcile the Romanian Orthodox and Uniate Churches. It is interesting that, apparently, now is considered the right time to evoke problems that were not mentioned in the volume of recollections printed in 1974. (4)

The poet's first trip to Russia was in March 1917. He was bound for Petrograd, «on a mission that has never been clear to me,» according to Ghibu. (5) However, according to Vasile Curticăpeanu, Goga allegedly submitted to the Russian Foreign Minister a memorandum in which he expressed his admiration for the Russian Revolution as follows:

I came to Petrograd guided by the feeling of piety entertained by the whole of mankind in the face of the Russian Revolution... The liberating movement of the Russian people represents a step forward made by modern society so far as the evolution of feelings is concerned... This is how we Romanian democrats feel about the recent movement in Russia, which we are happy to see directing itself toward the establishment of conditions for a new life. Following the practical implementation of the principles of the Russian Revolution, we shall see in Petrograd a second Paris, which will provide mankind with a second glorious page in modern world history. (6)

The «Two Lives» article, however, casts some doubt on the authenticity of this alleged memorandum and Curticăpeanu admitted that he only had a typed, undated copy of it, made available to him by Veturia Goga, the poet's widow. While Ghibu gives an account of Goga's views on the Russian Revolution, related to him by his friend in Chişinău (Russia), (7) there is unfortunately no way of comparing this version of Goga's views with the ideas expressed in Curticăpeanu's alleged memorandum since *Viaţa Românească* cut the relevant part of the text, replacing it by ellipses.

In Curticăpeanu's view Goga's visit to Petrograd was aimed at «helping improve relations between the Romanian and Russian governments.» In this connection the memorandum stated that:

current Romanian-Russian relations are not quite clear, /Prime Minister / Ionel Brătianu's assurances are not reassuring and, therefore, a way should be sought to force the hand of the government, so that it should be aware one hour in advance of when the offensive would be triggered. (8)

It is not easy to explain why Goga, who was carrying a diplomatic passport, should have expressed himself in these terms about Ionel Brătianu, the head of his country's government. The most plausible hypothesis is that Goga's first mission, in his capacity as a Transylvanian and volunteer in the Romanian Army employed by the Army General Headquarters for press and propaganda purposes, had been to get permission from the Russian government to recruit as volunteers as many Romanian soldiers as possible who had fought in the Austro-Hungarian Army and were then being held as prisoners on Russian territory. On his return from Petrograd Goga again stopped over in Chişinău to meet Ghibu. On 5 May 1917 they returned together to Iaşi, where three days later Goga was to make a speech at a meeting of prisoners who had returned from Russia. (9) In any case, Goga's alleged memorandum was submitted to Pavel Nikolaevich Miliukov, foreign minister of the provisional government established on March 15, and not to the Petrograd Soviet of Workers' and Soldiers' Deputies. According to the text of the memorandum to Miliukov, who was a liberal historian and the strong man in Prince Lvov's democratic cabinet,

The Russian Revolution is finding in the souls of our peasants and intellectual proletarians, liberated of any feudal ballast, an echo of the closest spiritual relationship... That is why today, when we are watching red flags along the streets of Petrograd, our hearts feel the impulse of fraternal union. (10)

In quoting this text Curticăpeanu was attempting to prove that Goga had been an admirer of the communist revolution since October 1917. This was also the purpose behind his use of an excerpt from an article published by the poet in 1917, entitled «The Revolutionary Petrograd.» Referring to the consequences of the Petrograd events of the winter of 1917, Goga emphasized that «180,000,000 people, over a boundless area, are debating all the conceivable values of mankind.»

However, these excerpts from Goga could not refer to the revolutionary events of the *winter* of 1917, since both the memorandum and the article which appeared in the daily *România* (No. 115 of 30 May 1917) (11) were written before the October Revolution. It therefore follows that if Goga did have sympathetic things to say about the Russian Revolution, he was writing about the democratic revolution of the spring of 1917, and not the Bolshevik revolution of October.

Among the ideas circulating in Russia in 1917 that Goga could have agreed with was that of national self-determination, which was applicable not only to his native Transylvania but also to Bessarabia. Thus, in the summer of 1917 he toured Russia and the Ukraine, visiting Kiev, Petrograd, and Odessa, and negotiating the repatriation of Transylvanian and Bucovinian prisoners who happened to be there. (12) His trip was most successful, since in this way Romania was able to supplement its army with soldiers from the Austrian-Hungarian provinces. On 8 June 1917, 1,500 volunteers, recruited from among former Transylvanian prisoners in Russia, arrived at Iaşi, and on November 11 the corps of Transylvanian volunteers numbered 11,000. (13)

From Ghibu's notes published in *Viaţa Românească* something can be learned for the first time about Goga's pro-Bessarabian activities. Goga apparently contacted Bessarabian political leaders who were in favor of union with Romania: in 1916 the poet Ion Buzdugan, who was an interpreter for the Russian General Headquarters in Iaşi and two years previously had published a poem dedicated to Goga; and later Ion Nistor, with whom he signed a petition to the Great Soviet of the Moldavian Republic. (14) Goga joined Ghibu in his attempts to establish a printing office with Latin characters for the Bessarabians and also had printed in Kiev the daily *România* in Latin characters for Transylvanian prisoners, thus facilitating pan-Romanian communications. He also had a large say in significant matters for Bessarabia of that time, writing, for instance, «an excellent article in which, in really prophetic terms, he appreciated the role of the new publication *Ardealul,* in the Bessarabian capital.» (15) Unfortunately, the cuts made in Ghibu's text prevent one from establishing Goga's views, expressed on 1 October 1917, «almost a month before the new proletarian revolution inaugurated by Lenin.» (16) Goga kept in touch with Prime Minister Ionel Brătianu, with Minister of the Interior Alexandru Constantinescu, and with Saint-Aulaire, the French Minister Plenipotentiary, «with a view to calming down the anarchy in Bessarabia.» (17) During the spring and summer of 1918 Goga made several trips to Chişinău, contributing poems and articles to the daily *România Nouă.* (18) Finally, he was instrumental in sending thousands of Transylvanian and Bucovinian intellectuals (teachers, priests, professors, doctors, engineers, lawyers, economists, and journalists) to Bessarabia to contribute to the national organization of the new Moldavian Republic. This was one of the most interesting acts of support for Bessarabia with which his name has been connected, (19) although at this point in the history of Bessarabia one could still be both a revolutionary and a Romanian patriot, and hence the conducting of Romanian nationalist activities was not in itself right- wing.

In the historical studies devoted to Octavian Goga and the problem of the Russian Revolution we are faced with two distinct stands: the older one, in which Goga appears as an admirer of the communist revolution and a more recent one, that emphasizes the national Romanian character of his political activity. In order to support the first thesis, chronological confusion is deliberately created, for instance, when it is noted that in his memorandum of February 1917 Octavian Goga expressed «his adhesion to the lofty social and political upheaval in Russia,» (20) which in fact occurred only in October 1917. The object of this distortion is to ascribe to the right-wing politician Goga a pattern of thinking «placing him at the head of his contemporaries in the field of public life,» (21) at a time when Veturia Goga, the poet's widow, was benefiting from various privileges granted her by the regime, being the administrator of Ciucea Castle where the poet is buried.

The manner in which Goga crossed Russia in 1918 and then went to Paris to plead the cause of the union of all Romanians suggests that his relations with the Bolsheviks were not very good. He was obliged to grow a beard, carry a forged passport on the name of Gheorghe Oprescu, and assume a false identity as a representative of the Romanian Marxists. In this way he could travel safely to Moscow, in a special carriage of a commissar of the Russian government. When he got to Petrograd he again forged his papers so that he could cross the border to Finland and travel from there, by an indirect route, to Paris. (22)

The picture of Goga by Ghibu in *Viaţa Românească* is more in keeping with the work and political views of this controversial poet and politician. The contradiction between the two presentations is emphasized in an editorial footnote in *Viaţa Românească,* saying that Ghibu's notes, «written after Curticăpeanu's study had appeared, but not yet published, still maintain their topicality to this day". The publication of Ghibu's original manuscript, entitled *Other Recollections on Octavian Goga,* will certainly provide more information about his views on the Russian Revolution and the Bessarabian problem. It is likely that the book will not confirm the thesis that Goga was in favor of the Bolshevik Revolution and will confirm recent revelations that he was a staunch supporter of the Bessarabian cause. Hence the hesitation to publish the full text of Ghibu's later work on Goga, the omission of his more sensitive confessions, and the decision to defer publication of the full text.

Situation Report No. 21,
Munich, 16 October 1981,
Radio Free Europe Research.

BIBLIOGRAPHY:

1) Ion Dodu Bălan, "Goga Centenial", *Flacăra* No. 14, 2 April 1981; Pompiliu Marcea, "Octavian Goga Today", *Transilvania* No. 3, 1981; Mihai Ungheanu, "Goga's Literary and Political Destiny", *Luceafărul* No. 14, 1981; Constantin Ciopraga "We" *Tribuna* No. 14, 1981
2) Şerban Cioculescu, "90 Years Since Octavian Goga's Birth", *România Literară* No. 17, 1917.
3) Onisifor Ghibu, "Two Lives", *Viaţa Românească* Nos. 4-5, April-May 1981, pp. 78-91.
4) Onisifor Ghibu, *Amintiri despre Octavian Goga* /Recollections on Octavian Goga/, (Cluj. Dacia Publishing House, 1974).
5) Ghibu, "Two Lives..."
6) Vasile Curticăpeanu, "Octavian Goga's Struggle for the Implementation of the Romanian Unified State", *Studii, Revista de Istorie* No. 5, 1969, p. 941.
7) Ghibu, "Two Lives", p. 81.
8) Curticăpeanu, *op. cit.,* p. 941.
9) Ghibu, "Two Lives..."
10) Curticăpeanu, *op. cit.,* p. 941.
11) *Ibid.*
12) Ghibu, "Two Lives", p. 82; and Curticăpeanu, *op. cit.,* p. 940.

13) I. Gheorghiu and C. Nuţu, *Adunarea Naţională de la Alba Iulia, 1 Decembrie 1918 /The National Assembly of Alba Iulia, 1 December 1918/* (Bucharest. Editura Politică, 1968), pp. 81 and 86.
14) Ghibu, "Two Lives", pp. 87-88.
15) *Ibid.,* pp. 82 and 88.
16) *Ibid.,* p. 82.
17) *Ibid.*
18) *Ibid.,* p. 83.
19) *Ibid.,* p. 89.
20) Curticăpeanu, *op. cit.,* p. 941.
21) *Ibid.*
22) Ion Dodu Bălan, Preface to *Octavian Goga, Opere,* Vol. I (Bucharest. Editura pentru Literatură, 1967), pp. LV-LVI.

IX

BESSARABIA'S PLACE IN NICOLAE TITULESCU'S FOREIGN POLICY

March 4 marked the 100th anniversary of the birth of Nicolae Titulescu, a diplomat of European stature, in the city of Craiova. Titulescu is noted especially for having been – in 1930 and 1931 – the Chairman of the General Assembly of the League of Nations and a leading figure supporting the policy of collective security in Europe between the two world wars. "This minister of a small state who is conducting a large-scale policy," (1) as Edouard Herriot used to say, was commemorated both in Romania, in numerous deferential articles and at a festive gathering on March 16, (2) and in various capitals, especially Paris, under the auspices of the International Diplomatic Academy, (3) whose chairman he had been.

Ceaușescu is Extolled during the Titulescu Commemoration

In present-day Romania, dominated by Ceaușescu's personality cult, the celebration of the centennial of Titulescu's birth turned, in fact, into a laudation of the RCP's present secretary-general and of his foreign policy. Foreign Minister Ștefan Andrei emphasized, with the authority of the position he holds: "We notice with a feeling of profound satisfaction that all the progressive elements in the thinking and work of Nicolae Titulescu are being happily implemented, on a higher level, by the foreign policy of socialist Romania, which incorporates the basic interest and aspirations of the Romanian nation and, at the same time, of all mankind." (4) Moreover, the commemoration on March 16, devoted in principle to Titulescu, in fact was turned into a eulogy of Ceaușescu's foreign policy, with the speakers emphasizing that his particular abilities "had stamped his personality on international politics; as a result, current international policy could hardly be imagined without the contribution of socialist Romania, and of President Nicolae Ceaușescu." (5) At the commemorative exhibition at the Museum of the History of the Republic, the panels presenting scenes from the life of the celebrated diplomat were accompanied by an apotheosis of Nicolae Ceaușescu.

In fact, the exhibition proclaimed that the worldwide prestige enjoyed by Romania "is everywhere associated with the name of the President of our country, Nicolae Ceauşescu, with the clear-sightedness and realism of his thinking." (6)

Patriotism as the Basis of International Relations

Nicolae Titulescu started his political career shortly before World War I as a member of the Conservative Party, supporting the idea that in order to achieve the national unity of all Romanians the country had to enter the war on the Allied side. The acquisition and retention of Transylvania within the national borders could be said to form the cornerstone of his entire political thinking and efforts. An excerpt quoted from a speech he made in 1915 in Ploeşti can be used as an illustration: "Romania cannot be complete without Transylvania. This region is the cradle that has protected it in childhood, the school that molded the nation, the charm that supports its life existence... Transylvania is not only the heart of political Romania, Transylvania is the heart of geographical Romania."(7)

In his capacity as Romania's first delegate at Paris peace conference Titulescu signed the peace treaty between the Allied powers and Hungary on 4 June 1920, wich legalized the union of Transylvania with Romania. Later, during his 20 years of diplomatic activity, he persevered in defending Romania's rights to Transylvania against all those who wanted to modify the peace treaties, resorting to every possible legal means in his efforts. (8) His diplomatic career was devoted to progressively coordinating Romanian policy with that of states with a similar interest in maintaining the postwar European status quo. (9) Quotations from Elena Văcărescu, outstanding Romanian cultural figure in Paris between the two world wars, and from Lucian Blaga, the poet-philosopher of modern Romania, were used during the anniversary celebrations to strengthen the image of Titulescu as a diplomat-patriot. (10) And, as a conclusive argument, it is emphasized that in his last will Titulescu asked to be buried in Transylvania, in Braşov, the province for whose retention he had devoted his entire life. (11) For the time being, he is still buried in Cannes, despite regime's attempts to bring him home. The present government also made attempts to bring home the bodies of George Enescu and Constantin Brâncuşi.

For a Settlement of the Romanian-Hungarian Dispute

Patriotism did not push Titulescu into jingoistic nationalism, for he pleaded for the settling of local differences and for the building of an international society that would be based on the force of right, and not on the right to force. Even during the heated discussions of 1922-1930, known under the name of the "Optants' problem", when the legality of Romania's expropriation of some 500

Hungarian landowners in Transylvania was raised in international circles, Titulescu presented the problem within a framework that went beyond bilateral Romanian-Hungarian relations, emphasizing that the Romanian government's agrarian legislation was helping stabilize the situation in southeastern Europe. (12)

Titulescu responded to the Hungarian campaign to have the post-World War I borders revised with the singular argument that revision was not a peaceful solution but rather a warlike one, for it would create other malcontents as a substitute for the present ones. Therefore, he suggested that instead of revising the Treaty of Trianon the situation created by it be improved through the political and economic rapprochement of the peoples living in the same geographical area:

The present-day Romanians and Hungarians are not responsible for the whole historical past which has separated them throughout the centuries. I think that instead of wasting energy on modifying your positions and expanding your political assistance you should use that energy to seek a formula that would allow us to walk side by side. (13)

From Balkan Entente to the Denuclearization of the Balkans

The attempted conversion in 1933 of the Little Entente from a system of alliance into a multilateral international body, with a unified political and diplomatic policy, constituted an early application of Titulescu's views on regional understanding. The economic cooperation within the Entente, open to those involved in other alliances as well, should have prevented Europe from being divided into rival blocs, but its members could truly cooperate in practice only on the subject of containing Hungary and blocking a Hapsburg restoration.

The Balkan Entente treaty, signed on 4 February 1934 in Ankara, represented another regional agreement to whose creation Titulescu made a decisive contribution. This agreement is particularly interesting because its basic points are still being supported. In fact, recent articles emphasize that the proposal to turn the Balkans into an area of cooperation and good-neighborly relations free of nuclear arms has been advocated in many party and state documents, as well as in Ceauşescu's speeches. (14) Recently, during Ceauşescu's meeting with Turkish head of state Kenan Evren, the secretary-general called for a top level meeting of Balkan leaders to strengthen confidence in the Balkan area. Such a meeting would be regarded as a positive step in Europe. (15)

Former Foreign Minister George Macovescu emphasized that the 1934 Balkan Agreement did not have an anti-Soviet character, although the opposite had been asserted at the time. He said that a secret clause in the Balkan Agreement included a declaration by the Turkish Foreign Minister who, speaking in the name of his government, specified that Turkey did not wish to become involved in any anti-Soviet moves. Macovescu went on to say that the Foreign Ministers of Romania, Yugoslavia, and Greece had stated in writing that the Turkish declaration did not run counter to the agreement creating the Balkan Entente. Therefore, the Balkan Entente was not designed as an instrument through which to conduct a policy hostile to the Soviet Union. (16)

Romanian-Soviet Relations and the Problem of Bessarabia

The policy of maintaining good-neighborly relations with the Soviet Union, adopted by Titulescu, was based on the premise that a small state like Romania could not afford the luxury of conducting a policy hostile to a neighbor as big as the Soviet Union. In Titulescu's opinion, if a conflict had erupted with the USSR, Romania would have been isolated, and no Western country would have come to its assistance merely in order to protect its interests. (17) However, a Romanian-Soviet rapprochement was made more difficult by the Soviet failure to recognize the union of Bessarabia with Romania and by the lack of diplomatic relations between the two countries. By 1931 the Polish government had asked the Romanian whether it was prepared to sign a bilateral nonaggression treaty with the Soviet Union, similar to the Polish-Soviet draft of nonaggression treaty. The difference between the two countries was that the Romanian-Soviet frontier, unlike the Polish-Soviet border, had not been recognized by Moscow. Consequently, the Romanian-Soviet draft treaty, submitted by Bucharest to Poland, included a provision designed to ensure "the integrity in practice and the present political independence of the other contracting party." When informed by Polish sources about the negotiations then under way, Titulescu drew attention to the danger to Romania's integrity presented by the clause providing that "all the problems and differences of any kind that will /arise/ between them... should be submitted to conciliation and arbitration." (18) Put in charge of conducting all Romanian- Soviet negotiations in 1932, Titulescu did not give in to Polish pressure to sign the nonaggression treaty in a form that seemed to him dangerous for the security of Romania, "opting for a continuation of a significant, independent policy of the Romanian government." After 1932, when he became Foreign Minister, Titulescu was never willing to recognize the existence of litigation or differences with the Soviet Union, and refused to recognize that Romania's sovereignty in Bessarabia was being weakened. (19)

Within this pre-established framework, which was meant to guarantee Romania's fundamental rights, the convention for the definition of aggression, which safeguarded the national territory against any act of violence, was signed in 1933 in London. Then, in July 1934, Titulescu re-established diplomatic relations with the Soviet Union. In an exchange of letters, the Romanian and

Soviet governments mutually guaranteed respect for each other's sovereignty and declared that neither would interfere in the domestic affairs of the other. Finally, in the fall of 1934, Titulescu met in Evian with Soviet Foreign Minister Maxim Maximovich Litvinov, to discuss the invitation to the Soviet Union to become a member of the League of Nations. (20) In this way, an attempt was made to claim that Romania helped introduce the Soviet Union to international relations through the League of Nations.

The campaign for a Romanian-Soviet rapprochement culminated in the conclusion of a treaty of mutual assistance between Bucharest and Moscow. Gheorghe Brătianu questioned Titulescu in parliament, asking him whether he was negotiating the passage of Soviet troops across Romanian territory under specific conditions. On 13 December 1935 Titulescu categorically denied the existence of such negotiations. Finally, on 21 July 1936 in Montreux, Titulescu and Litvinov initiated the text of a pact of Romanian-Soviet assistance which provided for the transit of troops across the territory of the signatory states, only at the request of the relevant government. (21) In such case, troops that had given assistance had to withdraw as soon as they were requested to do so. (22) However, this agreement did not become final, for on 29 August 1936 Titulescu was dismissed from his position. (23) The conditions under which these events occurred have never been properly clarified and in this respect George Macovescu wrote:

The time will come – in the not too distant future – when all archives will be examined and objective analyses will be made to evaluate (these events) and to draw conclusions in accordance with the historical truth. (24)

For Sovereignty, against a Superstate

In Titulescu's view, the policy of friendly and good-neighborly relations with the Soviet Union did not mean making his country a vassal to its powerful Eastern neighbor. Titulescu stated this peremptorily:

We should like to be on friendly terms with all big powers – France, Great Britain, Italy, Germany, and the Soviet Union. We are ready to provide them all with concrete proofs of our sincere wish to have peaceful and friendly relations with them. On the other hand, we shall never give up, in favor of any of them, and not even in favor of all the big powers put together, the principle of the equality of states, that is, of the sovereign right of each one of us to handle our own fate and never to accept a decision regarding us to which we would not agree. (25)

Titulescu explained this attitude by saying that the Romanians, like all nations that have achieved independence recently, reject dependence as a concept running counter to their feelings of national dignity. (26)

Therefore, Titulescu based Romanian policy regarding the USSR on the principles of equality and national sovereignty, similar to those of the present-day policy of the Bucharest regime vis-à-vis Moscow. Moreover, although in his concept of the organization of international society he advocated the integration of state entities in increasingly broad organizations, "from national through regional, to universal," (27) he nevertheless considered that the abolition of national feeling and sovereignty are chimerical solutions which would throw the world into chaos and anarchy. (28) As for integration into a political system that would sacrifice national sovereignty, Titulescu's views were just as resolutely negative when he said that "in the present-day organization of the international community there is no room for a superstate," (29) adding that relations between states are governed by an international law of coordination, not of subordination; of independence, not of dependence.

Commenting on Titulescu's views on national sovereignty, former Foreign Minister Macovescu said that after more than half a century, after mankind has gone through a world war, has flown to the moon, and gone through revolutionary changes in technology and science, the principle of observing the sovereignty of states, as formulated by his predecessor Titulescu, continues to be valid. Maco-vescu added:

As long as nations exist – and the end of this historic era is not visible yet – states will also exist, and as long as these states exist, their sovereignty will also, for there is no other way. A state deprived of sovereignty and independence is no state at all, but something else: a colony, a province, a dominion, a pashalik, but not a state. (30)

At a time when analysts wonder whether the policy of the Bucharest regime vis-à-vis the Soviet Union will suffer or will not any essential changes under the pressure of the economic crisis and of the need for foreign assistance and relief, a recalling of Titulescu's political views may serve as an indirect means to provide an answer. National interests stemming from problems posed by geopolitical realities rarely change sharply.

Situation Report No. 7,
Munich, 20 April 1982,
Radio Free Europe Research.

BIBLIOGRAPHY

1) Jacques de Launay, "Nicolae Titulescu, the Man," *Magazin Istoric* No 1, 1982.
2) "Centennial of Nicolae Titulescu's Birth, Commemorative Gathering *Scînteia,* 17 March 1982.
3) Agerpress, 17 March 1982.
4) Ştefan Andrei, "The Foreign Policy of Socialist Romania, Continuity, Innovative Spirit, and Responsibility," *Lumea* No. 12, 18 March 1982.
5) "Centennial of N. Titulescu", *Scînteia,* 17 March 1982.
6) "The Permanence of Romanian Foreign Policy; Nicolae Titulescu's Centennial Exhibition," *ibid.,* 19 March 1982.
7) Mircea Muşat and Vasile Arimia, "Nicolae Titulescu, Defender of Unity, Independence, and National Sovereignty," *Anale de Istorie* No. 1, 1982, p. 54.
8) Mircea Muşat, "A Brilliant Romanian Diplomat, a Great Man of His Time," *Scînteia,* 16 March 1982; Gabriel Iosif Chiuzbăian, "The Creative Ideal of Nicolae Titulescu," *Săptămîna,* No. 589, 26 March 1982; Vasile Netea, "In the Service of the Fatherland," *Rumänische Rundschau* No. 1, 1982, pp. 94-99.
9) Ion Isaiu, "Romania Has Paid Too Heavy a Price for Its Right to Existence Ever to Renounce It", *Familia* No. 2, 1982.
10) Valentin Lipatti, "Testimonies on Titulescu", *România Literară* No. 10, 3 March 1982; Lucian Blaga, "The Intimate Fire", *Rumänische Rundschau* No. 1, 1982, pp. 121-127.
11) Ion Greceanu, "The Last Wish of Nicolae Titulescu," *Magazin Istoric* No. 3, 1981.
12) George Macovescu, "The Diplomatic Efforts of Nicolae Titulescu," in *Nicolae Titulescu, Documente Diplomatice /Diplomatic Documents/,* (Bucharest: Editura Politică, 1967), p. 28.
13) Mircea Muşat and Vasile Arimia, *op. cit.,* p. 60.
14) Ion Fântânaru, "The Foreign Policy of Socialist Romania, an Expression of the Enduring Aspirations of the People for Freedom and National Independence, Peace, and Progress throughout the World," *Scînteia,* 16 March 1982.
15) AP, 8 April 1982.
16) George Macovescu, "Romania Has Paid Too Heavy a Price for Its Right to Life Ever to Renounce It", *Contemporanul* No. 10, 5 March 1982.
17) George Macovescu, "Peace Is One of the Best Means of Preserving Our National Unity," *ibid.,* No. 11, 12 March 1982.
18) Teodor Popescu, "On a Volume of Documents Devoted to Romania's Foreign Policy," *Anale de Istorie* No. 5, 1981, p. 174.
19) *Ibid., p.* 176.
20) Petre Bărbulescu, "A Great Romanian Diplomat," *Lumea* No. 10, 4 March 1982.
21) George Macovescu, "The Diplomatic Efforts...," *op. cit.,* p. 48.
22) Savel Rădulescu, *Nicolae Titulescu, 1882–1941* (Bucharest: Casa Scînteii, no date), p. 428.

23) Valter Roman, "Notes on Nicolae Titulescu," *România Literară* No. 12, 18 March 1982.
24) George Macovescu, "Peace Is...," *op. cit.*
25) *Flacăra* No. 6, 12 February 1982.
26) George Potra, "The Vital Strength of the Principles of International Law," *Era Socialistă* No. 5, 1982.
27) Alexandru Cernatoni, "National and Universal Concepts in a Political Destiny," *Contemporanul* No. 11, 12 March 1982.
28) *Flacăra* No. 6, 12 February 1982; Constantin Turcu, "A Champion for the Extension of Romania's Foreign Relations," *Rumänische Rundschau* No. 1, 1982, pp. 72-76.
29) Martin Niciu, "Nicolae Titulescu and World Peace," *Tribuna* No. 11, 18 March 1982.
30) George Macovescu, "I Want Romania To Live," *Contemporanul* No. 8, 19 February 1982.

X

40TH ANNIVERSARY OF ANNEXATION OF BESSARABIA AND NORTHERN BUCOVINA

Germany Stands Aside

The Soviet ultimatum of 26 June 1940, worded in unusually harsh terms, came as a surprise to Romania and under conditions which left no option other than acceptance or war. Although Soviet intentions had been fairly well veiled, the disintegration of the European collective security arrangement first organized after World War I by France and, to a lesser extent, Great Britain, the establishment of the Third Reich's «new order» in its place meant important political changes in Eastern Europe. Since Romania was caught between the Soviet Union in the East and the Third Reich, which was extending its dominion to the West, King Carol II approached Berlin in spring of 1940 to see how much he could rely on German support as a counterweight to Soviet pressure and its claims to Bessarabia. (1) The answer received from German Foreign Minister Joachim von Ribbentrop was hardly encouraging, however, for he said bluntly that the question «whether and to what extent Romania might be disposed to agree to any revisionist demands by its neighbors, as for example by Russia on the Bessarabian question,» (2) was a prerequisite for German support.

The Soviet Union Raises the Bessarabian Question

As a matter of fact, the Bessarabian question had been raised by Soviet Foreign Minister Viacheslav M. Molotov about two months earlier, in a speech delivered on March 29 to the Supreme Soviet, in which the Soviet Foreign Minister said:

> Of the neighboring southern states I have mentioned, Romania is one with which we have no pact of non-aggression. This is due to the existence of an unsettled dispute, the question of Bessarabia, whose seizure by Romania the Soviet Union has never recognized, although we have never raised the question of recovering Bessarabia by military means. (3)

Shortly after these statements, which presaged no good for Romania, Friederich Werner von der Schulenburg, the German Ambassador to Moscow, reported to the Foreign Ministry in Berlin that Molotov had told him the following on June 23:

The solution of the Bessarabian question brooked no further delay. The Soviet government is still striving for a peaceful solution, but it is determined to use force should the Romanian government decline a peaceful agreement. (4)

In order to justify this change in Soviet attitude Molotov pointed out the «long time» that has elapsed since his speech to the Supreme Soviet, with Romania doing nothing to help find a solution to the Bessarabian problem. Von der Schulenburg replied that he had not expected this new decision by the Soviet government, that Soviet claims to Bessarabia were not contested by Germany, but that, since Romania was then supplying Germany with very large amounts of essential military and civilian raw materials, difficulties in its foreign relations would lead to a serious encroachment on German interests. Consequently, he requested Molotov not to take any decisive step before the German government had decided on a stand concerning the intentions of the Soviet government. That same day Molotov let von der Schulenburg know that the Soviet government would wait until June 26 for the German government's reply on the matter.

Commenting on von der Schulenburg's communication, Ernst von Weizsaecker, State Secretary of the German Foreign Ministry, defined Germany's attitude to Moscow and Bucharest as follows:

With regard to the matter itself, the Russians already knew that we agree to their demand for Bessarabia; however, there has been no discussion of Bucovina thus far. (5)

He thought that direct negotiations should be conducted between Moscow and Bucharest, adding that:

Molotov could be told that we knew that Romania was prepared in principle to negotiate and that Germany could, if desired, suggest that we, on our part, induce Romania to send a plenipotentiary at once.

According to Weizsaecker, it would be said in Romania that «the Romanian government was not apparently aware of the gravity of the situation and was counting, at least in part, on our help against Soviet Russia.» In reality, the Third Reich was «fully sympathetic to the idea of settling the Bessarabian problem,» as Foreign Minister von Ribbentrop wrote to his ambassador to Moscow.

His only concern was to salvage German economic interests in Romania, which was a good source of supply of oil and grain for the Third Reich. For this reason, von Ribbentrop added in his communication to von der Schulenburg:

Please point out clearly, once again, to Mototov our great interest in Romania's not becoming a theater of war. (6)

On June 21 Wilhelm Fabricius reported to Berlin that the Soviet Envoy to Bucharest, Anatolii Iosifovich Lavrentiev, had arrived in Bucharest, but that the Romanian government did not know what he was going to demand of it. If he demanded Bessarabia, Romania would have to draw Germany's attention to the danger threatening the Balkans; if he demanded bases, Romania was fully aware of the sad experience of the Baltic countries. In any case, the Romanian government was hardly disposed to abandon the population of Bessarabia, the majority of whom were ethnic Romanians, to Bolshevism and Russification.

Reporting on a discussion he had with Premier Gheorghe Tătărescu on June 26 Fabricius, the German Minister to Bucharest, said that the Romanian premier had confirmed to him that, were Lavrentiev to claim Bessarabia during his audience with the king, «the Romanian government and the king were determined to fight rather than simply give in.» (7) Tătărescu added that:

The surrender of this region would, therefore, mean handing over 2,000,000 of their own people to Soviet Russia, to say nothing of all the other dangers it would entail for the Danube region in the wake of Russian influence penetrating beyond the Dniester.

Tătărescu thought of offering the Soviet Union an exchange of populations which would not have affected the existing borders; possibly he would have confined himself to offering an exchange of Ukrainians, Russians, and Jews from Bessarabia for the «Moldavians» (Romanians) living east of the Dniester, but Fabricius considered that this solution would not satisfy the Soviet Union.

In another conversation on the same day (June 26) with Ion Gigurtu, who claimed that a Soviet invasion was imminent, Fabricius asked the Romanian Foreign Minister whether the Russians could be offered something more than the prime minister had told him. Gigurtu then mentioned Romania's frontier of 1856-1878, when Russia's Bessarabian frontier was pushed back from the Danube. But Fabricius replied that he could not take any stand on that issue, although it would be advisable, in any case, to find some peaceful compromise. (8)

An Ultimatum Full of Surprises

As a matter of fact, none of these anticipated scenarios came true, for the Soviet Union surprised diplomatic circles both with the speed and brutality of its June 26 move and with the extent of its claims.

At 11,00 hours on 26 June 1940, George Davidescu, Romanian Minister to the Kremlin, was summoned by Molotov, who handed him an ultimatum in which the Soviet Union called upon Romania to surrender Bessarabia and Northern Bucovina, claiming that Romania had taken advantage of Russia's military weakness in 1918 and wrested some of its territory, Bessarabia, away, «thus destroying the centuries-long union of Bessarabia, inhabited principally by Ukrainians, with the Ukrainian Soviet Socialist Republic.» The note went on to say that now, when the military weakness of the Soviet Union was a thing of the past, the Soviet Union considered it necessary and opportune, in the interest of re-establishing justice, to reach, together with Romania, an immediate solution concerning the restitution of Bessarabia. Consequently, the Soviet government proposed to the Romanian government: a. that Bessarabia be returned to the Soviet Union; and b. that Northern Bucovina, «as shown in the attached map,» be transferred to Soviet jurisdiction. The note ended with the following sentence: «The Soviet government expects the reply of the Romanian government in the course of June 27.» (9)

Davidescu tried to counter the statements in the ultimatum, replying that up to 1812 Bessarabia had always been an integral part of the Principality of Moldavia. He also protested that such a grave issue should be raised in the form of an ultimatum, without having previously been submitted to negotiation between the parties concerned, which still, nevertheless, maintained correct relations. Finally, Davidescu added that the deadline set for a reply to the note handed him so late in the evening was too short and that he was unable to convey to Bucharest the plan attached to the ultimatum on time. (10)

Molotov accepted none of these arguments. His tactics were to launch a strong attack, without allowing Romania any alternative but surrender or war. There was nothing left for Davidescu to do but to send a coded message to the Romanian Foreign Ministry. This message began: «The following is the text of the ultimatum which was handed to me this evening at 22,00 hours by Molotov.» At that point, telegraphic connections with Moscow broke off abruptly and the interruption lasted 7 hours, thus reducing the deadline from 24 to 17 hours. Alexandru Cretzianu, who was then Secretary-General of the Romanian Foreign Ministry, said that he and newly appointed Foreign Minister Gigurtu went to see Prime Minister Gheorghe Tătărescu to discuss how to reply. Since theFranco-British forces had been eliminated from the continent following the collapse of France and the British evacuation, the only possible counterforce capable of opposing the Soviet Union was to be sought in Germany and Italy. Tătărescu decided to inform the German and Italian governments that Romania could not accept an ultimatum of a military character, and that his country was determined to defend itself, declaring a general mobilization. At that time Fabricius reported to Berlin: «war is to be expected.» (11)

Germany and Italy Abandon Romania

At 10,00 hours on June 27 Fabricius was summoned to the royal palace where Prime Minister Tătărescu read the text of the Soviet ultimatum to him in the presence of King Carol II and Foreign Minister Gigurtu. King Carol II told the German representative that Marshal Hermann Goering had given him (the king) clearly to understand (during the king's 1938 visit to Germany) «that a Romanian rapprochement with Germany excluded a rapprochement between Romania and the Soviet Union.» Consequently, the king considered that Germany «bore some responsibility for the present situation.»

He called on Germany and Hitler to seek «some way to assist Romania.» (12) But during the audience with King Carol II, who was trying in this way to get German help to save Bessarabia from Soviet annexation, Fabricius received an urgent telephone message from von Ribbentrop in Berlin, who ordered him to convey a message to the Romanian Foreign Minister. Basically, Ribbentrop said: «In order to avoid a war between Romania and the Soviet Union, we can only advise the Romanian government to yield to the Soviet government's demands.» (13) Upon hearing this the king «launched forth into criticism of our policy. How could they ask him to cede one third of his territory without fighting? After all he had obtained the Führer's word. One cannot depend upon the Reich» King Carol was so angry that Fabricius had to interrupt him; interjecting that, in his capacity as a representative of the Reich, he «could not listen to such rash words from His Majesty». (14)

At 15,00 hours of the same day Radu Crutzescu, Romanian Minister to Berlin, unaware of events in Bucharest and following instructions which had become obsolete, went to the German Foreign Ministry and asked Weizsaecker whether Germany would be prepared to act as mediator in the Bessarabian issue. The reply was that his question was out of date in the wake of Fabricius's step. (15) Using King Carol II's reproaches as a pretext, despite the fact that Prime Minister Tătărescu had apologized to Fabricius, (16) Hitler informed the Romanian king that Germany had never had any political interest in Romania, and therefore refused to exert any influence in the current dispute. To make his refusal the more categorical, Hitler added that Romania had for decades been a steadfast and active ally of the German Reich's enemies. (17)

Half an hour after Fabricius had delivered his disappointing message, Italian Minister to Bucharest Pellegrino Ghigi reported to the Royal Palace conveying the advice of the Italian government: Romania was advised to accept the Soviet ultimatum and execute it without offering any resistance, although earlier Italian advice had been to resist any Soviet attack in the interest of civilization and of the Latin world. (18) In fact, on June 26 Italian Foreign Minister Galeazzo Ciano, informed by German Ambassador Hans Georg Mackensen about the June 25 Molotov –von der Schulenburg meeting, «remarked that he did not see any reason why the Italians should not suggest to the Russians that they should not close the door to a peaceful solution, and offered to exert their influence in Bucharest, if this is desirable for us or for the Russians.» Ciano added that he was going to talk to Mussolini on the following day about the whole issue and was confident that the latter would agree. (19) As expected, the Duce expressed agreement with this handling of the Bessarabian question and concurred with the German position.

Fears of a Concentric Attack

Romania might possibly have resisted the Soviet Union if Bucharest had received assurances from Germany that Hungary and Bulgaria would not take advantage of a war on Romania's eastern frontier to attack it for the sake of their own claims to Romanian territory (i.e., Transylvania, Crişana, Maramureş, and the Banat for Hungary, and Southern Dobrogea for Bulgaria). The Romanian government therefore asked Berlin, through Minister Crutzescu, «whether the German government would be in a position to indicate if Hungary and Bulgaria would refrain from any move in the event of a Russo-Romanian war.» Weizsaecker gave an evasive answer. He said that «the question regarding the attitude of Hungary and Bulgaria is based on an assumption of something that we wish to see avoided, a Russo-Romanian war,» (20) which did not mean that Germany committed itself in any way.

The Bulgarian government was following the evolution of the Bessarabian question with particular interest, and the Bulgarian Minister to Berlin Parvan Draganov informed Ernst Woermann, Director of the Political Department in the German Foreign Ministry, that

Tzar Boris III and the Bulgarian government would find themselves in an extremely difficult position if they did not take advantage of the present moment. (21)

The Hungarian government, in its turn, submitted a memo to the German Foreign Ministry in which it said that

In the opinion of the Hungarian government, if Romania, on its own initiative, enters into agreements with another state on territorial questions, Hungary must also be included. (22)

The possibility of opening a second front was also taken into consideration by the Crown Council when it reached a decision on 27 June 1940.

The Crown Council Answered Evasively

The Crown Council, made up of advisers of King Carol II, met at the royal palace immediately after the German answer was received. At this meeting the historian Nicolae Iorga spoke categorically in favor of resistance at any cost, claiming that a country willing to surrender a part of its territory without fighting would run the risk of losing everything. His opinion was shared by the representatives of Bessarabia, Bucovina, and Transylvania. The majority of the council's members, however, realized that Romanian resistance would have no chance of success, for Romania stood quite alone politically. According to this viewpoint, which was presented by the Ministry of War and strongly supported by the Chief of the General Staff, even if Romania would succeed in resisting the first frontal Soviet attack, it could never mount a resistance of any duration, for there was no way for it to obtain supplies of military material. In fact, Germany had agreed, according to the terms of the Ribbentrop-Molotov Pact, not to supply arms and war material to any country at war with the Soviet Union. This meant that Romania could not hope to become a second Finland. Consequently, the decision to give in, made by the Crown Council, was justified as follows:

Because of its desire to preserve peaceful relations with the Soviet Union, the Crown Council approves of the decision of the Romanian government to ask the Soviet government to set a time and place where the delegations of both governments could meet to discuss the Soviet note. (23)

The Second Soviet Ultimatum

This answer did not mean explicit acceptance of the Soviet ultimatum, but neither could it be regarded as a refusal. It left the question of deciding on the substance of the matter, the Soviet claims, up to the forthcoming negotiations. Under such conditions, since the Crown Council's announcement that it would send plenipotentiaries to discuss the Soviet conditions might be considered unacceptable by the Kremlin, the Soviets might have invaded.

On June 27 Molotov told Davidescu that the Soviet government considered the Romanian government's reply of June 27 unacceptable, since it made no direct reply to the question whether it accepted the Soviet government's proposals of an immediate transfer to the Soviet Union of Bessarabia and Northern Bucovina. When Davidescu replied that the Romanian answer meant acceptance, Molotov demanded that the Romanian authorities evacuate Bessarabia and Northern Bucovina within the next four days, starting at 14,00 hours on June 28. Romania had 12 hours in which to respond to this new ultimatum. On that day – June 28 – the Red Army was going to occupy key positions in the claimed areas Chişinău, Cernăuţi, and Cetatea Albă. Romania would be held responsible for any damage caused to communications, warehouses, airports, factories, etc. (24) Molotov added:

My colleagues, especially the military, are very dissatisfied with the answer of the Romanian government, for it does not seem to have a clear understanding of the situation on the frontier. The Soviet government expects a reply before noon tomorrow. After that hour we shall proceed to act. (25)

Implicit and Explicit Romanian Reservations

On June 28 at 11,00 hours the new Romanian Foreign Minister Constantin Argetoianu sent the final reply, reproduced on June 29 by Tass as follows:

The Romanian government, in order to avoid the grave consequences of recourse to force and the commencement of hostilities in this part of Europe, is constrained to accept the demand that it withdraw from the territories specified in the note of the Soviet government.

Romania did, however, request that the deadline be extended, since it would have been extremely difficult to complete evacuation of the territory in four days because of damage caused by rains and floods. Molotov conceded that in case of need a newly created Romanian-Soviet Commission, which would meet in Odessa, could take up the question of postponing the evacuation for a few hours.

From the text of the answer delivered by Davidescu it emerges that Romania had only accepted the demand that it withdraw from those territories, without, however, recognizing any legal justification for the act of surrendering the territories.

Prime Minister Tătărescu told parliament that the government rejected the historical and ethnic arguments invoked in the Soviet ultimatum to justify the annexation of Bessarabia. He said:

Bessarabia is a Romanian province torn away from the territory of Moldavia in 1812 and returned to the fatherland in 1918 by the will of a population which, after a century of oppression, had not forgotten its forefather's language, had not allowed its feelings or mores to become alienated. The union of Bessarabia with Romania was not an act of conquest but one of liberation, based on rights which have been and still are inalienable in the eyes of our nation.

Speaking about the ethnic character of Bessarabia the Prime Minister added:

Some 1,800,000 Romanians live in Bessarabia. This province has been and still is one of the oldest bastions of the Romanian nation, and the foreign populations which have settled there have changed neither its character nor its appearance. Bessarabia, with its free peasants, its fortresses and other buildings from the days of the voivodes, has been and still is Romanian.

Tătărescu went on to say that capitulation in the face of superior force had been the real reason why Bessarabia had been surrendered:

In the final hour when we still had time to give our answer, we decided to accept. I declare here, before this parliament and the country: we have decided to withdraw from Bessarabia and Northern Bucovina in order to save the Romanian state and not to jeopardize the future of the Romanian nation. I declare here that we made this decision under pressure, at one of the gravest moments of our history, leaving it to the future to pass judgement on our act. (26)

Therefore, the stand adopted by the Romanian government in the Bessarabian crisis in 1940 was to agree not to the cessation of Bessarabia and Northern Bucovina, but only to evacuate those territories under the threat from a greater force, which did not entail transfer of the legal title of possession to that territory. Romania considered that, in this way, it would preserve its historical and national rights to the provinces occupied by the Soviet Union, rights that could be reclaimed under more favorable conditions.

Brutal Enforcement of the Ultimatum and Its Consequences

At the beginning of June 1940 numerous Soviet divisions, backed by armored brigades, had been concentrated along the Dniester River and in Northern Bucovina. On June 25 these units were operationally ready and had gone on the alert. According to the program prepared by the Russians, the Romanian army and authorities were to withdraw in four stages, one per day, back to previously set lines. During this operation Romanian and Soviet troops were to be kept separated in order to avoid any incidents. Nevertheless, the Soviet troops failed to observe the timetable set by their own government. They advanced at a far quicker pace, with some units reaching the Pruth River at 13,00 hours on June 30 instead of on July 3. During their advance the Soviet units acted in a provocative and hostile manner to the Romanian troops, who had been categorically ordered not to resort to arms. Under such conditions King Carol II complained to Hitler that the Soviet troops had insulted and disarmed Romanian soldiers and asked for Germany to help by sending a German military commission to Bucharest. (27)

The withdrawal of Romanian troops under constant pressure from the Soviet army, which tried to cut off their route in order to confiscate Romanian supplies, ammunition, and war material, as well as the abandoning, without struggle, of the population, humiliated the Romanian army.

Prime Minister Tătărescu told Fabricius the following about the mood of the Romanian public:

The people are extremely indignant, and the king has called the Russian demands unbearable, while a large part of the Romanian nation is willing to go to war and will not forgive the government for unconditionally ceding the entire area.

The Error of Too Heavy a Red Pencil

Molotov had given Davidescu a 1/1,800,000 scale map on which the new Romanian-Soviet border was traced with a heavy stroke of red pencil which covered a seven-mile-wide band of territory. As a result, the new demarcation line inadvertently cut Herța and the northern corner of Romania off, a territory that belonged neither to Bessarabia nor to Northern Bucovina, since it was a part of Dorohoi County in Moldavia.

The Romanian government proposed to the Kremlin that a mixed commission should meet to negotiate a definitive settlement in a friendly way of this additional territory, while Prime Minister Tătărescu asked Germany to bring its influence to bear upon Moscow to leave at least this territory to Romania. However, his attempt failed. (28) The Soviets ignored these Romanian suggestions so that Herța, which had not been mentioned in the Soviet ultimatum, was nevertheless occupied by Soviet troops. This is how the Soviet Union came to appropriate a 10-kilometer-strip of territory (about six and a quarter mile) that belonged to Moldavia. In Herța Soviet units disarmed two Romanian battalions and killed two officers and four soldiers of the 16th Cavalry Regiment who died not knowing what mischief a heavy Soviet pencil had caused.

Bessarabia – a Victim of the Soviet-German Non-aggression Treaty

In point of fact, the dice deciding the fate of Bessarabia had been cast even before the Soviet ultimatum was sent, under Article 3 of the Secret Protocol to the 23 August 1939 Soviet-German Non-aggression Treaty establishing zones of influence partitioning Europe. The article reads as fallows:

With regard to southeastern Europe the Soviet Union calls attention to its interest in Bessarabia. Germany declares its complete lack of any political interest in that area. (29)

In partitioning Europe into zones of influence according to the terms of the Secret Protocol, Bessarabia, together with Finland, Estonia, Latvia, Lithuania, and eastern Poland, fell into the Soviet sphere. Ribbentrop explained that when the spheres of interest in southeastern Europe were marked out the Russians had expressed their interest in Bessarabia and the southeastern parts of the continent. He allegedly did not want to «put down in **explicitly written form** recognition of the Russian claim to Bessarabia because of the possibility of indiscretion» . . . and he preferred a formulation of a **general nature** for the protocol (emphasis in the text). He went on to say that he had proceeded in accordance with the general instructions given by the Führer about southeastern Europe and with a special directive, received before his departure for Moscow, «in which the Führer authorized me to declare that Germany was not interested in the territories of southern Europe, even, if necessary, as far as Constantinople and the Straits. The latter, however, were not discussed.» (30)

Romania's leaders in 1940 did not know of the existence of the Secret Protocol. That is why they still placed their hopes on German support or mediation, unaware that Germany had formally declared itself not interested in the fate of Bessarabia, surrendering it to the Soviet Union. By yielding Bessarabia to the Soviet Union Hitler not only made an old wish of tzarist Russia to push its borders as far south as possible come true, but also made Romania less able to enter the forthcoming war at the side of France and Great Britain, by weakening its military, physical, and moral strength. Hitler expressed this opinion only a few days after the signing of the Soviet-German Non-aggression Treaty, when he wrote to Mussolini:

Thanks to these arrangements, Russia's favorable attitude in case of a conflict is guaranteed and the possibility of Romania's joining such a conflict is eliminated as of now. (31)

Mussolini shared this view, for he replied:

The Moscow treaty blocks Romania and might modify Turkey's stand...(32)

The Gold Reserves of the National Bank Withheld as «Reparations»

When Molotov informed von der Schulenburg on June 26 of the Soviet decision to occupy Bessarabia militarily, the German ambassador told him that the cession would be facilitated if the Soviet Union were to refund to Romania the gold reserves of the National Bank, which had been transferred to Russia for security reasons during World War I. These were the reserves of the Romanian National Bank on which constituted the guarantee for the issuing of 314,580,446 lei worth of gold. (33) On the basis of the protocol signed between Russian Minister Poklevsky Koziell and Romanian Minister of Finance Nicolae Titulescu on 27 July – 9 August 1917, the Romanian treasury contained a total declared value of 7,000 million gold lei. (34) When Romanian-Soviet diplomatic relations were resumed in 1934 the Soviet Union returned only a few symbolic items that had belonged to the Romanian treasury (a standard meter /lyardstick/ and kilogram weight, and nine highly accurate thermometers). Later, around 1956, the Soviet government returned to the Bucharest authorities several artistic items from the Romanian treasury in Moscow: 35,000 old coins, 1,400 paintings, ecclesiastical objects, etc., (35) but nothing of the gold reserves of the National Bank. However, von der Schulenburg's suggestion brought no response, for the Soviet Foreign Ministry replied:

There can be no such discussion, for Romania exploited Bessarabia for a fairly long time. (36)

Why Was Northern Bucovina Annexed?

The Soviet claim to Northern Bucovina took both the Romanians and the Germans by surprise for that territory had never belonged to tzarist Russia – it had also not been included in the zone of Soviet influence established by the Secret Protocol in 1939.

When Molotov informed Ambassador Schulenburg that the Soviet Union claimed not only Bessarabia but also the whole of Bucovina, the latter replied that a peaceful solution would be considerably facilitated «were the Russians to give up Bucovina, which has never been a part of tzarist Russia.» Molotov responded by arguing that

> *Bucovina is the last missing part of a unified Ukraine and it is on this account that the Soviet government is obliged to attach particular importance to a simultaneous settlement of this issue with that of Bessarabia. (37)*

Molotov apparently did not plead convincingly enough for Schulenburg concluded that:

> *I was left under the impression that Molotov had not completely closed the door to the possibility of giving up Bucovina during the negotiations with Romania. (38)*

Furthermore, when meeting with Italian Ambassador Augusto Rosso, Molotov did not say a word about Bucovina when discussing Soviet claims to Romanian territory. (39)

In any case Molotov again summoned von der Schulenburg on June 26. Referring to the discussion they had on the previous day, he said that the Soviet government had decided to limit its demands to the northern part of Bucovina and the city of Cernăuți:

> *According to Soviet opinion, the boundary line should run from the southernmost point of the Soviet western Ukraine at Mt. Kniatiasa, east along the Suceava /River/ then northeast to Herța on the Pruth /River/ whereby the Soviet Union would obtain a rail connection from Bessarabia via Cernăuți to Lvovo. (40)*

Even after Romania had received the Soviet ultimatum the Romanian government called upon Germany «to make attempts to have the Soviets agree to leave Romania Cernăuți,» noting that a large part of its population was made up of Germans. (41) The reply of the German Foreign Ministry to that question read:

> *The question of Cernăuți is not to be mentioned under any circumstances whatsoever in the telephone conversation with Minister Fabricius. (42)*

Writing to Weizsaecker about the atmosphere prevailing in the diplomatic corps in Moscow, von der Schulenburg remarked that news of the action against Romania had been greeted with general surprise precisely because the Soviet Union had also demanded the northern part of Bucovina, although there had never been any earlier Soviet claims to that region. In von der Schulenburg's opinion, this claim had been raised by the Ukrainian circles in the Kremlin. Although he could not say for sure which Ukrainian had so much influence in the Kremlin, the German ambassador thought that young Pavlov, from the Soviet Embassy in Berlin, could be the man: «he is a special pet of Stalin and Molotov; Stalin once described him to me as our little Ukrainian.» (43) In any case the justification given in the Soviet ultimatum for its claim to northern Bucovina was that acquisition of this territory would serve as compensation for the damage caused to the Soviet Union and to the population of Bessarabia by the 20-year-long Romanian «dominion» over Bessarabia. Therefore, in addition to withholding the gold reserves of the Romanian National Bank, the Soviet Union was granting itself compensation by occupying a part of Romanian territory without any historical justification. The occupation and exploitation of Northern Bucovina as «compensation» for the damage allegedly caused by Romania has now lasted 40 years.

Bucovina – An Apple of Discord

After Molotov first claimed the entire territory of Bucovina he then reduced his demands to Northern Bucovina. Later, however, he reverted to his original demand and, in a memo handed to von der Schulenburg on September 21, also claimed Southern Bucovina, so that the Soviet Union could take possession of the entire province. This new territorial claim was made after the Vienna arbitration and after northern Transylvania had been surrendered to Hungary. Molotov allegedly said that «for the present» the Soviet government had confined itself to claiming Northern Bucovina, which meant that it reserved for itself the right to raise the question of Southern Bucovina on another occasion. Von der Schulenburg declared, however, that he could not remember this short sentence, a fact which caused Molotov to draw in his horns a bit, saying that, «apparently, he had made this remark in an indefinite form at the time.» (44)

The claim to Southern Bucovina was the subject of extensive discussions during the meeting between Hitler and von Ribbentrop with Molotov and Vladimir Georgievich Dekanosov (Deputy People's Commissar for Foreign Affairs). On that occasion Molotov again maintained that although the Soviet Union had at first confined its claims to Northern Bucovina, under the present circumstances Germany must nevertheless understand the Russian interest in Southern Bucovina. Instead of replying to this point Germany guaranteed the territory of Romania, «completely disregarding Russia's wishes concerning Southern Bucovina.» In fact, Hitler answered that according to an oral agreement the former Austrian territories in that region should be included in the German sphere of influence. The territories which were included in the Soviet zone were listed by name (Bessarabia, for example), but there was no mention of Bucovina as being included in the Soviet sphere of influence. The fact that a part of Bucovina was nevertheless occupied by Russia meant «a considerable concession on the part of Germany.» So far as Molotov's objection that the territorial revision claimed by the Soviet Union was small when compared to the various revisions Germany had made by force of arms, Hitler emphasized that the latter type of revisions had not been the subject of any German-Soviet agreement. (45)

Therefore, Bucovina turned into an object of political divergences between Germany and the Soviet Union, with Germany maintaining that the claim to Bucovina constituted an encroachment of the provisions of the Secret German-Soviet Protocol of 23 August 1939 on the delimitation of the zones of influence and spheres of interest of the two big powers which had partitioned East Europe.

Consequences of the Ultimatum

According to Molotov, the immediate consequences for the Soviet Union of the Soviet ultimatum were the annexation of Bessarabia, with a surface area of 44,500 square kilometers and a population of 3,200,000, and Northern Bucovina, with a surface area of 6,000 square kilometers and a population of 500,000. «As a result the frontier of the Soviet Union had now been shifted westward and has now reached the Danube which, next to the Volga, is the biggest river in Europe and one of the most important commercial routes for a number of European countries.» (46)

So far as Romania was concerned, it not only lost Bessarabia and Northern Bucovina but also Northern Transylvania and Southern Dobrogea, for, as Ribbentrop put it:

It is right that the Hungarian and Bulgarian revisionist demands on Romania should be set in motion by the occupation of Bessarabia and Northern Bucovina. (47)

This opinion was also shared by the German ambassador to Moscow, who had played the role of an intermediary between Moscow and Berlin during the surrender of Bessarabia. He said:

The Soviet Union really opened up a great complex of questions by its settlement of the Bessarabian matter with unexpected speed, and it has thereby forced us, in order to avoid military complications in the Balkans, to take quick decisions on the matter of the Romanian-Hungarian dispute. (48)

The Third Reich's unfriendly attitude to Romania was explained by both Ribbentrop and by Hitler as being due to the pro-Western policy adopted by Romania between the two world wars and especially on the eve of World War II when Bucharest accepted the French-British guarantees (1939). Ribbentrop said that

Romania must blame its own policy for the crisis caused by the Bessarabian problem. Last year the Romanian government accepted England's promise of a guarantee and welcomed it very enthusiastically in both official statements and in the press, though this promise of a guarantee was aimed directly against Germany. (49)

The same argument – Romania's anti-German policy, based on the acceptance of the British guarantee – was also used by Hitler. (50)

While Romania, as a victor state of the first world war, had generally followed a pro-Western policy and was part of the French alliance system during the interwar period, the real reason for its dismemberment was that its geographical location, oil, and agriculture made it an important bargaining chip in a repartition of Europe between two totalitarian, aggressive states.

Background Report No. 183,
Munich, 23 July 1981,
Radio Free Europe Research.

BIBLIOGRAPHY:

1) See the Telegram sent by German Minister to Bucharest Wilhelm Fabricius to the German Foreign Ministry, dated Bucharest, 29 May 1940, in *Documents on German Foreign Policy, 1918-1945,* (London: Her Majesty's Stationery Office, 1956) Vol. IX, pp. 466-467.
2) Joachim von Ribbentrop's Telegram to the German Legation in Romania, dated Berlin, 1 June 1940, *ibid.,* p. 493.
3) Viacheslav Mikhailovich Molotov's Speech to the Supreme Soviet, Moscow, 29 March 1940, in *Documents..., op. cit.,* Vol. X, (London: Her Majesty's Stationery Office, 1957), p. 3.
4) Friedrich Werner, Count von der Schulenburg's Telegram to the German Foreign Ministry, dated Moscow, 23 June 1940, *Ibid.,* p. 3.
5) Ernst Freiherr von Weizsaecker's Telegram to Wolfsschantz (code name for Hitler's East Prussian field headquarters) dated Berlin, 24 June 1940, *Ibid.,* pp. 7–8. While

Bessarabia had belonged to the Russian Empire between 1812 and the collapse of the tzarist order (with the temporary loss of Danubian Southern Bessarabia between 1856 and 1878), Bucovina was between 1775 and 1918 Hapsburg territory, acquired by Romania, along with the Banat, Crişana, Maramureş, Transylvania and Bessarabia, when the two neighboring empires collapsed in the wake of World War I.

6) Ribbentrop's Telegram to the German Embassy in Moscow (transmitted by telephone) (dated Berlin, 25 June 1940), *Documents..., op. cit.,* pp. 12-13.
7) Fabricius's Telegrams to the German Foreign Ministry (dated Bucharest, 21 and 26 June 1940) *op. cit.,* Vol. IX, p. 656, and Vol. X, pp. 19–20.
8) Summary of Fabricius's 26 June 1940 Telegram to the German Foreign Ministry, *Ibid.,* p. 20.
9) Tass Statement on the notes exchanged with the Romanian government concerning the transfer of Bessarabia and Northern Bucovina to the Soviet Union, *Mirovoe Khoziaistvo,* 29 June 1940, in Jane Degras, *Soviet Documents on Foreign Policy* (London, New York, Toronto: Oxford University Press, 1953, Vol. III, 1933-1941), pp. 458-460.
10) Grégoire Gafenco, *Preliminaires de la Guerre à l'Est. De l'Accord de Moscou (21 Août 1939) aux Hostilités en Russie* (22 Juin 1941) (Fribourg, Switzerland: Egloff, 1944), p. 337.
11) Alexandre Cretzianu, *The Lost Opportunity* (London: Jonathan Cape, 195 7), pp. 40–48: Fabricius's Telegram to the German Foreign Ministry (dated Bucharest, 27 June 1940), in *Documents..., op. cit.,* Vol. X, p. 28.
12) Fabricius's 27 June 1940 Telegram to the German Foreign Ministry, *Documents..., op. cit.,* Vol. X, p. 33.
13) Telephone Message from von Ribbentrop (on a special train) to Minister Paul Otto Schmidt in the German Foreign Ministry; the latter subsequently relayed it to German Legation Counsellor Gerhard Steltzer in Bucharest at 10.30 hours. *Ibid.,* p. 28.
14) Fabricius's 27 June 1940 Telegram to the German Foreign Ministry, *Documents..., op. cit., p.* 34.
15) Ernst Weizsaecker's Memorandum, *Documents..., op. cit.,* p.31.
16) Fabricius's 27 June 1940 Telegram to the German Foreign Ministry, *Documents..., op. cit.,* p. 37.
17) Adolf Hitler's Message to King Carol II (telephoned to Fabricius), Führer's Headquarters, 29 June 1940, *Ibid.,* pp. 58-59.
18) Gafenco, *op. cit.,* p. 393.
19) Hans Georg Mackensen's Telegram to the German Foreign Ministry, Rome, 26 June 1940, *Documents..., op. cit.,* Vol. X, pp. 18-19.
20) Weizsaecker's Memorandum, dated Berlin, 27 June 1940, *Documents..., op.* cit., pp. 37–38.
21) Ernst Woermann's Memorandum, dated Berlin 27 June 1940, *Documents..., op.* cit., p. 38. It should be recalled that Romanian acquired Southern Dobrogea from Bulgaria in the Second Balkan War of 1912-1913.
22) Memorandum, dated Berlin, 27 June 1940, *Ibid.,* p. 39.

23) Communiqué No. 4, from the royal palace, *Universul,* Bucharest, 28 June 1940.
24) Tass statement..., *op. cit.,* p. 461.
25) Alexandre Cretzianu, *La Politique de Paix de la Roumanie a l'Égard de l'Union Soviétique* (Paris: Institut Universitaire Roumain Charles I-er, 1954), p. 10.
26) "Statements of Gheorghe Tătărescu, Royal Adviser and Prime Minister", *Universul,* June 1940.
27) Fabricius's Telegram to German Foreign Minister von Ribbentrop, dated Bucharest, 2 July 1940, in Herbert Michaelis and Ernst Schraepler, *Ursachen und Folgen vom Deutschen Zusammenbruch 1918 und 1945 bis zur Staatlichen Neuordnung Deutschlands in der Gegenwart,* (Berlin: Dokumenten–Verlag Dr. Herbert Wendler & Co. n. d.), Vol. XIV, pp. 266–267.
28) Fabricius's Telegram to German Foreign Minister von Ribbentrop, Bucharest, 28 June 1940, *Documents..., op. cit.,* Vol. X, pp. 52-53.
29) Secret Protocol of 23 August 1939, in *Documents..., op. cit.,* Vol. V, p. 10.
30) *Ibid.*, pp. 10–11.
31) Lettre de Hitler à Mussolini, 25 August 1939, in *La Vérité sur les Rapports Germano–Soviétiques de 1939 à 1941* (Paris: The US Department of State, Éditions France–Empire, 1948), p. 86.
32) *Ibid.,* p. 88.
33) *The Romanian Encyclopaedia* (Bucharest: Imprimeria Naţională, 1943), Vol. IV, p. 514.
34) Ion Popescu-Puţuri, "For a Just Cause. Romania's Joining the War in August 1916" (II), *Anale de Istorie* No. 2, 1978, pp. 7-8.
35) "The Solemn Ceremony at which the Soviet Union Handed Over Historical Treasures of Romanian Art", *Scînteia,* 7 August 1956.
36) Von der Schulenburg's Telegram to the German Foreign Ministry, Moscow, 26 June 1940, *Documents..., op. cit.,* Vol. X, p. 26.
37) *Ibid.,* p. 21.
38) *Ibid.*
39) Molotov's Statement to Italian Ambassador Augusto Rosso on Soviet policy in southeastern Europe, Degras, *op. cit.,* Vol. III, pp. 457-458.
40) Von der Schulenburg's Telegram to the German Foreign Ministry, Moscow, 26 June 1940, *Documents..., op. cit.,* Vol. X, p. 26.
41) Telegram of German Legation in Romania to German Foreign Ministry, Bucharest, 28 June 1940, *ibid.,* p. 46.
42) Rudolf Steg (assistant to Minister Schmidt), Note dated Berlin, 28 June 1940, *ibid.,* p. 48.
43) Von der Schulenburg's Letter to the State Secretary, Moscow, 11 July 1949, *ibid.,* p. 195.
44) Von der Schulenburg's Memorandum to German Foreign Ministry, Moscow, 21 September 1940, *ibid.,* Vol. XI, pp. 137–138.
45) Memorandum by an official of the Foreign Minister's Secretariat, dated Berlin, 15 November 1940, *ibid.,* p. 553.
46) Von Ribbentrop to the German Embassy in Moscow, dated Berlin, 6 September 1940, *Documents..., op. cit.,* Vol. XI, p. 30.

47) Von Ribbentrop to the German Embassy in Moscow, dated Berlin, 6 September 1940, *Documents..., op. cit.,* Vol. XI, p. 30.
48) Von der Schulenburg's Telegram to the Foreign Ministry, dated Moscow, September 1940, *ibid.,* p. 18.
49) Von Ribbentrop's Telegram to German Legation in Romania, dated Berlin, 27 June 1940, *ibid.,* Vol. X, p. 35.
50) Adolf Hitler's Message to King Carol II of Romania, dated Führer's Headquarters, 29 June 1940, *ibid.,* Vol. X, pp. 58-59. (According to a notation on the document, this message was telephoned to Fabricius at 20,00 hours.)

XI

THE PROBLEM OF BESSARABIA AND NORTHERN BUCOVINA DURING WORLD WAR II

The Annexation of Bessarabia and Northern Bucovina by the Soviet Union

As a result of the Soviet ultimatum of 26 June 1940 (1) the Soviet Union annexed an area of land belonging to Romania amounting to 19,446 square miles and with 3,700,000 inhabitants: 17,146 square miles and 3,200,000 inhabitants in Bessarabia, and 2,300 square miles and 500,000 inhabitants in Northern Bucovina. The annexation of these territories immediately resulted in a considerable shifting of the native population, with about 300,000 Romanian refugees from Bessarabia and Northern Bucovina crossing the new border into Romania. (2) At the same time, an opposite migratory current built up when more than 150,000 people, particularly Jews, moved from Romania to the territories occupied by the Soviet Union. In addition, 80,000 Germans were evacuated from Bessarabia to Germany, together with about 30,000 from Northern Bucovina. (3)

The Romanians from Bessarabia and Northern Bucovina who did not flee when the Romanian troops withdrew were not allowed to opt in favor of their old citizenship and were obliged to stay on. Only Romanians of German descent in those areas were entitled to choose German citizenship, on the basis of an agreement concluded between the Soviet Union and Germany. (4) Both the deprivation of the right of Romanian citizens to opt for a specific citizenship and the conclusion of an agreement with a third state ran contrary to international law (though this was hardly unique in relations between great powers and smaller countries) since they ignored the existence of a sovereign state – Romania – which should have been party to any agreement directly concerning it. (5) At the same time, the understanding reached over Romania's head was indicative of the complicity of the Soviet Union and the Third Reich on the division of Europe into zones of influence and the relegation of Bessarabia and Northern Bucovina to the Soviet sphere.

Under a law of 2 August 1940 less than half of the Moldavian Autonomous Socialist Soviet Republic (MASSR), located beyond the Dniester, together with most of the districts of Bessarabia, particularly those with a predominantly «Moldavian» (Romanian) population, were merged into the Moldavian Soviet Socialist Republic, while the districts of Hotin, Cetatea Albă, and Ismail, as well as Northern Bucovina, and most of the former MASSR were attached to the Ukraine. (6) In 1940 the New Moldavian SSR consisted of 13,012 square miles with a population of 2,400,000. Finally, under a decree of 15 August 1940, the land, industries, and trade of the recently annexed territories were nationalized. (7)

The Soviet Union derived two economic advantages from the annexation of Bessarabia and Northern Bucovina: it gained both a considerable surplus of cereals and animal products, and control of a Danubian state, on the basis of which it could arrogate to itself – as it had, in fact, tried to do since the previous century – the control of the navigation of this major European thoroughfare. At the same time, the presence of the Soviet Union along the Danube represented a large step forward toward the Black Sea straits, (8) a continuation of the tzars' time-honored policy.

So far as Romania was concerned, as a result of the loss of Bessarabia and Northern Bucovina, the process of disintegration of the Romanian state was continued by the surrendering of Northern Transylvania to Hungary under the Vienna Award (30 August 1940) and of Southern Dobrogea to Bulgaria by the Treaty of Craiova (September 1940). Finally, General Ion Antonescu set up his military dictatorship (6 September 1940 – 23 August 1944).

Diplomatic Preparations for the Regaining of the Lost Territories

Following the fall of Romania's chief traditional Western ally, France, in June 1940 and in view of Britain's inability to provide effective aid, in order to conquer its lost territories, Romania adjusted its foreign policy to the new international circumstances, trying to win over the Third Reich's support for its territorial claims. As far back as the first meeting between Antonescu and Hitler on 22 November 1940, Antonescu had declared that «the main goals of my policy will be to restore Bessarabia, Northern Bucovina, and Northern Transylvania to the Fatherland.» (9) Within the framework of this policy, on 30 August 1940 Romania accepted a German-Italian guarantee of its new borders and, at the same time, welcomed on its territory a German military mission to help it «reorganize» its army. (10) The reaction of the Soviet Union to Romania's shifting into the German political orbit – Romania had been for some years in the Reich's economic sphere of influence – was not confined to a diplomatic protest; it also materialized in «intensive military preparation at all levels.» (11) During the visit to Berlin from 12 through 14 November 1940 of Soviet Foreign Minister Vyacheslav M. Molotov he told Hitler that

the Soviet Union had expressed to Romania its dissatisfaction with the fact that the latter had agreed to Germany's and Italy's guarantee without consulting Russia. The Soviet government expressed this opinion twice; it considered that this guarantee was directed against the interests of the Soviet Union, if he could put it so bluntly. Because of this, the question of cancelling this guarantee has been raised.

Hitler retorted to the suggestion of revoking this guarantee that it had been given because otherwise Romania would not have agreed to the surrender of Bessarabia. He added that the presence of German troops in Romania was necessary to ensure the protection of the Romanian oil area against possible British attack. (12) In any case, Molotov attempted to find out from Hitler whether the guarantee provided to Romania would also be valid in the event of a RomanianSoviet conflict. (13) Hitler said that the answer given to Molotov had been: «He did not suppose that Russia had the intention of attacking Romania,» adding that, according to the very letter of the guarantee, it was operative against any aggressor. (14)

Romania's adherence to the Tripartite Pact (23 November 1940), which the Soviet Union had refused to join, placed it in an alliance which took on an increasingly anti-Soviet character with the development of a Soviet-German diplomatic «tug of war» in the Balkans. (15) On the occasion Antonescu declared that this was not a mere formality, but a fundamental act testifying to the new orientation of Romanian foreign policy designed to rebuild Europe and defend present-day civilization. (16) Apparently, this declaration was aimed more at the Soviet Union than at the Anglo-Saxon powers, although such jargon was used by the European Right against both «Bolshevism» and liberal parliamentary democracy.

In order to pave the diplomatic way for the reconstitution of the Romanian borders with German aid, during their talks Antonescu lectured Hitler on the Latin origin of the Romanian people and on its role as a counterweight to the Slav peoples. As far back as his first meeting with Hitler, Antonescu had pleaded not only for the retrieval of Bessarabia and Northern Bucovina but also for a revision of the Vienna Award, calling for Northern Transylvania to be restored to Romania. Regarding the retrieval of the territories annexed by the Soviet Union, Hitler said that «he could already assure Antonescu that Romania would receive damages when the conflict came to an end; as far as Germany was concerned, there would be no limits to this territorial compensation.» (17) This implied that Romania was promised more than the retrieval of its lost territories, namely, the area beyond the Dniester known as «Transdnistria». So far as the revision of the Vienna Award was concerned, Hitler confined himself to saying that «naturally, no ideal solution had been found in the Vienna Award,» but that «the time was not yet ripe to reconsider this situation». However, he could assure Antonescu that he fully understood his feelings, anger, and grief. After all, history had not stopped in the year 1940. (18) It was thus to regain the territories lost in 1940 that Antonescu came to join Hitler's war against the USSR.

Reconquering Bessarabia and Northern Bucovina

As early as December 1940 Germany was reckoning with Romania's joining the war against the Soviet Union and siding with the German forces. According to the Barbarossa plan, which had been worked out by Wilhelm Keitel and Alfred Jodl in accordance with Hitler's instructions and was the first directive to deal with Russia

on the flanks of our operation we can count on the active participation of **Romania** *and* **Finland** *in the war against the Soviet Union /emphasis in the original/... It will be the task of Romania, together with the forces concentrated there, to pin down the enemy facing it and, in addition, to render auxiliary service in the rear area. (19)*

At his meeting with Hitler on 12 June 1941 Antonescu said that he had been eager to fight alongside Germany right from the first day of the war. Romania's declaration of war against the Soviet Union was dated 22 June 1941 and was accompanied by Antonescu's order of the day to the Romanian army. In a poetic and patriotic style it stated that the goal of the war was to liberate Bessarabia and Northern Bucovina: «Free your oppressed brothers from the red yoke of Bolshevism, bring all of Bessarabia and the woods of Bucovina, your fields and meadows, back into the Fatherland!» (20)

Strangely enough, the declaration of war was not handed over to the Soviet government by the Romanian ambassador to Moscow, who had not been informed by his government about the beginning of the hostilities and had only learned that a German-Romanian offensive had begun from a counsellor at the German embassy in Moscow. When, on June 24, Grigore Gafencu, the Romanian ambassador, was summoned by Molotov, he was surprised to learn that the latter had not been apprised also by the Soviet embassy in Bucharest of the breaking off of diplomatic relations between Romania and the Soviet Union. The Soviet Foreign Minister reproached the Romanian ambassador, saying: «Romania had no right to break off its peaceful relations with the Soviet Union. It knew that after settling the Bessarabian issue we would not have made any other demands on it.» Gafencu replied that, in fact, the Soviet Union was to blame for triggering off the war since,

by last year's brutal ultimatum, when it claimed not only Bessarabia but also Bucovina and some of old Moldavia, by the subsequent continual violations of our territory, by its skirmishes on the Lower Danube at the very moment when the new border was about to be established through negotiations, the Soviet Union destroyed any feeling of confidence and security in Romania; it aroused the justifiable fear that the very existence of the Romanian state was jeopardized. Romania has sought support elsewhere. Had it not been affected, had it not felt threatened, it would not have needed such support and would not have sought it. (21)

Defining the nature of the conflict in which Romania had been involved, Mihai Antonescu, the Romanian Minister of Foreign Affairs during World War II, said that the war had not been an aggressive, imperialist one, but one to defend Romanian territorial integrity and order. He added: «Our foreign policy is the policy of our territory and of our unity.» (22)

Romania therefore began military operations for the reconquest of Bessarabia and Northern Bucovina, throwing into the battle 2 armies consisting of 12 infantry divisions, 1 armored division, 6 independent brigades, 672 planes, and its fleet, including 3 destroyers, 2 submarines and other smaller vessels. (23) The Romanian troops started their offensive only on July 2, in accordance with the German strategic plan which provided for the main offensive to take place in northern Galicia, thus obliging the Soviet troops to fall back from Bessarabia and occupy new positions along the Dniester. (24) Various large towns were successively liberated: Cernăuţi on July 4, Chişinău on July 9, and Cetatea Albă on July 26. On July 26, within only a month of the start of the hostilities, the goal set at the beginning of the war – the reconquest of the territory lost in the east in the summer of 1940 – had been achieved.

When Romanian troops reached Bessarabia and Northern Bucovina the Romanian authorities considered that, from the point of view of international law, these territories had reverted to the *status quo ante* of 28 June 1940, for in its diplomatic note of that date the Romanian government specified that it had been **constrained** /emphasis added/ to accept the demand that it withdraw from these areas, thereby operating an evacuation actuated by force, and not a legal transfer of sovereignty. Consequently, as early as February 1941 the Antonescu regime appointed prefects for Bessarabia and Northern Bucovina, with the obvious intention of restoring the constitutional and administrative *status quo ante*. (25)

The British Stand

After World War I Great Britain came to support Romanian claims to Bessarabia and was one of the signatories to the Paris Convention of 28 October 1920 between the major Allied Powers and Romania, by which the latter's sovereignty over the territory between the Pruth and the Dniester was recognized. Although on the eve of World War II Neville Chamberlain's government offered Romania guarantees against a German attack, the Bessarabian issue created serious complications for Anglo-French diplomacy since it made the practical application of guarantees even more difficult. In fact, the British guarantees had been conceived within a system of mutual assistance in which British military support would have been combined with similar Soviet support. However, Romania opposed an agreement (as it had in 1938) which would have allowed Soviet troops to cross its territory, lest this military aid should become a pretext for the Soviet Union effectively to occupy Bessarabia, whose union with Romania had never been recognized *de jure* by the Soviet government. Winston Churchill had himself admitted before the beginning of World War II that Romania, Poland, Finland, and the Baltic countries were not sure what they had to fear more, German aggression or Soviet support. (26) After the Anglo-French guarantees had been granted, Viorel Tilea, Romanian Minister Plenipotentiary to Great Britain, told Lord Halifax, the British Secretary of State for Foreign Affairs, that it was necessary to decide whether the British and French guarantees to Romania would operate against Soviet as well as German aggression. (27) The British government declared that it was ready to extend this guarantee to Soviet aggression also, which would have been mainly aimed at Bessarabia, in the case that Turkey came to Romania's help and Italy will take action in the Balkan on the side of the Allies. The existence of a bilateral secret Italo-Romanian agreement, was also mentioned by Italian Foreign Minister Galeazzo Ciano during a meeting with US Undersecretary of State Sumner Welles, according to which

if Russia attacked Romania, Italy would at once come to the assistance of Romania, not through an open declaration of war on Russia, but through the furnishing of every form of military assistance, including the furnishing of troops and airplanes. (28)

The British authorities did not share Romania's opinion about the guarantees. While Lloyd George thought that Great Britain should provide Romania with guarantees, (29) Lord Ismay, Secretary of State for Imperial Defense, considered that the guarantees offered to Romania arrived «very late in the day.» (30) On the other hand, in the opinion of Lord Halifax, the foreign minister, they were in addition illusive, since the guarantor «had no means of making them effective». (31)

When the Soviet Union sent an ultimatum to Romania calling on it to surrender Bessarabia, the Anglo-French guarantees did not operate. King Carol II, together with Gheorghe Tătărescu, the Romanian Prime Minister, decided not to appeal for British and French support because France was disarmed and out of action while Great Britain was organizing the defense of its own territory with the paltry means still available to it. As Tătărescu said, one could not maintain that Great Britain had not fulfilled its obligations to Romania since it had only agreed to lend assistance if Romania decided to resist aggression by force and if it formally called for help from the guaranteeing powers. Since Romania did not turn for help to Great Britain, however, the latter had no obligations to fulfill. (32)

Consequently, Tilea informed the British Foreign Office that «it was clear.... that the circumstances of this unhappy story did not involve HMG / His Majesty's Government/ in the implementation of their guarantee.» The British answer was that «no occupation of the territory of a friendly government could be matter of indifference to HMG» (33) which suggested that Great Britain did not recognize the reannexation of Bessarabia by the Soviet Union.

The failure of France and Great Britain to hasten to Romania's assistance at a time when the Soviet Union claimed Bessarabia nevertheless resulted in a loss of British prestige not only in Romanian leading political circles but also at the grassroots. In this context, Franklin Gunther, US Minister to Bucharest, reported to US Secretary of State Cordell Hull that, as a result of the German-Soviet conflict in which Romania had been involved, the popular mistrust of German policy had lessened and the sympathy, until then obvious, of Romanian public opinion for the Anglo-Saxons had diminished.

Russia, particularly Bolshevik Russia, has always been considered by Romanians public enemy number one, and it is therefore not unnatural that a revision of public sentiment favorable to Germany should take place now that that country is Romania's ally in arms. At the same time it must be admitted that Great Britain and, to a lesser extent, the United States have lost sympathy possibly and, it is hoped, only temporarily, as a result of their announced friendliness for and desire to help Russia in its war against Germany. (34)

Gunther added that, nevertheless, the majority of Romanians continued to hope for an allied victory which would leave Russia, Germany, and Hungary weakened, so that none of these countries could constitute a threat to Romania for a long time to come. In other words, since at the popular level they were counting on the ultimate victory of Great Britain, there were hopes that Bessarabia could be reconquered with German help and Northern Transylvania with Anglo-Saxon help.

Although the Romanians had reoccupied Bessarabia and Romanian troops had penetrated into Soviet territory, nevertheless, the British Prime Minister, Winston Churchill, did not consider «that a declaration of war was the correct method of dealing with the situation.» (35) He therefore decided to turn directly to Stalin, to persuade him that it was better for Great Britain to avoid declaring war on the German satellite countries (Finland, Romania, and Hungary). He argued that Finland had many friends in the United States and that «the dictatorial regime of Antonescu would not last indefinitely.» Besides, Romania, like Hungary, was a country «full of our friends; they have been overpowered by Hitler but if fortune turns against /the German dictator/, they might easily come back to /the British/ side.» Churchill added that «a British declaration of war /would have/ only frozen / those friends / and made it look as if Hitler had been the head of a grand European alliance..» This stand was also adopted by the British dominions, Australia excepted. (36) Stalin's answer was that were Great Britain not to declare war on the German satellite countries, especially Finland, the impression would be created that there was a lack of unity among the allies, (37) and that Hitler's accomplices could «do their base work with impunity»; he added, however, that «with regard to Hungary and Romania, we can perhaps wait a little while.»

The Soviet ambassador to London related how angry the British Prime Minister was when Stalin's answer was conveyed to him: «I can't understand what Stalin wants. Bad relations? A rupture? Whom will that benefit? Now, when Germans are at the gates of Moscow and Leningrad is threatened with a blockade!» (38) A compromise was eventually reached, however, with Stalin explaining in a letter that he had not meant to insult the British Prime Minister, while the latter reluctantly pledged himself to send ultimatums to the satellite states, but to declare war only when the time limits expired and if Moscow still wished such a step. The British Prime Minister was not persuaded of the benefits to be derived from expanding the war and he wrote to his foreign minister: «My decision about the unwisdom of this measure remains unaltered.» (39) On November 28 the British Foreign Office had asked the United States, which represented British interests in Romania, to inform the Romanian government «that unless they had ceased military operations by December 5 and had in practice withdrawn from all participation in hostilities against the Soviet Union, the ally of Great Britain, HMG would have no choice but to declare the existence of a state of war between the two countries.» (40) The hesitation of Great Britain to declare war on Romania and Finland was also partly due to the fact that the latter's probable reason for beginning hostilities against the Soviet Union was the retrieval of parts of its national territory recently guaranteed by the British government. The fact that the ultimatum only called for the withdrawal of the Romanian troops along the Dniester and not along the Pruth implied that the Romanian claims on the territory between the Pruth and Dniester were not contested, since the evacuation of that territory was not required.

In fact, the Romanian reply to the British declaration of war emphasized the one-sided character of the war, specifying that it was directed only against the Soviet Union. Summoning Romanian journalists, after receipt of the British declaration of war, Marshal Antonescu declared: «I am the ally of the Reich against the Soviet Union. I am neutral between Great Britain and Germany.» (41)

The American Stand

After World War I, since, according to the official American doctrine, no territorial change would be recognized in the Soviet Union until a representative government had been established in Moscow, the US din not sign the Paris Treaty of 28 October 1920 by which the union of Bessarabia with Romania was recognized *de jure*. In 1933, when the US was about to recognize the Soviet government, Romania tried to obtain recognition of its union with Bessarabia before the US government recognized the Soviet regime. Cordell Hull, US Secretary of State at that time, proposed to President Roosevelt to recognize *de facto* the union of Bessarabia with Romania by the inclusion of that province within Romania's immigration quota (15 November 1933). (42)

Franklin Mott Gunther, the US Minister in Bucharest, reported to the US Secretary of State that the moment the surrender of Bessarabia began being discussed in diplomatic circles, Gheorghe Tătărescu had emphatically stated that Romania would and could put up a determined resistance to an eventual attack, even if it came from both the Soviet Union and Germany. Tătărescu added that the Romanian army numbered 1,200,000 men and that it was properly equipped and trained for resistance. (43) When the Soviet ultimatum was, in fact, submitted to the Romanian government, Gunther said that he thought it would be firmly rejected. (44) When, despite delays, the ultimatum was finally accepted, the American representative said that the decision «came as a great shock to the people who have been filled for 20 years with strong words against territorial cession of any kind and Romania's ability and willingness to defend her soil at any costs.» (45)

In the spring of 1940, therefore, shortly before Romania was presented with the Soviet ultimatum on Bessarabia, Romanian Foreign Minister Grigore Gafencu asked Washington, through the agency of Gunther, to ensure that Soviet intentions toward Bessarabia be clarified. At that time the Romanian government was perturbed by the realignment of Soviet troops on Romania's borders, by the Soviet Union's active building program of roads and railways facing in the direction of Romania, and by the evacuation of peasants from the frontier area. In Gunther's opinion, Romania's appeal to Washington had a political aim, i.e., it sought a way out of succumbing to Germany's offer of protection. (46) Following Gunther's information, Cordell Hull instructed Walter Thurston, the American Chargé d'Affaires in the Soviet Union, to convey to the Commissar for Foreign Affairs the United States's concern about the possibility of an extension of the war into the Balkans. (47) Thurston's reply was that:

Should conditions appear propitious (as a result of the general hostilities in the Balkans or otherwise), it is to be assumed that the Soviet government would seize the opportunity to recover Bessarabia. Whether its aspirations with respect to Romania go further is not known. (48)

Hull's final opinion communicated to Gunther was that «it would be inopportune and would serve no useful purpose for the American embassy in Moscow to take steps along the lines suggested». (49)

When Germany advised Romania to give in to the Soviet Union's demand for its withdrawal from Bessarabia and Northern Bucovina, Heath, the American Chargé d'Affaires in Berlin, wrote to the Secretary of State that official German circles were intimating that the Russian occupation of those territories should not be regarded as definitive and might possibly last only a few months. (50) After the Soviet Union had occupied Bessarabia and Northern Bucovina Ion Gigurtu, Minister of Foreign Affairs in the government which had received the Soviet ultimatum, and prime minister from 4 to 28 June 1940, told Gunther that the Romanian government should have abandoned the Franco-British guarantee, which was already meaningless, and followed up the offer of a German guarantee; it should then have told the Soviet Union that Romania was ready to settle the Bessarabia and Ukrainian minority question by negotiation. Gigurtu believed that with the German guarantee behind them the Romanians could have made a better bargain and possibly an independent, buffer zone of Bessarabia. (51) On the other hand, Constantin Argetoianu, the new Foreign Minister replacing Gigurtu, told Gunther that he was not at all sure Russia would stop on the Pruth River, pointing out that a much straighter and more easily defended line would be that of the Siret River, taking in all of Moldavia. Very likely in order to arouse the interest of the US in Romania's political issues of the time, Argetoianu added that he was also concerned about the possibility of a Soviet move southward, across the mouth of the Danube, to meet with the Bulgarians in the Dobrogea, with the attendant menace to Turkey and the Straits.

Continuing his mission Gunther conscientiously reported both the opinions prevailing in leading Romanian circles and the public mood on the eve of

Romania's joining World War II. For example, early in January 1941 he reported that during talks with General Antonescu the latter had complained that Romania was constantly harassed by Russia, that no progress was being made in the negotiations for the demarcation of the new Romanian-Russian frontier, and that the Russians had attempted to seize the mouths of the Danube. Gunther added:

The general is obviously obsessed with the danger, either real or imaginary, of Russia. He is evidently dealing with present-day Russian annoyances with great caution and temperance, but he has told me more than once that he would resist, come what may, any Russian attempt to occupy the mouths of the Danube. (52)

Antonescu explained to the American representative that «the poltroonery of ex-King Carol's government in not having opposed Russia's occupation of Bessarabia and Northern Bucovina, and the fact that Romania was still being threatened by Russia» (53) were the main reasons why he adopted a pro-German policy. On another occasion Antonescu said that he hoped to get back Bessarabia, Northern Bucovina, and even Transylvania with German help during the war which Germany was preparing against the Soviet Union, as testified by the concentration of German troops in Moldavia:

The general also said he could not understand why the United States was so opposed to Germany only, when Soviet Russia had acted in a much worse manner toward small countries such as Finland, the Baltic states, and Romania. Nevertheless, he seemed very well disposed toward us and referred good-naturedly to our blocking of Romania's funds. (54)

The American ambassador to Moscow also kept track of the evolution of Romanian-Soviet relations and reported to Washington that the Soviet Union did not seem to be hostile to the suggestion of a frontier rectification «based on the return to Romania of a limited amount of territory in Bucovina» and also seemed favorable to the conclusion of a Romanian-Soviet non-aggression pact. (55)

When the war for the reconquest of Bessarabia began Gunther reported to Washington the content of General Antonescu's two proclamations, to the people and to the army, briefly listing the reasons why Romania had joined the war: according to Antonescu, this was «to revenge the humiliation and injustice of Russia's seizure, just a year ago, of Bessarabia and Northern Bucovina, and to fight for the preservation of the civilization of the world.» (56) Some time later he said that Acting Prime Minister Mihai Antonescu had made «a plea to the Western democracies to find a formula for settlement with Germany in order to avert the danger to Europe of Communism, Pan-Slavism, and Russian-Imperialism." (57)

Just as Bessarabia and Northern Bucovina had been reconquered, Brutus Coste, Romanian Chargé d'Affaires in Washington, applied for an appointment with the Secretary of State, whom he informed, in the name of the Romanian government, that the military operations conducted by Romania did not constitute aggression since the sole aim of Romania had been to recover the territories seized by the Soviet Union a year earlier. Coste added that, having regained the territories in question, Romanian operations would henceforth be limited to the duties of an occupation force. For strategic reasons the Romanian Army had been obliged to advance beyond the reclaimed territories but that, even as an occupation force, their area of operations would be limited to the region between the Dniester and the Bug Rivers. Coste had also been instructed to say that the Romanian government had formally notified the German government of its position and had specified:

that Romania would be unwilling to agree to any territorial expansion to the east in exchange for a renunciation of Romania's claims against Hungary in Transylvania, which will be maintained as a matter of primary national priority. (58)

Without raising any objection to the reoccupation of Bessarabia and Northern Bucovina, Hull noted Romania's stand, commenting in his memoirs:

The Romanians soon assured us they intended only to occupy the territories Russia had acquired from Romania the year before and take up a strategic defensive position along the Dniester River, and they consider their obligations to Germany fulfilled.

At his meeting with Hjalmar Procopé, the Finnish Minister in Washington, Hull gave Romania as a model of conduct to Finland: «... Romania had informed us it would cease active hostilities against the Soviet government when Odessa had fallen and the former Romanian territory had been regained.» (59) Discussing the problem of the ceasing of hostilities between Finland and the Soviet Union with the British Chargé d'Affaires, Sir Ronald Campbell, Hull mentioned that he had told the Finnish minister that the Romanian government would cease hostilities against the Soviet Union as soon as the former Romanian territories were regained, suggesting that the Finnish government proceed in a similar way. (60) All this seems to imply that Hull regarded Romania's reason for entering the war as justif-ied.

In any case, on 12 December 1941 George Davidescu, Secretary General of the Romanian Ministry of Foreign Affairs, delivered to Webb Benton, the American Chargé d'Affaires in Romania, a note mentioning that the Romanian government was in a state of war with the American one, in this way «respecting the obligation of solidarity contained in the Tripartite Pact.» (61) Davidescu added:

«You understand that we are not taking such proceedings willingly. If we are parting today, it is in the hope of eventually fighting in the same camp." General Antonescu's secretary, who related this scene, said that the representatives of the two states which had become enemies parted after embracing one another. Romanian Foreign Minister Mihai Antonescu told Benton when the latter was about to leave Romania that it would «never commit any hostile act against the United States.» (62) Even General Antonescu made a point of resuming with a few alterations the formula he had used in the instance of the declaration of war on Great Britain: «I am the ally of Germany against Russia. I am neutral between Great Britain and Germany. I am siding with the United States against Japan.» (63)

It is interesting to note that the United States did not immediately take note of Romania's declaration of war. Cordell Hull provided the following explanation:

for the time being we would not ask the Congress for declarations of war against these satellites /Romania, Bulgaria, and Hungary/. We realize that their governments were puppets of Hitler and had merely jumped when the strings were pulled. (64)

The US government countersigned the declaration of war only at the prompting of the Soviet government and it did not do so until 5 June 1942. (65)

War Continued Beyond the Bessarabian Frontier

On 27 July 1941, the second day after the liberation of Bessarabia, Hitler wrote to the Romanian Prime Minister and head of the state, Ion Antonescu, from his general headquarters, congratulating him on his military successes. «The recovery of Bessarabia is the most natural reward for your efforts and those of your brave troops,» Hitler wrote. Apart from these congratulations, however, Hitler's note also included an ominous suggestion: «I should appreciate it if you would advance with your troops into the area southwest of the Bug and thereby also take over the protection of this area.» (66) Confronted with this proposal, Antonescu replied: «I shall fight on with the German Army until the final goal is attained. I, therefore, do not put forward conditions of any kind, nor do I have any proposals to make for a discussion of this military collaboration in a new field.» (67) Acting Prime Minister Mihai Antonescu immediately informed Franklin Mott Gunther, the American Minister in Bucharest, of General Antonescu's decision to continue the war beyond the Dniester as follows: «General Antonescu has no intention of going further beyond the Dniester than a reasonable distance – possibly to the Bug River, calculated to make Romania safe in the future from such recurrent Russian molestation as it has suffered in the past.» (68) Nevertheless, on 7 August 1941, at his meeting with Hitler, General Antonescu expressed his wish to occupy not only Odessa but also Sevastopol and the Crimea «in order thus to seize the air bases of the Russians from which the Russian Air Force could make heavy bombing attacks on the Romanian harbor of Constanţa.» (69)

Since the German forces met with more resistance in Russia than they had expected, Hitler was increasingly eager to involve Romanian troops in his East European campaign. He therefore wrote to General Antonescu on 14 August 1941: «Furthermore, it would be especially desirable if the mobile Romanian forces – Cavalry Corps and Armoured Brigade – and the Mountain Corps were to participate in the coming operations east of the Dnieper too.» (70)

Now General Antonescu's answer was more restrained. He agreed to take over responsibility for the protection, policing, and security in the territory between the Dniester and Dnieper, in which he insisted that the German authorities not interfere; he agreed to continue the campaign beyond the Dnieper as well, with a view to «saving civilization, justice, and liberty among nations,» but added that the Armoured Brigade, which had suffered considerable losses before Odessa, should only participate with reduced forces. Finallly, he stated bluntly:

I am not in a position, for lack of means and prepared personnel, to assume the responsibility for the administration and economic exploitation of any territory other than that between the Dniester and the Bug, the more so as the whole of Romania, as well as Bessarabia in particular, is in need of complete reorganization both administratively and economically. (71)

Transdnistria

After the fall of Odessa on 16 October 1941 the entire territory beween the Dniester and the Bug Rivers was conquered by German and Romanian troops. The problem then arose of organizing this territory, a question that had been the subject of previous talks among German high officials and between Hitler and Antonescu. As far back as December 1940 Hitler had told Marshāl Walter von Brauchitsch and General Franz Halder that in order to involve Romania even more in the East European campaign he had planned to give it some Ukrainian territory, besides the former Romanian territories – Bessarabia and Northern Bucovina. (72) In fact, at the conference held by Hitler with some of his political and military assistants, asked by Hermann Goering what territories he had promised other states, Hitler had replied: «Antonescu desired Bessarabia and

Odessa with a strip of land leading west-northwest from Odessa.» To the objections raised by Göring and Rosenberg against this concession Hitler retorted that «the new frontiers desired by Antonescu contained little outside the old Romanian frontiers.» (73) During the same conference Hitler had added that Germany's relations with Romania should be established on such bases that would not make Germany dependent in the future on Romanian good will, which could have meant that by giving the Romanians a strip of land that had not belonged to them they would feel obliged to bind their fate once and for all to that of Germany in the war. Hitler said:

Our present relations with Romania are good, but nobody knows what they will be at any future time. This we have to consider and we have to draw our frontiers accordingly. One ought not to be dependent on the good will of other people; we have to plan our relations with Romania in accordance with this principle. (74)

Under a Romanian government decree of 19 August 1941 the area between the Dniester and the Bug Rivers was passed over to the Romanian administration under the name of Transdnistria, an entity that had never existed before, with Gheorghe Alexianu as governor of this new province.

Agreements «regarding security, administration, and economic utilization of the territories between the Dniester and the Bug (Transdnistria), and the Bug and the Dnieper (Bug-Dnieper Territory)» were signed by representatives of the Romanian General Staff and the German High Command at Tighina on 30 August 1941. The Romanian troops beyond the Bug River mostly continued to remain under Romanian military command.

The Tighina agreement on the administration of Transdnistria was regarded by the Romanians as final, while the Germans regarded it as merely temporary. (75) Apparently, Hitler's «generosity» in offering Antonescu large areas of the Ukraine was not alien to his political intention to distract his Romanian ally from the goal of regaining Northern Transylvania by keeping the Romanians occupied with the East.

When Romanian Foreign Minister Mihai Antonescu complained to Hitler about incidents that had taken place in Transylvania and called for «a definitive solution to be found in relations with Hungary on a just basis,» the German leader replied that it was «tragic that ethnographic and historical claims were often incompatible, so that no delimitation of frontiers could do justice to all claims.» Nevertheless, he immediately added:

In the east, however, both Romania and Germany had tremendous areas to colonize. Romanian and German interests met here and forced one biological decision; i.e., Romania too would have to give as much of her own ethnic group as possible in the interest of preserving these newly acquired territories, and this to the furthermost frontier of these new areas. (76)

However, when on 11 September 1941 the American Minister in Bucharest asked the same Mihai Antonescu whether one could take seriously the rumor circulating in Hungary that a Romanian expansion beyond the Dniester would allegedly compensate for Romanian claims in the West and assuage Romanian-Hungarian relations, the Romanian Foreign Minister replied: «The Romanian people cannot consider this even as an assumption for discussions along that line, for our claims on Transylvania are the basis of our foreign policy.» (77)

Romanian Political and Military Opposition to Expansion Beyond Bessarabia

In a letter to General Antonescu, Iuliu Maniu, Chairman of the National-Peasant Party and the real head of the Romanian democratic opposition, supported the reconquest of Bessarabia: «The current watchword is to remake the country's frontiers.» (78) Ion Mihalache, Vice-Chairman of the National-Peasant Party, joined the eastern campaign as a volunteer in token of his party's adherence to a policy of reconquest of Bessarabia and Northern Bucovina. (79) A couple of days after the declaration of war Maniu told Gunther, the American Minister in Bucharest, that he «looked forward with great satisfaction to the announcement that all Bucovina and Bessarabia had been occupied.» (80) Less than a week after war had been declared, however, since Bessarabia had not yet been entirely reconquered, Maniu insisted on specifying that he was against conducting a war beyond the Romanian ethnic frontiers, more exactly, beyond the Dniester, categorically declaring: «The Romanian Armies must not overrun territories that have not belonged to them. Romanian imperialism would be condemned by everyone.» (81) On 1 July 1941, at a meeting with Gunther, Maniu emphasized that he was strongly opposed to any advance by the Romanian Army beyond the Dniester.

He added that he had urged Antonescu to be satisfied with the return of Northern Bucovina and Bessarabia, neither of which was, however, absolutely certain in as much as Hitler apparently planned to create a German-controlled Ukrainian state. Bearing in mind the possibility that Germany was planning to use and decimate the Romanian Army in the Russian campaign, Maniu protested strongly against the wholesale incorporation of large Romanian contingents and asked that the Romanian Army should fight separately and independently from the German Army. When Gunther raised the possibility of Hungary taking advantage of the fact that the Romanian Army had moved off from its bases at home «to steal a further march on Romania,» Maniu seemed fully aware of this contingency. (82)

In a letter to General Antonescu (18 July 1941), Maniu again raised the topic of going beyond the Bessarabian frontier. He elaborated on the reasons why he opposed Romania's involvement in the Russian campaign:

We are categorically against Romania's pursuing aggressive goals, Maniu said. It is inconceivable for us to appear as aggressors against Russia, now an ally of Great Britain.... that is, as companions-in-arms of Hungary and the Axis which, through an arbitrary act, unjustified by anyone, had torn away a considerable strip of our country, violating our territory, national pride, and honor.... We have no Romanian soldiers to sacrifice for alien goals. We must spare our army for our own, Romanian goals which are many, significant, and of tragic topicality, to be achieved in the very near future.

The head of the democratic opposition went on to draw General Antonescu's attention to

the idea that has been increasingly spread by the Hungarian press and in influential circles that Romania's living space extends east of the Carpathians, while Hungary's stretches west of them. It is inconceivable for us to come up with arguments and justifications to support those who are planning to push us eastwards, moving us away from the natural fortress of Transylvania, the cradle of the Romanian people; moreover, it is inconceivable for us to bind our fate with the Axis through wars of conquest and aggression. (83)

Maniu continued to expound his opinions on the danger of Romania's increasing involvement in the eastern war. This is evident from the notes of former Foreign Minister Grigore Gafencu, who on 3 August 1941 wrote:

In Maniu's opinion, our army should stop at the Dniester. We don't care for what is happening beyond our border. The Germans are doing their best to involve us in the problem of Transdnistria in order to bind us even more closely to their fate, to implicate us even more in their war and oblige us to stay, no matter what happens, under their dominion and dependence. (84)

Iuliu Maniu's opinions were also shared by the representatives of the National Liberal Party. Gheorghe Brătianu, vice-chairman of that party, joined the eastern war as a volunteer. Dinu Brătianu, Chairman of the National Liberal Party, and Iuliu Maniu did not confine themselves to sheer political analyses; they also enjoined General Antonescu to change his policy thus preserving the future of the nation, especially the regaining of Northern Transylvania. In one of their letters, after elaborating on the well-known thesis of sacrificing Northern Transylvania following the struggles conducted in the Russian steppes, Maniu and Brătianu came to the practical conclusion: «Therefore withdraw troops from Russia! Reconstitute your army!» Only in this way, they believed, could Romania go back to its former frontiers and become the master of its own destiny. (85)

The belief that Romania should not continue the eastern campaign beyond the borders of Bessarabia was also shared by some Romanian generals, such as Nicolae Ciupercă, Alexandru Orăşeanu, Iosif Iacobici, and Nicolae Rădescu. (86) In 1942 General Iosif Iacobici was dropped from his position as Chief of the General Staff, because in a report to Ion Antonescu he had expressed his disagreement with the continuation of the war beyond the Dniester, maintaining that a war waged beyond the country's borders would be unpopular. (87) When Manfred von Killinger, the German Ambassador to Bucharest, pubicly declared that all those who spoke out against the continuation of the war beyond Bessarabia's frontiers were "mean politicians", General Rădescu retorted that it was the foreigner who, dissatisfied with the attitude of the patriots, took advantage of the privileged position he held and was "mean" – not the patriots who were considering how to spare the people, at least some of its sufferings. (88) For his opposition to the continuation of the war beyond the Dniester and in particular for offending the German ambassador, Rădescu was sent to a concentration camp.

Apparently there was some plan by such Romanian military and political leaders to stop the military campaign along the Dniester, for, according to a report sent to the Army General Staff by the secret intelligence service in July 1941, «some of the political leaders, together with the generals, would allegedly militate for the idea of ceasing hostilities, since their continuation would be meaningless.» (89)

In any case, not only the democratic opposition to General Antonescu and some higher military circles, who were afraid lest the Romanian Army be plowed down in the Russian campaign, but also the soldiers, who were no longer eager to fight, expressed their reluctance to continue the war beyond the Dniester. This fact has been noted by some Soviet historians as well, for example, N. I. Lebedev who said:

The crossing of the Dniester, the participation of the Romanian Army in the fighting many hundreds of kilometers away from Romania's frontiers, opened the eyes of many soldiers and officers to the aggressive character of the war. Discontent with the anti-Soviet war began to spread on a large scale in the Romanian Army. (90)

Great Britain about to Give in?

Just a few weeks after the hostilities on the eastern front had been triggered off, the Soviet Union began to be concerned about the conclusion of a political treaty with Great Britain by which its new ally was to recognize at least its frontiers recognized by Hitler in 1941. Since the Anglo-Soviet agreement for a joint action of 12 July 1941 did not include any territorial clauses, in September 1941 Stalin suggested to Lord Beaverbrook, while the latter was visiting Moscow, that Great Britain and the Soviet Union should conclude a political agreement of a more far-reaching character than the first one, covering not only the war but also the postwar period. (91) In November 1941 relations between Churchill and Stalin had grown worse because Stalin was attempting to link the visit of two British generals, sent by the British government to take up the issue of military cooperation, with talks on postwar policy, which exceeded the two generals' mission. Acting as a messenger for the Soviet claims, Stafford Cripps, the British Ambassador to Moscow, called on Churchill to send Eden, the British Secretary of State for Foreign Affairs, to Moscow to take up with Stalin peace objectives and postwar cooperation; otherwise he threatened to resign. Under these circumstances, Eden went to Moscow on 15 December 1941, charged with exploring the possibilities of some kind of political agreement and discussing certain postwar problems. In order to clear the way for Eden's talks in Moscow, but after much hesitation, on 5 December 1941 Great Britain decided to declare war on Romania, Finland, and Hungary. (92)

During the negotiations in Moscow and the following ones in London and Washington the Bessarabian problem was not raised as an independent issue but rather within the broader framework of the talks on the Soviet Union's western frontiers.

Eden left for Moscow armed with a memorandum and a draft declaration which would provide the Soviet Union with assurances that its interests would not be ignored at the conclusion of the hostilities. According to the memorandum, it was premature to attempt a postwar territorial settlement; however, the territorial changes would have to take into account the freely expressed wishes of the peoples concerned, in line with the principles contained in the Atlantic Charter. The declaration also referred to the principles of the Atlantic Charter. In addition it quoted a Soviet government statement of 6 November 1941, according to which the Soviet Union «could not have such war aims as the seizure of foreign territories.» (93) However, right at the beginning of the talks, on December 16, apart from a draft of alliance providing for military assistance during the war and an agreement on the postwar reconstruction of Europe and the content of the peace treaties, Stalin also proposed a secret protocol to the agreement, in which he drafted the postwar map of Europe. Among other territorial changes, this secret protocol emphasized that Bessarabia and Northern Bucovina would be taken away from Romania, which in the future would be allied to the Soviet Union and allowed to maintain Russian military bases on its territory. (94)

The Soviets demanded that the surrendering of Bessarabia and Northern Bucovina as well as their frontier with the Baltic States and Finland be immediately recognized by the British government; they only agreed to a postponement of talks on the Soviet-Polish border since Poland was the ally of Great Britain, for the sake of which the latter had, in fact, joined the war. (95)

Eden declared that he could not sign the secret protocol since Great Britain, through the voice of its prime minister, had publicly claimed that this country «could not acknowledge during the war any changes of sovereignty that had been made since the beginning of the war.» He added that his country was also committed to the United States not to bind itself to any decision upon European frontiers before the end of the war and without consultation with them. The British Foreign Secretary maintained that if Stalin were to propose the pre-September 1939 frontiers as the western frontiers of his country there would be no difficulty in agreeing to them, whereas accepting the changes that had taken place during the war while it was still going on would run counter to the principles of the Atlantic Charter, to which both the United States and Great Britain had subscribed. In fact, the first three points of the Joint Declaration of the Atlantic Charter read: «First, their countries seek no aggrandizement, territorial or other; second, they desire to see no territorial changes that do not accord with the freely expressed wishes of the peoples concerned. Third, they respect the right of all peoples to choose the form of government under which they will live, and they wish to see sovereign rights and self-government restored to those who have been forcibly deprived of them.» (96)

When informed about the Soviet claims Churchill reacted sharply. He wrote to the Lord Privy Seal:

Stalin's demand about Finland, the Baltic States, and Romania are directly contrary to the first, second, and third articles of the Atlantic Charter, to which Stalin has subscribed. There can be no question whatever of our making such an agreement, secret or public, direct or implied, without prior agreement with the US. The time has not yet come to settle frontier questions, which can only be resolved at the peace conference when we have won the war. (97)

Even before Eden left for Moscow, suspecting that under the pretext of negotiations for a political agreement Moscow was aiming, in fact, at the recognition of Soviet territorial claims, on December 5 the State Department sent John G. Winant, the American Ambassador to London, a telegram approved by President Roosevelt, instructing him to inform Eden that «insofar as our postwar policies are concerned, it is our belief that these have been delineated in the Atlantic Charter, which today represents the attitude not only of the United States but also of Great Britain and of the Soviet Union.» (98)

Since Stalin maintained that the signing of the secret protocol was a condition *sine qua non* for the signing of the other two documents and since Eden had not been empowered to sign any agreement including territorial clauses, he left Moscow without signing any military or political agreement. Nevertheless, he promised Stalin to submit his proposals to the British and American governments and to the governments of the dominions.

Back in London, on January 28 Eden submitted to the British war cabinet a memorandum on postwar cooperation with the Soviet Union, suggesting how Stalin's demands could be met.

Our first step, therefore, should be to ask Mr. Roosevelt for his opinion. If he were unwilling to accept the whole of Russian demands, we could propose that Great Britain and the United States would support after the war either the acquisition by the Soviet Union of bases in territories contiguous to the Soviet Union, and especially in the Baltic and Black Sea regions, or the control by the Soviet government of the foreign relations and defense of the Baltic States. The question of the absorption of the Baltic States, Bessarabia, and parts of Finland would be free for decision at the peace conference. The Russians would be free to propose such a measure; we should be free to accept or reject it. (99)

It is notable that Eden's memorandum contained no mention of Northern Bucovina, which was one of the Soviet demands, although for practical purposes it may have simply been understood as falling under the «Bessarabia» heading.

American Intervention Postpones the Issue

In anticipation of the British soundings on the Soviet territorial claims, the State Department instructed two of its senior officials, James Dunn and Ray Atherton, to draft a memorandum on this issue. The memorandum stipulated that the USA and Britain would «not recognize any territorial change that had been made in European frontiers since the outbreak of the World War and /would/ not enter into any commitments of a territorial nature in Europe that might hamper the proceedings of the postwar peace conference. (100) The prescient memorandum went on to say that there was «no doubt that the Soviet government had tremendous ambitions with regard to Europe and that at some time or other the United States and Great Britain would be forced to state they could not agree, at least in advance, to all its demands.» (101) Moreover, the memorandum said that as soon as the Soviet Union saw that its demands had been met it would come up with new ones regarding frontiers, territories, and spheres of influence, and that the existence of a precedent would destroy one of the most important clauses of the Atlantic Charter, throwing a shadow on the sincerity of the Anglo-Saxon policy. Roosevelt accepted the State Department's view that «such an accord would be both dangerous and unwise» and informed Churchill of his opinion. (102)

When Cordell Hull fell ill, Sumner Welles, in charge of the department, continued to oppose territorial concessions. In a verbal exchange with Lord Halifax, the British Ambassador to Washington, he said on February 18: «If that is the kind of world which we have to look forward to, I do not believe that the people of the United States would wish to be a party thereto.» (103)

However, despite the American intransigence, Churchill changed his mind, on the one hand, because he feared that Stalin might conclude a separate peace with Hitler and, on the other, because, in the military sphere, he could not introduce Allied troops into Western Europe to comply with the Soviet Union's demand.

From Moscow the British Ambassador, Sir Stafford Cripps, exerted pressure on Churchill for Great Britain to conclude an agreement with the Soviet Union «based on full recognition of the Soviet claims to the three Baltic States, Bessarabia, and Moldavia /sic/, and bases in Finland. (104) Great Britain was about to give in as regards the western Soviet frontiers established with Hitler's consent. Maisky, the Soviet Ambassador to London, was aware of this change of attitude: « In my negotiations with Eden I could see that from meeting to meeting his resistance to our requirement was weakening.» (105) It was under these circumstances that on March 7 Churchill sent a message to Roosevelt suggesting that, owing to the «increasing gravity» of the situation, «the principles of the Atlantic Charter ought not to be construed so as to deny Russia the frontiers which she occupied when Germany attacked her.» (106) on March 26-27 instructions were sent to Lord Halifax to explain to President Roosevelt that in view of the military situation the British government considered it necessary to satisfy the Soviet demands.

We appreciated, Mr. Roosevelt, the difficulties but, as a European Power, for whom postwar collaboration with Russia is essential, we could not neglect any opportunity of establishing intimate relations of confidence with Stalin. (107)

On April 1 Welles told Lord Halifax that Roosevelt's opinion remained unchanged and that concessions on the frontier question would only encourage more demands. Despite the American opposition, on April 8 Eden told Maisky that the British government was ready to negotiate a treaty on the basis proposed by Stalin, that is, acknowledging the territorial changes which included the assignment of Bessarabia to the Soviet Union. The negotiations were to take place during a visit paid by Molotov to London, because Stalin considered that it would be «necessary to exchange views regarding the text of the respective suitable agreement» (108) since the British drafts «reveal fresh divergencies of opinion » (109) Even before the Soviet Foreign Minister's arrival in London, Maisky asked Eden to attach a secret protocol to the political treaty, with an indication of future Soviet frontiers as mapped out by Stalin during his meetings with Eden in Moscow. Under that protocol the British government would state its willingness to agree to Soviet-Romanian and Soviet-Finnish pacts of «mutual assistance» under a guarantee of Romanian and Finnish independence, and the Soviet government would agree to similar pacts between Great Britain and Belgium and the Netherlands. (110) Eden also objected to a mutual assistance pact with Romania and Finland: according to him, such a «demand had never been made when I was in Moscow and.... it was despairing to negotiate with the Soviets when they invariably raised their price at every meeting.» (111)

Molotov arrived in London on 20 May 1942. During his talks with Eden he insisted that without the guarantee of mutual assistance pacts with Romania and Finland, no one in the Soviet Union would approve of the political treaty with Great Britain. (112) He also objected to the clause in the British draft of the political treaty dealing with the question of frontiers, which emphasized that Great Britain would have «full regard to the desire of the Union of Soviet Socialist Republics for the restoration of its frontiers violated by Hitlerite aggression.» (113) The London talks, at which Molotov brought up Soviet claims to «Eastern Poland» and «the recognition in a secret agreement of Russia's claims on Romania... though most friendly, therefore moved toward a deadlock.» (114)

From his sickbed Secretary Hull sent a strong memorandum to President Roosevelt in which he expressed the belief that the signing of the proposed Anglo-Soviet treaty, including the territorial clauses, «would be a terrible blow to the whole cause of the United Nations.» Hull added that if the treaty in its proposed form were signed, the United States might not be able to remain silent since silence might give tacit consent, and threatened to issue a separate statement, clearly emphasizing that the United States did not subscribe to its principles and clauses. (115) Roosevelt accepted Hull's views and cabled to Winant in London to inform the British government accordingly. Following the American intervention Molotov began backing off, and the Russians « dropped their proposal for a secret agreement relating to Romania and Finland, but proposed instead that a clause be inserted whereby Britain would recognize Russian special interests in those countries.» At a meeting with Molotov US Ambassador Winant told the Soviet Foreign Minister that Roosevelt was opposed to the introduction of frontier problems in the Anglo-Soviet treaty; however, he was ready to discuss with Molotov various commercial problems, a relief program for the Soviet Union, and even the introduction of Allied troops into Western Europe. After this conversation Molotov asked Stalin's permission to negotiate an agreement with Great Britain on the basis of Eden's draft, including a long-term alliance but excluding the secret protocol. (116)

On May 26 the Anglo-Soviet treaty was signed in London without mentioning the frontier problems. When he learned about this Hull wrote: «I was enormously relieved.» (117) Churchill commented: «This was a great relief to me and a far better solution than I had dared to hope.» (118) Only Maisky did not understand the ins and outs of this arrangement and wondered at the concession made by Moscow. «I don't know what obliged Stalin so sharply to change his attitude, but, however, that might be, the change has been made.» (119) Even Eden, the negotiator of the treaty, thought that the reason why the Soviets had changed their attitude remained «obscure.» (120) On the other hand, Churchill could write to Roosevelt that the concluded agreement was consistent with the Atlantic Charter. (121) However, Cadogan, a veteran Foreign office official, noted that the London treaty «merely postponed what Churchill later called the brute issue until a time when the Russians were better placed to enforce their claims.» (122)

Reorientation of Romania's Foreign Policy

Romania's sovereignty over Bessarabia and Northern Bucovina, reacquired in 1941, did not last long, for in 1943 the Soviet Army went on the offensive on the Eastern Front and was thus poised to reconquer the provinces.

The Soviet victories at Stalingrad, on the Don, and at Kursk opened the way to Romania and Poland for Soviet troops, thus making the question of the USSR's frontiers with those countries of immediate, practical importance. The Romanians, who up to November 1943 had lost over 250,000 men on the Eastern Front, saw the battle line draw nearer to the Dniester; they felt that not only the future status of Bessarabia and Northern Bucovina but perhaps also broader political issues would be raised very soon. As a result, some Romanian leaders, to be found among both those in power and those of the opposition, sought a way to save Romania by detaching it from the alliance with Germany and negotiating with the Allies. The prime Romanian goal was, following the example of the country's switch of sides in World War I, to move to the winners' side as painlessly as possible and with as much territory as could be secured. In concrete terms, this meant the restoration of northern Transylvania, which was lost to Hungary in 1940, and Bessarabia and Northern Bucovina, which had been taken by the Soviets in 1940 but reassigned to Romania by Hitler in 1941.

With Marshal Antonescu's assent, Romanian Foreign Minister Mihai Antonescu started negotiations to join Romania to its neighbors in federations bordering on the Dniester River, while Iuliu Maniu, a prominent Transylvanian politician, leader of the National Peasant Party, a former Prime Minister, and at that time also head of the national opposition, hoped to negotiate a separate peace with the Western Allies, including recognition of Romania's claim to Bessarabia and Northern Bucovina. Romania hoped the Western Allies would be amenable to such a move, one that was obviously to Moscow's detriment. Although Marshal Antonescu had promised Hitler at their 10–12 January 1943 meeting that Romania would continue to fight alongside Germany and would supply 19 fresh divisions to the Eastern Front, the Romanian leader had doubts that the German Army could stop the Soviet offensive in the East, by then supported by the allied offensive in the West, and was considering informing the Allies of the newly created situation, and in a scarcely disinterested vein warning them against the danger of Soviet expansion. (123) Hitler himself admitted that the Romanian army, which, after retaking Bessarabia and Northern Bucovina and acquiring the newly designated "Transdnistria" had to fight well beyond its frontiers, was in a difficult predicament. He told the Hungarian leader, Admiral and Regent Miklos Horthy: "It will surely not be easy for the sons of Romanian peasants to understand why they still should fight far away from their fatherland or from the areas conquered by them."(124)

Iuliu Maniu had always maintained that "the political aims of the Axis are not those of Romania," and had demanded that Romania withdraw from the war once Bessarabia and Northern Bucovina were regained resuming friendly relations with Great Britain and the USA. (125) The Soviet victories had confirmed Maniu's forecasts that the Allies would win. The government made use of the opposition's policy and to some extent cooperated with it during the negotiations to obtain the territorial settlement desired.

Mihai Antonescu's Attempts to Get Romania out of the War

On 19 January 1943, a few days after his return from Hitler's general headquarters, Wolfschanze, Mihai Antonescu informed Renato Bova Scoppa, Italian minister in Bucharest, with whom he was on good terms, that the atmosphere within the German leadership was depressing and that the German leaders had been forced to fall back from the idea of a *Blitzkrieg* to that of total defense of "Fortress Europe". Mihai Antonescu who, in November 1942, had arrived at the belief that Romania must keep in close contact with Italy so that the two countries could detach themselves from the Axis, decided to take steps. Accordingly, Bova Scoppa prepared a memorandum in which he set forth the Romanian minister's foreign policy views, winding up by saying that "the essential point at this decisive time for our destiny is to keep directly in contact," to save Europe from the threat of communism and from anarchy. (126) In a practical manner, Mihai Antonescu suggested that Italy sound out the Western Allies, together with Romania, regarding a separate peace with them, one directed against the USSR. Dino Grandi and Duke Pietro of Acquarone, who six months later were implicated in an anti-Mussolini plot, enthusiastically approved Bova Scoppa's memo. (127) In turn, Ciano submitted the memo to Mussolini, to whom he presented his own views on seeking a way out of the war. Mussolini retorted that he was confident the Germans would be able to resist, and rejected the Romanian proposal, saying that "the Danube is not the road" for Italy to follow. (128) Later, Ciano told Bova Scoppa that Mussolini had approved of Mihai Antonescu's views advocating the establishment of direct contact with the Western Allies, reproaching him by saying that "your memo of January 15 has been responsible for my demotion from the ministry."(129)

The Romanian foreign minister also suffered as a result of his initiative, for Hitler, upon learning about Mihai Antonescu's schemes at his 12 April 1943 meeting with Marshal Antonescu at Klessheim asked the Romanian leader to replace his foreign minister. (130) Nevertheless, after a brief punitive "leave of absence," Mihai Antonescu was able to revive his project of saving Romania by attempting to pull it out of the war in a move that would be initiated by Italy. On 5 June 1943 Bova Scoppa submitted a second memorandum that contained the views of the Romanian foreign minister reiterating the suggestion that Italy place itself at the head of the group of small countries, for no one imagined that Great Britain and the USA would stand guard in Europe against Slavism for several generations to come. Bova Scoppa maintained that he himself had prepared the report which had received prior approval by King Victor Emmanuel III. He added, however, that he had presented it to Undersecretary of State Giuseppe Bastianini as conceived by Mihai Antonescu in order to lend it more weight. He even reproached the Romanian Foreign Ministry for failing to be up to such a historic mission and failing convincingly to present the ideas on which they had agreed at their Rocca delle Camminate meeting with Mussolini. (131)

On June 15 Bastianini informed Bova Scoppa that "Il Duce had agreed with Mihai Antonescu on several points of your memorandum," but he would like to wait for two more months before taking any action. Eventually, Mihai Antonescu succeeded in presenting his plan to Mussolini directly, during a five-hour conversation which he had with the Italian dictator on 1 July 1943 at Rocca delle Camminate. By then Mussolini was apparently more convinced by the Romanian foreign minister's plea and promised to talk to Hitler in two months' time about convening a conference of neutral and belligerent states to discuss Europe's destiny. (132) But the allied landing in Sicily killed the plan.

Mihai Antonescu believed that the foundation of a bloc of the small states of the Danube Basin or the Balkans in order to impede the Soviet advance would have been favorably received by Germany, which was withdrawing from the Eastern Front, as well as by the Western Allies, who, he felt, would not be very keen to see Russia extend its sphere of influence to the Danube Valley and the Balkans. Mihai Antonescu would also have liked to get Italy's consent to a project of this type. Since in this respect, at least, Romania's interest was identical with Hungary's, Romania was ready to cooperate with its Western neighbor, although the Transylvanian issue did not exactly make for an atmosphere of mutual trust. Noting Romania's eagerness to cooperate with Hungary, Count Ciano said that "the Germans would do well to keep an eye on the Romanians, because the sudden desire to achieve reconciliation with Hungary seems suspicious to me." (133)

Mihai Antonescu's project to pull Romania out of the war on the best terms possible by resorting to a political solution, such as the setting up of a bloc of small states, had no chance so long as none of the big powers supported it. Informing von Ribbentrop of the Turkish project for a Balkan Federation, Franz von Pappen, the German Ambassador to Ankara, expressed his opinion that such a solution would be of considerable advantage to Germany, were the retreat on the Eastern Front to be continued. Hitler himself raised this point at his March 1943, meeting with tzar Boris of Bulgaria, but no concrete results were achieved. (134)

It was clear that this idea also interested British circles, for on 10 March 1943 Anthony Eden sounded out Ivan Maisky, the Soviet Ambassador to London, on the Soviet Union's attitude to a European federation. Maisky retorted that Moscow might not oppose the idea of a Balkan Federation, provided Romania were ruled out of the arrangement. (135) After the November 1943 Cairo Conference, Turkish Foreign Minister Numan Menemençoglu complained to Alexandru Cretzianu that "overnight, at a frown from Stalin," even Churchill gave up the idea of a federative reorganization of Europe, in which Turkey would have played a significant role, within a Balkan Federation.(136) Later, on 1 December 1943, during the Teheran Conference, Churchill asked Stalin what he thought about the project for a Danubian Federation. Stalin replied that a Danubian Federation would not be viable, that the Germans would take advantage of this "by putting flesh on something that is only skeleton, thus creating a great new state." (137) The Soviet dictator also wanted to know whether Romania and Hungary would be members of such a federation.

Iuliu Maniu Places his Hopes on Negotiations with the Western Allies

Starting from the idea that the Germans and Russians would decimate each other during the lengthy wear and tear of the war, Iuliu Maniu thought that World War II would end in an Allied, but especially Anglo-American, victory. Accordingly, after the Romanians got beyond their pre –1940 border of the Dniester River, Maniu made an effort to pull his country out of the war. But since he was persuaded that he could not get the Kremlin's recognition of the border along the Dniester, he did not enter into direct negotiations with the Soviet Union; he chose the indirect way, negotiating with Great Britain and the USA.

Early in 1942 Maniu had established contact with Great Britain, stating he wanted to engineer a coup d'état to overthrow Antonescu's regime at an appropriate moment – whenever the Allies landed in the Balkans. In return for this change of alliance, Maniu asked that the Allies guarantee the existence of an independent Romanian state, with the prewar borders, including Bessarabia and Northern Bucovina. (138) His British contacts did not seem too optimistic, for they thought that the Soviet Union would not give up the provinces concerned. That is why, when in the summer of 1942 it was rumored that the Soviet Union had agreed to setting up a plebiscite on Bessarabia and Northern Bucovina, the British Foreign office commented as follows: "We have heard nothing to corroborate this... which strikes us as extremely improbable. In any case, a plebiscite run by the Soviet government would be as valuable a guide to opinion as an announcement that the inmates of a German concentration camp had subscribed to a Christmas present for Himmler." (139) Nevertheless, Maniu persevered in his plans to save Bessarabia and Northern Bucovina through the agency of the Allies and, in a note to the British Foreign office, he said that public opinion in Romania was favorable to the allied cause, the border issue being the sole obstacle on which the American and British governments would have to act to bring about a change in Romania's alliance. He added that, were the Anglo-Americans to guarantee Romania's border, the Romanian army would also be won over for a change in the Allies' favor. (140) The answer from the British Foreign Office was that Romania's eastern borders would be determined by the United Nations, in conformity with the Atlantic Charter and the provisions of the Anglo-Soviet treaty. (141) Since the Anglo-Soviet treaty specified that the need for Soviet security would be borne in mind, this meant that the Soviet Union would have at least a broad say in setting Romania's eastern borders.

In February 1943 Maniu again informed the British government, through Suphi Tanrioer, Turkey's minister to Bucharest, that Romanian public opinion, which had favored entry into the war but then objected to the continuation of the campaign beyond the Dniester, now felt that Marshal Antonescu should be asked to bring back his troops and change the country's military and foreign policy, adding that "Romania's national movement would like to know the British and American viewpoint on Romania's borders and the role to be assigned to it in the future." (142) As time went by and the Soviet Army continued its advance toward Central Europe, however, hopes for preserving Bessarabia and Northern Bucovina with Anglo-Saxon support diminished. At least as far back as the spring of 1943 Great Britain considered that Romania fell predominantly within the Soviet sphere. Eden's briefing on Romania before his March 1943 visit to Washington stated: "Our policy toward Romania is subordinated to our relations with the Soviet Union and we are... unwilling to accept any commitments or take any action except with the full cognizance and consent of the Soviet government." (143) During Eden's visit to Washington Roosevelt also agreed to the Soviet claim to Bessarabia on the ground that the Soviets would be entitled to regain this province "as it had been Russian throughout most of its history," (144) an assertion that is, of course, historically incorrect.

Along with the efforts to persuade the Allies to guarantee Romania's eastern border along the Dniester, Maniu also started exerting pressure on Marshal Antonescu to convince him to withdraw Romanian troops to the same river line. On 10 July 1943, in a memo to the marshal also signed by Constantin I.C. Brătianu, Maniu reiterated his wellknown arguments: "Romanian public opinion approves moves for the defense of its natural borders, but not conquest. At the same time, Romania cannot remain committed to an action directed against the Western democracies, which had provided decisive support for the creation of Greater Romania." (145) In another memo to Marshal Antonescu of 12 August 1943, the two Romanian democratic leaders reiterated their request for the Romanian army to withdraw "within the country's borders," that is, to the line of the Dniester. (146) Then, on 30 September 1943, in a letter to the Marshal in which he condemned recognition of Mussolini's rump Social Republic, Maniu categorically declared: "Romania's most fervent wish has been to entertain friendly relations with those powers to whom it owes its national unity, through the liberation of Bessarabia and Northern Bucovina," (147) a reference to Western support in the post-World War I peace settlements.

Former Romanian Foreign Minister Grigore Gafencu, who was then living in Switzerland and kept in touch with Iuliu Maniu, wrote in his diary on 15 December 1943 that the Romanian leader "was following a policy of national reintegration, instead of one of national salvation." Unlike Maniu, Gafencu advocated direct contact with the Russians, without seeking any Anglo-American mediation. (148)

Nevertheless, Iuliu Maniu's perseverance yielded some results. Toward the end of 1943 Marshal Antonescu informed the National Peasant leader that he was ready to retire from the country's leadership and surrender his position to him, provided Maniu could obtain from Great Britain and the USA terms guaranteeing

Romania's independence and integrity. Maniu replied that he could not obtain such terms as long as he, or someone representing him, had not contacted the Allies. (149) Therefore, Marshal Antonescu agreed to allow someone named by the opposition to go abroad to try to obtain the best political and territorial terms, in exchange for Romania's withdrawal from the war.

The Soviet Union Enter into the Negotiations

Alexandru Cretzianu was the first Romanian emissary to contact the Allies on behalf of Iuliu Maniu, of the opposition, and of King Michael. Cretzianu had been appointed Romanian minister to Ankara and entrusted with this secret mission by Foreign Minister Mihai Antonescu. Before leaving Romania he called upon the King, Maniu, and Marshal Antonescu, realizing that the latter two still hoped for an Allied landing in the Balkans to facilitate Romania's pullout of the war. Marshal Antonescu revealed to him that Romania had reorganized its armed forces after the defeats in the Soviet Union and now had 21 properly equipped divisions available. This confirmed the foreign minister's belief that in an emergency Romania could cope with a German countermove. (150)

When he arrived at Istanbul on 15 December 1943, however, Cretzianu realized that the real state of affairs in the world was entirely different from what the Bucharest politicians felt it to be. Turkish Foreign Minister Menençoglu informed him that Eden, whom he had met in Cairo early in November, did not mention any landing in the Balkans; neither did the Turkish official learn anything about any interest of the Western Allies in Soviet frontier questions in the Balkans. So far as Romania was concerned, Eden had told him that it had no choice but to capitulate. The Moscow Conference had decided that any capitulation was to be made to all three allies; no separate peace with the West would be possible. Some time later, on 1 February 1944, Cretzianu learned from Lieutenant Colonel Ted Masterson of the Middle East Command that the best Romania could hope for from the negotiations with the Allied countries would be a Soviet promise not to cross the line of the River Pruth, which meant that Bessarabia and Northern Bucovina were going to be lost again. (151)

The system of tripartite consultation among the Allies had been in operation since 1943, after the Moscow Conference. Therefore, on 21 November 1943, the State Department was informed by the British ambassador to Washington that in a message to Great Britain Iuliu Maniu had expressed his wish to send one or several delegates abroad to discuss arrangements for a political changeover in Romania. The State Department consented to have the USA represented at any conference that might be held in Cairo with Maniu's representative by Lincoln MacVeagh, ambassador to the Greek and Yugoslav governments in exile in Egypt. (152) Great Britain also informed the Soviet Union about Maniu's communication. In its answer, the Soviet government indicated that it considered "absolutely necessary" the presence of a Soviet representative at any negotiations that might be held with Maniu's representative. (153) The fact that the presence of the Soviet Union was binding for the negotiations, in view of concluding an armistice with Romania, obviously reduced the latter's chances of retaining Bessarabia and Northern Bucovina.

Nevertheless, the State Department continued to express itself in vague terms on the future status of the above-mentioned provinces, and did not consider their occupation by the Soviet Union as an "ultimate settlement," although it cannot be said that official Washington gave much thought to that area. In a document sent by the director of the State Department's office of European Affairs to the American ambassador to London (a document that had been passed by the Working Security Committee and cleared through the State Department, but not yet by the Joint Chiefs of Staff) (154) mention was made of the evacuation of the occupied territories. These "Provisions for Imposition upon Romania at the Time of Surrender" stipulated that "without prejudice to the ultimate settlement of disputed territorial claims," the Romanian armed forces should be withdrawn from all areas other than the territory held by Romania on 21 June 1941. The withdrawal of Romanian forces would be conducted according to a schedule laid down by the "occupation authorities," (155) which meant the Soviet authorities. From this text it follows that, were the Soviet troops to advance in this area, the status of Bessarabia and Northern Bucovina was going to be that of a province under military occupation. In fact, the above-mentioned document added that the Soviet occupation authorities could retain in Bessarabia and Northern Bucovina, those Romanian officials whose "presence was desired by the occupation authorities," whereas "individuals or units in such areas might be designated to be held as prisoners of war." The American stand was more clearly defined in an explanatory document in these "Provisions for Imposition upon Romania," that provided the following: "If geographical and military consideration should make it inevitable for these disputed areas to be placed under Soviet occupation until the conclusion of the final settlement, it should be stipulated among the three principal Allies that these areas are to be occupied in the interest of the United Nations (a term that, at that time, effectively meant the US, Great Britain, and the USSR, but which was widely used at the insistence of the Roosevelt administration) and are not to be assimilated with the status of a national territory until their final disposition has been agreed upon as part of the general peace settlement." (156)

It should, however, be recalled that Eastern Europe, except perhaps Poland, was of minor importance in Washington's eyes, while Britain really cared only about Greece of all the countries in the area, going along with the Americans on

Poland in order to obtain concessions elsewhere. Roosevelt's chief preoccupations were the Pacific War and the postwar international order, while Churchill concentrated on protecting time-honored British interests in Europe, the Middle East, and elsewhere. Romania, however, was a traditional concern of St. Petersburg, Vienna, and later Berlin, and following World War I of France, USSR, and eventually of Hitler's Germany.

The Problem of Northern Bucovina

According to the explanatory document, a clear-cut distinction was to be made between Northern Bucovina and Bessarabia, for the first "had never been a part of Russia before 1940, and the Soviet claim to it had never been recognized by any of the United Nations." Accordingly, the American proposal was that Northern Bucovina should be administrated under the United Nations military government in the interest of the United Nations, pending a general peace settlement. In any case, it was emphasized that "the disposition of Northern Bucovina is closely connected with that of Eastern Poland and both problems should be considered together as part of the general peace settlement." (157)

Apparently, the American stand toward Northern Bucovina had been influenced by the views expressed by General Wladyslaw Sikorski, head of the Polish government in London, during the meeting held in Washington in 1942. On that occasion, the Polish prime minister condemned the stand adopted by Great Britain in the negotiations with the Soviet Union on the Western frontiers of the Soviet Union, for, giving in so far as the Romanian provinces were concerned, London was later to be "confronted by additional and greater demands, involving not only Soviet sovereignty over Bucovina and Bessarabia, but probably Eastern Poland and, eventually, the Dardanelles, the Balkans, and Iran." (158) In a memo submitted to Anthony Eden on 24 March 1942, Sikorski elaborated on the reasons why Poland had been against the surrender of Northern Bucovina. He said that that area had never belonged to Russia and represented a useful link between Poland and Romania, that the cession of Bucovina and Lithuania would put Poland squarely in the Soviet pincers from north and south, just as Germany had surrounded it earlier by occupying Slovakia, and that, accordingly, he could not agree to the surrender of a territory for which he had earlier offered guarantees. Finally, he felt that the security argument invoked by the Russians was not valid, for no sea or Danubian bases could be set up in land-locked, non-Danubian Bucovina to threaten the Soviet Union. (159) In a conversation that he had with Eden, the Polish prime minister noted that, through the Anglo-Soviet draft treaty, Great Britain granted the Soviet Union borders analogous to those obtained under the Ribbentrop-Molotov Agreement of 1939, sacrificing the vital interests of a considerable part of Europe to the Soviet Union, whose ultimate objective was to provoke a worldwide revolution. (160)

In a memorandum that has never been published, the exiled Polish government apparently asked the American government to approach the British government with Poland's request to be present at the negotiations about the borders of Bucovina and Lithuania. (161) In his conversations, General Sikorski put forth a strong argument: that the annexation of Bucovina and Lithuania by the Soviet Union had been a death blow to the project of a Central European federation. In turn, Count Edward Raczyinski insisted that confirming Soviet sovereignty over Bucovina would render more difficult the participation of Romania and Hungary in a future Central European federation. Since the project of that federation had not been implemented, however, this argument carried little weight. (162)

The British foreign minister also rejected the idea that Great Britain was politically and morally responsible for guaranteeing Romania's territory, saying that, "As regards Bucovina, the British government rejects the legal Polish argument on that point. Romania rejected the British guarantee and chose to collaborate with Germany. Britain subsequently declared war on Romania and does not feel bound by obligations existing under its former guarantee." (163) Great Britain maintained the same negative attitude on the future status of Northern Bucovina when it received the American document suggesting that the United Nations be entrusted with the administration of that territory. The American ambassador to London informed the Secretary of State that the British were definitely opposed to introducing the provision that the withdrawal of Romanian forces from certain areas be without prejudice to disputed territorial claims, for "they do not wish to imply that such a settlement must await a general peace treaty, and they would ask that this subject not be raised in any way in connection with Romanian surrender terms." (164)

The US finally came around to the British position, which regarded Romania as an enemy state whose interests could easily be sacrificed to Moscow in order to speed Germany's defeat and to win diplomatic concessions from Stalin on other issues. When Edward R. Stettinius, Jr. went to London from 7-29 April 1944 for discussions with members of the British government, the State Department's Division of Southern European Affairs prepared a memorandum on Romania which said that "the British and American governments might consider the desirability of reaffirming their expectation that Romania and the other Axis satellites should exist in future as independent states within reasonable frontiers,"... "assuring as far as possible Romania's continued existence as a state with such territories as would enable it to make its way as an independent country." More exactly, dealing with the status of Bessarabia, the above-mentioned memorandum said that the US might contemplate the separation of that region from Romania, while the Soviet claim to Northern Bucovina was justified only on Soviet strategical grounds, supported by general ethnic arguments. In the case of Bucovina, however, the memorandum added that "there is no indication that Moscow would permit this question to be opened." Therefore the State Department also considered Bessarabia and Northern Bucovina virtually lost for Romania, taking a firmer stand only in case the Soviet Union would claim still more Romanian territory. "It would however be difficult for us to acquiesce in any further extension of Russian claims to Romanian territory, even if Moscow were to offer to compensate the Romanians by supporting their demands for the return of Transylvania." (165)

The Romanians Put forward their Claims

Although Iuliu Maniu had expressed his wish to send a delegate abroad to discuss the terms for Romania's pulling out of the war as early as 23 November 1943, the negotiations did not start until March 1944. In fact, it was on 17 March 1944 that the meeting between Prince Barbu Ştirbey, Maniu's representative, and those of the Allies, Walter E. Guinness, Lord Moyne, British Deputy Minister of State for Foreign Affairs and Minister Resident in the Middle East, Lincoln MacVeagh, the American Ambassador to the Yugolav government in exile, and Nikolai Vassilievich Novikov, Soviet Ambassador to Cairo, began.

Romania was conducting negotiations for an armistice under difficult conditions, for in the spring and summer of 1944 the balance of forces had changed markedly in favor of the Allies. On March 26 the Soviet Army on the Second Ukrainian Front reached some points on the River Pruth and, continuing its offensive, crossed to Suceava and Botoşani Counties, as well as part of Iaşi County. (166) The political conditions were also particularly unfavorable, for Churchill and Roosevelt had decided in Casablanca (14-26 January 1943) that their adversaries would have to capitulate unconditionally; the Moscow Foreign Ministers' Conference (5-6 November 1943) had made consultation among the Allies compulsory, while at the Tehran Conference (28 November-2 December 1943) the idea of an Allied landing in the Balkans was finally abandoned.

On his way to Cairo, Ştirbey stopped over in Ankara where Alexandru Cretzianu told him about the seriousness of Romania's position. Cretzianu thought, just as those who had sent him, "that Romania would rather perish fighting than have history show that its current rulers had surrendered unconditionally to Russia." (167) At the first round of conversations, Ştirbey informed the Allies that Maniu was willing to stage a coup d'état, but before undertaking it he wanted an assurance from the Allies not only that Romania's independence would be maintained but also that its territorial rights would be respected. When asked about "territorial rights," he said that this term covered Transylvania and that the future of Bessarabia should eventually be decided by a plebiscite. (168)

The Allies reacted in different ways to the message of the head of the Romanian democratic opposition. Lord Moyne considered that "if Romania will work its way home its independence would at least be saved though boundary questions cannot be gone into at this time." (169) In its turn, the State Department thought that the proposals submitted by Ştirbey were more encouraging than expected and specified the following American viewpoint on Romania's eastern border: "Romanian territorial rights will, in principle, be respected; the proposal for a plebiscite in Bessarabia (and Northern Bucovina) is reasonable..." (170) A different opinion was expressed by the Soviet government, through the agency of its Foreign Minister Viacheslav M. Molotov, who insisted that there were no grounds for attaching importance to Ştirbey's statements, because he did not appear to represent Maniu. Molotov added that it was now clear Maniu was not one of those leaders who might oppose Antonescu and that very likely his moves were undertaken with Antonescu's permission. (171)

The Soviets had always been reserved toward Maniu, not only because the latter had preferred establishing contacts with Great Britain, instead of the Soviet Union, but also because the National Peasant leader proved to be inflexible on the Bessarabian issue. The information on his political stand was reported to Moscow by the Romanian Communist Party. As early as 26 January 1942 the RCP CC addressed an appeal to the Chairman of the National Peasant Party "to cooperate and join the common struggle to safeguard the Romanian people and its army, to create a National United Front of all patriots." Maniu demanded a prior guarantee by the Soviet government recognizing Romania's frontiers as they existed before the Soviet ultimatum of June 1940, and a public RCP declaration to that effect, as conditions for agreeing to "cooperation and joint struggles'. (172) Later, in the spring of 1943, during a discussion with RCP CC delegates Mihai Magheru and Petre Ion, Maniu claimed that Romania could not be considered an aggressor state, in the sense adopted at Geneva, supporting this claim with the argument that the British and American governments had not taken a stand against Romania at the time it entered the war but only from the moment its army crossed the Dniester, i. e., moved beyond the country's pre-1940 frontiers. He added that his party would not give up the claim to Romania's old borders. (173) The guarantee of the frontier along the Dniester is a recurring theme in both the correspondence and in the negotiations between Maniu and the RCP, and a communist writer stated that "it testified once more to the head of the bourgeois opposition's lack of broad-mindedness and political realism." (174) Maniu had long placed his hopes in an Anglo-American landing in the Balkans which would have led, he felt, to a tripartite occupation of Romania. When this hope was shattered after the Tehran Conference, Maniu turned to the Anglo-Saxons, through Ştirbey, asking for airborne troops and air forces in a resistance area, in Oltenia and the Banat, in order to have the possibility of a retreat into Yugoslavia. (175) Nevertheless, Molotov sent a letter to the British Ambassador to Moscow in which, after calling Romania the worst of the satellites, he offered at the request of the British government to continue to deal with Stirbey. (176)

The Soviet Union Assumes the Leadership of Negotiations

The proposals Molotov advanced through the British government provided for the establishment of immediate contact between the Romanian and Soviet commands and the surrender of Romanian troops in contact with the Soviet army. The proposals further said that the Romanian Army formations in the Dniester and Crimea regions would be sent to the River Pruth area after the surrender, to be returned to Romania for use against the Germans. (177) Denoting the River Pruth as a dividing line between the Soviet Union and Romania suggests clearly that the Soviet Union intended to annex Bessarabia and Northern Bucovina immediately, without awaiting the final decision of a peace conference. When examining the Soviet proposals, Admiral William D. Leahy said on behalf of the Joint Chiefs of Staff that "the Russian proposal in effect leaves the matter of Romania's surrender exclusively in Russian hands, but considered it from a military viewpoint; this is only natural and to be expected since Russian forces are the only ones prepared to implement and take advantage of the surrender terms." (178) Military considerations were thus still primary over eventual political ones.

The Soviet proposal was approved by Great Britain as well, then submitted by Ştirbey to Maniu for Antonescu, via British channels, (179) which meant that all three Allies had indirectly agreed to having the River Pruth constitute the frontier between Romania and the Soviet Union. As a matter of fact, at the time when these notes were being exchanged the Soviet Army had already reached the River Pruth.

On 2 April 1944 the Soviet press published a declaration of the Soviet government that began by stating that the River Pruth was the frontier between Romania and the Soviet Union. The fact that the Red Army was approaching the River Pruth "signifies the beginning of a full reestablishment of the Soviet state border established in 1940 by a treaty between the Soviet Union and Romania." (180) Reporting that Soviet troops had crossed the River Pruth at several points, thus entering territory recognized even by the Soviets as Romanian, the communiqué of the Soviet government stated that it was not pursuing "the aim of acquiring any part of Romanian territory." Commenting on this communiqué the

Chief of the State Department's Division of East European Affairs noted that "as far as Romania is concerned, this statement signifies that the Soviet government intends to reincorporate all of Bessarabia and all of Bucovina into the USSR." (181)

The arrival of Soviet troops on Romanian territory immediately enhanced the Soviets' role in the armistice negotiations with Romania. Sir Archibald Clark Kerr, British Ambassador to Moscow, informed the Soviet government that the British presumed that in negotiating with Romania for the surrender of the Romanian Army, the Russians would regard themselves as acting on behalf of the three principal Allies. (182) Cordell Hull expressed himself more subtly when he said that the Romanians should realize that the three principal Allies were acting after mutual consultation and in common agreement, and "that the future of the Romanian nation is not left exclusively in the hands of the one power with which Romania has been directly engaged in combat." (183) Following its enhanced role in the negotiations with Romania, on 8 April 1944 the Soviet Union submitted to the representatives of Great Britain and the US, through Novikov, the armistice terms proposed by the Soviet government. One of the main points of the Soviet document stipulated "the re-establishment of the Romanian-Soviet frontier in accordance with the 1940 agreement." (184)

The State Department received the Soviet proposals with reservation, considering that "the terms are essentially Russian, not allied or tripartite; they are frankly based on the practical premise that the war with Romania is Russia's own business... The Russian proposals differ drastically from those prepared in the State Department, worked over in the "Working Security Committee" and approved by the Joint Chiefs of Staff for submission to the "European Advisory Commission..." "The Russian terms were at variance with the American views on territorial questions: a) whereas the Soviet government is acting on the assumption that Bessarabia and Northern Bucovina lie within the Soviet state frontiers, we have entertained the view that the status of Bessarabia is at least open to question and that the basis of the Russian claim to Northern Bucovina is still more dubious..." (185) Nevertheless, on 14 April 1944 Cordell Hull reported to MacVeagh that the American government had given its assent to the presentation to the Romanians of the proposed terms; however, it mentioned that "we should have preferred that the definitive settlement of the status of Bessarabia and Northern Bucovina be held over for later discussion." (186) Hull added that one must assume that the Russians would be unwilling to give any consideration whatever to a modification of the article concerning its frontiers with Romania, in view of the frequent public reiteration of Russian claims to those regions.

A Maniu Government in Moldavia (Bessarabia)?

On 14 April 1944 the Soviet armistice terms, approved by Great Britain and the US, were handed over to Marshal Antonescu and Iuliu

Maniu.(187) The diplomatic notes published to date indicate that around April 14 Ştirbey had made the unexpected suggestion to Novikov that, should the negotiations with Marshal Antonescu fail to yield the anticipated results, Maniu should remove to Russian territory in Moldavia and establish a government in opposition to Antonescu. (188) This time Moscow did not object to the Romanian leader but asked Great Britain and the US to assent to a formal proposal to Maniu along that line. The instructions that Cordell Hull gave to MacVeagh included the following: "If he accepted the proposal to remove to Russian territory in Moldavia, Maniu would be placing himself, as well as whatever governmental and administrative bodies he might set up, under the protection and auspices of the Soviet government, at least until the time British and American representatives could arrive. For this reason it is important that you should give Mr. Novikov clearly to understand the position of this government as set forth in the State Department's note of 23 April 1944, that in conformity with the known American policy of deferring the settlement of boundary issues until the conclusion of hostilities, we have been unwilling to look upon any dispositions of territory effected during the course of the war as being definitive, preferring to regard them as pending final examination and settlement at the close of hostilities." (189)

The suggestion of establishing a Maniu government in Moldavia again implicitly raised the issue of Romania's eastern border and that of the future of Bessarabia. The Soviets suggested that Maniu transfer to "Russian territory in Moldavia." Since Moldavia is the name given by the Soviets to Bessarabia, it was evident that they already considered Moldavia (Bessarabia) Russian territory. Reiterating this expression, the State Department put it in quotation marks, "Russian territory", which suggests that it had not adopted it.

When he received the State Department communication Novikov asked "whether the State Department meant its remarks to apply to Bessarabia, altering its previous acceptance of the 1940 boundary." The American ambassador answered: "In my belief, the State Department was merely repeating its known policy of deferring boundary issues until the conclusion of hostilities with special reference to this particular proposal regarding Moldavia... and that the question of Bessarabia, already agreed, did not arise." (190)

Moscow declared itself satisfied with MacVeagh's interpretation that suggested American acceptance of the Soviet position on Bessarabia and clearly answered that the territorial jurisdiction of the eventual Maniu government had no bearing on Bessarabia and must be based on the known declaration of Soviet Foreign Minister Viacheslav Molotov concerning the preservation of the Romanian-Soviet frontier, as established in 1940. (191) The discussions on the establishment of a Maniu government in Moldavia under Soviet occupation ended in the explanation given by Molotov to Harriman, the American Ambassador to Moscow. Molotov said that although that proposal was acceptable to the soviet government, nevertheless, "it was not considered as having been made seriously." Molotov added that there were yet no definite indications that Maniu would follow such a course. (192)

Apparently, this diplomatic episode was used by Maniu as a test of Soviet intentions, to check whether in case a government under Soviet aegis were to be established, the Kremlin would agree to leaving Bessarabia under Romanian sovereignty. A similar probing on eventual Soviet concessions over the issue of Bessarabia and Northern Bucovina had been done in December 1943, through the agency of Czechoslovak President Eduard Benes. Evoking in a conversation with Molotov the issue of Romania's postwar frontiers, Benes urged the restoration of Northern Transylvania, but was more reticent regarding Bessarabia. He said: "I always show them (the Romanians) a map and say that no compromise is possible over your (Soviet) frontiers." (193)

The Soviets' Own Negotiations

On 11 April 1944, that is, a few days before the armistice terms had been reported to Marshal Antonescu and Iuliu Maniu, Frederic Nanu, the Romanian Minister to Stockholm, was informed by Aleksandra Mikhailovna Kollontai, the Soviet Ambassador to Sweden, under the seal of absolute secrecy, that "Stalin has realized that in order to achieve a lasting peace he has to win the friendship of neighboring nations. He therefore intends to treat Romania kindly and even to help it repair the damages of war." (194) These declarations came one day after Semionov, the Soviet Chargé d'Affaires in Stockholm, had reproached Nanu because the Romanians preferred to deal with the Anglo-Saxons instead of directly dealing with the Soviet Union, which was their neighbor. Nanu's impression was that the Soviets, who were eager to deal with the Romanian government via Stockholm, and not with its opposition, tried to persuade those concerned of the advantages of direct negotiations over those conducted through the agency of the Western Allies. That Moscow was willing to talk to the Antonescu government and offer better terms than were presented in Cairo shows the primacy the Soviets still attached to military, rather than purely political, considerations, even at that stage of the war. (195)

On 13 April 1944, that is, one day after the armistice terms had been handed to the Romanians in Cairo, they were conveyed to Nanu in Stockholm as well. Certainly, these terms, edited by the Soviet Union, also included the clause of re-establishing the 1940 Romanian-Soviet frontier, that is, the annexation of Bessarabia and Northern Bucovina by the Soviet Union. As the Stockholm negotiations continued, the Kremlin eventually granted the representative of the Romanian government more favorable terms than those offered in Cairo. After eventually accepting the Cairo armistice terms, Iuliu Maniu called on the Allies to improve their terms in the note he sent to Alexandru Cretzianu on June 12, along the lines of the concessions made by Moscow during the Stockholm negotiations. Commenting on Maniu's request for an improvement of the armistice terms, MacVeagh, who was not acquainted with the bilateral Romanian-Soviet negotiations, said: "The Allied representatives are at a loss to understand the last sentence above, since they promised no ameliorations to the armistice terms." (196) Maniu then notified them that "definite information exists that so far as Antonescu is concerned modifications were agreed to." (197)

The Stockholm negotiations again provided the Romanian government with an opportunity to raise the question of the future status of Bessarabia, for in replying to the Soviet armistice proposals, Mihai Antonescu urged Nanu to demand that a plebiscite be held in Bessarabia and Northern Bucovina. The verbal instructions given by Mihai Antonescu on this point were worded as follows in the memorandum edited by Nanu: "Since it is our aim not only to re-establish peace but also to establish lasting friendship with Russia and since the Allies, including Russia, have solemnly supported the principle of self-determination, the Romanian government believes the fate of Bessarabia and Northern Bucovina should not be decided before the end of the war, when the methods of application of that principle will be decided for all disputed territories." (198) When he received the copy of the memorandum submitted to the Soviet Union, the Romanian Foreign Minister insisted on specifying that, in any case, "we could not give up Bessarabia and Bucovina." (199) Finally, in a new verbal message sent to Stockholm on August 5 Mihai Antonescu added that the conduct of the Russians in occupied Moldavia had hardly been encouraging, and therefore it would be better to settle the fate of Bessarabia at the peace conference. (200)

Certainly, the last moment attempt in Stockholm to persuade the Soviets to defer settling the problems of Bessarabia and Northern Bucovina had no chance of success, particularly since this time the Romanians could no longer rely even on a well-disposed attitude such as that displayed by the State Department. By that point, the Soviet Union was dealing directly with Romania, and with almost discretionary powers. The Soviets thought they were entitled to proceed in that way since on 5 May 1944 Eden had suggested that the Soviet Ambassador to London proceed to a demarcation of the relevant zones of activity in the Balkans, according to a line which left Romania and Bulgaria within the sphere of Soviet interest, while Greece and Yugoslavia remained in the British. (201) As early as May 18 the Soviet Ambassador to London reported to Eden that the Soviet Union had tentatively accepted this division of the Balkans; later, on May 31, Churchill asked Roosevelt for his "blessing" to a plan to assign wartime responsability for Romania to the USSR and for Greece to Britain. (202) Even before the october 1944 conference, when the Churchill-Stalin agreement was penned, giving the USSR 90% of influence in Romanian affairs, (203) Moscow, as the dominant allied military power in the area, made singlehanded decisions on the fate of Bessarabia and, within certain limits, even of that of the entire Romanian state.

The Government and the Opposition on the Brink

Neither the Romanian government nor the leaders of the opposition had any knowledge of the agreement concerning the inclusion of their country in the sphere of influence of the Soviet Union. They wishfully believed until the last moment that the Anglo-Saxons would not abandon Romania and join in its military occupation, if not through troops landed in the Balkans, at least through symbolic airborne forces. In the last contacts Mihai Antonescu had with the Allies he adopted the American viewpoint that the problem of the frontier with the Soviet Union be deferred till the conclusion of a peace treaty. In a message sent in July 1944 to Harrison, the American representative in Bern, through the agency of Vespasian Pella, Romania's Minister to Bern, Mihai Antonescu said that Romania was ready to cease hostilities with the Soviet Union provided its national sovereignty, its territorial rights, and its institutions were respected. If these terms were not accepted, Romania would be obliged to continue the struggle "with the risk of succumbing with dignity." In that case, however, "the Anglo-Saxon powers would bear the responsibility for its sacrifice and the destruction of European equilibrium and having the war won only by the Soviets." In his message to the United States the Romanian Foreign Minister added that practical possibilities for getting out of the war would increase if a statement were made agreeing to leave to the peace conference the decision regarding Bessarabia and Northern Bucovina, and if the United States and Great Britain could, at the right moment, provide effective military help by debarking troops, landing paratroops, and building air bases. Finally, according to the above-mentioned message, the Soviet Union offered in Stockholm to enter into bilateral negotiations on territorial questions, claiming that the 1940 frontier was primarily a question of prestige and in no way excluded the possibility that a peace conference would return Bessarabia and Northern Bucovina wholly or in part, and wound up with the statement that Romania was prepared to join new regional, continental, and worldwide organizations, especially a European or Balkan federation. (204)

At the last meeting Hitler had with Marshal Antonescu on 5 August 1944 at his general headquarters in Wolfsschanze, he tried to persuade the Romanian leader that Romania, Hungary, Bulgaria, Yugoslavia, Turkey, and Finland could be saved from Bolshevism only by binding their fate to that of Germany, rather than under a British protectorate. (205) Despite Hitler's insistence, with many technical details, on the superiority that Germany would acquire over its enemies by turning out and using new destructive weapons, Marshal Antonescu declared to his assistants on the train taking him back to Romania that "Germany has lost the war. Now, we must concentrate our efforts not to losing it ourselves." (206) To be sure, Marshal Antonescu who had declared war on the Soviet Union in order to conquer Bessarabia and Northern Bucovina, could not easily sign any armistice recognizing the loss of those provinces. That is why, at the decisive meeting he had with King Michael on 23 August 1944, he declared he would not accept an armistice unless assurances were given him that he could retain Bessarabia and Transylvania. For lack of such guarantees, Marshal Antonescu declared that he would then continue to fight in the Carpathians. (207)

The acceptance of the armistice terms was one of the first foreign policy decisions made by the regime established after the palace coup of August 23; these terms provided that Romania's border would be that set under the Soviet-Romanian Agreement of 28 June 1940. Although the new Romanian government was willing to sign the armistice immediately, (208) the document was nevertheless not signed until 12 September 1944 in Moscow. Article 4 confirmed the RomanianSoviet border along the River Pruth. (209) In Moscow the former democratic opposition, now joined by representatives of the Romanian Communist Party, realized that Romania was firmly within the Soviet sphere. Cordell Hull informed Ambassador Harriman in Moscow of the data supplied by American military sources about the immediate impact of the Romanian negotiations in Moscow. "Government officials and businessmen in Romania feel that Britain and the United States have broken their promises and have abandoned Romania to Russia." Returning members of the Romanian armistice delegation spread the story that the negotiations in Moscow were dominated by the Russians, with the British and American representatives refusing to discuss the terms without conferring first with the Russian representatives. (210) Moreover, Lucrețiu Pătrășcanu, the communist representative of the Romanian delegation sent to Moscow, complained to American Ambassador Harriman that although Molotov had received him he had nevertheless not discussed the terms of the armistice with him. (211)

The report supplied by American military sources emphasized that "Maniu is reported disappointed in Great Britain, having expected more consideration and easier armistice terms." (212) The extent of Iuliu Maniu's disappointment is clear from what he said two months later to Burton Berry, the American representative in Bucharest to whom, on the evening of 8 December 1944, he said that "if he had known the Soviets were to be given a free hand in setting the armistice terms he would not have advised the king to sign the armistice." He argued that his pressure and the Romanian action that resulted from it had actually advanced the Focșani-Galați line, which might have been held a long time, to the very gates of Budapest." Berry's report went on as follows: "With considerable emotion, Maniu asked if America and Great Britain wished Romania to become a part of the Soviet Union? If so, please advise me accordingly, for this can easily be arranged and even today, late as it is, I could arrange it to the better advantage of Romania than can the Romanian Communists. Then he repeated that, if it were our intention to abandon Romania, we owed him the obligation of telling him so and he owed the Romanian people the obligation of obtaining the best possible terms for them." After claiming that Maniu had been a steady friend of the Allies, Berry wound up saying: "Because of what he has been and what he is, it seems important that he be preserved from slipping into sharing the general conviction that the dissolution of the Romanian state is now in progress." (213)

Conclusion

The postwar fate of Bessarabia and Northern Bucovina had been established under the armistice terms submitted by the Soviet government through the agency of Novikov in Cairo on 8 April 1944. Since then the diplomatic documents dealing with this subject had merely reiterated the sentence which consisted in reestablishing the Romanian-Soviet frontier of 28 June 1940. At its 8 May 1946 meeting the Paris conference of the foreign ministers of the Soviet Union, the US, Great Britain, and France established that the Romanian-Soviet frontier would continue to be that of 28 June 1940. The representatives of the four major powers agreed comparatively quickly on this, for, generally speaking, the frontier problem was not a central point in the negotiations.(214) On 2 September 1946 Gheorghe Tătărăscu, head of the Romanian delegation at the Paris conference, declared before that conference that "the frontiers assigned by the peace treaty to Romania remove all possibility of conflict in that part of Europe." (215) At the Paris peace conference the official Romanian delegation did not allude to the problem of Bessarabia and Northern Bucovina at all. The reason why the Romanian representatives behaved so passively was that they had agreed with the Soviet delegation to settle all issues of the treaty draft concerning Romania's relations with the Soviet Union in bilateral discussions either with that delegation or with the Soviet government in Moscow and not to raise them at the conference's plenary sessions. (216)

The only problem raised in connection with the Romanian-Soviet frontier – and even this merely in the discussion held prior to the peace conference – was the need for a more detailed and precise description of it, since the exact line of this frontier, settled under the so-called agreement of 28 June 1940, was only known after a small-scale map was prepared and published by *Izvestiia,* along with the Soviet ultimatum. Since the work on precisely defining the frontier and the question connected with the transfer of territory were still underway in 1940, when the Romanian-Soviet war broke out, it was especially necessary to specify the line of the frontier. Therefore, on 16 September 1946, Romania addressed a note to the Paris conference of the allied foreign ministers in which it asked that the Romanian-Soviet border be clearly marked on the map annexed to the peace treaty, but that note was not even distributed among the members of the Political and Territorial Commission for Romania. (217) Since there were rumors in 1945 that the Soviets had set up frontier posts across the Danube on the Romanian side and tried to establish control over the Sulina, the only navigable branch of the Danube, and eventually to bring about a territorial union with Bulgaria across the narrow Dobrogea, the Anglo-Saxon Allies tried to obtain a promise from the Soviet Union that it would more precisely define its frontier with Romania. The fear lest the Soviet Union extend its sovereignty beyond the imprecise limits of the 1940 agreement grew when the Soviet chairman of the Allied Control Commission in Bucharest refused to permit General Schluyer, the US representative on that commission, to visit the area on the grounds that it was under the jurisdiction of the Soviet High Command. (218) Under these conditions, on 24 September 1946 the US and British representatives noted at the Paris conference of the allied foreign ministers that the map indicating the Romanian-Soviet border was too small and reserved for themselves the right to express their remarks on a larger scale map. Eventually, the Soviets submitted a new map, and the problem was not subsequently raised at the New York allied foreign ministers' conference. This map became the appendix number I of the Paris Treaty, where it got approval without any objection. Despite this recognition the US was aware of the fact that "the frontier that had been forced on Romania in 1940 by no means corresponded to the ethnic dividing line between the Romanians and the Ukrainians." (219)

Since the official Romanian delegation did not actively contest the Soviet position, the task of raising the problem of Bessarabia and Northern Bucovina at the Paris peace conference (1947) again fell to the Romanian democratic opposition, particularly to Iuliu Maniu. The National-Peasant and National-Liberal Parties sent to Paris formal declarations reiterating their well-known views on Romania's eastern border, which they felt had to correspond to the ethnic dividing line. Iuliu Maniu's declarations and the comments of the National-Liberal Party were handed, along with an explanatory letter, to the various delegations at the Paris peace conference through the Paris *emigré* political group headed by one of former King Carol's foreign ministers, Grigore Gafencu. (220)

Recently a Bucharest publication gave partly favorable mention to the campaign conducted by the democratic opposition at the Paris peace conference: "Although the representatives of the government coalition severely and justly criticized the campaign initiated by the opposition, nevertheless, they did not denounce the major problems correctly raised by the latter in the first document or in the remarks to the draft treaty." (221) The American delegation to the peace conference could only take note of the stand expressed by the

Romanian democratic opposition without embracing its viewpoint as regards the frontier question.

> Background Reports Nos. 61, 136 and 329,
> Munich, 3 March, 12 May and 21 December 1981,
> Radio Free Europe Research.

BIBLIOGRAPHY:

1) See chapter X of the present book.
2) Memorandum on the Conversation between Hitler and Romanian Prime Minister General Ion Antonescu in Berlin, 22 November 1940 in Andreas Hillgruber, *Staatsmänner und Diplomaten bei Hitler* Vol. I (Frankfurt am Main: Bernard und Graefe Verlag, 1967), p. 355.
3) See David J. Dallin, «*Soviet Russia's Foreign Policy 1939-1942*» (New Haven: Yale University Press, 1947), pp. 239-240.
4) See German-Russian Agreement on the Settlement in the German Reich of the Population of German origin from the Territories of Bessarabia and Northern Bucovina, 5 September 1940, in Margaret Carlyle, *Documents on International Affairs,* 1939-1946, Vol. II (London, New York, Toronto: Oxford University Press, 1954), pp. 59-68.
5) See Joseph B. Schechtmann, «The option Clause in the Reich's Treaties on the Transfer of Population,» in *American Journal of International Law* Vol. XXXVIII, 1944, pp. 371-372.
6) Stephen Fischer-Galati, «The Moldavian Soviet Republic in Soviet Domestic and Foreign Policy» in Roman Szporluk ed., *The Influence of East Europe and the Soviet West on the USSR,* (New York: Praeger, 1976), p. 236.
7) A.M. Lazarev, *Moldovskaya Sovetskaya Gosudarstvennost i Bessarabskiy Vopros,* Vol. VI (Chişinău: Cartea Moldovenească, 1974)
8) W. Gordon East, «The New Frontiers of the Soviet Union,» *Foreign Affairs,* July 1951, p. 601.
9) Gheorghe Barbul, *Mémorial Antonescu, le Troisième Homme de l'Axe* (Paris: Editions de la Couronne, 1950), p. 51.
10) See Herbert Michaelis and Ernst Schraepler, *Ursachen und Folgen vom Deutschen Zusammenbruch 1918 und 1945 bis zur Staatlichen Neuordnung Deutschlands in der Gegenwart* (Berlin: Documenten-Verlag Dr. Norbert Wendler), pp. 303-304.
11) See Joachim von Ribbentrop's Telegram to the German Embassy in Moscow, dated Berlin, 21 June 1940, in *La Vérité Sur les Rapports Germano-Soviétiques de 1939 à 1940* (Paris: Editions France Empire, 1948), p. 249.
12) Memorandum on the talks between Adolf Hitler and Viacheslav Molotov, in the presence of Joachim von Ribbentrop and Dekanosov, Berlin, 13 November 1940 in *La Vérité...,* pp. 180-181.

13) Memorandum on the talks between Adolf Hitler and Romanian Prime Minister General Ion Antonescu at Obersalzburg on 14 January 1941, in A. Hillgruber, *op. cit.*, pp. 433-434.
14) Memorandum on the talks between Adolf Hitler and General Antonescu in Munich, on 12 June 1941, in A. Hillgruber, *op. cit.*, p. 587.
15) Vojtech Mastny, *Russia's Road to the Cold War* (New York: Columbia University Press, 1979), p. 30.
16) See H. Michaelis and E. Schraepler, *op. cit.*, p. 586.
17) Hillgruber, *op. cit.*, p. 591.
18) *Ibid.*, pp. 361-362.
19) M. Carlyle, *Documents on International Affairs...*, pp. 69-70.
20) Dallin, *op. cit.*, p. 378.
21) Grégoire Gafenco, *Préliminaires de la Guerre à l'Est. De l'Accord de Moscou (21 Août 1939) aux Hostilités en Russie (22 Juin 1941)* (Fribourg: Egloff, 1944), pp. 359-361.
22) Mihai Antonescu, *Im Dienste des Vaterlandes* (Bucharest: 1942), p. 27.
23) Aurica Simion, *Preliminariile Politico-Diplomatice ale Insurecției Române din August 1944 /Political-Diplomatic Preliminaries of the August 1944 Romanian Insurection/*, (Cluj- Napoca: Dacia, 1979), p. 143.
24) See Adolf Hitler's Letter to Ion Antonescu of 18 June 1941 in *Documents on German Foreign Policy 1918-1945,* Vol. XII, (London: Her Majesty's Stationery Office, 1962), p. 1049.
25) Malbone W. Graham, «The Legal Status of Bucovina and Bessarabia,» *The American Journal of International Law* Vol. XXXVIII, 1944, p. 672.
26) Winston S. Churchill, *The Second World War,* Vol. I, *The Gathering Storm* (London: Cassel and Co., 4th edition, 1955), p. 325.
27) David Dilks, *The Diaries of Sir Alexander Cadogan O.M. 1938-1945* (London: Cassel and Co., 1971), p. 236.
28) Report by Sumner Welles on his special mission to Europe, Rome, 26 February 1940, in *Foreign Relations of the United States,* 1940 Vol. I, (Washington: United States Printing Office, 1959), p. 26, and also Cadogan, *op. cit.*, p. 240.
29) D. Dilks, *op. cit.*, p. 173.
30) *Memoirs of General Lord Ismay* (Lionel Hastings), (London: Heinemann, 1960), p. 95.
31) The Earl of Halifax (Edward Frederick Lindley Wood), *Fullnes of Days* (London: Collins, 1957), p. 205.
32) See G. Gafenco, *op. cit.*, p. 393.
33) Paul Quinlan, *Clash over Romania: British and American Policies Toward Romania: 1938–1947* (Los Angeles: American Romanian Academy of Arts and Sciences, 1977), p. 63.
34) Telegram of 17 July 1941 in *Foreign Relations of the United States, Diplomatic Papers 1941,* Vol. I (Washington: United States Printing Office, 1958), pp. 321-322.
35) Churchill, *op. cit.*, Vol. III, *The Grand Alliance*, p. 167.

36) Churchill to Stalin, 4 November 1941, in *ibid.*, p. 468.
37) Stalin's Telegram to Churchill of 23 November 1941, in *ibid.*, p. 473.
38) Ivan Maisky, *Memoirs of a Soviet Ambassador, the War 1939-1943* (New York: Charles Scribner's Sons), pp. 199-204, Vol. III, p. 473.
39) Churchill to Eden, 28 and 29 November 1941, *op. cit.,* Vol. III, p. 473.
40) Quinlan, *op. cit.,* p. 72.
41) Barbul, *op. cit.,* p. 140.
42) *Foreign Relations of the United States, 1933* Vol. II, (Washington: United States Printing Office), pp. 656-682.
43) Franklin Mott Gunther's Telegram to Cordell Hull, Bucharest, 17 April 1940, *ibid.*, 1940, Vol. I, p. 462.
44) Gunther's Telegram to Hull, Bucharest, 27 June 1940, *ibid.,* p. 480.
45) Gunther's Telegram to Hull, Bucharest, 29 June 1940, *ibid.,* p. 485.
46) Gunther's Telegram to Hull, Bucharest, 27 May 1940, *ibid.,* Vol. I, p. 468.
47) Hull's Telegram to Walter Thurston, Washington, 29 May 1940, *ibid.,* p. 470.
48) Walter Thurston's Telegram to Hull, Moscow, 1 June 1940, *ibid.,* p. 471.
49) Hull's Telegram to Gunther, Washington, 7 June 1940, *ibid.*, p. 473.
50) Heath's Telegram to Hull, Berlin, 29 June 1940, *ibid.,* p. 487.
51) Gunther's Telegram to Hull, Bucharest, 2 July 1940, *ibid.,* p. 489.
52) Gunther's Telegram to Hull, Bucharest, 10 January 1941, *ibid.,* pp. 274-275.
53) Gunther's Telegram to Hull, Bucharest, 20 February 1941, *ibid.* p. 286.
54) Gunther's Telegram to Hull, Bucharest, 25 February 1940, *ibid.,* pp. 291-292.
55) Laurence Steinhardt's Telegram to Hull, Moscow, 22 April 1941, *ibid.,* p. 306.
56) Gunther's Telegram to Hull, Bucharest, 22 August 1941, *ibid.,* pp. 315-316.
57) Gunther's Telegram to Hull, Bucharest, 22 August 1941, *ibid.,* p. 325.
58) Memorandum of Conversation among Brutus Coste, Cordell Hull, and Cavendish W. Cannon of the European Division, Washington, 4 September 1941, *ibid.,* pp. 326-327.
59) Cordell Hull, *The Memoirs of...*, Vol. II, (London: Hodder and Stoughton, 1948), pp. 977-978.
60) Memorandum of Conversation between Cordell Hull and Sir Ronald Campbell, Washington, 17 September 1941, *ibid.,* p. 69.
61) Webb Benton's Telegram to Hull, Bucharest, 12 December 1941, *ibid.,* p. 591.
62) G. Barbul, *op. cit.,* pp. 140-141.
63) Quinlan, *op. cit.,* p. 75.
64) C. Hull, *op. cit.,* Vol. II, pp. 1,114, 1,175, and 1,176.
65) A. Simion, *op. cit.,* p. 147.
66) Hitler's Letter to Ion Antonescu, Hitler's Headquarters, 27 July 1941, in *Documents on German Foreign Policy, 1918-1945,* Vol. XII (London: Her Majesty's Stationery Office, 1962), pp. 225-226.

67) Ion Antonescu's Letter to Adolf Hitler, Bucharest, 30 July 1941, *ibid.*, pp. 266-267.
68) Gunther's Telegram to Cordell Hull, Bucharest, I August 1941, in *Foreign Relations of the United States,* Vol. I (Washington: United States Printing Office, 1959), p. 323.
69) Record of the Bestowal of the Knight's Cross on General Antonescu by Hitler in the School at Berdichev (Ukraine) on 7 August 1941 in *Documents on German Foreign Policy,* Vol. XII, p. 299, and A. Hillgruber, *Staatsmänner und Diplomaten bei Hitler,* Vol. I, (Frankfurt am Main: Bernard und Graefe Verlag, 1967), p. 619.
70) Hitler's Letter to Ion Antonescu, Hitler's Headquarters, August 1941, *Documents on German Foreign Policy...,* p. 317.
71) Ion Antonescu's Letter to Hitler (no location), 17 August 1941, *ibid.,* pp. 324-325.
72) Andreas Hillgruber, *Hitler, Konig Carol und Marschall Antonescu: die Deutsch-Rumänischen Beziehungen 1938-1944* (Wiesbaden: Franz Steiner Verlag, l954), p. 139.
73) Memorandum of a Conference Attended by Hitler, Hermann Göring, Alfred Rosenberg, Hans Heinrich Lammers, Wilhelm Keitel, and an Unknown Participant, Hitler's Headquarters, 16 July 1941, in Margaret Carlyle, *Documents on International Affairs, 1939-1946,* Vol. II (London, New York, Toronto: Oxford University Press, 1954), p. 232.
74) *Ibid.*
75) Hillgruber, *Hitler, Konig Carol...,* pp. 140-141.
76) Record of the Conversation Between Hitler and Mihai Antonescu, Berlin, 3 December 1941, in *Documents on German Foreign Policy,* Vol. XII, pp. 892-893.
77) Aurică Simion, *op. cit.,* p. 209.
78) *Ibid.,* p. 207.
79) Traian Udrea, «The Policy of Alliance of the Romanian Communist Party: the Setting up of the National Democratic Bloc in June 1944,» *Revista de Istorie* No. 6, 1979, p. 1,018.
80) Paul Quinlan, *Clash over Romania: British and American Policies Toward Romania: 1938-1947* (Los Angeles: American-Romanian Academy of Arts and Sciences, 1977), p. 70.
81) Simion, *op. cit.,* p. 207.
82) Mott Gunther to Cordell Hull, Bucharest, 1 July 1941, *Foreign Relations of the United States,* Vol. I, pp. 319-320.
83) Simion, *op. cit.,* pp. 208-209.
84) *Ibid.,* p. 214.
85) Iuliu Maniu's and Dinu Brătianu's Letter to Ion Antonescu (without location), January 1942, in Caryle, *op. cit.,* p. 327.
86) *România in Războiul Antihitlerist /Romania in Anti-Hitlerite War/,* (Bucharest: Editura Militară, 1966), p. 26.

87) Gheorghe Zaharia, «The Unanimous Will of the People,» *Magazin Istoric* No. 8, 1979, p. 10.
88) Simion, *op. cit.*, p. 215.
89) Vasile Mocanu, «New Data on the Anti-Hitlerite Attitude of the Romanian Army: Essential Prerequisite of the Victory of the August 1944 Insurrection,» *Anale de Istorie* No. 4, 1976, p. 40.
90) N.I. Lebedev, *Rumyniia v Gody Vtoroi Mirovoi Voiny, Vneshnepoliticheskaia i Vnutrepoliticheskaia Istoriia Rumynii v 1938-1945 gg.* (Moscow: Izdatelstvo Imo, 1961), p. 121.
91) Llewellyn Woodward, *British Foreign Policy in the Second World War*, Vol. II (London: Her Majesty's Stationery Office, 1971), p. 40.
92) Ivan Maisky, *Memoirs of a Soviet Ambassador, the War 1939-1943* (New York: Charles Scribner's Sons 1968) p. 218.
93) Woodward, *op. cit.*, Vol. II, pp. 220-221.
94) *Ibid.*, p. 223.
95) *Ibid.*, p. 232.
96) The Atlantic Charter, 14 August 1941, in Walter Consuelo Langsam, *Documents and Reading in the History of Europe Since 1918* (Chicago: Lippincott, 1951), p. 920.
97) Churchill to Lord Privy Seal (without location), 20 December 1941, in Winston S. Churchill, *The Second World War*, Vol. III, *The Grand Alliance* (London: Cassel and Co., 1950), p. 559.
98) «British-Soviet negotiations looking forward to the conclusion of a treaty of a political character with particular reference to the Soviet suggestions that certain territories taken over by the Soviet Union during the period 1 September 1939 – 22 June 1941 be recognized as Soviet territory (Washington), 4 February 1942,» *Foreign Relations of the United States*, Vol. I, p. 507.
99) Woodward, *op. cit.*, Vol. II, p. 237.
100) «British-Soviet negotiations....,» in *Foreign Relations of the United States*, Vol. I, p. 509.
101) *Ibid.*, p. 510.
102) Hull, *op. cit.*, Vol. II, p. 1,170.
103) *Foreign Relations of the United States*, Vol. III, (Washington: US Government Printing Office, 1961), p. 520, and Gaddis Smith, *American Diplomacy During the Second World War, 1941-1945* (New York, London, Sydney: John Wiley and Sons, 1965), p. 42.
104) Walter Thurston's Telegram to State Secretary Kuibishev, 5 January 1942, *United States Foreign Relations*, Vol. III, p. 491.
105) Maisky, *op. cit.*, p. 261.
106) Churchill to Roosevelt (without location), 7 March 1942, in Churchill, *op. cit.*, Vol. IV, *The Hinge of Fate* (London: Cassel and Co., 1951), p. 293.
107) Woodward, *op. cit.*, Vol. II, p. 241.
108) Stalin to Churchill (without location), 15 March 1942, in Churchill, *op. cit.*, Vol. IV, p. 294.

109) Stalin to Churchill (without location), 23 April 1942, in Churchill, *op. cit.,* Vol. IV, p. 296.
110) Maisky, *op. cit.,* p. 263 and 266, and Woodward, *op. cit.,* Vol. II, p. 247.
111) Earl of Avon, *The Eden Memoirs* (London: Cassel and Co., 1965), p. 326.
112) *Ibid.,* p. 328.
113) Woodward, *op. cit.,* Vol. II, pp. 249-250
114) Churchill, *op. cit,* Vol. IV, p. 296.
115) Hull, *op. cit.,* Vol. II, p. 1,172.
116) *Ibid.,* p. 1,173.
117) *Ibid.,* p. 1,174.
118) Churchill, *op. cit.,* Vol. IV, p. 300.
119) Maisky, *op. cit.,* p. 267.
120) Avon, *op. cit.,* p. 329.
121) Churchill to Roosevelt (without location), 27 May 1942, in Churchill, *op. cit.*, Vol. IV, p. 302.
122) Cadogan, *op. cit.,* p. 439.
123) Andreas Hillgruber, *Hitler, König Carol und Marschall Antonescu* (Wiesbaden: F. Steiner, 1954), pp. 153, 155, and 167.
124) Record of the Conversation Between Adolf Hitler and Miklos Horthy, Klessheim, 16 April 1943, in Andreas Hillgruber, *Staatsmänner und Diplomaten bei Hitler* Vol. II, (Frankfurt: Bernard and Gräfe, 1970), p. 252.
125) Iuliu Maniu's Letter to Ion Antonescu, Bucharest, 30 September 1943, in Margaret Carlyle, *Documents on International Affairs (1939–1946),* Vol. II, *Hitler's Europe* (London: Oxford University Press, 1954), pp. 327-328.
126) Renato Bova Scoppa, *Colloqui con Due Dittatori* (Rome: Ruffolo, 1949), p. 75.
127) *Ibid.,* p. 80.
128) Galeazzo Ciano, Diario, 1937-1943 (Milan: Rizzoli, 1980), p. 691.
129) Bova Scoppa, *op. cit.,* p. 109.
130) Record of the Conversation between Adolf Hitler and Marshal Antonescu, Klessheim, 16 April 1943, in Hillgruber, *Staatsmänner und Diplomaten...,* Vol. II. pp. 217-223.
131) Renato Bova Scoppa, *La Pace Impossibile,* (Turin: Rosenberg and Sellier, 1961), pp. 205 and 213.
132) Bova Scoppa, *Colloqui...,* pp. 107, 110, 113, and 114.
133) Ciano, *op. cit.,* p. 688.
134) F. W. Deakin, *The Brutal Friendship: Mussolini, Hitler, and the Fall of Italian Fascism* (New York: Harper and Row, 1962), pp. 253-255.
135) The Earl of Avon, *The Eden Memoirs* (London: Cassel, 1965), p. 371.
136) Alexandre Cretzianu, *The Lost Opportunity* (London: Jonathan Cape, 1957), p. 114.
137) Winston Churchill, *The Second World War,* Vol. V, *Closing the Ring* (New York: Bantam, 1977), p. 144.

138) Paul A. Quinlan, *Clash over Romania: British and American Policy Toward Romania, 1938-1947* (Los Angeles: American-Romanian Academy, 1977), p. 83.
139) *Ibid.*
140) Aurică Simion, *Preliminariile Politico-Diplomatice ale Insurecției Române din August 1944 /Political-Diplomatic Preliminaries of the August 1944 Romanian Insurection/*, (Cluj-Napoca: Dacia, 1979), p. 274.
141) *Ibid.*, p. 275.
142) *Ibid.*
143) Quinlan, *op. cit.*, p. 84.
144) Herbert Feis, *Churchill, Roosevelt, and Stalin* (New Jersey: Princeton, 1957), p. 123.
145) Aurică Simion, *op. cit.*, p. 312.
146) *Ibid.*, p. 313.
147) Iuliu Maniu's Letter to Ion Antonescu, Bucharest, 30 September 1943, in Margaret Carlyle, *op. cit.*, pp. 327-328.
148) Simion, *op. cit.*, p. 345.
149) *Ibid.*, p. 352.
150) Alexandre Cretzianu, *op. cit.*, pp. 93-98.
151) *Ibid.*, pp. 113, 125, and 126.
152) Cordell Hull's Telegram to John Winant, Washington, 8 January 1944, in *Foreign Relations of the United States (F.R.U.S.). Diplomatic Papers 1944*, Vol. IV, *Europe* (Washington: Government Printing Office, 1966), p. 134.
153) Averell Harriman's Telegram to Cordell Hull, Moscow, 11 January 1944, *ibid.*, p. 135.
154) James Clement Dunn's Communication to John Winant, Washington, 2 February 1944, *ibid.*, p. 136.
155) Provisions for Imposition upon Romania at the Time of Surrender (without location), 13 January 1944, *ibid.*, p. 137.
156) Aspects of the Romanian Surrender Requiring Agreement Among the British, Soviet, and American Governments (no location), 14 January 1944, *ibid.*, p. 143.
157) *Ibid.*, p. 144.
158) Memorandum on Conversation Between Wladyslaw Sikorski and Acting Secretary (Washington, 25 March 1942), *ibid.*, p. 124.
159) *Ibid.*, p. 128.
160) Anthony J. Drexel Biddle's Telegram (American Ambassador to the Polish Government in Exile) to Sumner Welles, London 24 April 1942, *ibid.*, p. 141.
161) Sumner Welles to President Roosevelt, Washington 14 April 1942, *ibid.*, p. 139.
162) Anthony J. Drexel Biddle's Telegram to Cordell Hull, London, 24 and 27 April 1942.
163) Anthony J. Drexel Biddle to Sumner Welles, London, 27 April 1942, *ibid.*, p. 143.

164) John Winant's Telegram to Cordell Hull, London, 15 February 1944, *ibid.,* p. 145.
165) Memorandum by the Division of Southern European Affairs, Washington, (no day) March 1944, *ibid.,* p. 146.
166) Ion Enescu, *Politica Externă a României în Perioada 1944-1947 /Romania's Foreign Policy During the 1944-1947 Period/,* (Bucharest: Editura Ştiinţifică şi Enciclopedică, 1979), p. 28.
167) Lincoln MacVeagh's Telegram to Cordell Hull, Cairo, 3 March 1944, in F.R.U.S., Vol. IV, p. 148.
168) A 17 March 1944 Telegram, *ibid.,* p. 150.
169) A 18 March 1944 Telegram, *ibid.,* p. 151.
170) Memorandum of Cloyce Kenneth Hudson of the Division of Southern European Affairs, Washington, 21 March 1944, *ibid.,* p. 152.
171) Averell Harriman's Telegram to Cordell Hull, Moscow, 23 March 1944, *ibid.,* p. 154.
172) A. Simion, *op. cit.,* p. 426.
173) *Ibid.,* p. 433.
174) A. Simion, "Pînă la orice Sacrificiu în Interesul Poporului Român", /Down to the Last Sacrifice in Interest of the Romanian People/, *Magazin Istoric,* Vol. X, No. 7, July 1976.
175) Lincoln MacVeagh's Telegram to Cordell Hull, Cairo, 25 March 1944, in F.R.U.S., Vol. IV, p. 156.
176) Memorandum of Cavendish Cannon (Assistant Chief of the Division of Southern European Affairs) to James Clement Dunn (Director of the Office of European Affairs), Washington, 27 March 1944, *ibid.,* p. 159.
177) *Ibid.*
178) William D. Leahy to Cordell Hull, Washington, 28 March 1944, *ibid.,* p. 161.
179) Lincoln MacVeagh's Telegram to Cordell Hull, Cairo, 30 March 1944, *ibid.,* pp. 162-163.
180) Statement of the Soviet Government Issued to the Press, Moscow, 2 April 1944, *ibid.,* p. 165.
181) Memorandum of Charles Eustis Bohlen to Cordell Hull, Washington, 1 April 1944, *ibid.,* p. 166.
182) Cordell Hull's Telegram to Averell Harriman, Washington, 5 April 1944, *ibid.,* p. 168.
183) *Ibid.*
184) Memorandum by Cloyce Kenneth Huston of the State Department's Division of Southern European Affairs, Washington, 11 April 1944, *ibid.,* pp. 172-173.
185) *Ibid.*
186) Cordell Hull's Telegram to Lincoln MacVeagh, Washington, 11 April 1944, *ibid.,* p. 174.
187) Lincoln MacVeagh's Telegram to Cordell Hull, Cairo, 14 April 1944.
188) A 16 April 1944 Telegram, *ibid.,* p. 175.

189) Cordell Hull's Telegram to Lincoln MacVeagh, Washington, 18 April 1944, *ibid.*, p. 176.
190) Lincoln MacVeagh's Telegram to Cordell Hull, Cairo, 24 April 1944, *ibid.*, p. 177.
191) *Ibid.*
192) Averell Harriman's Telegram to Cordell Hull, Moscow, 25 April 1944, *ibid.*, p. 177.
193) Vojtech Mastny, "The Benes-Stalin-Molotov Conversations in December 1943," new documents in *The American Historical Review*, Vol. XVII, No. 5, December 1972, p. 392.
194) Frederic Nanu, "The First Soviet Double-Cross," *Journal of Central European Affairs,* Vol. XII, No. 3, october 1952, p. 249.
195) Vojtech Mastny, *Russia's Road to the Cold War* (New York: Columbia University Press, 1979), pp. 154-156.
196) MacVeagh's Telegram to Cordell Hull, Cairo, 13 June 1944, *ibid.* p. 181.
197) A 29 June 1944 Telegram, *ibid.,* p. 183.
198) Nanu, *op. cit.,* p. 251.
199) *Ibid.,* p. 253.
200) *Ibid.,* p. 254.
201) William Hardy McNeil, *America, Britain, and Russia: Their Cooperation and Conflict, 1941-1946* (London: Oxford University Press, 1953), p. 422.
202) Winston Churchill, *The Second World War,* Vol. 6, *Triumph and Tragedy* (New York: Mantam, 1977), p. 62.
203) *Ibid.,* p. 197.
204) Harrison's Telegram to Cordell Hull, Bern, 20 July 1944, in F.R.U.S., Vol. IV, p. 186.
205) Record of the Conversation Between Adolf Hitler and Marshal Antonescu, Wolfsschanze, 5 August 1944 in Hillgruber, *Staatsmänner...,* p. 493.
206) Gheorghe Barbul, *Mémorial Antonescu, le Troisième Homme de l'Axe* (Paris: Editions de la Couronne, 1950), p. 163.
207) Nicolette Franck, *La Roumanie dans l'Engrenage* (Paris: Elsevier Sequoira, 1977), p. 32.
208) Shanz's Telegram to Cordell Hull, Cairo, 25 August 1944, in *F.R.U.S.,* Vol. IV, p. 195.
209) Emil Ciurea, *Traité de Paix avec la Roumanie, 10 Février 1947,* (Paris: Pedone, 1954), p. 236.
210) Cordell Hull's Telegram to Averell Harriman, Washington, 30 September 1944, in *F.R.U.S.,* Vol. IV, p. 243.
211) Averell Harriman's Telegram to Cordell Hull, Moscow, 3 September 1944, *ibid.,* p. 214.
212) Cordell Hull's Telegram to Harriman, Washington, 30 September 1944, *ibid.,* p. 243.
213) Burton Berry's Telegram to Cordell Hull, Bucharest, 9 December 1944, *ibid.,* pp. 279-280.
214) Ion Enescu, *op. cit.,* p. 224.

215) Tătărăscu's Speech at the Opening of the Paris Conference, in *F.R.U.S.*, Vol. III, p. 197.
216) Ştefan Lache and Gheorghe Ţuţui, *România şi Conferinţa de Pace de la Paris din 1946, /Romania and the 1946 Paris Peace Conference/*, (Cluj-Napoca: Dacia, 1978), p. 242.
217) *Ibid.*, p. 270.
218) John Campbell, "The European Territorial Settlement," *Foreign Affairs* Vol. XXVI, Nos. 1-4, october 1947–July 1948, p. 210.
219) *Ibid.*, p. 199.
220) Grigore Gafencu's Letter to Iuliu Maniu, Geneva, 8 September 1946, Hoover Foundation Archives.
221) Titus Georgescu şi Matei Gheorghe, "The Assistance Granted to Romania by the Soviet Union at the Paris Peace Conference", *Studii. Revista de Istorie şi Filosofie* No. 1, 1954, p. 105.

XII

ROMANIA'S 35TH ANNIVERSARY OF AUGUST 1944:
The Role of National Forces and Soviet Army in Romania's «Liberation War»

I. Political Events and Leaders Reconsidered in Romania

The true conditons under which the 23 August 1944 royal *coup d'état* was conceived, organized, and carried out have never been described objectively and in detail in Romania in official speeches, the press, or even in specialized studies. A significant role, well out of proportion to its real one, has been assigned to the communist party, while the essential roles of the democratic parties and of King Michael have been played down. Over the years various articles and studies have appeared with new facts and interpretations, coming ever closer to the historical truth.

This year /1979/ Romanian historians have gone further than ever before using official documents, notes, and entries from private diaries, some of which had never been published before. Although Romania's joining the war against the Soviet Union still is condemned, they nevertheless suggest that the war might have been justified. Because it aimed at pushing Romania's frontiers up to the Dniester and retaking Bessarabia, it was a popular war. Reviewing the events of 35 years ago has provided Romanian historians with the opportunity to reconsider, at least in part, several political and military personalities such as Iuliu Maniu, Marshal Antonescu, and Grigore Gafencu, who at times are depicted as patriots.

The 35th anniversary of the August 23 royal *coup d'état* has been celebrated in the Romanian press according to a long-standing formula, crediting the RCP with a primary role in organizing the political coup and the armed insurrection against German troops in Romania. (1) However, in contrast to this routine coverage of the dailies, the specialized historical magazines are bringing out a great many new facts and assessments which contrast with the standard official view of August 23 from the declaration of war to the signing of the armistice.

A War to Recover Bessarabia

On the basis of German-Romanian political-diplomatic documents it is now revealed that the Barbarossa project originally did not provide for the participation of Romanian units. Hitler was ready to offer the Romanians Bessarabia and even some territories beyond the Dniester (Transdnistria) in exchange for deliveries of oil and food. In his talks with Nazi leaders in January 1941 Marshal Antonescu refused the «minor» role assigned to Romania, asking that his country be allowed to join the anti-Soviet war directly and from the start. (2) Although the historians of the 23 *coup d'état* maintain that Romania's joining the war was «entirely unjustified», a statement made in the same context is worthy of note: Romania was tempted with the «territory surrendered in June 1940» and even more. The impression that Romania had freely joined the war to acquire territory is strengthened by the following statement:

In order to put more emphasis on the approval for throwing Romania into the war, I. Mihalache (former Chairman, and beginning in December 1937 Vice-Chairman of the National-Peasant Party) and Gheorghe Brătianu, Vice-Chairman of the National-Liberal Party, joined «the Eastern campaign» as volunteers. Through their presence, the leaders of the two political parties had, in fact, expressed their agreement with the war adventure into which Antonescu had dragged Romania. (3)

Present-day historians reveal another new element: the National-Peasant and Liberal Parties, which had supported Romania's joining the war against the Soviet Union, had nevertheless asked that the Romanian army not move beyond the Dniester, thus limiting the war to liberating Bessarabia. The historian Traian Udrea added that this stand had been adopted to please Great Britain and influential economic and political circles in the West (particularly in the United States) which considered that after reaching the Dniester, «the vital forces, including the army, had to be preserved to liberate Northern Transylvania.» Finally, under the influence of the leaders of the two democratic parties, some generals, who were in command of large units, had also asked that the troops stop at the Dniester.

Another historian, Gheorghe Zaharia, has revealed that the head of the army general staff, General Iosif Iacobovici, was a member of that group and was discharged following a report to Antonescu in which he disagreed with continuing the military operation and maintained that a war beyond the country's borders was unpopular, (4) implying that the war for Bessarabia was a popular one. Now the RCP claims to have realized at the end of July 1941 that, on the basis of the stand adopted by the bourgeois parties and by some higher officers who supported a limited war to the Dniester, a unified front against Antonescu could be organized. (5)

The Armistice Battle

The August 23 royal coup was preceded by the so-called armistice battles in Moldavia and Bessarabia from August 19 through 23. General Ilie Şteflea, who was then head of the army general staff, said that several Romanian divisions had been intentionally shifted to the Tîrgu Neamţ – Dealul Mare line south of Iaşi, in order to hold this line until the armistice was concluded. Nevertheless, this front was broken before the armistice was signed; contrary to Şteflea's opinion, the German Command stripped the strong position on Dealul Mare of troops, prompting Şteflea to ask to be replaced. (11)

General Titus Gîrbea, Romanian general staff representative to the OKW (Wehrmacht High Command), arrived in Romania on 21 August 1944 and informed Marshal Antonescu and General Sănătescu that Germany would not send a single soldier to Romania, since all its reserves had been moved to Poland. (7)

Nevertheless, the German Command did not think that all was lost, and it organized the 641,000-man Southern Ukraine Army Group, composed of 47 divisions, of which 22 divisions, 3 regiments, and other units were provided by Romania. According to the historians Ştefan Lache and Gheorghe Ţuţui, who describe fairly objectively and with documentation the military and diplomatic events leading up to the August 23 coup, a fortified line had been organized between the southern Carpathian bend and the Danube. In January 1944 this line was 30 km deep and included 1,660 concrete casemates, with cannons and automatic armaments, to defend the Danubian plain and Bucharest. Early in August, 11 battalions from the casement units and other reserve units were transferred to those positions and put on alert, in case of a Soviet attack. (8) Antonescu would have liked to continue the armistice negotiations from these fortified positions.

Marshal Antonescu's Armistice Negotiations

These military developments followed lengthy armistice negotiations about which more and more accurate details have been coming to light. Two sets of parallel talks were conducted: one by Marshal Ion Antonescu with his Foreign Minister Mihai Antonescu as intermediary; and the other, with Ion Antonescu's approval, by Iuliu Maniu in the name of the democratic opposition.

As early as the fall of 1943 Romanian diplomats in Portugal, Spain, and Turkey were instructed by Mihai Antonescu to establish official contacts with the local Allied embassies. Relevant authorities in Switzerland, Finland, and the

Vatican were approached, while the Hungarian and Bulgarian governments were consulted without, however, reaching the goal of concluding a separate peace with the US and Great Britain. In July 1943 Mihai Antonescu, seeking a way out, approached Mussolini. Since negotiations with the Western powers had come to a deadlock, at the end of 1943 and early in 1944 the Antonescu government contacted Alexandra Kollontai, the Soviet Ambassador to Stockholm, to inquire about possible Soviet armistice conditions. However, the negotiations with the Soviets broke off in February 1944 when it was decided, with the agreement of the opposition leadership headed by Maniu and Brătianu, to send Prince Barbu Știrbei as an unofficial emissary to Ankara and then to Cairo. The Soviet government considered that, as a result of this mission, the Romanians had given up negotiations with the USSR and they no longer felt bound by any of the proposals they had offered the Soviets. In April 1944 the Romanian-Soviet contacts nonetheless were resumed via Stockholm at the Soviet initiative with V. Semionov giving the Soviet armistice proposals to Frederic Nanu, Romanian Minister to the Swedish capital.

One of the terms, point 2, provided for re-establishing the Romanian-Soviet border as set down in the 1940 treaty. Dealing with this last problem, Lache and Țuțui, who provide these extensive details on the armistice negotiations conducted by Antonescu, argue that in June 1940 no treaty had been concluded between Romania and the Soviet Union; there had only been an exchange of diplomatic notes. They say that on 15 May 1944, the Antonescu government officially rejected these conditions, without specifying that Antonescu's refusal to surrender Bessarabia had been the reason for the rejection. However, Antonescu's relations to the Soviets via Stockholm were not broken, because on 29 May 1944 Nanu submitted a memo to the Soviet Embassy drawn up on the basis of instructions from the Romanian Foreign Ministry, according to which the Romanian government sought a 15 day grace period following the conclusion of an armistice, in order to negotiate the evacuation of German troops in Romania with the German government. The memo added that after the armistice the Antonescu government would resign, making room for a civilian government with headquarters in an area not under Soviet occupation. The Antonescu government suggested that the boundary questions be settled at the future peace conference.

On 2 June 1944 the Soviet government accepted Antonescu's proposals, even agreed to Romania's wish to remain subsequently neutral. It asked the Romanian government to send a delegation to the Soviet Union to sign the armistice.

Lache's and Țuțui's report on the armistice negotiations is objective and, in broad lines, corresponds to the description by the American historian Paul Quinlan, (9) whose work has been based on documents from the American and British archives. Quinlan's work, incidentally, has received good reviews in Romania for providing comprehensive and original material, «presenting new viewpoints on the international circumstances under which the Romanian insurrection was prepared and succeeded in August 1944.»

Another new disclosure is that on the evening of August 22, Marshal Antonescu asked Germany, through its intermediary Kurt Clodius, that freedom of political action be restored to Romania. In a German Foreign Ministry note of 24 August 1944 Clodius stated that «the Marshal wishes to have a free hand in order to make a desperate attempt to pull out of the war but only if the front collapses.» (11) According to the same study, Hitler's confidence in the unconditional loyalty of Antonescu was shaken in the summer of 1944, and at an August 5-6 meeting Hitler asked the Romanian marshal whether or not he was ready to follow Germany to the bitter end.

Reappraisal of Marshal Antonescu

This actually constitutes a political re-evaluation of Ion Antonescu, who is described as a patriotic leader, since he had entered the war in order to reconquer Bessarabia. When he saw that the German cause was lost, moreover, he tried to detach the country from the alliance and conclude an armistice with the Western allies and the Soviet Union. This, therefore, continues the positive reevaluation which began in literature with Marin Preda's novel *The Delirium* in which the Marshal's moves against the radical-right Iron Guard, and his attitude on the Jewish problem were favorably described. Now it is noted that «Antonescu opposed Killinger when he was told to send the Romanian Jews to camps» and that «he put the nose of the Iron Guard member who had killed /noted Professor Nicolae/ Iorga out of joint.» However, he still is accused of «allying himself with the Germans and joining the Axis without previously obtaining any assurances about Romania's future, » and «of submitting himself to the Vienna arbitration treaty» which had not yet begun to be implemented when he came to power on 6 September 1940. (12)

Nevertheless, the description of Antonescu is far from negative. One of the characters of the novel, the communist Ilie Dragomir, who apparently represents Emil Bodnăraș, considers that Antonescu's biggest mistake was crossing the Dniester: «Who wanted him to cross the Dniester? Or to give up the freedom of action of our army?" (12) This implies that, had the Romanian army under Antonescu's command stopped at the Dniester, no charges would have been brought against him.

On the other hand, however, the same Antonescu appears as a loyal military man when, for the sake of rescuing his country, he agreed to leave the Axis and surrender his power to the democratic opposition. Lache and Țuțui quoted Alexandru Cretzianu, one of the envoys sent by the Antonescu government and the opposition to Ankara to contact the representatives of the Western powers, as saying that Antonescu had admitted that «he would never fight the Germans» but «would surrender the helm of the state to Maniu, were the British and Americans to advance toward the Danube, and ask him to do so.»

The Democratic Opposition Negotiates the Armistice

Lache and Țuțui describe at length the role played by Chairman of the National-Peasant Party Iuliu Maniu in organizing the *coup d'état*. They emphasize the shifts during the negotiations, his reluctance to deal directly with the Soviet Union, and his wish to negotiate with the Western powers, from which he hoped to recover Bessarabia:

Neither Maniu nor Brătianu believed in a German victory and did not wish it; they reckoned on the Germans and Russians plowghing each other down and on an Anglo-American victory. Hence the vacillations and shifts of Maniu and Brătianu, the mistaken belief that, after Germany's defeat, peace conditions, including the new map of Europe, would be dictated by the US and Great Britain. The one-sided character of the bourgeois opposition leaders' plans stemmed from their anticommunism. (13)

At first the National-Peasant and National-Liberal Parties rejected the RCP proposals for unity and cooperation in the antifascist struggle; the prerequisites for joint action were created only in June 1943 after the Third International was dissolved. Therefore, only in the spring of 1944 did Maniu and Brătianu agree to cooperate with the RCP in a patriotic and national front, the authors write.

Lache and Țuțui stress that Maniu and Brătianu had seen in Ion Antonescu's assumption of power an alternative for the brief period of German domination in Europe, after which Antonescu would surrender his leadership. For this reason, during Antonescu's dictatorship the two democratic leaders did not remain inactive. They maintained contacts with a number of generals and top officials of the army and the state administration, particularly the Foreign Ministry, who informed them about the military and political situation, and supplied the Western powers – the US and Great Britain – with military and economic data.

With regard to the armistice negotiations, the authors write that on 18 December 1943, when Gheorghe Tătărescu asked Maniu to accompany him to Moscow to negotiate Romania's exit from the war with the Soviets, the leader of the National-Peasant Party asked for three days to think it over, after which he stated that he did not agree to the suggested project. On the other hand, in February 1944 Maniu and Brătianu agreed, with the assent of the Antonescu government, that an unofficial envoy, Prince Barbu Ştirbei, be sent first to Ankara and then to Cairo, to inform the three Allied powers about the terms under which Romania would leave the Axis. Quoting A. Cretzianu's *The Lost opportunity,* Lache and Ţuţui said that one of the conditions set by the leaders of the democratic opposition was that their country should not be occupied by the Red Army. Apparently, the Americans supported this, because as early as 14 November 1943 the Romanian legation in Spain had sent the Romanian Foreign Ministry a summary of a discussion with the US Ambassador to Spain:

According to the information of the US General Staff, the Russian offensive is taking on huge proportions and the German army will be unable to stop it. Therefore, our country is obviously running the risk of being occupied by the Soviet troops. Romania is interested in avoiding at any price an occupation which might jeopardize its future existence. Were the Romanian government to agree to the conditions mentioned below, the American government would be in a position to give us assurances that at least some of its territory would be occupied by the Anglo-American troops, which would constitute the only possibility of salvation for Romania. (14)

According to the same authors, both the Antonescu government and the opposition led by Maniu and Brătianu based their political plans on the opening of a new front in the Balkans and on the penetration of Western troops into that area, including Romania. However, the Balkan landing operation was not accepted by the Teheran Conference. Drawing the political consequences of this military decision, and since the Soviet army was going to enter Romania anyway, the British and American governments recognized Soviet pre-eminence in the negotiations with Romania. Prince Ştirbei was notified of the Soviet Union's armistice conditions on 12 April 1944, in Cairo, one day before Nanu was notified. On 25 May 1944, Maniu sent a memo to Cairo via C. Vişoianu; it gave the opposition's objections to the armistice terms and made the following demand: Romanian territory outside the war zone, Bucharest included, should not be occupied by the Allied forces; the Romanian territory occupied by the Russians should remain under Romanian administration; and Northern Transylvania should be returned to Romania. The Allies refused to discuss these demands, which suggested to them Romanian reluctance to sign the armistice immediately.

Lache and Țuțui add that the false assumption of a Balkan landing and the expectation that the Anglo-American troops would maintain a bourgeois regime in Romania explain why the leaders of the National-Peasant and Liberal-Parties had been reticent in establishing direct contact with the Soviets as per the Cairo proposal. For that reason Maniu turned down a Soviet invitation, sent through Czechoslovak President Edward Benes, for a delegation of the democratic opposition to go to Moscow to discuss the armistice conditions. Maniu advised Romanian Foreign Minister Mihai Antonescu not to inform Tătărescu about the decision because Tătărescu was not opposed to going. At the Council of Ministers meeting of 15 and 16 September 1944 Lucrețiu Pătrășcanu blamed Maniu for the failure of the Soviet negotiations, saying: «One person is guilty of it, and I will speak quite openly: one person is to blame for Romania's failure to conclude the armistice on the basis of the /Soviet/ proposals in April, and you, Mr. Maniu, are this person.» Maniu answered this charge, saying: «Whoever, like me, has already made a revolution/i.e., bringing Carol II back to Romania in 1930/, will not make a second one: you know how to start it, but you don't know how to end it.» (15)

Partial Rehabilitation of Iuliu Maniu

Despite the charges brought by Pătrășcanu against him, Maniu's political standing did not diminish because he had tried under difficult circumstances to obtain the best armistice conditions for Romania. Literary texts also emphasize that some of the actions undertaken by Maniu at home won him considerable prestige in various circles. Novelist Dumitru R. Popescu quotes extensively from a memo addressed by Maniu to Antonescu, asking that Romania leave the war. Maniu's argument, according to Popescu, is that:

our country is threatened by danger with which it can no longer cope. The defeated German armies can no longer protect themselves against a Russian invasion, and the aid we can offer to prevent it is entirely inadequate. Continuing to cooperate with the German armies would mean uselessly sacrificing the remnants of our military power, and provoking reprisals and irreparable destruction from the Bolshevik armies. (16)

There is another allusion to Maniu in connection with a memo from the university teaching staff to Antonescu, calling for Romania's exit from the war. Popescu adds, not without respect, that Maniu «ordered all members of the National-Peasant Party on the teaching staff to sign it.» (17)

The Maniu-Antonescu relationship was ambiguous, with Maniu sometimes wanting the Marshal to remove Romania from the war, and at others to remove Romania from the war and Antonescu from power. In an excerpt from the diary of former Romanian Foreign Minister Grigore Gafencu, published now for the first time, emphasis is put on Maniu's insistence on continuing the Cairo negotiations with the Western Allies while neglecting the Soviet factor to the end which «would be unforgiveable.» (18)

Rehabilitation of Former Foreign Affairs Minister Gafencu

Taking advantage of the August 23 anniversary, *Magazinul Istoric* began to rehabilitate Gafencu's reputation by publishing a eulogistic biography and a picture. In the past, a biographical note had stated that Gafencu, along with a group of former Romanian political leaders and diplomats living in the West, whose activities were coordinated with those of the bourgeois National-Peasant and Liberal Parties at home, had submitted several memos to the Paris Peace Conference expressing their views on various Romanian issues. Of course, the note did not specify that the memos included the reasons why Bessarabia should be a part of Romania. Gafencu's biographer confined himself to stating that, «although his stands were distorted by an undisguised hostility to the new regime, by the revolutionary changes in Romania, nevertheless, some of his views coincided with or were close to those of the Romanian delegation.» (19)

According to Gafencu's Diary (23 August 1944, written at Geneva) it appears that he had advised both Maniu and Mihai Antonescu against the Cairo talks because «the Cairo action is not all, and the Russians have their own opinions and conditions. My impression was, however, that Maniu insisted on Cairo.» (20) In any case, there were two parallel negotiations, one with the Western Allies, and the other with the Soviet Union; and Romanian politicians generally preferred the former.

Profile of General Sănătescu, Marshal of the Royal Palace

General Constantin Sănătescu is another actor in the August 23 coup who figures prominently in the new disclosures. At that time he was marshal of the Royal Palace. From the diary of General Titus Gîrbea it seems that, as early as March 17-18 Sănătescu had revealed that «we» /that is, the Palace/ «do not want to share the destiny of the Nazi Reich» and, consequently, fast action should be taken before it is too late. Gîrbea, who maintained contacts with the OKW (Wehrmacht High Command) and the OKH (Army High Command), kept Sănătescu informed about the German projects for the military occupation of Romania (30 March 1944) and about the plan of General Friessner, the new commander of the "South Ukraine" German armies to ask Hitler to assign him the command of the Romanian troops as well (16 August 1944). (21)

The August 23 Coup

Lache and Țuțui, who provide such extensive, hitherto unpublished information on the domestic and foreign conditions under which the August 23 coup occurred suggest that, prior to August 20, the democratic opposition led by Maniu had worked hand in hand with Marshal Antonescu to withdraw Romania from the war. «Until 20 August 1944 the leaders of the National-Peasant and National--Liberal Parties had considered that setting down the final text of the armistice agreement and signing it had to precede the overthrow of Antonescu and Romania's withdrawal from the Hitlerite war /i.e., that the Antonescu government would sign the Armistice/. Certainly, this type of alternative was desirable from Romania's viewpoint, however, it proved to be unfeasible.» (22) The same authors describe the coup as follows:

on August 20 the Soviet Army launched its big offensive on the southern wing of the Soviet-German front. In the night of August 21-22 a meeting took place at the Royal Palace to set up the insurrection for August 26 considering that, toward the end of the week, the security measures would be relaxed. A cable was sent to the Allied powers, via Cairo, asking them to bomb the German targets in Romania from the air, while the Soviet offensive would keep the German troops engaged on the east Carpathian front up to the Dniester River. Before noon on August 23 Marshal Antonescu summoned a Council of Ministers meeting at Snagov, near Bucharest, where he reported about the situation on the Moldavian front which he had inspected on August 21 and 22; he said he had ordered the evacuation of government agencies from the capital and continued resistance to the Soviet troops along the east Carpathians and the fortified Focșani-Nămoloasa, Galați-Danube Delta line.

At this point there is a gap in Lache's and Țuțui's account, for they fail to explain that the coup was moved up from August 26 to 23 on King Michael's initiative and without the knowledge of the leaders of the political parties, for fear that, if Bucharest were evacuated, the Marshal would establish his headquarters at some place difficult to reach. (23) That is why the August 23 coup took everybody by surprise: Antonescu, the Germans, the Soviets, the Western powers, and even the representatives of the opposition parties, who had expected it to come later. The August 23 coup is thus the work of the Royal Palace, a fact which is not explicitly stated in specialized Romanian historian literature even to this day.

Romanians Fight the Germans Alone

The German military reaction to the coup was not long in coming; General Alfred von Gerstenberg, head of the Luftwaffe in Romania, immediately ordered the bombing of Bucharest. For eight days, from August 23 through 31, the Romanian army cleared Romanian territory of German troops, liberating 150,000 square kilometers, an area as large as Denmark, Belgium, the Netherlands, and Switzerland together. (24)

A thesis advanced in 1961 by the Soviet historian V.B. Ushakov, who attributed Romania's liberation exclusively to Soviet troops, overlooked the role of the Romanian armed insurrection. (25) This provoked objections from Romanian historians, who emphasized that both Romanian troops and patriotic groups fiercely fought the Germans not only in the Bucharest area to capture the capital, but also in the oil producing area of Ploiești and other regions of the country. (26) Since then, this view of the role of the armed insurrection in Romania's liberation has been stressed by many specialized studies and articles, and has finally prevailed. However, the polemics over who liberated Bucharest began afresh when East German television presented a Russian documentary film attributing to the Soviet army a decisive role in liberating southeastern Europe. (27) Leslie Collitt, Berlin correspondent of the *Financial Times,* wrote that the Romanians reacted to the film with a number of articles insisting that the credit should go to the Romanian army and the patriotic formations. (28) In some articles printed in *Scînteia* and in other Romanian publications authors such as Haralamb Zincă and General Marcel Olteanu point out the role of the Romanian army in the liberation of Bucharest. (29) Furthermore Major-General Constantin Olteanu notes that without Soviet participation Romanian troops started an offensive in northeast Transylvania, toward Ilieni-Sfîntu Gheorghe-Odorhei on August 30, and another on September 9 in central Transylvania. In the Banat Romanian troops resisted the German-Hungarian offensive alone until September 18-20 when Soviet troops arrived. (30)

A book published in Bucharest on the eve of the August 23 anniversary concluded that internal factors played a decisive role in Romania's liberation while the external factors only gave support. (31) This version is very different from that of the Soviets who purport that only the powerful Soviet army offensive on the Iași and Chișinău fronts liberated Romania. (32)

Rehabilitation of the Head of Antonescu's General Staff

Romanian historians now write that after the coup all German attempts to find commanders of Romanian units who would stand by the Third Reich and to build up a pro-German government, which would arrest the members of the new Sănătescu government, failed. This can now be confirmed both by German documents dealing with Hitler's order on August 23 or 24, to take such action, and by the answers of the attaché of the German embassy in Romania Albrecht von Hohenzollern and Edmond Wesenmayer, SS head under the German Foreign Ministry, who reported that those plans could not be implemented. (33)

Among other materials now published, mention should be made of a memo signed by the former head of the general staff of the Romanian army, General Șteflea, who like Gafencu is now being at least partly re-evaluated. This text suggests that Șteflea had tried to persuade Antonescu not to send additional Romanian troops to the Russian front, so that a fairly strong military force could be maintained at home, to be used in a possible campaign against Hungary to liberate Northern Transylvania. After Marshal Antonescu turned down this project asking, «Are these the brains of the army?,» Șteflea organized a campaign to sabotage the war in the East, submitting forged military reports both to Antonescu and to the German authorities. He admitted that, in this way, he had succeeded in stopping 566,000 soldiers from being sent to the front and in storing large amounts of war material so that, when he left office on 23 August 1944, the Romanian army was much stronger than when he had been appointed to that position on 20 January 1942. (34) This explains why, immediately after August 23, Romania was able to join the campaign against Hungary and Germany with fresh forces. It lost 170,000 of the 540,000 troops it provided, and became, in number of participants – according to Romanian statistics, the fourth partner of the Allied coalition, after the Soviet Union, the US, and Great Britain. (35)

Role of King Michael Played Down

As in the past, the latest works on 23 August 1944 mention that King Michael had played a role without, however, admitting that he had been a major protagonist. The RCP had established links with the palace circles as far back as August 1943, a year before the coup actually took place. According to Lache and Țuțui, there was a certain amount of hostility between the king and Antonescu owing to the fact that, as far back as September 1940 when he took power, the Marshal had assumed some royal prerogatives and systematically excluded Michael from any decision-making role in domestic or foreign policy. (36) At the first meeting with the representatives of the king, Lucrețiu Pătrășcanu, who was responsible for contacting the palace, said that: «Although the communist party is maintaining a republican stand, it nevertheless considers that the issue of monarchy versus republic is not topical; and should the king take action to remove Romania from the Hitlerite war, the communist party will be ready through its Central Committee, to support him with all its might.» (37)

To some extent, the king's decision to put an end to Antonescu's dictatorship was influenced by the Italian events of July 1943, when, following a palace coup, Mussolini was demoted and replaced by a government under Marshal Badoglio. (38) Even current Romanian publications recognize that the king had planned to prepare the country to withdraw from the war as far back as March 1944 (39). The palace circles advised that Antonescu be replaced by a government under Ion Gigurtu, who allegedly would remove the country from the anti-Soviet war with Hitler's assent, while the communists suggested the alternative of overthrowing Antonescu by force and turning on Nazi Germany. (40) Moreover, King Michael's proclamation, broadcast on August 23, had been discussed and approved at a joint meeting of representatives of the Block of Democratic Parties and the Palace. (41)

The king's participation in the coup is explained as a way to save the monarchy in the difficult times through which Romania and the throne were passing. (42) Without giving up its republican convictions, the RCP supported Michael, believing that he enjoyed great popularity among the military circles, some of the peasants, and the *petite bourgeoisie*. (43)

As a rule, recently published studies about the historical conditions under which the coup took place include only brief mention of the Soviet Army's role. Nevertheless, they state that the Soviet military command had not been informed of the preparation of the insurrection and that there had been no co-ordination between the Soviet offensive on the Iași-Chișinău front and the Romanian insurrectionists. (44) The articles and studies published this year present in a new and more favorable light many of the political and military participants in the 23 August 1944 coup who have been gradually rehabilitated whenever the subject arises of who was or would become a declared adversary of the regime.

Background Report No. 205,
Munich, 25 September 1979,
Radio Free Europe Research

BIBLIOGRAPHY:

1) *România Liberă,* 12 August 1979; *Scînteia,* 28 July and 19 August 1979; Radio Bucharest, 18 August 1979.
2) Traian Udrea, «The Alliance Policy of the RCP. The Establishment of the National Democratic Block in June 1944,» *Revista de Istorie* No. 6, 1979.
3) *Ibid.*
4) Gheorghe Zaharia, «The Unanimous Will of the People,» *Magazin Istoric* No. 8, 1979.

5) Udrea, *op. cit.*
6) General Ilie Şteflea, «The Head of the General Staff Resisted the Pressure of the Wehrmacht,» *Magazin Istoric* No. 8, 1979.
7) General Titus Gîrbea, «Meetings with General Sănătescu,» *Magazin Istoric* No. 8, 1979.
8) Ştefan Lache and Gheorghe Ţuţui, *România şi Conferinţa de Pace de la Paris din 1946 /Romania and the 1946 Paris Peace Conference/*, (Cluj-Napoca: Dacia, 1978), p. 74.
9) Paul D. Quinlan, *Clash over Romania: British and American Policies Toward Romania, 1938-1947* (Oakland: American–Romanian Academy of Arts and Sciences, 1977), p. 173.
10) G. Buzatu, «The History of the Romanians in Some Recent Foreign Works,» *Cronica* No. 8, 23 February 1979.
11) Florin Constantiniu, «Aspects of the Crisis of the Antonescu Regime on the Eve of the National Anti-fascist and Anti-imperialist Armed Insurrection,» *Revista de Istorie* No. 7, 1979.
12) Dumitru Radu Popescu, «The Porphyrogenite,» *Transilvania* No. 4, 1979.
13) Lache and Ţuţui, *op. cit.*, p. 50.
14) *Ibid.*, p. 50.
15) *Ibid.*, p. 71.
16) D.R. Popescu, «Looking at Himself,» *Viaţa Românească* No. 1, 1979.
17) D.R. Popescu, «The Porphyrogenite...»
18) Grigore Gafencu, « Romania's Exploit – an Act of Justice,» *Magazin Istoric* No 8, 1979.
19) Ion Călăfăteanu, «Gafencu's Biography,» *Magazin Istoric* No. 8, 1979.
20) Gafencu, *op. cit.*
21) Gîrbea, *op. cit.*
22) Lache and Ţuţui, *op. cit.*, pp. 70-71.
23) Nicolette Franck, *La Roumanie dans l'Engrenage*, (Paris, Brussels: Elsevier Sequoia, 1977), p. 76.
24) Colonel Constantin Căzănişteanu, « Romania's Comprehensive and Substantial Contribution to the Final Victory over Fascism, » *Scînteia*, 6 July 1979.
25) V.B. Ushakov, *Hitlerite Germany's Foreign Policy* (Moscow: Publishing House of the Institute of International Relations, 1961), p. 270.
26) A. Niri and V.B. Ushakov, «Hitlerite Germany's Foreign Policy,» *Analele Institutului de Istorie a Partidului de pe lîngă CC al PMR* No. 5, 1962.
27) Gerd Prokot, «The Decisive Front: from the Balkans to Vienna", *Neues Deutschland*, 9 August 1979.
28) Leslie Collitt, «Romania and Russia Argue over the Past, *Financial Times*, 10 August 1979.
29) Haralamb Zincă, «Through the Archives of Hour 'H',» *România Literară*, 9 August 1979; Marcel Olteanu, «Bucharest, Ineradicable City,» *Contemporanul* No. 34, 22 August 1979.

30) Constantin Olteanu, «Romania's Military Contribution to the Defeat of Nazi Germany,» *Era Socialistă* No. 16, 20 August 1979.
31) Agerpres, 25 June 1979.
32) Radio Moscow in Romanian, 26 August 1979.
33) Mircea Muşat and Vasile Arimia, «German Documents on August 23: A Well-Defined Day in the History of the War,» *Magazin Istoric* No. 8, 1979.
34) Şteflea, *op. cit.*
35) Căzănişteanu, *op. cit.*
36) Lache and Ţuţui, *op. cit.*, p. 52.
37) *Ibid.*, p. 53.
38) G. Zaharia, *op. cit.*
39) T. Gîrbea, *op. cit.*
40) Aron Petric, «The Romanian Communist Party: Leader of the Revolutionary Struggle for National and Social Liberation,» *Era Socialistă* No. 16, 20 August 1979.
41) G. Zaharia, «The Entire Country Called to Arms,» *Magazin Istoric,* No. 7, 1979.
42) Zaharia, «The Unanimous Will...»
43) Petric, *op. cit.*
44) Zaharia, «The Entire Country...»

XIII

THE POLICY OF RUSSIFICATION

Russification as a political doctrine and as administrative practice is something common both to the tzarist and the Soviet regimes. Its aim is the assimilation of non-Russian peoples by the Great-Russian nation, considered to be superior to all others living in the Muscovite empire.

Russian nationalist ideology and the techniques of assimilation have evolved over the years, but the aim remained the same: the creation of a single Russian people through the amalgamation of other nations.

The Great-Russian people, in the middle of the Muscovite empire, enjoys a favorable position from which to attain domination over other peoples in Europe and Asia, despite the fact that they today represent only 53% of the empire's population. (1) Scattered about the urban centers from the Amur River to the Dniester, and from Vladivostok to the Sea of Azov, the Great-Russians, who have acquired over the centuries the technique of governing, persist in imposing upon other peoples their language, culture, and way of life. In order better to attain this aim, the tzarist Russification policy made use of certain ideas, such as Russian nationalism, the Christian-Orthodox messianism, and the myth of Moscow being the third Rome. (2) The tzarist motto «pravoslavie i narodnost» – Orthodoxy and nationality – impregnated by the idea of world domination inherited from the Mongols and Tartars, served as an ideological front for Russian expansionism. If the declared aim of tzarism was to liberate the Christian peoples from the Ottoman yoke, the real aim was their cultural Russification and economic exploitation by means of a centralistic administration and persevering colonization.

The Soviet regime took up this policy, using Great-Russian nationalism and Slavophile ideas, in order to proclaim Soviet Russia as the contemporary worlds' champion of intelectual and moral progress. Religious messianism was thus replaced by proletarian messianism, the Moscow-is-the-Third-Rome myth by the

Kremlin is the Mecca-of-International-Communism. Communism adds to the tzarist arsenal of Russification a centralized party and the policy of forced industrialization for underdeveloped regions.

The Soviet doctrine of Russification appears neither in Lenin's, nor in Stalin's works of 1913, in which the latter advocated equal rights for all the nations of the Russian Empire and went as far as to recognize the right of cessation. (3) It was not until the Second World War that Stalin encouraged and exploited Russian patriotism, mobilizing it against the Germans. Immediately after the war, he commenced the «political education» of the population in the spirit of proletarian internationalism, by fighting the «bourgeois ideology.» In other words, he concouraged Russian nationalism, but condemned non-Russian patriotism.

The new Stalinist nationalities doctrine was formulated in the famous speech delivered by the red dictator on May 24, 1945, when he proclaimed the Russian people to be the most «eminent» nation of the USSR. This speech was the starting signal for a propaganda campaign exalting the virtues of the Russian people as the leading nation of the Soviet Union.

The campaign of intensive Russification unleashed by Stalin was slowed down by Beria, who probably hoped to get the support of the other nationalities to consolidate his own position in the power struggle. Under Khrushchev and Brezhnev, the policy of forced Russification was resumed in a new form, recruiting the Ukrainians and Byelorussians into the process. In this latter phase, Russification gives way to the Slavicization of non-Russian nations dominated by the Muscovite empire.

The tzarist and communist Russification policies proved effective to a certain extent, thanks to continuity and to the means of «persuasion» used. As a result of these policies, the number of ethnic groups in the Soviet Union was considerably reduced – from 186 in 1926, to some 100 in 1970 – and this considering those groups which were sufficiently important to be called nationalities. (6) With the Soviet census of 1970, the number of non-Russians who declared Russian to be their mother tongue began to rise until it reached 13,800,000, which is 3,600,000 more than in the 1959 census. This proves the success of linguistic Russification, which represents the first step in the process of ethnic Russification. The pace of Russification is more rapid in the border regions of Asia and Europe, where Moscow needs to create a powerful ethnic Russian belt loyal to the regime. One of the highest rates of Russification is that in Soviet Moldavia, where the number of Russians is growing faster than that of the other nationalities of the republic, despite the fact that the Russians are as alien there as the French in Africa.

In the days of the tzars, Russification registered a certain degree of success among the Moldavian boyars, who changed their nationality in order to obtain certain privileges, but it never engulfed the peasantry. (9) Under the Soviet regime, the peasants are also threatened with the loss of national identity, particularly as they have to choose between instant assimilation and Siberian exile. However, together with the Ukrainians and the Jews, the Moldavians are among those nations of the Soviet Empire most likely to cause difficulties for the Moscow regime. This at least is the impression of George Savor, a recent traveller in Soviet Moldavia, (10) confirmed by an American study which concluded that Moldavian nationalism tends to equal the most powerful form of nationalism found anywhere in the Soviet Union, the nationalism of the Baltic countries. (11) An analysis of the articles published by the Moldavian press also betrays anxiety of the Soviet authorities in the face of the degree of national reaction to the policy of forced Russification. In general terms, Zbigniew Brzezinski ascertains the existence among non-Russian intellectuals of a growing sensitivity to the kind of Russification resulting from the industrialization of the Soviet Union. Further on, the author believes that the communist leaders are beginning to realize the potential danger represented by local nationalism, which could become an even more serious problem for the Soviet Union than the racial issue in the United States. (12) A study of the tools used and of the results obtained by the policy of Russification is of interest, because failure in this field could mean a serious setback in the evolution of the Soviet system.

Administrative methods

Soviet Russification methods are both more subtle and more brutal than those of the tzars. Among the first measures to be adopted in order to facilitate the Russification of the Moldavian population was the isolation of the province by a total severance of communications between the new republic and Romania. Some 50,000 Bessarabians had left their province after the Soviet occupations of 1940-1941 and 1944. Others would have followed them, had the Soviet authorities not made it impossible to cross the Pruth. To reach Romania, fugitives had to cross strips of plowed and mined land 50 to 100 meters wide, they had to bypass guards in watchtowers, armed with machine guns and equipped with search-lights. Furthermore, a would-be refugee had to cross a barbed-wire fence guarded by police dogs, disable a modern alarm system, and finally swim the river. In other words, the Moldavian Republic was turned into a sealed camp. Besides, successful escape was no better than being caught, for, instead of forced labor in Siberia, the successful fugitive would have been sent to work on the dreaded Danube-Black Sea Canal project. Never before was the Pruth border so tightly guarded as under the Soviet regime. In the days of the tzars, numerous intellectuals, such as Alexandru Donici, Zamfir Arbure, Bogdan Petriceicu Haşdeu, Constantin Stere, etc., managed to leave Bessarabia and settle in Romania where they promoted the cause of their province. Under the Soviet regime, the Bessarabians, already settled in Romania, were forcibly repatriated and the slightest allusion to Bessarabia was severely punished. It was not until the 1950s that official contacts between the Moldavian Republic and Romania started becoming more numerous, without, however, attaining a normal level. Visas for official journeys and visits with relatives and friends residing in the USSR were only waived in March 1966, two years after the elimination of the need for visas between Romania and Yugoslavia /September 1964/, and one year after the need for visas between Romania and the DDR had been abolished. To this date, visits between relatives and friends living on the two banks of the Pruth is sporadic, and so are tourism and cultural exchanges, despite the ties and the linguistic and cultural unity existing between Bessarabia and Romania.

Another step toward the Russification of Bessarabia was the division of the province's territory. Unlike the tzars, who had preserved the administrative unity of the province, the Soviets parcelled it up, taking away the districts of Akkerman (Cetatea Albă) and Izmail now called Belgorod-Dnestrovski from the south and Khotin (Hotin) from the north. (13) These districts were annexed to the Ukraine, together with the Northern Bucovina. A similar policy had been applied in Central Asia, where the administrative borders of the republics do not coincide with the ethnic ones. This practice caused discontent among the nationalities concerned. By breaking up the unity of the Moldavian block, Moscow hopes to be able to apply more pressure on the population, in order to accelerate the denationalization process. The Russification of the Moldavians annexed by the Ukraine should be easier, because of the simple fact that the administration there is alien and the official languages are Russian and Ukrainian. In reality, it seems that these measures do nothing but exasperate the population, causing it to opt for a life of complete isolation and to view the administration in the way a prisoner regards his guards.

By the law of August 2, 1940, part of the Autonomous Moldavian Republic founded in 1924 on the left bank of the Dniester was taken away from the Ukraine and attached to the new Socialist Republic of Moldavia. In reality, only 936.3 square miles of the territory of the formerly autonomous republic had been surrendered to the new Socialist Republic: the districts of Dubassary (Dubăsari), Rybnitsa (Ribnița), Slobodzeya (Slobozia) and Tiraspol. The rest of the 1,200 sq. miles were annexed by the Ukraine. From existing statistics, it appears that the new Moldavian Socialist Republic had, at the time of its establishment, 4,071 sq. miles of territory and some 164,000 inhabitants less than Bessarabia, i.e., 13,203 sq. miles and 2,700,000 inhabitants in 1941, as compared with the 17,274 sq. miles and 2,864,402 inhabitants of Bessarabia in 1930. The Soviets administratively carved up Soviet Moldavia and through the territorial exchanges between the USSR and the Ukraine, created a reason for tension between the Moldavians and the Ukrainians – sowing the seed of discord in order to be able to govern them better. The new administration proceeded immediately to Russify the names of towns, villages, and districts and did it so thoroughly that one has difficulty in recognizing in the Cyrillic spelling the old Moldavian names of Latin resonance like Românești, today Romanova; Sângerei, today Synzhereya; Volintiri, today Volintirova; or Cărpineni, changed to Karpinyani, etc.

The Government

Soviet Moldavia was given a government and a Communist Party whose programs do not support the interests of the Moldavian nation, but only its complete Russification. In spite of its federal organization, the Soviet state is centralistic, leaving little to the jurisdiction of the governments of the socialist republics. These are simply instruments of the central government. The entirely Russian or Russified administration of the Moldavian Autonomous Republic (1924–1940) had already achieved notoriety through the terrorist methods used against the Moldavian population by Commissar Shiroky for Internal Affairs. A declaration published in January 1939 announced that Commissar Shiroky and his aides had forced, by criminal means, a great number of teachers and young Moldavians to confess that they belonged to an imaginary counterrevolutionary organization, allegedly called "The Moldavian Fascist Youth". Abuses were so flagrant that the chiefs of the local NKVD had been punished for crimes perpetrated under Stalin. (14) Even after the establishment of the Moldavian Socialist Republic, the key position of chief of the Moldavian KGB was never entrusted to a Moldavian but rather to Russian-Ukrainian career policemen, hard, confident men who proceeded to arrest and deport en masse the Moldavian bourgeoisie, intellectuals, and peasants. The importance Moscow attaches to the position of chief of the KGB is underlined by the fact that one of the most recent of those bosses, the Ukrainian J. T. Savchenko, was promoted, after serving in Socialist Moldavia (1959–1966), to All-Soviet Minister of Public Order. In his place came another Ukrainian, P. V. Chvertko, hitherto chief of the KGB of the Kirghiz Republic. (15)

The prerogatives left to the Government of the Moldavian Socialist Republic by the central government are quite insignificant.

Indeed, in May 1954 the republic's Supreme Soviet approved amendments to the Moldavian Constitution, reinforcing administrative centralism, which was already asphyxiating. Similar measures had been adopted by the Baltic, Caucasian, and Central Asian Republics, with the common aim of strengthening Moscow's control over local administration in view of the Russification and Sovietization of the non-Russian republics. Soviet Moldavia has two kinds of ministries: the "unionist" ministries, whose heads are simply the respective ministers of the USSR exercising their authority locally through an intermediary residing in Chişinău, and the "republican" ministries, whose heads are appointed by the Supreme Soviet of Moldavia. Moscow exerts absolute control over the Moldavian government by virtue of the fact that the main ministries are of the "unionist" variety: internal affairs, foreign affairs, defense, justice, commerce, finance, agriculture, food industry, consumer goods industry, industrial control of the state, timber, transportation, automobiles and roads, culture, and health. Ministries subordinate to the Moldavian Supreme Soviet are relatively minor ones: the ministries of social welfare, local administration, civic construction, local industry, and education. (16) Even in such cases, however, representatives of the central authorities, attached to the republican ministries, reduce to nil the role of the Moldavian executives. Moscow's control over republican activity was strengthened in 1954 by the creation of sections dependent on the Ministry of the Interior, attached to the local Soviets, and also by the rule that the municipal and regional attorneys must be confirmed by the attorney general of the USSR.

In 1954, the majority of the members of this government, deprived of any real authority, were Russians and Ukrainians with names like Gherasim Rud (Chairman of the Council); A. Melnik, N. A. Scalekos, and Ustik (vicechairmen); J. L. Mordovet (Internal Affairs); F.S. Koval (Agriculture); P. A. Beliaev (Commerce); Atamenko (Local Industry); A. Baranovschi (Public Education); etc. Even while the Prime Minister was a Moldavian (the case of Aleksandr Filipovich Diorditsa (Gheorghiţă) who raised to this position in 1958), the satisfaction granted the natives was purely formal, for the Transdniestrian Gheorghiţă was notorious for having participated in the Sovietization of Moldavia beginning in 1940.

The Party

The communist Party of the Soviet Union proved to be an even more powerful instrument of Russification. The Soviet state is a state of a single party, unitary and centralistic, ruling supreme over all other administrative bodies. To this strongly centralized and very disciplined party are subordinated all the Republican Communist Parties. From the very beginning, the Communist Party of the USSR has been under the influence of the Great-Russians, who dominate it numerically as well as ideologically.

When the Soviets founded the Moldavian Autonomous Republic on the left bank of the Dniester in 1924, with a plan to use it as a base for lending support to an irredentist movement in Bessarabia, they had difficulties in recruiting members for the new Moldavian Communist Party. The peasant population of the new republic was profoundly religious and felt no attraction whatsoever for an atheistic party which was getting ready, moreover, to collectivize the land. (17) The party was hardly established when Stalin hurried to decapitate its national leaders. Numerous functionaries of the party and numerous Moldavian economists were shot in the days of the personality cult; the Chairman

Vorovic of the Central Executive Committee; Chairman Borisov of the Council of People's Commissars; as well as the Territorial committee secretaries Golumb, Buchman, and Docul, to whom should be added the Bessarabian émigrés Milev and Kriworukov. (18) This purge of the cadres of the Communist Party of Moldavia, as well as those perpetrated at the same time in the parties, governments, and intellectual circles of other non-Russian nations, brought about the annihilation of the national elites which had represented an obstacle to forced Russification.

The Communist Party of the new Moldavian Socialist Republic faced similar difficulties in its endeavor to broaden its base, in order to be able to solve the problems of an enlarged republic. In 1945, there were only 130 rural communist cadres for the whole of Socialist Moldavia, of whom 38 were for ex-Bessarabia. Three years later, it was decided to send 1,000 communists from the towns to the villages, in order to activate propaganda among a peasant population growing in number and hostility to communism. (19) Despite these efforts, by 1953 the party consisted of only 10,000 members, most of them recruited from among the Russians and the Ukrainians. (20) In 1961, the membership of the Moldavian Communist Party began to grow at the rapid rate of 41% per year, which was not surpassed for the period under discussion (1961-1965) except in the case of the Latvian party (45%). On January 1, 1965, the membership of the Moldavian Communist Party attained the figure of 85,379, representing 1 Party member for every 35 inhabitants. This was a lower proportion than the 26 existing in the Baltic countries and the 27 to 30 existing in Central Asia. (21) The Moldavian Communist Party does not reflect the ethnic structure of the republic – the Moldavians represent less than 40% of the members, while constituting 65.4% of the population. It is presumed that an effort to "Romanize" took place in 1965, when the membership of the Moldavian Communist Party grew by more than 10% in a single year, reaching the figure of 94,574. It is probable that an attempt was made partially to satisfy the native element by recruiting an increasing number of Moldavians. At any rate, the operations of this improvised party leave a lot to be desired, as confessed by Yuri Melkov, one of the secretaries, who complained to the Central Committee that certain organizations did not hold meetings or did so only perfunctorily. (22)

Improvised and fragile, the Moldavian Communist Party was to also be shaken by frequent changes at the top. In 1951, three of the five secretaries of the party (N. G. Kovalj, the first secretary; F. I. Karnikov, and M. M. Radul) were replaced. (23) The new first secretary of the Moldavian Communist Party was Leonid Brezhnev, who was to become First Secretary of the Communist Party of the USSR, a personality – therefore of the first magnitude proving the importance Moscow attached to Soviet Moldavia. Before surrendering his position to Dimitri Spiridonovich Gladky on october 25, 1952, Brezhnev read the general report at the 14th Congress of the Moldavian CP. The Secretariat counted among its members the following newly elected persons: B. A. Gorban, A. A. Melnik and A. M. Lazarev. They were joining D. G. Tkack and P. F. Teresenco, who retained their positions. (24) The only Romanian in this Secretariat seems to have been, judging by his name, Gorban. The 1951 reshuffle of the Moldavian CC was of the same significance as the changes made in the same period in Lithuania.

The Russian-Ukrainian elements loyal to the Kremlin were reinforced, so that they could more effectively counter manifestations of local nationalism in the non-Russian republics.

The composition of the Moldavian CC changed again in 1954, when the function of first secretary was taken over by another Ukrainian, Zinovi Timofevich Serdyuk, and that of second secretary by Gladky (demoted). Maxim Vasilovich Scurtul was the only Romanian in the new CC. (25) On June 18, 1954, the Central Committee elected two new secretaries: Ivan Dimitrievich Kozacov and the old secretary Dimitri Grigorovich Tkack. (26) This change, which came so shortly after the 1951 reshuffle, is evidence of Moscow's discontent and nervousness vis-à-vis Moldavian nationalism. Serdyuk held out in the function of first secretary until 1961, when he was summoned to Moscow and given some job at headquarters. The first secretaryship of the Moldavian Party was then given to the Trans-dniestrian Moldavian Ivan Ivanovich Bodyul (Bodiul), who occupies the position to this day. As in the case of Gheorghiță, the significance of the promotion of Bodyul, designed to satisfy Moldavian nationalism, is merely formal, since Bodyul is a docile instrument of Moscow. A member of the Communist Party of the Soviet Union since 1937, he is also a member of the Soviet Central Committee. Yet, even a man as trustworthy as Bodyul is seconded by a Russian. Nikolai Afanasyvich Melnikov was transferred directly from the Soviet Party central apparatus and named Second Secretary of the Moldavian Communist Party in 1961. In 1963, the Russians and Ukrainians represented a large majority in the Moldavian CC, holding approximately 60% of the seats. Their number grew further in March 1966 when the Russian-Ukrainian percentage rose to 65%. (27)

The names of the section chiefs of the Moldavian CC show that not a single Moldavian was present among them in 1952; Chernenko was charged with agitprop; Koroltov with controlling the administrative bodies; Korotnyan with planning, finance, and commerce; Ilyasenko with education; Volkov with science and higher education; Klimanov with transportation; Vorobeyev with industry; Pisarenko with the indoctrination of women; and Darienko with literature and the arts. (28)

When the Moldavian Barbulat somehow managed to become chief of agitprop, he did not last long in that position. Accused of inefficiency, he was replaced by the Russian Anton Konstantinov (February 13, 1969). (29)

The composition of the Congress of the Moldavian CP also betrays a numerical preponderance of Russians and Ukrainians. Thus, at the seventh Congress of the party, 263 Moldavians, 214 Russians, 153 Ukrainians, 9 Ruthenians, and 39 Bulgarians and Gagautzs, were present. This makes for 61.22% non-Moldavians, who represented a mere 34.6% of the population. (30)

The rekindling of Moldavian nationalism places the Soviets in a dilemma: to leave the Moldavian Party and its leadership in the hands of Russo-Ukrainian elements enjoying Moscow's confidence but provoking more nationalist reaction, or to Romanize the party and its cadres thus risking the strengthening of Moldavian national sentiments.

The Cadres

The administrative machinery of Soviet Moldavia is also in the hands of Russian und Ukrainian functionaries. They guide and control the republic. Stalin at one time encouraged and even accepted having the economic and cultural life of the non-Russian republics guided by national cadres, familiar with the language and local customs. (31) This principle however was never reflected in practice and Moldavian Prime Minister Gheorghiță found nothing wrong with the preponderance of Russo-Ukrainian employees, explaining that, since the "reunification" of Bessarabia with the Soviet Union, the majority of Moldavians had been found to be illiterate. (32) In this context, one should not forget that it was the Russians who kept the Moldavians in a state of profound ignorance for a whole century, aiming, of course, at delaying their national awakening. Russian statistics of 1897 show that 89.5% of the Moldavian men and 98.3% of the women were illiterate. (33) The situation was somewhat improved during the 22 years of Romanian administration (1918–1940), thanks to the introduction of obligatory primary education and the construction of numerous elementary and secondary schools, for both Romanians and the minorities. (34) Nevertheless, in 1930, there were still many illiterate people (48.6% men and 74.9% women) particularly among those above 30 years of age who had been beyond school age in 1918 when Bessarabia was united with Romania. On the other hand, one should not forget that the Soviet Union could have formed an intellectual elite and leading cadres for Moldavia, in the schools of the Moldavian Autonomous Republic (1924–1940) and of the Moldavian Socialist Republic during more than three decades of Soviet domination. Instead, the Soviet Union continued to apply in Moldavia the same policy of discrimination which the tzars had inaugurated in Bessarabia, favoring admission to school of Russian and minority children. In 1959, the director of a Communist Party school declared before the Moldavian Central Committee that his school had instructed 4,800 functionaries, of whom 2,338 were recruited from among the local population. (35) The same policy was being applied in the other republics. Supporting his argument with statistics, Svyatoslav Yosypovych Karavansky (36) denounced the Russification of Ukrainian schools and requested the General Attorney of the Ukrainian Republic to bring judicial action the Minister of National Education for having infringed upon the principle of national equality. (37) The minister was not condemned, but Karavansky himself was. He received a sentence of eight years and seven months in a forced labor camp, in addition to his condemnation in 1945 to 25 years in prison as a result of the accusation of having acted as an agent for the Romanian secret service. (38)

Gheorghiţă, however, was content with his explanation, based on the shortage of Moldavian cadres, and was made even happier when the Soviet CC and the Kremlin sent a great number of industrial, agricultural and cultural specialists to Soviet Moldavia, as well as party cadres – qualified Russian, Ukrainian, Byelorussian and other employees and workers – for they were going to accomplish the "extraordinary feat of elevating" the level of Moldavian production and culture. Of the 627,000 Moldavian employees counted in 1965, only 264,000 were recruited from among the local population. (39) The flood of cadres imported from the Soviet Union, therefore, has attained a total of 363,000 persons, which reveals the magnitude of the effort invested in the Russification of the Moldavian administration. The number of Russian and other minorities employees is even greater if one takes into account the fact that many of the locally hired employees had to be Russian, Ukrainian, Bulgarian, etc.

In the Moldavian Republic, Moldavians find it very difficult to attain the envied position of government employee – the Russians are given priority. Bodyul furnished some information concerning the proportion of Moldavians in the national economy when he specified that only 30% of the specialists (i.e., 35,000 out of a total 113,000) were Moldavian, and that in the rural areas, where the Moldavians represent 75% of the population, the percentage of Moldavian kolkhoz heads was 54%. It should be noted that Bodyul's opinion was not different from Gheorghiţă's, since he found that these percentages were "high" and that those who demanded priority for the Moldavian national element were wrong, because a "free" exchange of cadres contributes to the economic progress of the republic. Justifying the Russification of his republic's administration with the argument of the shortage of qualified Moldavian cadres, the Moldavian leader was himself in error. The truth is that the Moldavians have hardly any access to public functions and when they do, they have to be satisfied with lower positions. A knowledgeable traveller, George Savor, found that at the Cahul Cellulose Plant, the director, the chief engineer, and the technicians were Russian, while the workers were Romanians and Ukrainians. (40) This discriminatory policy vis-à-

-vis the Moldavian population provoked the reaction of the indigenous population, which resents being kept from running its own affairs. The problem of the distribution of labor is a serious source of tension between the Moldavians of the one hand and the Russians and Ukrainians on the other. This tension will continue to grow as long as the Moldavians are treated as a colonized people.

The new employees brought from Russia are preferably installed in towns, which explains why the Russification of the urban area is ahead of the process in the villages. It is a known fact that towns have always been a powerful factor of denationalization – a phenomenon noted and condemned by Stalin in the very Ukraine where the towns were and remain strongly Russified. The Russification of towns is also to be found in the republics of Central Asia, where the Russians represent the preponderant element in the urban areas, which are constantly growing because of industrialization. In Soviet Moldavia, the progress of industrialization also facilitates the penetration of the Russian specialist into the countryside, through the installation of fruit, vegetable, and meat canneries producing for the whole of the USSR. Seventeen canneries were built in the center and south of the republic and five others appeared in the north, the latter situated in Florești, Camencea, Glodeni, Soroca and Edinița. (41)

The Russification of the countryside will be further facilitated if the project for the concentration of Moldavian villages is implemented. The plan is to concentrate, within the next 20 to 25 years, the 1,800 villages and hamlets of Moldavia into 880 rural centers, which would lend themselves better to administrative control and constraint. (42)

Mariage and Military Duty

The nationalities melting pot represented by towns and industrial centers favors mixed marriages between Russians and minorities and between the different minorities themselves. These unions, encouraged by official propaganda and by the Soviet authorities, should represent 102 per 1,000 for the whole of the Soviet Union, 158 per 1,000 in Latvia, 150 per 1,000 in the Ukraine, 144 per 1,000 in Kazakhstan, etc. (43) As the industrialization and urbanization of Soviet Moldavia progresses, the number of mixed marriages in the republic will grow and with it the Russification of Soviet Moldavia will advance to the satisfaction of the Kremlin. This method, too, is a legacy of the tzars, who used to send Moldavian recruits to Poland, to the Baltic provinces, to Russia itself, to the Caucasus, and even to Siberia. The young soldiers had to stay in those places three to four years, subjected to a severe military discipline and forced to listen to and speak only Russian. (44) In our own day, it emerges from letters sent to the Chișinău newspapers by Moldavian soldiers, that they are scattered throughout the Soviet Union, from the far north to the easternmost frontiers of Siberia. (45) The Russian Army could have avoided complications, deriving from the fact that many recruits do not speak Russian and bring with them their specific regional mentality, by adopting the territorial formations system with instructors using the local languages and respecting the customs of the land. But the Russian Army wants to be a unitary *national* army and to instill into soldiers not only military instruction, but also political education in the Russian language. It is a known fact that Russian instructors have had serious difficulties in instructing Turkmen soldiers. Now, Colonel V. Filonski, chief of the political section of the Moldavian Republic's Military Commissariat, complains of the trouble he is having with instructing Moldavian soldiers. He quotes the case of a soldier from Criuleni who refused to take the oath of allegiance because he had already sworn the oath to God. (46)

Deportations

Among the many efficacious and inhumane administrative methods used to denationalize an ethnic group, deportation occupies first place. Beginning in 1940, Bessarabia and its successor, Soviet Moldavia, have been the scene of heartrending human dramas, which still have to find a sensitive enough and informed chronicler to bring them to the attention of the world, as was done for the Tartars – with authority and courage – by General Piotr Grigorenko. (47)

Let us mention, however, the moving description of the deportation of Romanians from Northern Bucovina and their mishaps in Siberia by the peasant author Dumitru Nimigeanu. (48)

Lacking official statistics regarding the number of deportees, we shall make use of estimates advanced by various researchers. During the one-year occupation of Bessarabia (June 28,1940–June 22, 1941), the Soviets deported representatives of the local bourgeoisie, as well as persons who had played a political role in Romania. Alexandru Nicolae, and others along with them who have studied the problem, estimate 300,000 Romanian nationals were transferred from Bessarabia and Northern Bucovina to the north of the USSR during that period. (49) Calculating on the basis of Romanian statistics, we arrive at a different result. The statistics of 1938 showed Bessarabia to be inhabited by 1,758,000 Romanians. (50) In 1941, when Romania recovered the province, 1,793,493 Romanians were registered, *i.e.,* 35,493 more than before. The population growth figure for Bessarabia for the 1930–1938 period was 1.15% per annum. It follows that in 1941 the Romanian population of the province should have been roughly 1,820,000 people. The difference of some 25,000 is probably the number of Romanians deported during the period.

Population displacements also concern other ethnic groups inhabiting Bessarabia – notably the Jews and the Germans.

According to expert estimates, some 150.000 Jews left from Bessarabia and Northern Bucovina in 1941, before the German advance. (51) Approximately 50,000 of these fugitives died on the way, while 10,000 were later located in Siberia, where they had been deported. (52) Of the 126,000 Jews who remained in Bessarabia, 109,000 were deported to Transdniestria, of whom 54,500 perished there. This latter estimate corresponds more or less to the Soviet estimate (63,000) of the victims of Fascism in Bessarabia. (52) At the end of the war, approximately 90,000 Jews returned from the USSR to their homes. The 1941 Romanian census showed Bessarabia as having 6,882 Jews. The Soviet census of 1959 listed 95,107 Jews in Soviet Moldavia.

The Germans, another ethnic group of Bessarabia, completely disappeared during the Soviet occupation of 1940–41. Following the Russian-German agreement of September 5, 1940, 93,548 persons were repatriated to Germany, which explains why the Romanian census of 1941 listed only 2,050 Germans in Bessarabia. In this group of repatriates, there were several thousand persons of other nationalities, who managed to leave the Soviet Union as Germans. The repatriation of German nationals who had been partly Romanized, the extermination of more than 100,000 Jews, and the deportation of thousands of others, depleted Bessarabia and Northern Bucovina of more than 200,000 inhabitants. In their place, the province was colonized by Russians and Ukrainians to speed up the process of Russification.

The second wave of deportations began in August 1944, when the Soviets reoccupied Bessarabia and Northern Bucovina. This time, the victims were the "collaborationists" and the Moldavian "nationalists". The pretext, with which the authorities tried to justify this large-scale operation, was that the fascist invaders had left behind in the Soviet Union armed gangs of "nationalists and common criminals", in order to disorganize socialist reconstruction, carry on anti-Soviet propaganda, and terrorize the population. (53) It was further said that the Soviet authorities in the liberated regions had undertaken to fight these enemies, as well as the "nationalist-bourgeois" ideology, liquidating "banditism". It is very difficult, if not impossible, to establish the total number of Moldavians executed or deported during this period (1944–1955) in which the population was subjected to the harshest administrative measures. According to George Savor, 200,000 Moldavians and Ukrainians were executed, sentenced to hard labor, deported, or colonized between 1944 and 1947, under the accusation of having collaborated with the German Nazis, the Romanian "fascists" and the local boyars, or of having carried out anti-Soviet, counter-revolutionary propaganda. (54) Alexandru Nicolae considers it quite probable that a total of 250,000 Romanian civilians were deported during the 1944 – 1948 period. That figure includes the 50,000 Bessarabians who fled to Romania in 1941 and 1944, and who were repatriated by force when the Russians entered Romania, after the August 23, 1944 coup; the 60,000 political prisoners sent to concentration and extermination camps; the 20,000 civilians taken away by the Russians, etc. (55) Brezhnev, at the time First Secretary of the Moldavian CC (1951–1952), is said to personally have supervised the deportation of the quarter-million Moldavians. (56) This second wave of deportations seems to have been harder and more devastating than the first because it was no longer aimed at the "class enemy" alone, but at the nationalities of the Muscovite Empire. The Soviets, victors in the Second World War, now had more time to carry out their plans and showed no compassion for the vanquished. From time to time there would be announcements that yet another group of Moldavians had taken the road of exile.

In the night of July 5, 1949, no fewer than 25,000 Moldavians were deported from the towns of Bolgrad, Cetatea Alba, Izmail, and Chişinău (Kishenev) and were sent to Siberia and Kazakhstan. (57)

The third wave of deportations began in 1955. It was less brutal, but just as effective as the first two. This time, the blow fell on the peasants. The reason then invoked was the economic necessity of working the wastelands of Siberia. The deportation of Moldavian peasants, euphemistically called "a planned transfer of labor" was carried out in apparently attractive conditions, designed to lure "volunteers" to the colonization of Siberia. Those who "volunteered" enjoyed free transportation to their new place of residence and could take with them up to two tons of belongings per family. They received 500 to 800 rubles in cash per family head and 150 to 300 for each other member; they were exempt from agricultural taxation and from obligatory deliveries to the state for the first two years, and could obtain credits repayable in ten years for the construction of their houses and in five years for the purchase of cattle. (58)

A very similar attempt to attract Moldavian peasants to Siberia, the Caucasus, the region of Amur and Turkestan had already been made in the days of the tzars, when colonists were promised 55 to 110 hectares of land, free transportation, exemption from taxation and provision of agricultural equipment. (59)

The Soviet credit of 2,000 rubles for the construction of a house proved wholly inadequate. And even those colonists who had enough money of their own to build a new home could not do so because construction materials were not available. As for the 150 rubles for the purchase of cattle, that kind of money was just enough for a suit and a pair of shoes. (60) Yet, many must have left their native province for the faraway kolkhoses of Astrakhan, Rostov, or Pavlodar, pushed to it by the misery reigning in Bessarabia and enticed at the same time by the hope that administrative control would be more relaxed in the distant regions being colonized.

The aim of this new form of disguised deportation was not purely economic, because, while Moldavians were sent to Astrakhan, Rostov, and Kazakhstan, inhabitants of these regions emigrated to Moldavia. (61) It is difficult to explain this population exchange by maintaining the Moldavians were better at working the soil of Kazakhstan than that of Bessarabia and that the Kazakhs were more productive in Moldavia than their native regions. The purpose of the planned transfer of Moldavian peasants was none other than to reduce the number of Moldavians in Moldavia, in the general framework of the Soviet nationalities policy based on the disaggregation of ethnic groups (Balts, Caucasians, Asians, etc.). A look at the list of the Moldavian districts favored for the recruiting of "volunteers" for deportation shows that the choice went to the most Romanian regions of orhei, Soroca, Lăpuşna and to the south of the district of Hotin which had been left to the Moldavian Republic.

The tzars had proceeded in the same manner to reduce the native element. Colonists were being recruited from Ataki (Atachi; Hotin), Beltzi (Beltsy; Bălţi), Bravitchy (Bravicea; Orhei), Britchansk (Briceni; Hotin), Grodiansk (Glodeni; Bălţi), Drokien (Drochia: Soroca), Iedinetz (Ediniţa; Hotin), Zgouritz (Zguriţa; Soroca), Kalavach (Călăraşi; Lăpuşna), Korpensk (Cărpineni; Lăpuşna), Kishinev (Chişinău; Lăpuşna), Notovsk (Hânceşti; Bălţi), Kotienpansk (Coşeni; Bălţi), Oknitz (Ocniţa; Hotin), Nisporiensk (Nisporeni; Lăpuşna), Resnik (Rezine; Orhei), Soroki (Soroca; Soroca), Strachensk (Străşeni; Lăpuşna), Souslensk (Susleni; Orhei) and Tyrnow (Tarnova; Soroca).

On April 14, 1955, Anton Crihan, former member of *Sfatul Ţării* (the parliament which had voted in 1918 for the Union of Bessarabia with Romania), protested to the Assembly of Captive Nations against the planned deportation of the Moldavian population. (62) The Assembly of Captive Nations brought the problem to the attention of the United Nations, and the UN, in its turn, informed all its delegations, as well as the State Department. Similarly, the Romanians living in the West denounced before the world the deportation of the Moldavian population and demanded an immediate end to the process. (63) The experience of the Tartars had already shown that the pressure of public opinion exerted on the Kremlin did not alleviate the fate of the deportees, but rather aggravated it. (64) The Kremlin did not show any sign of relenting in the case of the Moldavians, the deportation of Romanian peasants resumed with a vengeance between 1960 and 1963. This time, the pretext was the need to amalgamate the numerous middle-sized Moldavian kolkhozes into 650 large kolkhozes and 72 sovkhozes.

On the occasion of this agrarian reorganization, thousands of peasants had to choose between the integration of their possessions – land, cattle, equipment – in the giant new agricultural units, where they would lose all claim to independent living, and emigration to Siberia, where they were promised land, houses, credit, and a freer life. A communiqué published in the daily *Moldova Socialistă (Socialist Moldavia)* on January 29, 1965 sought to convince the peasants to participate in the development of Kazakhstan. In reality, the final destination of the new deportees was not only the Kazakh republic, but also the Amur region and Sakhalin Island. (65) Some peasants took the bait, particularly as the authorities exerted all sorts of pressures on them to make them leave Moldavia (heavy taxation, obligatory deliveries of agricultural produce, labor participation in public projects). It is believed that, this time, the peasants left Moldavia at a rate of 100,000 per year, totaling in all 300,000. (66) Once the country's economic reorganization was accomplished, the departure of colonists slowed down, particularly as the news from Siberia showed that the life of a "mamalishnik" (Polenta-eater) in Moldavia was preferable to the life of a colonist in Siberia. However, up until 1965 the Soviet authorities continued to publish advertisements for emigration to the region of Pavlodar in the Moldavian Press. (67)

The fourth wave of deportations was unleashed in 1964 and was directed particularly toward the Moldavian intelligentsia. The graduates from Moldavian colleges, institutes, and universities were scattered throughout the Soviet Union, in the Urals, Central Asia, and the Far East. Those who refused the jobs they were assigned lost the right to exercise their profession and became unqualified workers. At the same time, the regime transferred to Soviet Moldavia Russian doctors, lawyers, pharmacists, engineers, technicians, economists, etc. Many expatriated Romanian intellectuals married Russians, settled far from their republic, and ended by being assimilated by the Russians. The Russians transferred to Soviet Moldavia, on the contrary, formed themselves into the local intelligentsia and strongly contributed to the Russification of the republic.

Finally, there was a fifth form of deportation, that of young Moldavians dispatched to various so-called youth *gantries* for "voluntary" labor. Let us mention, as an example, the 3,000 young Moldavians who worked at Tavda-Sotnik, in the region of Tyumen, building a railway, while others were constructing the automobile works Togliatti, on the Volga, labored in the Barnaul tyre factory, or in the tractor plant of Pavlodar. (68)

The grand total of Moldavian deportees was evaluated by Alexandru Nicolae at 1,000,000. At first glance, one could believe that this is a Romanian exaggeration, but an approximate calculation on the basis of Soviet and Romanian statistics seems to confirm this figure. The counting is difficult, because of the many administrative reorganizations of Bessarabia, but one can arrive at realistic conclusions by studying the Moldavian demographic dynamics in the Ukraine and Soviet Moldavia. The Romanian census of 1930 shows that some 460,000 Moldavians inhabited the districts of Bessarabia and Bucovina later to be incorporated into the Ukraine – 72,000 in Izmail; 62,949 in Cetatea-Albă; 81,691 in Hotin (without the district of Briceni, which remained in the Moldavian Socialist Republic); 78,589 in Cernăuți; 57,595 in Storojineț; 45,000 were half of the population of the Department of Rădăuți, divided between Romania and the

Ukraine; and 61,804 in the district of Herţa. (69) Considering that the index of Bessarabian demographic growth for the 1930 –1938 period was 1.15% per annum, it follows that the number of Romanians annexed by the Ukraine in 1940 was about 500,000. The Soviet census of 1926 shows that two Moldavian groups already existed in the Ukraine – one on the left bank of the Dniester, of 172,419 people, and another scattered throughout the rest of the Ukraine.

The Russian census of 1897 showed that, at that time, the latter Moldavian group comprised 147,801 people at Kherson, 8,453 at Ekaterinoslav (Dnepropetrovsk), 2,895 in Taurida, etc. According to more modest estimates, in 1926 this group contained a total of 257,794 Moldavians. (70) At a rate of growth of 1.15% per annum, one should arrive at an approximate total of 500,000 in 1940. One can conclude, therefore, that some 1,000,000 Moldavians lived in the Greater Ukraine of 1940 – 500,000 in the territories annexed by the USSR in June 1940, and 500,000 dispersed. Calculating with the same index of growth of 1.15% per year, 1,000,000 Moldavian-Romanians should have become 1,243,000 by 1959. But the Soviet census of 1959 showed 342,000 inhabitants for this territory: 100,863 Romanians, and only 241,650 Moldavians – 204,000 in the oblasts odesskaya (Odessa), Chernovitskaya (Cernăuţi) and Kirovogradskaya (Kirovograd), 12,200 in the Ukainian, industrial oblast of Donets, where they had been deported to work in the mines; and another 25,450 scattered in unspecified areas. The salient fact emerging from this evidence is the absence of some 900,000 Moldavians, probably deported from Southern Bessarabia and Northern Bucovina with a view to changing the ethnic structure of those provinces.

A different reckoning permits the verification of this result for the entire territory inhabited by Moldavians in the USSR. In 1940 the total number of these Moldavians was approximately 2,520,000, *i.e.*, 2,020,000 surrendered by Romania to the USSR in Bessarabia and Northern Bucovina (72), and 500,000 living in Autonomous Moldavia and in the Ukraine. A Moldavian population of 2,500,000, with a demographic growth of 1.15% per annum, should have given a total of 3,075,000 in 1959. But the Soviet census of 1959 shows 2,229,081 Moldavian-Romanians, of whom 1,886,566 were in Soviet Moldavia and 342,515 in the Ukraine. Some 846,000 people are missing.

The figure proposed by Alexandru Nicolae seems, therefore, to be confirmed, with the specification that the deportation hit the Moldavians living in the regions annexed by the Ukraine particularly hard. The number of deportees who perished on their way to Siberia, travelling in cattle cars, without food and water, exposed to the elements and disease, cannot be established. Neither do we know how many of those who arrived at their destinations survived the conditions prevailing in the forced labor camps, in a hostile climate, deprived of medical care. In the same regions, the result of colonization by the tzars was, according to Russian sources: "long rows of graves". (72) The Tartars of the Crimea say they have lost, following their deportation and the first two years of hardship in Uzbekistan, 46.3% of their people. (73) If one applied this percentage to the Moldavians, one would have to assume that 392,000 Moldavians died as a result of the deportations. Where the 454,000 remaining Moldavians are continues to be an open question. The Soviet census of 1959 tells us that 62,200 Moldavians lived in unspecified centers of the Russian Republic and that another concentration of Moldavians, 15,000 strong, lives in Kazakhstan. The remaining Moldavians, scattered in the various Soviet republics, are not mentioned in official statistics. Occasionally, sporadic information regarding the fate of surviving deportees filters through. Thus, an article on the Moldavian linguistic map tells us that the purest Moldavian language was found by the authors not only at 168 spots in the Moldavian Republic, but also in 24 towns and villages of the Odessa region (therefore, Southern Bessarabia), 19 places in the Cernăuți region (Northern Bucovina), 4 in the region of Nikolaev, 1 in Dniepropetrovsk, 1 in Lugansk (Voroshilovgrad), 2 in Donetsk, 1 in Zaporozhye, and 5 in Kirovograd. (74) But the dispersion of Moldavians goes beyond the neighboring Ukraine, where the above-mentioned places are situated, because the linguistic inquiry was taken as far as the Russian, Kazakh, and Kirghiz Soviet Socialist Republics. The places in question are situated in the following republics, regions, and districts: Abkhaz 1; Krasnodar 2; Omsk 2; Aktyubinsk 2; Primorsk 8; and Frunze 1. In Primorsk, there is a large Romanian colony, consisting of eight villages situated near the Chinese border, to which the Soviet regime continues to invite Moldavians, promising them all sorts of advantages. (75)

Here we find, therefore, Moldavians entrusted with the mission of defending the eastern frontier of the USSR against the Chinese threat! The Moldavian language was preserved in these villages in its purest form, because of the isolation of the area, situated far from all modern means of communication. A Romanian linguist, finding that Romanian is spoken today in Zaporozhye, in the Caucasus, in Turkestan and in Vladivostok, concluded that the dislocation of "Romania" begun in the third century, has not ended and that a Far Eastern "Romania" was constituted on the territory of the Soviet Union. (76) As a matter of fact, the formation of the Far Eastern "Romania" began a long time ago, with the descent of Romanian shepherds from the Carpathian Mountains toward the Black Sea, the Dobrogea and the Crimea. In this folk movement, they arrived at the Sea of Azov, pushed on toward the Caucasus, the Caspian Sea, and the trans-Caspian steppes. This migration with the herds was the basis for Romanian agricultural colonization beyond the Dniester. (77) In the 19th century, Romanian colonists dispersed throughout Russia were strengthened by the flow of Moldavians deported in the days of the tzars to Siberia, Turkestan, the Amur Region, the Caucasus, and the Urals. (78)

Another important movement of Moldavian deportees to Siberia occurred after the revolution of 1905. (79) Victor Buescu (80) identified pure Moldavian villages between the Urals and the Altai Mountains; in the region of Orenburg and Turgai (Turkestan) 32,000 Moldavian families were settled before the First World War. In addition to the Romanians of the Austro-Hungarian Army captured by the Russians in the First World War, the many Romanian prisoners of the Second World War and the deportees of Stalin, Khrushchev, and Brezhnev have strenghthened the Romanian element in Asia to the point where one can speak today of the Romanians of Asia as a linguistic reality. Buescu mentioned among the Romanian villages in Asia: Berdyansk, Abjarsk, Orkheievka (founded by the inhabitants of Orhei), as well as villages situated in the neighborhood of Samarkand, Omsk, and Akmolink. One can still find Romanian settlements in the region of Tomsk and in eastern Siberia, in the vicinity of Irkutsk, as is the case with Ceremhovo, founded by the peasants of Soroca, Hotin and Tighina, or with the settlements north of Vladivostok and in the Ussuri Valley, bearing Romanian names like: Teiul, Zâmbreni, Bogatârca, Chişinovca, Bălcineşti, Dunai (Dunărea), Basarabia Nouă, Logăneşti, Timofeievca, Alexeievca, Tritiacova, and so forth. These villages are inhabited by some 30,000 Romanians, cattle raisers and producers of a famous Wallachian cheese known locally as "Moldovanskij syr." Finally, the same author informs us of the existence of another Romanian-Siberian center, situated near Khabarovsk and the group of villages called Inul, Aur, and Dunărea, whose inhabitants live from fishing. Many Moldavian fishermen work in the collective fisheries of the Pacific coast, while 20,000 farmers have settled in Manchuria. To these Romanian centers in Siberia, listed by V. Buescu, let us add an important group of Moldavian peasants working in the forests of the Arkhangelsk (Archangel) region. (81)

When one considers the immensity of the Euro-Asian space sown with islets of Moldavian deportees, their survival to this day suggests the collapse of the Soviet system in less than a generation. Indeed, the continuing policy of deporting Moldavians, inaugurated by the tzars and perpetuated by the Soviets, doggedly pursues its implacable aim of diminishing the number and the strength of Moldavians in Soviet Moldavia – or, to be exact, Bessarabia – in order to facilitate their Russification and to condemn the deported Moldavians to a slow, but sure Russification.

Colonization

The conquest of many peoples and foreign territories, be it under the tzars or under communism, poses the problem of governing the world's largest empire. Marx, Engels, and even Lenin denounced Russian colonialism as the peak of hypocrisy and cynicism, because it used noble language in order to deceive, dominate, and exploit other nations. Instead of confirming this condemnation expressed by the founders of communism, the Soviet regime chose to rehabilitate the imperialist and colonialist ideology of the tzars, seeking to consolidate and modernize the Russian empire which became, for the sake of the cause, the Union of the Soviet Socialist Republics. One can say today, like W. Kolarz, that Soviet power depends on the success of the policy of colonization. (82) The cohesion of the Soviet empire is maintained by means of Great-Russian imperialism, of union around the idea of the special mission of the Russian nation which places itself in the center of and above the peoples to be colonized. Russian colonialism differs from the old British and French forms, because it undertakes to assimilate the conquered peoples. Beginning with 1928, the Soviet regime inaugurated a policy of planned colonization, aimed in the first place at the populations of the Urals, Eastern Russia, Siberia, and Central Asia.

Industrialization facilitated Russification, because the new urban centers became focal points for the assimilation of the non-Russian peoples. Industrial colonization was soon joined by agricultural colonization, meaning an army of peasants and youth dispatched to reinforce the Russian element in the militarily vital regions.

The first wave of Soviet colonists emerged in Soviet Moldavia with the arrival of government and party cadres: activists, secret police, control bureaus, army units, military garrisons, etc. As the majority of the employees had left for Romania or had been deported by the province's new masters, the implantation of the new Soviet administration was massive and fast.

The second wave of colonization took place between 1946 and 1953, when 250,000 were transferred to Soviet Moldavia to replace the Moldavian "collaborationists" and "nationalists" who had been deported to the Soviet Union. Seeking to give a more pronounced Slavic character to Moldavia, these colonists were recruited mainly from the Slavic nations of the empire, from among the Great-Russians, Ukrainians, Ruthenians, with a net predominance of Russians from Tambov, Saratov, Voronezh and Smolensk. (83)

In a third phase (1954 – 1959), thousands of demobilized soldiers were settled in Moldavia, where they were given the houses abandoned by the deportees, jobs, credits, and various other advantages. To accelerate the change in Bessarabia's ethnic structure, the new colonists were encouraged to marry Moldavian women. This time, the colonists had been recruited not only from among Slavs, but also from among the Turkoman nationalities – Tartars, Bashkirs, Chuvaks. (84)

The new colonists found in Soviet Moldavia the descendants of the colonists lured there by the tzars who had offered them the following advantages and facilities: 66 hectares of arable land per family, free timber for the construction of a house, long-term credits, and exemption from military service. Tzarist colonization was multinational – which explains the variegated character of the Bessarabian population. Many of these colonists (Lipovans, Jews, Bulgarians, Gagauzs) had sought refuge from religious persecutions. Others, the Russian peasants, Germans, etc., had escaped serfdom or had come to Bessarabia in search of more land than they possessed at home. All arrived in the hope of finding in Bessarabia an oasis of peace – many were disappointed.

The most prosperous among them, the Germans, who arrived in 1822 and 1835 from Bavaria, Württemberg, and Switzerland, disappeared from Moldavian soil. Besides the colonists in search of more land, there were French and Swiss veterans who remained in Russia after Napoleon's 1812 campaign and even mystics, who, frightened by the doomsday predictions of Pietist preacher Bengel, had stopped in Bessarabia on their way to heaven. (85) These colonists settled in the south of Bessarabia and founded villages bearing strange names which recalled Napoleonic battles or their religious preoccupations: Paris (capitulations of 1814 and 1815), Arciz (Arcis-sur Aube, the bloody battle of March 1, 1814), Leipzig (the battle of 1813), Borodino (the Battle of Moscow –September 7, 1812), Berezina (crossing of the river between 26th and 29th November 1812), Chelmno «Kulm» (defeat of General Vandamme – August 29–30, 1813), Brienne (Brienne-le-Château – French victory of January 29, 1814), Strasbourg, Luxembourg, FerşampenuazMare and Ferşampenuaz-Mic (from Fère-Champenoise), Gnadenfeld, Friedens-tahl, Friedensfeld, etc. Many model farms thus appeared in the Cetatea-Albă district, where the land was cultivated according to modern methods of agriculture by the colonists whom the Romanians considered "their best children". (86) In 1941, however, these colonists disappeared faster than they had come, leaving behind abandoned farms and villages, proof of how ephemeral the achievements of colonization are irrespective of its value and in spite of having lasted more than a century.

Another ethnic group, that of the Jews, had a tragic destiny. In fleeing the Russian persecutions and pogroms, many Jews had believed that Bessarabia would become for them a new Promised Land. (87) Initially, they easily acquired the right (which had been refused them in Russia) to settle in towns on an equal basis with the Russian citizenry. Their number grew rapidly from 19,130 in 1817 to 267,000 in 1919. The 1930 census and the 1940 estimates based on it showed that 204,858 Jews lived in Bessarabia (1930) and 247,000 in the entire territory surrendered to the USSR in 1940. (88) These figures were underestimates, because many Jews declared themselves to be Russians. Within the interval of a year, they disappeared almost completely from Bessarabia, where, in 1941 we find only 6,882 Jews. A great part of them returned later and, in 1970, there were 98,000 Jews in Soviet Moldavia, (89) half of whom (42,934 in 1959) lived in Chişinău. (90) The fate of the Bessarabian Jews is related to that of the Soviet Jews, whom the Kremlin wants to have assimilated at any price. The Soviet census of 1970 showed that the number of Jews in the USSR had decreased from 2,268,000 in 1959, to 2,151,000, *i.e.*, by 5% in 11 years, as a result of forced Russification. In Soviet Moldavia their number has slightly increased: 95,000 in 1959, 98,000 in 1970. They seemed fated to stagnation and Russification, however, despite the fact that their strong national sentiment seems to withstand the powerful administrative pressures to which they are being subjected.

The third ethnic group of Bessarabia is that of the Turkomans: Gagauzs, Tartars, Bashkirs and Chuvaks. The Gagauzs, probable descendants of the Cumans, are an extremely religious people who settled in Bessarabia at the beginning of the 19th century, coming from Bulgaria to which they had fled from Ottoman persecution. In Bessarabia, they succeeded not only in keeping their language and religion, but also in augmenting their number from 1,205 in 1817, when they represented 0.25% of the population, to 115,683 in 1941, 96,000 in 1959 and 125,000 or 3.50% of the population in 1970. These two last statistics do not include those Gagauzs inhabiting the southern districts of Bessarabia, incorporated into the Ukraine. Their national identity was sanctioned by the Fifth Congress of Soviet Writers which, at the beginning of July 1971, mentioned the birth of a new literature, that of the Gagauzs.

The position of the Gagauzs was strengthened by the arrival of new Turkoman colonists – the Tartars, Bashkirs and Chuvaks. The Gagauzs and the Chuvaks have the best chances to understand each other, since both peoples represent a branch of the Christian Turkomans (except for a Chuvak faction which remained pagan). The Chuvaks were transplanted to Bessarabia from the Upper Volga – *i.e.,* from a region which Moscow has been trying to Russify since the days of the tzars. The Bashkirs came from a region south of the Urals also subjected to forced Russification. Indeed, in 1905, no fewer that 180,000 Russian colonists invaded the Bashkir lands, starting a colonizing effort which continues to this day. Finally, the Tartars came from the Volga and Ural regions, in the wake of their ancestors, whom Suleiman the Magnificent had led into the Bugeac, the south of Bessarabia. The Tartars belong to that group of minorities which are most persecuted in the USSR, their Autonomous Republic of the Crimea having been dissolved in 1944 and its population deported to Uzbekistan. The 1970 census does not show the number of Turkomans living in Soviet Moldavia; it included them under the general denomination "other nationalities", which totaled 47,000 inhabitants. It is likely that a greater number of Turkomans were settled in southern Bessarabia which today belongs to the Ukraine, for in 1970 this republic comprised 758,000 inhabitants of other nationalities. Because of their numbers and economic and cultural activity, the Turkomans represent the most important minority in the Soviet Union, and have a national consciousness of their own and moral concepts fundamentally opposed to Communist ideology. There is no doubt that the Tartars, Bashkirs and Chuvaks dream of leaving Soviet Moldavia and the south of Bessarabia, in order to return to their lost lands. This may happen one day, for their ethnic group demonstrates unique vitality. The Turkomans of Central Asia augmented their numbers by 52% in the period between 1959 and 1970. In the same period, the Russian population grew in the same regions by 13%, this percentage including, besides births, the flow of new colonists arriving from Russia. (91) There are, therefore, chances that the Turkomans of Soviet Moldavia will successfully resist Russification. Their resistance promises to be facilitated if they join the indigenous population in the fight against Moscow's policy of general assimilation.

The most powerful group colonizing Soviet Moldavia is that of the Slavs: Russians, Ukrainians, and Bulgarians – amounting to some 1,000,000 inhabitants out of a total of 3,569,000. The Bulgarians form a sort of connecting link between the Turkomans and the Slavs, being of Turkoman origin, but using the Slav language and being of the Cristian faith. They are related to the Chuvaks, the Bulgarian branch of whom remained on the banks of the Volga when the Protobulgarians left those regions and went to settle, in the seventh century, between the Dniester, the Danube, and the Black Sea. The Bulgarians of today's Soviet Moldavia, 74,000 of them, representing 2.07% of the population, returned to Moldavian lands more recently, in the 19th century, when they crossed from Dobrogea (then under Turkish domination) into Bessarabia, fleeing Otoman persecution. During their 124 years' stay in Bessarabia, their numbers multiplied by a factor of 145, from 1,205 in 1817, to 177,647 in 1941. Normally, one could have discussed the complete transfer to Bulgaria of the Bulgarian population living in Romania on the occasion of the signing of the Craiova Treaty (1940), when southern Dobrogea was surrendered to Bulgaria. However, at the time of the Craiova Treaty, Bessarabia no longer belonged to Romania. Today, the Bulgarian population of Soviet Moldavia is less important than it was in Bessarabia (74,000 inhabitants in 1970 in Soviet Moldavia, as compared to 177,647 in 1941 in Bessarabia), because an important group of Bulgarians inhabit the south of Bessarabia, now belonging to the Ukraine. The grand total of the Bulgarians living in the Ukraine is 234,000. The Bulgarian population of Soviet Moldavia is growing at a slower pace than the other nationalities and today represents 2.07% of the population, as compared to 2.15% in 1959. Used as an auxiliary factor of Russification in the past, the Bulgarians were treated by the Russians as a most favored minority, and managed to preserve their language and traditions, but lost, in the administrative reorganization of Bessarabia, their former role and importance.

The Ukrainians of Soviet Moldavia constitute the most important minority of the province. Their number rose in 1970 to 507,000. The Ukrainians are the only minority coming from a land adjacent to Bessarabia. This means that the danger of the Ukrainization of Moldavia is real, more so since the Ukraine is one of the

Soviet Union's most important republics, both from the economic and the demographic standpoints. The Ukrainian people have shown a powerful national sentiment and civil courage every time they were put to the test and it was an error that neither the First World War nor the Second put an end to the servitude of the Ukraine, through the creation of an independent national state which the Ukrainian people have never ceased to desire. This great people must content itself with the role of a junior partner to Russia which, on one hand, carries on a merciless policy of Russification against the Ukrainians of the Ukraine and the Russian Republic, and, on the other, uses the Ukrainians for the Slavization of Crimea, Kazakhstan, and Soviet Moldavia. In the framework of this policy, the Ukraine was granted in 1940 the south and the north of Bessarabia, as well as Northern Bucovina, and in 1954 the Tartar oblast of the Crimea, undertaking in exchange to participate in the colonization of eastern Siberia and northern Kazakhstan. By resorting to this type of territorial carousel, the Great Russians aim at the Slavization of the Tartars, Kazakhs and Moldavians, at the same time using these three peoples against the Ukrainians, in order to remain, alone, the final beneficiaries of this policy of division.

Tzarist, Romanian, and Soviet statistics all show that the number of Ukrainians is growing continually, both in Bessarabia and in Soviet Moldavia. In Bessarabia, they rose from 30,000 in 1812 to 669,542 in 1941 (a 22-fold increase in 129 years). In Soviet Moldavia, the Ukrainians increased in number from 421,000 in 1959 to 507,000 in 1970, a growth of 86,000 in 11 years. The Moldavians and the Ukrainians, neighboring peoples, mix spontaneously. Large numbers of Moldavians live on the Ukrainian side of the Dniester and can be found on the Bug and Dnieper, while the Ukrainians have salients into Bessarabia – particularly in the departments of Hotin, Cetatea-Albă, and Northern Bucovina. At the citizen's level, the Moldavians and the Ukrainians lived and still live in harmony in the mixed villages, where the Moldavians have been Ukrainianized and the Ukrainians Romanized.

The same good understanding marked Romanian-Ukrainian relations during the short period of Ukrainian independence. on June 26, 1919, "Rada" of Kiev, the Ukrainian Parliament, unequivocally recognized the Union of Bessarabia with Romania: "The Ukrainian government declares that it does not wish in any way to bring into discussion the present border between the two states and considers the Dniester to be the final frontier; it wishes to establish better neighborly relations along this border." (92) Unlike the unjust Curzon Line which was used to mark in 1923 Poland's eastern border, the Dniester frontier coincides with ethnic reality, the number of Ukrainians inhabiting Bessarabia equaling the number of Moldavians living in the Ukraine. In 1930, there were approximately 577,000 Ukrainians and Ruthenians in Romania, to balance the almost 500,000 Romanians in the Ukraine. Those who dreamt of creating pure national states in a region of such ethnic interpenetration as Central and Eastern Europe could see no fulfilment of their vision except through the transfer of the Transdniestrian Romanians to Bessarabia and of the Bessarabian Ukrainians to the Ukraine – a senseless operation, since the two peoples concerned coexist in the best spirit of understanding.

After the Second World War, some concessions were made to the Ukraine, to satisfy the national feelings of a nation which had manifested its desire for independence through the formation of a government (1941) and of a national committee (1944) of its own and whose partisans had fought both the Germans and the Russians. The Ukraine, therefore, expanded its borders and became the Greater Ukraine, at the expense of Poland, Romania, and Hungary. It became a member of the United Nations and had the satisfaction of seeing a Ukrainian, P. Ye. Shelest, occupy the position of the First Secretary of the Ukrainian Communist Party. It also took its revenge on the Russians, when another Ukrainian, Khrushchev, became First Secretary of the Communist Party of the USSR. The Ukrainians, however, have not forgotten the confession of Khrushchev, that they had barely escaped the Stalinist deportations, simply because they were too numerous and he had not found enough space to settle them forcibly elsewhere. (93) They know that a reversal of Soviet policy is always possible, that they are always threatened by Russification, in danger of being sent to colonize the Soviet Union's eastern frontier and face the Chinese threat. The Ukraine, too, aspires to self-determination under a Western type, democratic regime as advocated by Taras Shevchenko or under a worker-and-peasant regime like the one proposed by Trotsky. (94)

The latest manifestation in favor of an independent Ukraine dates from 1960 when a Ukrainian opposition "party", active within the Soviet Union, had the courage to criticize the imperialist and chauvinistic policy of Soviet Russia and to demand the segregation of the Ukraine, which was to be formed into a socialist and independent state. (95) The Ukrainian people, who had managed to survive 300 years of Russian domination, the forceful collectivization of its lands, Stalinist terror, the deportation of its peasants and intellectuals, the arrest and purge of its Communist cadres, etc., seems difficult to Russify and is disinclined to play the thankless role of a "Russifier" to other nationalities. A tacit understanding between the peoples of the Ukraine and Moldavia, who are equally threatened by Russian imperialism, would help them both to preserve their national identities.

The essence of the problem of Russification of the Moldavians is reduced, therefore, to the conflict between the Romanian nation and the Great-Russian nation. Bessarabia and Soviet Moldavia are merely the battlefields of the confrontation between the Moldavians – the avant-garde of the Romanian nation – and the Great-Russian colonizing imperialism, strengthened by some ethnic groups of the Soviet Empire. The confrontation between Russian imperialism and Romanian nationalism, understood as the right of the Romanians to preserve their own identity, occurs under abnormal circumstances. On the one hand, Russia and the Russian people have no common border with Romania and use the Ukrainians as an instrument for their policy; on the other hand, the Romanian authorities lack the courage and the means openly to oppose the policy of forced assimilation of the Bessarabian Romanians, because, as communists, they feel bound to accept the policy set by Moscow.

A look at the Soviet census statistics of 1959 and 1970 tells us that the Russification of Soviet Moldavia is progressing, because the percentage of Russians grew from 10.16% to 11.6%, while those of other nationalities decreased as follows: Romanians from 65.41% to 64.56%; Ukrainians from 14.59% to 14.21%, Jews from 3.29% to 2.75%, and Bulgarians from 2.15% to 2.07%. During a period of 11 years (1959–1970), the growth of the Russian population in Soviet Moldavia was 41.3%, while the comparable process did not surpass 8% in the Russian Federal Republic. The Russian demographical jump in Soviet Moldavia – from 293,000 inhabitants in 1959 to 414,000 in 1970 – is not simply due to births; it is mostly due to immigration.

When the Russians got hold of Bessarabia, in 1812, they were represented in the province by 6,000 souls, mainly Lipovans belonging to the sect of the Old Believers who had rejected the ritual reform proposed by Patriarch Nikon. Part of the Old Believers had found in Moldavia the religious freedom which was denied them in Russia until 1971, when the new Patriarch Pimen was elected. It was proposed then that the excommunication pronounced upon them in 1656 and again in 1667 be rescinded. (96) Soviet sources admitted unequivocally that, after the annexation of Bessarabia, Moscow began the colonization and Russification of the province: "Nachdem Bessarabien mit Russland vereinigt worden war, wurde es rasch besiedelt. Hierher strömten die Ukrainer und russische Umsiedler." (97)

The number of Russians, employees and simple colonists grew rapidly, attaining the figure of 155,774 in 1897 (8.05%) and 164,410 in 1941 (6%). Yet, the effect of the forced Russification practiced under the tzars was superficial. It was barely noticed in the spoken language, where only a few Russian words had been introduced, mainly in the administrative and ecclesiastical vocabularies. One should mention the disappearance of the national dress of the peasants (except in the Hotin region and certain villages on the Pruth) but these changes had not in the least affected the Moldavian national consciousness.

The Soviet regime continues its policy of Russification in the territories annexed in Europe and in the Asian republics, for purely political reasons. It does so in spite of the slackening of the Russian population growth and against the advice of economists and sociologists, who draw attention to the saturation of the labor market in the colonized regions and to the shortage of labor on the Russian-Ukrainian market, which provides the colonists. Despite the intensive

Russification of Soviet Moldavia during the last three decades, the ethnic composition of the republic has not been profoundly changed – the Moldavians continue to represent the absolute majority of the population (2,304,000 inhabitants, or 64.56%, of a total of 3,569,000). Taking into account the fact that the Russian people is beginning to show signs of demographic fatigue, one can hope that Moscow will not be able to carry on its policy of colonization and Russification together on both the European and Asian fronts, that the colonized peoples, the Baltic, Turkoman, Kazakh, Tartar, Uzbek, Moldavian, etc., will take their revenge demographically, surpassing in number the invaders, in order finally to assimilate them. Thus, Moscow, the Third Rome, would be sharing the fate of the first Rome, which spent itself in trying to colonize conquered regions and collapsed just when it seemed to have attained its goal.

Language and Culture

The policy of Russification did not rely exclusively on the brutal means of denationalization, like deportations, colonization, and administrative pressure. It also used more subtle ways, such as substituting the Russian language, culture, and living style for the culture, customs, and civilization of the colonized peoples. History teaches us that nations which begin to ignore their own language and finally abandon it are about to disappear. In the days of the tzars, Bessarabia passed the test of the preservation of the Romanian language with flying colors and for more than a century kept it alive and without fundamental alteration.

Beginning in 1843 the Romanian language was forbidden in the administration and banned from all schools in 1871. (98) However, the peasants continued to speak Romanian (Moldavian), while the intellectuals – such as the poet Al. Mateevici (1888–1917) – treasured their national language as the most precious possession of the Moldavian people. In the end, it was Moldavian, not Russian, that became the language of communication between the various ethnic groups of Bessarabia. (99) This fact is recognized even by Russian intellectuals, such as Buttovich. (100)

The Soviet regime allowed the use of national idioms for practical reasons. In the first place, because one could not eliminate the national languages overnight without provoking grave reaction. Besides, communist propaganda was easier to disseminate among members of ethnic groups in their own languages. The regime started, however, a vast project to Russify national languages and, furthermore, to achieve the linguistic unification of all the peoples of the empire. Beginning in 1936, Russian became a compulsory subject in all secondary schools of the Soviet Union. It dominated party life, economic and administrative activity, trade, the press, radio broadcasts. After Bessarabia's 1941 and 1944 annexations, Russian established itself as the master language.

Moldavian (Romanian) – the only Latin language of the empire – was already being used in the Moldavian Autonomous Republic, where it had been submitted to a sophisticated process of Russification. Thus, Romanian begins to be described as Moldavian and is isolated from the language spoken in Romania. Romanists, however, are unanimous of the opinion that Romanian is a unitary language to the extent that one cannot speak of Moldavian as being even a dialect. At most, one can distinguish, in the region situated between the eastern Carpathians and the Dniester, a different pronounciation of certain vowels, the palatization of labials and a small number of lexical peculiarities. The thankless task of creating a Moldavian language as distinct from Romanian was assigned to "Moldavian" philologists, but their attempts were fruitless. The *Moldavian Grammar* of 1930, written by L. A. Madan of Tiraspol, was an attempt to create an artificial language, inventing words which no one had used before, such as "călduro-măsurător" for thermometer, "mâncătorie" for dining room, "multuratic" for plural, etc. (101)

Cold-shouldered by the people, this language remains a still-born philological curiosity. The creation of a Moldavian language was a purely political act meant to serve as a basis for further fictions, such as that of a Moldavian nation and state.

On the other hand, the substitution of the Cyrillic alphabet for the Latin proved to be a more durable change. This reform managed partially to isolate Moldavian from Romanian, which uses the Latin alphabet, and somehow to bring it nearer to the Russian. The confrontation between two alphabets was not new in the Soviet Union. The Latin alphabet had been introduced around 1920 in Azerbaijan, in place of the Arabic. (102) This reform had been imposed on other Turkoman peoples, for political reasons, because communist propaganda was easier to disseminate in the Latin alphabet than in Arabic script. But, beginning in 1930, the Latin alphabet lost ground and was finally replaced in the Turkoman nations with Cyrillic, which became the universal alphabet of the Soviet Union.

In order to consolidate "Moldavian", spelling rules were adopted which emphasize the local pronounciation and, whenever possible, Romanian words and neologisms of Latin origin have been replaced by neologisms borrowed from the Russian. A campaign was unleashed in favor of Russian, which was presented as the language of communication among the peoples of the Soviet Empire, the language of culture and technology spoken "by the most advanced people of the world." The peak of Russification came in the period dominated by the linguistic theories of N. Ya. Marr.

During the epoch when Stalin proceeded to organize a socialist economy inside his empire without awaiting the triumph of the International Revolution, Marr proposed a parallel drive on the linguistic front, in order to unify the various languages of the USSR. It was to serve until the International Revolution would lead to the formation of a single world language. Up to 1950, Marr's theory served as a "scientific decoy for the fusion of the various languages of the USSR with the Russian language, the latter being earmarked for universal use in the future, as Latin had been in the past. This was the epoch when one did not hesitate to make use of administrative means in order to bring about the supremacy of the language of Ivan the Terrible over others. During the 1937–1950 period Moldavian was considered a language without a history or any importance, a Slav-Roman dialect fated to evolve, sooner or later, into pure Slavic.

On June 20, 1950, Stalin, who had initially approved Marr's theory, repudiated it publicly (for opportunistic reasons), putting an end to the dictatorship of the Russian language. He had found it advisable to spare the susceptibilities of the peoples of Central Europe who had fallen under Soviet domination and particularly those of the peoples of China, where communism had triumphed. It was important to avoid giving these peoples the impression that they were all earmarked for Russification. Without renouncing his final goal, Stalin advocated a more subtle method, which gave the peoples of the USSR, including the Moldavians, a moment of respite. Constrainit, once relaxed, led to the triumph of common sense and Moldavian began to be considered as not merely *related* to Romanian, but *identical* with it. "The Romanian literary language and that of Socialist Moldavia are the same," declared "Moldavian" poet Emilian Bucov in June 1956, at a writers' congress held in Bucharest. (103)

Once the Moldavians were permitted to utilize Romanian again, they developed a national literature of their own. Indeed, in the absence of a Moldavian language, it had been impossible to speak of Moldavian literature in the small Moldavian Autonomous Republic. Besides, although after the annexation by the USSR the number of authors and readers grew, sterilizing aesthetics prevented the development of a Moldavian (Romanian) culture. At the time, literary creativity was dominated by the dogma that there was only one true culture, the proletarian culture. "Proletarian culture" meant, of course, Russian culture. The literatures of the non-Russian nationalities were mere re-editings of Russian culture. Moldavian cultural activity began to prepare itself for the needs of propaganda. In Chişinău, the capital of the republic, a printing shop producing books and magazines in Moldavian and Russian was established. There is a Writers' Union, an Institute for Scientific Research in history, language, and literature, a branch of the Academy ol Sciences of the USSR, etc. The Romanian (Moldavian) language is taught in every second elementary school of Soviet Moldavia, while Russian is used by the teachers in nine out of ten grammar schools, colleges, institutes, and universities. (104)

First Secretary Bodyul of the Moldavian Communist Party declared, toward the end of 1965, that the Russian language was understood by all the inhabitants of Soviet Moldavia, young and old, and that the majority of Moldavians spoke it fluently. (105) Yet, the role of the rulers of Moldavian culture proved as thankless as that of the linguists who were forced to create an artificial Moldavian culture, from scratch, independent of Romanian culture. Initially, the Moldavian writers' aberrations matched the aberrations of the philologists. They considered the chroniclers Grigore Ureche (1590–1647), Miron Costin (1633 – 1691), and Ion Neculce (1672 – 1745), as well as the Romanian writers Costache Negruzzi (1808 – 1868), Vasile Alecsandri (1821 – 1890), Ion Creangă (1837 – 1889), Mihail Eminescu (1850 – 1889), etc., who were all born in that part of Moldavian territory which was never annexed by Russia, to be Moldavian classics. The case of Mihail Eminescu is even stranger, since he had denounced Russian imperialism in a series of virulent articles published in the daily *Timpul*.

The purpose of the new Moldavian literature was to present an apology of the Soviet man and of the Soviet system. Chairman Lupan of the Moldavian Writers' Union declared before the congress of writers that the relationship of Moldavian writers to Moscow guarantees literary perfection. (106) It was the epoch when it was considered that the "Moldavian" classics had not been subjected to any other influence than that of Russian literature and when the contemporary "Moldavian" writers could follow no other example than that offered by Russian literature. Those who did not respect the aesthetic standards dictated by Moscow were severely criticized – the poet Emil Bucov for having idealized Moldavia before the Russian annexation, P. S. Darienko for praising Moldavia without mentioning the socialist transformations, the poet Bogdan Istru for having maintained, in his poem "Stalingrad", that the Moldavians had fought there out of love for their Dniester, without mentioning Mother Russia. In 1952, the Secretary of the Moldavian Communist Party also criticized the writers of his republic who showed: "political indifference, lack of ideological orientation, and a narrow-minded national sentiment".

The Moldavian historians' task was no easier, for they had to demonstrate the existence of a history of Soviet Moldavia, delimited by the River Pruth and Dniester, distinct from that of the Moldavia situated between the Carpathians and the Dniester. They had no choice, however, but to establish that the Moldavian princes had reigned over the whole Moldavian territory from the very formation of the principality, toward the middle of the 14th century, until 1812, when the tzars annexed the eastern half, which they named Bessarabia, and which later, in 1940, became Soviet Moldavia. All attempts to invent local heroes, proper to Soviet Moldavia, failed. Thus, the obscure "great Moldavian hero" Grigore Ivanovich Kotovski, one of the organizers of the Moldavian Autonomous Republic, who fought for the "liberation" of his country from under "the yoke of the Romanian occupiers" and for the union of the Moldavian people "in a single Soviet Socialist Republic", (107) continues to be ignored by the population.

While interpreting contemporary events, the "Moldavian" historians indiscriminately attack all historians searching for the truth outside the Soviet canon, be they Western (such as the American Richard V. Burks who explained that the Moldavians are Romanian), Romanian from Romania (such as Andrei Oțetea, G. Georgescu-Buzău, Dumitru Almaş and Aron Petric who used the expression "annexation of Bessarabia" or Romanians who escaped Soviet control and chose to study Russian-Romanian relations in the west. (108) Unlike the Ukrainian historians Valentyn Moroz and Ivan Dziuba, who fought against the Russification of their country, the majority of "Moldavian" historians identified themselves with Russian interests, with the exception of N.A. Nartov, who was accused of Russophobia and paid for his spirit of independence with his life.

This policy, which partly goes back to the epoch of the tzars, resulted in the promotion of the Russian and Ukrainian elements, at the expense of the Romanian. Thus, the English author W. Kolarz found that Bessarabia produced more personalities representative of Russia than of Romania. Kolarz cites as examples geographer Lev Semionovici Berg (1876 – 1950), Marshal Semion Konstantinovich Timosenko (1895 – 1970), chemist Nikolai Dimitrievich Zelinski (1861–1953), and architect Viktorovich Schtchusev (1873 – 1949), the designer of Lenin's mausoleum, of Moscow's Kazan Railway Station, and of the Tashkent opera house.

It is forgotten that even before the annexation of Bessarabia there were Moldavians who played important roles in the cultural life of Russia, such as Antioch Cantemir (1708–1744), writer and diplomat, one of the promoters of Russian literature's classicism; poet Mihail Mateevich Heraskov, alias Mihai Herescu (1733–1807), etc. After the annexation of the province, the Moldavians rose only with difficulty to positions of responsibility, because they had been kept in the dark by the obscurantist policy of the tzars. Finally, one must not forget the considerable number of Bessarabian Romanians who succeeded in political, social, and cultural life in Romania. A good example is that of writer Al. Russo (1819–1859), one of the pioneers of Romanian literary criticism. Others are: writer, linguist, and historian Bogdan Petriceicu Haşdeu (1838 – 1907), one of the most prestigious representatives of Romanian culture in the 19th century; the theoretician of rural democracy Constantin Stere (1865 – 1936), author of the notoriously long novel *On the Eve of the Revolution*; Marshal Alexandru Averescu (1859-1938), commander in chief of the Romanian Army in the First World War, etc.

Beginning in 1954–1956, conditions improved for the development of a Moldavian (Romanian) national culture, because artists and researchers were permitted to show an interest other than political in the people and problems. Taking advantage of the new, more liberal atmosphere, the Moldavian people vigorously affirmed its vitality and creative spirit and demanded, through the literary critic V. Coroban, the right of the Moldavians to have their own artistic conceptions. Later, the "Corobanist spirit" was condemned as revisionist, nationalist, and reactionary. Nevertheless, Moldavian literature entered a more active phase, generally being credited in 1959 with the publication of no less that 847 works with a total circulation of 8,000,000 copies. But quality improved, too. Thus, *Frunze de Dor* by Ion Druță elevated, according to Klaus Heitmann, Moldavian literature to the level of world literature. (109) Thus, Heitmann counts Moldavian culture as the 11th of the 10 Latin cultures known to date. (110) Moldavian literature, invented to eulogize Russian Communism, established the foundations of a culture which demonstrates the ethnic, linguistic, and cultural unity of Moldavians and Romanians.

Results and Perspectives

Deportations, colonizations, administrative pressures, industrialization, and the urbanization of rural life, Russification of the Moldavian language and culture – all these means of denationalizing a nation, will they succeed in making the Moldavians lose their identity and melt into the Russian masses?

The idea of an historic community – the Soviet people – based on a community of economic, political, and cultural interests of various peoples, constitutes the aim of the Soviet nationalities policy at the moment. Presented most recently by Brezhnev at the 24th Congress of the Communist Party of the Soviet Union, this policy was long debated by Moldavian "ideologists" – according to D. S. Cornovan (111) and I. I. Bodyul (112) – whose political work it has been to encourage a melding of the Moldavian nation with the Soviet people or "narod." Such is the fate reserved by Moscow for the 2,817,000 Romanians (Moldavians) who today live in the USSR. Their chances of survival are slimmer under the present regime than they were under the tzars, because the techniques of Russification have been perfected and honed to a keen edge made both harsher and more effective.

There are, however, circumstances working in the opposite direction, favoring the survival of Romanians (Moldavians) as a nation distinct from the Soviet people. The prime in importance among these circumstances is the demographical factor. During the last 11 years, the number of Romanians inhabiting the Soviet Union rose by 494,000 persons, from 2,323,000 in 1959, to 2,817,000 in 1970. (In 1959, there were 2,217,000 Moldavians and 106,000 Romanians, and in 1970 – 2,698,000 Moldavians and 119,000 Romanians in the Soviet Union).

In the entire Soviet Union, the Romanian population increased by 17.54% as compared to an increase of 8% for the Russians. The growth factor of the Romanian population is, therefore, twice that of the Russians. True, due to colonization, the growth factor of the Russian population in Soviet Moldavia was, in the same period, 41.30% (from 293,000 to 414,000), compared to the Moldavian factor of 22.1% (from 1,887,000 to 2,304,000). Nevertheless, due to their growth of only 8%, the Russians, who total 129,000,000, represented in

1970 53% of a total of 241,700,000 Soviet inhabitants. Or, in 1939, the Russians formed 58.4% of the Soviet population, and in 1959 they still represented 55%. This variation is explained partly by the effects of territorial annexations – the Baltic countries, eastern Poland, Bessarabia, Northern Bucovina. The variation of the last decade, however, points to a relative fall in the birthrate among the Russians, as compared to the other nationalities of the USSR. As a matter of fact, the two causes, annexations and birthrate, have cumulative effects, decreasing the chances of Russian domination.

For the first time in Russian history, the urban population (135,991,514) surpassed the village population (105,728,620). This is bound to lead to a further lowering of the birthrate. Children under the age of 5 already represent no more that 8.5% of the population, as compared to 10.1% in 1959. Under such circumstances, it will not only be difficult to maintain the Russian colonization effort at its present level, but it is probable that the Russian colonists will themselves be assimilated by the local populations. Indeed, in the Asian republics, the Moslem populations – such as the Uighurs and Dungans – have doubled their number from one census to the next. Moldavia, thanks to the demographical factor, preserved its predominantly Romanian character.

The Moldavians have always stubbornly refused to be extinguished as a nation. It may be true that the present leaders accept the task of denationalizing their own people, but the peasants, the workers, and the Moldavian intelligentsia reject this proposition. There are many signs that national sentiment is stronger today than ever. The resistance of the Moldavian peasants takes on the form of numerous acts of sabotage which are not coordinated by anyone organization, but are initiated individually, and whose perpetrators remain anonymous. The Soviet authorities invited party activists, teachers, writers, and historians to fight Moldavian nationalism, which "has nothing in common with Communist ideology, with the noble sentiments of internationalism and friendship with the other peoples of the USSR." (113) The Moldavians, on the other hand, demanded more participation in the management of their economy, in the leadership of the Communist Party, in the administration and governing of their republic. This is the same as asking for more economic and administrative decentralization pending political autonomy.

The Moldavians look spontaneously to Romania, although Bucharest is not in a position to encourage them without breaking the solidarity of the communist parties and jeopardizing its relations with the Soviets. Yet, in 1964, Bucharest indirectly raised the Moldavian problem, by publishing the notes of Karl Marx on the Romanians. (114)

These notes condemn Russian claims to Bessarabia (115) and arm the Romanians with arguments against the annexation of Bessarabia countersigned by the father of Communism. The attitude of the Bucharest regime during the Czechoslovak crisis and the manifestations of independence by the Romanian communists could also incite the national pride of the Moldavians and strengthen Romanian patriotism on the left bank of the Pruth. Finally, the installation in Iași of a powerful radio transmitter, capable of bringing to all Moldavian homes Romanian music, language, and literature, indirectly supports the Romanian patriotism of the Moldavians.

The assertion of Moldavian nationalism and its presumed connections with the national communism of Romania worry Moscow, which then reacts through the Moldavian intermediaries on its payroll. Thus, Bodyul complained that west of Soviet Moldavia – could that be Romania? – there are renewed attempts to demonstrate that Bessarabia had united with Romania (116) of its own free will. In November 1970, a book published in Chișinău (117) criticized historian Andrei Oțetea (who had published the notes of Marx), because he spoke of the "annexation" of Bessarabia by the Romanians, instead of speaking of its "military conquest." Some saw in these polemics between communist comrades the first signs heralding a major dispute between Romania and the Soviets over Bessarabia. It was even suspected that the Romanians had formally claimed the territory and that the Soviet leaders had replied, via the Moldavian press, that Bessarabia was Russian territory, occupied by the Romanians for two decades (1918 – 1940). (118) It is highly unlikely that Bucharest would have claimed Bessarabia. But it is possible that Soviet Moldavia will become, some day in the future, an object of discord between Romania and the USSR.

Moldavian nationalism is not an isolated issue. It is one of many movements at work in the Muscovite empire. Like tzarist Russia, the Soviet Union continues to be a vast prison for peoples awaiting the propitious moment to assert their identities. Moldavian nationalism becomes stronger as time passes, because the Moldavians are aware of the fact that they are not alone in their fight for selfdetermination, that their struggle is also that of the Estonians, Latvians, Lithuanians, Ukrainians, Byelorussians, Georgians, Armenians, Turkomans, not to speak of the Jews, whose struggle takes place in part in Moldavia, notably in Chișinău. General Piotr Grigorenko has already shown the Tartars that they should establish contacts with the "progressives of other nations", so that their struggle becomes more effective. (119) Recent history points to the fact that every time the central authorities in Moscow suffer a major crisis, the nationalities of the Russian empire become restive, striving for complete independence.

Since the collapse of the tzarist empire, we have witnessed no fewer than 16 proclamations of republics: Finland, the Baltic countries, the Byelorussians, Armenians, Kazakhs, Tartars, Georgians, etc. These peoples did achieve, for limited periods of various lengths, their national dream. The hope of toppling Russian imperialism had a period of revival during the Second World War, when soldiers of the Soviet Army belonging to various national groups crossed "en masse" into the German camp and formed national legions. However, Hitler's racist and totalitarian regime could no more bring freedom to others than it could tolerate it at home. The abundance of condemnations pronounced by Soviet courts for nationalist agitation and the fact that the majority of the prisoners in labor camps belong to non-Russian ethnic groups show that nationalism has lost nothing of its fighting power.

The awakening of the non-Russian nationalities of the Soviet empire and a coordination of their efforts could force the transformation of the union into a democratic federation, with the national republics being free to join it or leave it. This is actually how Lenin conceived the federation, recognizing the right of the non-Russian peoples to leave the union, notably in the case of Finland and Poland. Toward the end of his life, Lenin confirmed this right to self-determination when he demanded that the right to secede should not remain merely a bureaucratic formulation, incapable of actually defending the non-Russian nationalities against Russian chauvinism. (120) A return to the Leninist nationalities policy is being considered even today by certain Russian (121) and Ukrainian (122) intellectuals, who see in it the solution to the problem of nationalities in the USSR. Stalin was the one who perverted the Leninist doctrine and began to persecute the non- Russian leaders, accusing them of treason and counterrevolutionary activities.

The judgement passed against Stalin at the 20th Congress of the Communist Party of the USSR should have extended to his nationalities policy, which should have been replaced by the Leninist policy. The Moldavians inhabiting the land of Lenin find in him an ally of outstanding prominence against Russian imperialism, which Vladimir Ilitch vowed to fight to the death.

Leninism is, however, not the only solution envisaged today in the Soviet Union, against the impasse toward which the nationalities problem seems to be heading. A recently born current of opinion, inspired by Christian doctrine and liberal ideology, preaching democratic change in the Soviet Union, is gradually taking the form of a veritable opposition to the regime. (123) It is conceivable that this current of opinion, called "the Democratic Movement", should end by spreading from the Russian intelligentsia to that of the other nationalities. Milovan Djilas, a heedful observer of the communist society's evolution, is convinced that "nationalist grievances" will appear in the Soviet Union at the same time as a "democratic thrust." (124) In principle, the evolution of the Soviet Union toward democracy should be of interest to the United States, if only because the understanding and maintaining of peace would be easier with a democratic Russia than with a totalitarian Soviet Union. To this day, the United States, however, has treated the Soviet Union as if it were a homogeneous state, taking no notice of the multinational character of the Soviet empire and of the aspirations to liberty and independence of its oppressed, non-Russian peoples. If the

United States abandons the premise that the USSR is a unitary state, the non-Russian nationalities of the Soviet empire should find in Washington, the same kind of support for their struggle that the African and Asian peoples found while they were fighting the British and the French. In this context, Soviet Moldavia, this political fiction, invented to serve as a "cradle for a Soviet Romania", a stage of Russian imperialism's advance toward the Straits and the Mediterranean, would have the possibility to demand selfdetermination.

Besides the return to Leninism or the evolution toward democracy, one can imagine yet another solution to the nationalities problem: the disintegration of the Soviet Union through armed conflict. The Russian historian Andrei Amalrik believes a Russo-Chinese conflict to be inevitable and that it would take the form of a guerrilla war of vast proportions. Under such circumstances, Communist China would know how to exploit the discontent of the non-Russian peoples of the Soviet empire, making them rise against the Russian dictatorship. Amalrik foresees that the peoples of Eastern Europe would sense the weakness of a Soviet Union engaged in a war of attrition in the Far East and would reclaim the territories which Stalin snatched from them at the end of the Second World War. Taking advantage of this opportunity, Romania would claim Bessarabia.

The problem of Bessarabia, or that of Soviet Moldavia, remains open, therefore, even in the eyes of a representative of the Russian intelligentsia, because the policy of Russification to which this province fell victim after its third annexation by Russia has not managed to change its ethnic character or to erase the national consciousness of its inhabitants. The Bessarabian problem will be raised in the future in the general framework of the situation of the non-Russian peoples of the Soviet empire, of colonial peoples in search of a national life of their own choice. Up to now, the struggle of peoples for their national independence has always ended in defeat for the imperialist powers, and the demographic decline of the Russian population shows that the Soviet Union is no exception. It will be sooner or later forced to bow to the fact that it has been exhausted by the process of forced Russification and has only exacerbated the national feelings of the non-Russian peoples. It will have no other choice but to concede, of its own free will, autonomy and independence to the non-Russian nations, or to provoke a violent explosion of their nationalism.

Aspects des Relations Sovieto-Roumaines,
1967-1971, Sécurité Européenne
(Paris: Minard, 1971), pp. 170-207.

BIBLIOGRAPHY

1) Theodor Shabad, "Soviet 1970 Census", *New York Times,* 17 April 1971.
2) Roman Smal-Stocki, *The Captive Nations. The Nationalism of the Non-Russian Nations in the Soviet Union* (New York, Bookman Assoc., 1960), p. 29.
3) I.V. Stalin, "Marxism and the National Question", *Works II* (Moscow: Foreign Languages Publ. House, 1960), p. 766.
4) *History of the Communist Party of the Soviet Union* (Moscow: 1960), p. 766.
5) Frederick C. Barghorn, *The Soviet Nationalism* (New York: Oxford Univ., 1956), p. 43.
6) David Nagy, "Soviet Census Shows Birth Rate Still Falling", UPI, 17 April 1971.
7) Strana Sovetov, "Biografiia Rosta", *Izvestia,* 17 April 1971.
8) George Savor and Léo Heiman, "Moldavia: a Russian Satellite", *The Ukrainian Quarterly* No. 2, 1956, pp. 167 and 189.
9) Ion G. Pelivan, *Les Droits des Roumains sur la Bessarabie* (Paris: Imprimerie des Arts et des Sports, 1920), p. 21.
10) George Savor and Léo Heiman, *op. cit.,* p. 161.
11) "Nationalism and Party Squabbles in Moldavia", *Radio Free Europe Research, USSR,* 6 February 1970.
12) Zbigniew Brezinski, *Between Two Ages. America's Role in the Technotronic Era,* (NewYork: The Viking Press, 1970), p. 162.
13) Makarow, "Die Eingliederung Bessarabiens und der Nord Bukovina in die Sowjet-Union", *Zeitschrift für ausländisches öffentliches Recht und Völkerrecht* Nos. 1-2, p. 358-359.
14) Walter Kolarz, *Russia and her Colonies,* (London: Philip, 1952), p. 150.
15) Fritz Ermarth, "A Note on Personnel Changes in Moldavia", *Radio Free Europe Research, USSR,* 17 March 1967.
16) "Session of Supreme Soviet of Moldavian Socialist Republic", *Cronica Românească* No. 7, 1954, p. 18.
17) Walter Kolarz, *op. cit.,* p. 150.
18) "Soviet Polemics with Romanian Historians", *Radio Free Europe Research, USSR,* 18 January 1971.
19) Walter Kolarz, *op. cit.,* p. 151.
20) George Savor and Léo Heiman, *op. cit.,* p. 163.
21) Fritz Ermarth, "The View from Moscow". *Radio Free Europe Research, USSR,* 6 July 1965, p. 24.
22) "Nationalism and Party Squabbles in Moldavia", *op. cit. supra.*
23) "What Do Bessarabia and Northern Bucovina Signify to Us?", *Cronica Românească* No. 6, 1951, p. 96.
24) *New York Times,* 22 May 1951.

25) "The Leaders of the Moldavian Soviet Socialist Republic", *Cronica Românească* Nos. 4-5, 1954, p. 30.
26) "Session of Supreme Soviet of Moldavian Soviet Socialist Republic", *op. cit.*, p. 30.
27) Fritz Ermarth, "Anti-Soviet Nationalism in Moldavia", *Radio Free Europe Research, USSR,* 18 April 1960.
28) "Bessarabia under the Soviet Regime", *Cronica Românească* No. 12, 1952, p. 18.
29) "L'U.R.S.S. Rejette les Prétentions Roumaines sur la Bessarabie", *Le Monde,* 16 March 1967.
30) Dionisie Ghermani, *Die Bevölkerungsfrage Bessarabiens in Geschichtlicher Perspektive* (Munich: 1961), Manuscript, p. 107.
31) I.V. Stalin, "Report at the Fourth Conference of the CC with Nationalities Officials, 10 June 1933, on the Practical Measures for Applying the Resolution on the National Question of the Twelfth Party Congress", *Changing Attitude in the Soviet Russia. The Nationalities Problem and the Soviet Administration. Selected Reading on the Development of the Soviet Nationalities Policies. Selected, Edited and Introduced by Rudolf Schlesinger* (London: Routledge and Kegan Paul, 1956), pp. 65 and 76.
32) Aleksander Filipovich Diorditsa, "Vedinoi Bratskoi Zemlie Narodov USSR", *Sovietskaia Moldavia,* 28 March 1965.
33) Gheorghe Murgoci, *La Population de la Bessarabie. Étude Démographique avec Cartes et Tableaux Statistiques. Préface par Em. de Martonne* (Paris: 1920), p. 54.
34) *Facts and Comments Concerning Bessarabia, 1812- 1940,* (London: 1941), p. 52.
35) *Moldova Socialistă,* 17 April 1959.
36) "Opposition in the Ukraine", *Radio Free Europe Research, USSR,* 3 March 1971.
37) Ivan Dzyuba, *Internationalism or Russification,* (London: Weidenfeld and Nicolson, 1968), p. 125.
38) "Opposition in the Ukraine", *op. cit.*
39) Ivan Ivanovici Bodyul, "Condition of Marxist- Leninist Education of Working People in the Republic and Measures for Its Improvement", *Cultura,* No. 2, 1966.
40) George Savor and Léo Heiman, *op. cit.,* p. 160.
41) M. Bazin, "Sotsialno-Ekonomicheskie Preobrazovania Moldavskogo Sela", *Kommunist Moldavii* No. 11, 1970.
42) V. Mendec, "Rural Constructions", *Cultura* No. 8, 1965.
43) "Nationalities Policy: Burning Problem, Publicistic Panacea", *Radio Free Europe Research, USSR,* 8 March 1971.
44) Ion Pelivan, *La Bessarabie sous le Régime Russe (1812-1918)* (Paris: Lahure, 1919), p. 52.

45) Ion Dumitru, *Forme de etnocid în URSS* /Forms of Ethnocide in the Soviet Union/, (Munich: Avdella-Cenad, 1969), pp. 28-30.
46) "Anticommunist Resistance in Bessarabia. A Soviet Colonel about the Bessarabian Recruits," *Stindardul,* Nos. 78-79, 31 January 1964.
47) Piotr Grigorenko, "La Deportation des Tartares de Crimée et ses Conséquences" *Michel Slavinsky, La Presse Clandestine en URSS, 1960-1970* (Paris: 1970), p. 121-122.
48) Dumitru Nimigeanu, *Însemnările unui Țăran Deportat din Bucovina* /Notes of a Peasant Deported from Bucovina/, (Paris: Fundația Regală Universitară Carol I, 1958), p. 246; English Issue, *Hell Moved Its Borders* (London: Blandford Press, 1960), p. 168.
49) Alexandru Nicolae, "Der Angriff auf die Menschliche Substanz Rumäniens", *Zeitschrift fur Geopolitik,* Band XXII, 1951, p. 419.
50) Ion Frunză, *Bessarabien. Rumänische Rechte und Leistungen* (Bucharest: Dacia, 1941), p. 30.
51) Sabin Mănuilă and W. Filderman, "Jewish Population in Romania 1940-1957", *România* No. 18, 1957.
52) Afanasij Lukic Odud, *Sowjet Moldawien* (Berlin: SWA-Verlag, 1949), p. 49.
53) *History of the Communist Party of the Soviet Union* (Moskow: Foreign Languages Publ. House, 1960), pp. 591-592.
54) George Savor and Léo Heiman, *op. cit.,* p. 163.
55) Alexandru Nicolae, *op. cit.,* p. 419-420.
56) Mircea Opreanu, "Russifizierungsaktion in Bessarabien stärker denn je", *Stindardul* No. 93, 1966.
57) *România* No. 72, 1963.
58) "Glavnoie Upravlenie po Preseleniiu Organizovannomu Naboru Rabochih pri Soviete Ministrov Moldayskoi SSR", *Sovietskaia Moldavia,* 31 March 1955 (French Translation in *La Nation Roumaine,* 15 May 1955).
59) Ion Pelivan, *op. cit.,* p. 51.
60) Hans-Jurgen Wagener, "Commentary", *Radio Liberty,* 17 october 1969.
61) *Pro Bessarabia and Bucovina* (London: 1958), p. 12.
62) Anton Crihan, "Le Dernier Crime des Soviets. La Deportation Planifiée de la Population Roumaine de Bessarabie", *La Nation Roumaine,* May 1955.
63) *Pro Bessarabia and Bucovina, op. cit.,* p. 14.
64) Piotr Grigorenko, *op. cit.,* p. 129.
65) Mircea Opreanu, *op. cit.*
66) George Savor and Léo Heiman, *op. cit.,* p. 164.
67) "Communiqué of the General Directorate for the Permutation and organized Hiring of Workers, Attached to the Council of Ministers of Moldavian SSR", *Moldova Socialistă,* 24 January 1965.
68) *Moldova Socialistă,* 27 April 1969.

69) *Recensământul General al Populaţiei României din 29 Decembrie 1930,* Vol. II, Ist Part /General Census of Romania's Population of 29 December 1930/, (Bucharest: 1939), pp. 48, l00, 124, 216, 264, 268, 300 and 462.
70) Klaus Heitmann, "Rumänische Sprache und Literatur in Bessarabien und Transnistrien", *Zeitschrift für Romanische Philologie,* Vol. 81, p. 100-107.
71) *Geopolitica şi Geoistoria* Nos. IX-X, 1941, p. 31, *apud* "What Do Bessarabia and Northern Bucovina Signify to Us", *Cronica Românească,* No. 6, 1951, p. 95.
72) Ion Pelivan, *op. cit.,* p. 51.
73) Piotr Grigorenko, *op. cit.,* p. 51.
74) R. Udler and V. Komarnitki, "Moldavian Linguistic Atlas", *Cultura* No. 16 June 1965.
75) "New Deportations of Population into Bessarabia", *România* No. 13, 15 March 1957.
76) Eugène Lozovan, "La Roumanie Extrème-Orientale", *Festschrift Walter von Wartburg zum 80. Geburtstag,* (Tübingen: 1968, p. 85).
77) Simion Mehedinţi, *La Roumanie à la Frontière Orientale de l'Europe,* (Bucharest: Dacia, 1942), p. 19.
78) *Délégation Bessarabienne. Les Roumains devant le Congrès de la Paix. La Question de la Bessarabie* (Paris: 1919), p. 8.
79) Gheorghe Murgoci, *op. cit.,* p. 49.
80) Victor Buescu, "Les Roumains d'Asie", *Stindardul* Nos. 8-9, March-April 1954 and Nos. 102-103, April-August 1968.
81) *Radio Chişinău,* 22 March 1954.
82) W. Kolarz, *op. cit.,* p. 13-15.
83) George Savor and Léo Heiman, *op. cit.,* p. 158.
84) *Ibid.,* p. 163.
85) Lodewyk Hermen Grondijs, *Bessarabia* (Bucharest: 1940), p. 14.
86) Carl Uhling, *Die Bessarabische Frage, eine Geopolitische Betrachtung* (Breslau: Ferdinand Hirt, 1926), p. 82.
87) Aldo Garosci, "Alla Ricerca della Verità", *Gli Ebrei nell' URSS* (Milano: Garzanti, 1966), p. 33.
88) "What do Bessarabia and Northern Bucovina Signify to Us", *op. cit.,* p. 95.
89) Strana Sovetov, "Biografiia Rosta", *Izvestia,* 17 April 1971.
90) Alec Nove, "La Populazione Ebraica nell' URSS; Consistenza, Struttura Professionale ed Istruzione". *Gli Ebrei nell' URSS,* (Milano: Garzanti, 1966), pp. 49-57.
91) David Nagy, *op. cit.*
92) *Mémoire Concernant la Bessarabie et la Bucovine du Nord (avec une Carte Ethnographique),* (Bucharest: 1940), p. 6.
93) N.S. Khrouchtchev, "Extrait du Rapport au XX-e Congrès du PC US", Roy Medvedev, *Faut-il Réhabiliter Staline?* (Paris: 1969), p. 87.

94) Léon Trotsky, "La Question Ukrainienne, pour une Ukraine Soviétique, Ouvrière et Paysanne, Unique, Libre et Indépendante", *Samizdat* No. 1, (Paris: Seuil, 1969), p. 494.
95) Ivan Kandyba, "Le Programme de l'Union Ouvrière et Paysanne d'Ukraine", *Samizdat* No. 1 (Paris: Seuil, 1969), p. 500.
96) Henry Shapiro, "Russian Orthodox Church to Elect new Patriarch and end Schism", UPI, 2 June 1971; "Russian Prelate Urges Removal of the Curses on the Old Believers", *New York Times*, 2 June 1971.
97) A. Odud, *op. cit.*, p. 25.
98) Ştefan Ciobanu, *La Bessarabie, Sa Population, Son Passé, Sa Culture* (Bucharest: Académie Roumaine, 1941), pp. 56-57.
99) Gheorghe Murgoci, *op. cit.*, p. 13.
100) *Pro Bessarabia and Bucovina, op. cit.*, p. 9.
101) Klaus Heitmann, *op. cit., p. 111*.
102) V. Aliev "The Victory of the Latin Script", *Changing attitude in the Soviet Russia, op. cit.*, p. 124.
103) Klaus Heitmann, *op. cit.*, p. 124.
104) George Savor and Léo Heiman, *op. cit.*, p. 167.
105) Ivan Ivanovici Bodyul, "Condition of Marxist-Leninist Education... ", *op. cit.*
106) "Congress of Writers of Moldavian SSR", *Cronica Românească,* No. 10, October 1954, p. 23.
107) "Decade of Moldavian SSR", *Cronica Românească* Nos. 5-6, May-June l953, p. 18.
108) E. S. Grosul, "The Dark Years of Romanian-Landlords' Occupation. The Socio-Economic and Political Condition of Working People on the Territory of Occupied Bessarabia, Reflected in a New Work of Moldavian Historians", *Moldova Socialistă,* 3 December 1970 and *Sovetskaya Moldavia,* 18 December 1970.
109) Klaus Heitmann, *op. cit.*, p. 156.
110) *Ibid.,* p. 102.
111) Dimitry Kornovan, "The Friendship of the Peoples of the Soviet Union, Source of Strength in the Struggle for Communism", *Comunistul Moldovei,* January 1967, p. 50.
112) Ivan Ivanovici Bodyul, *op. cit.*
113) Dimitry Kornovan, *op. cit.*
114) Karl Marx, *Însemnări despre Români* /Notes on Romanians/, (Madrid: Carpaţi, 1965).
115) Max Frankel, "Romania out for Herself Now", *New York Times,* 19 December 1964.
116) Ivan Ivanovici Bodyul, "Speech at the Moldavian CP CC on 13 February 1967", *Moldova Socialistă,* 16 February 1967.
117) *Sovetskaya Moldavia,* 18 February 1970.

118) L'Explication des Difficulteés entre Moscou et Bucarest. L'URSS Rejette les Prétentions Roumaines sur la Bessarabie", *Le Monde,* 16 March 1967.
119) Piotr Grigorenko, "Pour le 72-e Anniversaire d'Alexis Kosterine", *Samizdat* No. 1, (Paris: Seuil, 1969), p. 515.
120) Vladimir Ilitch Lénine, «Trois Lettres au Congrès. La Question des Nationalités ou "l'Autonomie"», *Samizdat* No. 1, (Paris: Seuil, 1969), p. 487.
121) Piotr Grigorenko, *op. cit.,* p. 512.
122) Ivan Dzyuba, *op. cit.*
123) Andrei Amalrik, *L'Union Soviétique Survivra-t-elle en 1984?* (Paris: 1970), p. 63.
124) Milovan Djilas, *Une Société Imparfaite. Le Communisme désintégré,* (Paris: Kalmann-Levy, 1969), p. 238.

XIV

THE NEW CONSTITUTION OF THE MOLDAVIAN SOVIET SOCIALIST REPUBLIC

At its Extraordinary Session of 15 April 1978, the Supreme Soviet of the Moldavian Socialist Republic unanimously adopted a new republican Constitution, to replace the old Constitution of 12 January 1941, including its subsequent amendments. The new Constitution consists of a Preamble and 172 articles, and was prepared as part of the whole project of adjusting all 15 republican Constitutions to the new Constitution of the Soviet Union of october 1977. The Constitution of the Soviet Union has been and will continue to serve as an obligatory model for all republican Constitutions, which simply lift entire chapters from the Fundamental Law of the USSR, merely replacing the Soviet Union by the name of the republic in question.

The campaign to educate the Moldavian citizens – to help them become acquainted with the provisions and spirit of the Soviet Constitution – began as far back as June 1940, immediately after the Soviets occupied Bessarabia, by means of a mass political campaign among the local population conducted through lectures and circles for the study of the Constitution. Over 32,000 circles – including 2,385 in Chişinău alone – for the study of the Soviet Constitution and of the Electoral Law were organized throughout Soviet Moldavia, and about 36,000 propaganda workers were engaged in the effort.

This drive and the holding of the first elections for the Supreme Soviet of the Moldavian SSR on 12 January 1941 to adopt the first Constitution «of the reunited Moldavian people» – as Soviet historian Lazarev put it – met with difficulties «arising from the specific conditions in the recently liberated territories,» namely, the existence of «exploiting classes,» which had not yet been liquidated, the existence of a large number of churches and monasteries, and of religious sects with large memberships. (1) According to Lazarev, the «bourgeois-nationalist elements,» the clergy, and the believers tried to influence the electorate, «slandering» the Soviet system and making attempts to put up their own candidates. The first Constitution of the Moldavian SSR, based on the principles and provisions of the Constitution of the Soviet Union, was adopted at the first session of the Supreme Soviet of the Moldavian SSR. The «Moldavian» (ethnic Romanian) deputies represented 56 per cent of the total number of representatives, compared to a «Moldavian» population that made up 65 per cent of all inhabitants of the republic.

Although the republican Constitutions are similar to each other in general outline and all conform to the pattern of the all-union document, nevertheless, there are some differences among them due to the specific features of each republic or the special conditions of its historical development. These distinctions appear more clearly in the sections dealing with administrative matters, such as Sections III and IX of the 1978 Moldavian Constitution. The number of the districts has been reduced from the 40 mentioned in Article 18 of the old Constitution to 36 listed in Article 77 of the current one. The names of 12 districts have been omitted from the new Constitution: Ataci, Bălți, Basarabi, Bender, Brătușani, Bulboca, Cărpineni, Lipcani, Olănești, Paraclia, Târnova, and Tiraspol. On the other hand, the names of eight new districts appear: Anenii Noi, Briceni, Cantemir, Dondușeni, Grigoriopol, Kutuzov, Slobozia, and Suvorov. Presumedly, these merely reflect changes of name or the redrawing of some administrative territories in the Moldavian SSR that resulted in the absorption of four districts in the remaining eight, since, according to Article 14(a) of the old Constitution, the frontier between Socialist Moldavia and any other union republic can be modified on the basis of mutual agreement.

Another administrative change has increased the number of cities directly subordinate to the state administration of the Moldavian SSR from four (Chișinău, Bălți, Bender, and Tiraspol) to nine, by placing the following urban centers in this category: Cahul, Orhei, Râbnița, Soroca, and Ungheni.

The new Constitution has also made a slight change in the crest of the republic, the hammer and sickle surmounted by sunrays and framed by ears of corn. The coat of arms has now been «finished off» with a garland of grapes and fruit – products which, along with grains, represent Socialist Moldavia's greatest agriculture wealth. Viticulture is so crucial to the economy of the republic that frost damage to the vineyards in the winter of 1976 caused a major shortfall in Moldavia's plan fulfillment in 1977. (2)

The 1941 Constitution of Socialist Moldavia reflected some of the republic's distinctive features that arose from the substantial differences between the levels of socioeconomic and political-cultural development in the two regions that Stalin had «united» in 1940 – Bessarabia (part of Romania since 1918) and the Autonomous Moldavian SSR (formed as part of the Ukrainian SSR in 1924). Thus, side by side with the socialist sector, the existence of a private capitalist sector represented by individual peasants and artisans, small private industrial and commercial enterprises, was recognized in the republic. The disappearance of the small individual peasant homesteads and the completion of co-operativizing the artisans removed the initial economic distinctions between Socialist Moldavia and the other Soviet socialist republics, a change also reflected in the Constitutions. Nevertheless, the wording of some chapters and sections varies from one Constitution to another. The Preamble of the new Constitution of the Moldavian SSR, for example, is shorter than that of the Constitution of the Soviet Union, and there is no mention of «a new historic community of people (which) has been formed – the Soviet people.» The statement that the people of the republic recognized itself "an inalienable part of the whole Soviet people", which appears in the Constitutions of the Russian Soviet Federative Socialist Republic, and of the Ukrainian and Azerbaijan SSRs – thus seemingly making the legal right of each republic to secede null and void – is also missing. (3)

The Preamble of the Constitution of Socialist Moldavia merely pays homage to the October Revolution and to the Constitution of the Soviet Union; it emphasizes the immense help granted by the Great Russians and mentions «the state unity of the Soviet people» in the Soviet Union «which closely unites all nations and nationalities, in order to build communism jointly.» Emphasis is therefore laid on «the nations and nationalities,» which are placed on a more or less equal footing, possibly to play down the position of the majority nation in the republic bearing its name.

In accordance with the provisions of Article 34, the citizens of the Moldavian SSR are given «the possibility of using their mother tongue and the languages of the other peoples of the Soviet Union.» Therefore, there is no mention of a right, but merely of a possibility, just as there is no mention of directly identifying the «Moldavian» language (Romanian written in the Cyrillic alphabet) as the first language in use in the Moldavian Republic, but merely as the mother tongue of some of its citizens. This language is thus placed on an equal footing with the approximately 130 other languages spoken in the Soviet Union. (4) The Constitutions of only three union republics – Armenia, Azerbaijan, and Georgia – mention the language of the titular nationality as the state language. Moscow made a concession to national sentiment in these three cases only in the face of public pressure. (5) The fact that this right has been granted to the three Transcaucasian republics may have made some «Moldavians» more concerned over the lack of official primacy of their language in their republic. Nonetheless, at present the «Moldavian» language thus has merely a limited official role, used in education, the legal system, and in some cultural publications. Article 43 provides «the possibility of school education in the mother tongue.» Once again, however, it is the possibility, not any specific right that is mentioned, and the use of the term «Moldavian» language is again avoided, preference obviously given to the more general wording of «mother tongue.»

A Reuter correspondent noted that « the Russian language dominates across the republic, and Moldavian fathers cheerfully admit to sending their children to schools operating in the Russian language to give them a better chance of getting top-level jobs when they become adults,» (6) thus reflecting a trend among many other nationalities of the Soviet Union.

A New China News Agency correspondent provides a harsher account:

In their efforts to Russify Moldavia, the old tsars tried in every way possible to destroy Moldavian culture. According to Volume 28 of the **Great Soviet Encyclopaedia** *(1954), under the pressure of tsarist authorities the Moldavian-language schools, which had existed in the first half of the 19th century, were closed, and Russian was proclaimed the official language. The new tsars made use of similar practices when they imposed Russian and stifled the use of Moldavian under the banner of the two-language system. According to the report of the first secretary of the Moldavian Communist Party CC published in the daily* **Sovetskaya Moldaviia** *(27 April 1973), Russian was to be taught at all educational levels – from kindergartens to institutions of higher education. The magazine* **Sovetskaia Etnografiia** *(No. 5, 1975) called for the popularization of the Russian language among the inhabitans of the Moldavian Republic. This policy condemns the Moldavian-language schools to an ever more all-encompassing decline. But even the first secretary of the Moldavian CP CC could not help admitting that there has been a certain amount of success in national education in some areas of Moldavia. (7)*

Chapter 3 of the new Moldavian Constitution, entitled Social Development and Culture, does not mention the right to a «Moldavian» culture, or even the possibility of having one. There exists a mass circulation Romanian-language newspaper published 300 times per year, called *Moldava Socialistă* (which also appears in a Russian–language version), just as there are youth, party, and literary periodicals printed in «Moldavian.» But the overall trends in Socialist Moldavia were presented, if in a predictably hyperbolic fashion, by the New China News Agency in the following terms:

The number of Moldavian-language periodicals is diminishing. According to the Soviet economic statistical yearbook, the number of Moldavian-language dailies decreased by 50 per cent during the 1960-1974 period, while the proportion of books written in the Moldavian language has dropped from 64 per cent of all books published in the Moldavian Republic in 1950 to 33 per cent in 1976. The Soviet revisionist authorities have even permitted themselves to forbid the use of Moldavian terms, denouncing them as attempts to replace unified internationalist scientific terminology by terms entirely alien to the nature of the mutual language relations among the Soviet peoples.

In its 27 September 1974 broadcast of the program «Answering Our TV Audience,» the all-union Soviet TV station revealed that TV viewers have complained that the indigenous language is virtually no longer used in Moldavia. The book **The Results of the Census of the Entire Soviet Union,** *published in the Soviet Union in 1970, admitted that the number of Moldavians considering Moldavian as their mother tongue has dropped in the 1959-1970 period. In order to speed up Russification and to increase their domination over Moldavia, the Soviet revisionists have transferred, under the pretext of reshuffling cadres, a large number of Moldavians away from their native parts. (8)*

In Socialist Moldavia legal proceedings are conducted in «Moldavian», in Russian, or even in the language of the majority of the population in a given locality. This provision, contained in Article 158 and similar to that in the old Article 84, corresponds to articles to be found in all other Constitutions of the Soviet Union. A codicil to this provision reads that any person concerned with a law suit who does not know the language in which the judicial proceedings are conducted is guaranteed the right to become fully acquainted with the evidence and all other pertinent material by being provided with copies translated into his own language, and, if taking active part in the case, to have the services of an interpreter, and the right to address the court in his mother tongue. These rights, granted to every person concerned with a law suit, pertain only to individuals, irrespective of their ethnic origin, but not to any ethnic group as a whole. Such provisions can be found, however, in more or less similar form in the current laws of all countries; for example, in the Romanian Penal Code. (9)

The Moldavian SSR is a sovereign state (Article 68) which enjoys – at least in principle – certain prerogatives of sovereignty. According to Article 73, it has the right to enter into relations with foreign states, to conduct negotiations with them, and to exchange diplomatic and consular representatives; finally, it has the right to join international organizations. The Moldavian Republic has not yet, however, begun to apply this article (corresponding to Article 15 (a) of the old Constitution) in actual practice: it has not appointed diplomatic representatives to any foreign capital, nor has it joined any international organization. One can hardly, therefore, speak of a Moldavian foreign policy. As a matter of fact, Article 28 of the new Constitution emphatically specifies that «in its foreign policy, the

Moldavian SSR will be guided by the goals, tasks, and principles of the foreign policy established by the Constitution of the Soviet Union, which means that, in fact, the all-union authorities retain their prerogatives so far as foreign policy is concerned.

Another right of sovereignty, the right to secede, contained in Article 69 (corresponding to the old Article 14), states that «the Moldavian SSR retains the right freely to withdraw from the Soviet Union.»

But since «the sovereign rights of the Moldavian SSR are protected by the Soviet Union» (Article 75), exercise of them by the Moldavian Republic itself is illusory. At the extraordinary Seventh Session of the Supreme Soviet of the USSR (4 october 1977), Leonid Brezhnev said that a new historic community – the Soviet people – has emerged in the USSR. Brezhnev added that some comrades therefore, proposed that the concept of a unified Soviet nation be adopted and written into the new Constitution, thus putting an end to the formal sovereignty of the union republics, and depriving them of the right to secede from the USSR, and of the right to engage in independent foreign relations. Although this extreme suggestion was not adopted and was attacked by Brezhnev as «erroneous,» the attribute of sovereignty in conducting foreign relations by the republics, included in their Constitutions, has remained a dead letter or is simply a utilitarian provision, designed to give the Soviet Union larger representation in some international organizations, such as the United Nations.

The Moldavian SSR has more comprehensive powers so far as domestic sovereignty goes. It has the right to prepare and adopt its own Constitution, to pass laws, to maintain order, to create and run republican and local bodies, to establish a unified socioeconomic policy, to run the economy, public education, and cultural agencies, to protect public health, etc. (Article 71). But its new Constitution does deprive Socialist Moldavia of one of its most important – if unused – theoretical rights, contained in Article 15(b) of the old Constitution, which stated: «The Moldavian SSR has its own republican military units.» Article 29 of the new Moldavian Constitution transfers the right to defense to the armed forces of the Soviet Union, which the Moldavian SSR helps to equip and train, according to Article 30. This major reduction in regional rights does not affect Socialist Moldavia alone, for all the other union republics are also in the same boat.

The all-union authorities now also have quite noticeably greater rights in the economic field as well, for emphasis is put on the fact that «the plan for economic and social development of the Moldavian SSR is a component part of the State

Plan for the Economic and Social Development of the Soviet Union» (Article 139). There was no such phrase in the old Moldavian Constitution. The same stipulation is now made regarding the state budget of the Moldavian SSR, which «is a component part of the unified state budget of the Soviet Union» (Article 145). Once again, these are not changes made in the Moldavian Constitution alone – they can be found in all the other republican constitutions too.

Chapter 6, on the Rights, Freedom, and Fundamental Duties of the Citizens of the Moldavian SSR, is one of the most extensive and detailed chapters in the new Constitution. It prompted the prominent Russian dissident Pyotr Grigorenko to say (obviously referring to the Constitution of the Soviet Union): «The Constitution guarantees the right to go to the movies, but avoids the crucial issues.» (10) The Constitution of Socialist Moldavia does mention: the right to work, to rest, to protection of health, to a guaranteed income in old age, to housing, to education, to make use of all cultural facilities, the freedom of scientific, technological, and artistic creativity, the right to participate in the management of political affairs, freedom of speech, press, assembly, and conscience, the right to protect the family, respect for the person, inviolability of the domicile, etc. (Articles 37 through 67). The Moldavian Constitution does not, of course, include among these numerous rights the right to strike, and it especially does not provide the right to appeal, i.e., allowing a citizen to challenge any infringement upon his Constitutional rights. On the other hand, it does state that «recourse to these rights and freedoms by the citizens should not harm the interests of society and the state, or the rights of other citizens» (Article 37). But, under the pretext of defending the interests of society and the state, all kinds of abuses and infringements of civil rights have been committed in the past.

The lack of acknowledgment of human rights in the all-union and republican Constitutions of the USSR has aroused a certain amount of criticism in the West. Since the problem of human rights remains one of the fundamental issues in the contemporary world, and has been the subject of international discussions at Helsinki and Belgrade, Brezhnev counterattacked against these Western critics of the Soviet Constitution, maintaining that their criticisms of the Soviet handling of the human rights issue are «stereotyped inventions, shameless fabrications, and blatant lies, which are a part of the general anticommunist crusade.» (11)

Although it lacks originality, the new Constitution of the Moldavian SSR will be proclaimed as the foundation of the republic's sociopolitical order and will govern the relationship between the citizen and the state, for it will represent the ultimate legal authority. Very likely, many of its positive provisions will be applied rarely, if at all, in practice, just as it may be supposed that official policy will continue to encourage the trends toward centralization and assimilation, to the detriment of the national individuality of the ethnic Romanians of the Moldavian SSR.

Background Report Nr. 140,
Munich, 28 June 1978,
Radio Free Europe Research.

BIBLIOGRAPHY

1) A.M. Lazarev, *Moldavskaia Sovetskaia Gosudarstsvennost i Bessarabskii Vopros,* (Chişinău: Cartea Moldovenească Publishing House, 1974), p. 60.
2) See Ann Sheehy, "Economic Performance of the Union Republics in the First Two Years of the 10th Five-Year Plan", *Radio Liberty Research Report / 60,* 20 March 1978.
3) Ann Sheehy, "The New Republican Constitution", *Radio Liberty Research Report* /82, 18 April 1978.
4) TASS, in English, 10 May 1978.
5) See Ann Sheehy, "The National Languages and the New Constitutions of the Transcaucasian Republics", *Radio Liberty Research Report* /97, 3 May 1978.
6) Reuter (Chişinău), 19 December 1975.
7) Radio Peking, in Romanian, 20 February 1976.
8) *Ibid.*
9) *Buletinul Oficial* Nos. 58–59, 26 April 1973.
10) UPI (Moscow), 8 October 1977.
11) TASS, 4 October 1977. The speech in question was carried live over Radio Moscow and Moscow TV and delivered before the Supreme Soviet of the USSR.

XV

WALEW'S PLAN RAISED AGAIN THE BESSARABIAN ISSUE

Romania's present position is characterized by some changes in its relations with the Soviet Union, especially in the economic field. The Romanian government is trying to keep from engaging in any economic projects similar to those which, for many years, have bled the country. The present measures must be contemplated in the light of years of exploitation, which, in the long run, became unacceptable.

One of Romania's most painful losses was the annexation, by the Soviet Union, of national territory: Bessarabia and Northern Bucovina – a total area of 50,072 sq.km. with a population of 3,409,191.

The loss of Bessarabia alone meant 24%, less cereal grains and oleaginous crops, 30% fewer vineyards, 6% less forests, etc., not to mention an industrial investment capital of 2,500 million lei and its yearly return of 4,100 million lei – representing Bessarabia's industrial output.

To these losses must be added the human sacrifices made by Romania in order to shorten the war by joining the so-called "campaign against Hitlerism." The Romanian press has lately published several articles detailing the country's human losses – 170,000 dead, wounded, and missing – during the military operations against Hitler's Germany, losses which cannot be expressed in lei or rubles.

What economic statistician could calculate the losses suffered by the Romanian state? There are no figures to cite regarding the amount of plundering, in the private and public sectors, as over 1,000,000 Soviet soldiers crossed the country to and from the Western Front. It is well known that the Red Army took more or less anything movable: chickens, geese and ducks from the peasants, carpets from middle class homes, wine by the barrel, all transported as "souvenirs" in military trucks, not to mention the watches, which in full daylight were forcefully taken from any passer-by.

This brutal and haphazard plundering was then supplemented by a system of compulsory purchases. Members of the Soviet Army, who had already proved themselves masters at armed plunder, appeared once more as peaceful customers in the shops, where they bought almost anything available for occupation rubles, if they even took the trouble to fork out any kind of money. The acceptance of the occupation currency was compulsory. In order to convert these sacks of occupation rubles, the Romanian National Bank had to increase its issue of paper money, and thus contributed to the rapid inflation of the national currency.

Another trick adopted by the Soviets was the requisitioning of foreign property, for the purpose of appropriation, which went far beyond the requirements of the troops and the economic capacity of the country. These goods, classified as "supplementary requisitions," confiscated and transported to the Soviet Union, were meant for the needs of the Soviet civil population, at the cost of the impoverished and famished Romanians. In spite of the fact that the war had long ended, the requisitions for the use of the Soviet troops stationed in Romania continued unabated. In 1964 the Romanian press published figures representing the war burden for the Romanian economy as amounting to 106,500 million lei, equal to 767,500,000 US dollars at 1938 evaluation, omitting the amount of requisitions taken by the Soviet military.

220,000,000 Dollars at one Single Stroke

Let us now contemplate the problem of reparations, which Romania had to pay for war damage. They were set at 3,000 million dollars, to be paid within six years.

The payments had to be made in cereal grains, timber, coal, oil-products, machines, equipment, etc. Moscow thereby obtained an initial financial gain by setting the price for the Romanian deliveries at the currency level of 1938, which meant a much lower price than in the postwar period. With a single stroke, the Soviets "earned" a surplus, within the reparations account, amounting to 220,000,000 dollars (520,000,000 instead of 300,000,000). An American delegate at the 1947 Paris Peace Conference produced proof that Romania had already paid, by the end of the summer of 1946, in services and goods, as war damages, the sum of 1,050 million dollars, which represented a disastrous amount considering the resources of the country.

Since some circles estimated the Soviet appropriations to be over 80% of the Romanian national income, this could not be carried out without impairing the country's productive capital. In fact, Moscow did not hesitate, between August 23, 1944 (the date of Romania's *coup d'état*) – and September 12, 1944 – (the signature of the armistice) – to appropriate the following: the entire of the Romanian Navy, a great part of Romania's Danube and Black Sea merchant shipping, 227 railway engines and 23,000 railway cars, practically all the aircraft, trucks and private automobiles, a substantial part of the cattle herds, technical installations, etc. Romania thereby lost all its long and hard earned production capacity, putting its economy in a state of paralysis.

Fraud in Style: Sovrom

After the voracious Soviets devoured Romania's economic reserves, new ways of exploiting the country were devised. These new means were supposed to be less brutal than the plunder, the requisitions, and the war reparations, but proved equally effective in absorbing the output of Romania's workers.

This new task was entrusted to the "Sovrom" Companies, the mixed Soviet-Romanian Enterprises, which, through maximum effort to increase Romanian production, served exclusively the interests of the Soviet Union. Any sensible regime or economic system exploits limited reserves with an eye on the quantities available, internal demand and export capacity, while protecting national interests. This was not the *raison d'être* of the Sovroms, whose main task remained the exploitation of the country by the Soviets, without any reference to the needs of the local population or the future of the Romanian economy.

Moscow made sure that the 16 most important industries came under the control of the Soviets. Moscow thus obtained control over the production of oil, coal, gas, timber, metals, uranium, the construction industry, chemicals, means of transport, coastal and deep-sea navigation, air travel, banking, insurance, and the film industry.

The Soviet depredation, with the help of the Sovrom Enterprises, started from the moment that the Soviets made an estimate of their share in the companies, supposed in principle – to be equal to that of the Romanians. In fact, the Soviet share amounted to zero, since Moscow "contributed" either Romanian goods requisitioned by the Soviet Army, or properties belonging to former enemies in Romania – German and Italian assets and, according to a Soviet interpretation of the Potsdam Agreement, even French, Belgian, and Dutch assets, for French, Belgian, and Dutch nationals were put on a par with former war enemies.

A New "Shady Business"

After stripping Romania of its natural riches and when the Kremlin noticed that Romania's economy was about to go under, Moscow came with a new shady proposal: it was willing to sell its share in the Sovroms, for a fraudulently overestimated price, which has never been officially disclosed.

Undoubtedly, Moscow did not waste this opportunity of extracting a last benefit, when liquidating the Sovroms, by forcing the Romanians to decree a monetary reform, on January 31, 1954, through which the value of the leu was increased vis-à-vis the ruble. The exchange rate was nearly doubled – from 2.80

lei to the ruble, to 1.50 lei to the ruble. By this simple measure, Moscow obtained nearly twice as much as the fictitious initial subscription share. Instead of keeping silent about this shady financial transaction, the Soviets publicized their so-called generosity and stated that the liquidation amount was thereby reduced by 4,300 million lei.

But the bleeding of Romania's economy did not end with the liquidation of the Sovroms. The exploitation was carried on under another, more subtle, disguise. The new method was discovered late, in 1960, when statistical data concerning the Soviet Union's foreign trade were published for the 1955-1957 period.

The new device of Soviet exploitation was the overpricing of Soviet goods sold to Romania, at above the international market level, and the underpricing of Romania's products imported by Moscow. This renewed extortionist manipulation became possible because of the special trade relations which the Soviet Union maintains with its satellite states, it is entitled to estimate the prices, particularly since Moscow assumed a dominant position in Romania's foreign trade; it was the RSR's most important source of raw materials – iron ore and coke – as well as the top buyer of the end products.

As Moscow managed thus to enjoy a sort of monopoly over Romania's foreign trade, there was no impediment to dictating overpricing of Soviet exports and underpricing of Romanian imports. The overpricing of Soviet goods could not be justified by superior quality. It is well known that the Soviet ores are not distinguished for their rich contents or purity; that Soviet industrial equipment very often needs repair and reassembly. The discriminatory prices could only be explained by the unequal relationship between Romania and the Soviet Union.

What is surprising is the fact that the present leaders in Bucharest took 20 years to admit the truth, which the most modest of Romanian citizens had already long perceived: that the country had been and still was being exploited by the Soviet Union.

The Efforts Towards Economic Independence

The decision to have Romania specialize in agriculture appears to have been shared, at least partly, by the Soviet leadership.

From a secret report submitted by Walter Ulbricht to the plenary meeting of his Central Committee, on July 29–30, 1963, it is known that an embarrassing exchange of words took place at the Moscow meeting of First Secretaries and heads of government of the Comecon countries between the First Secretaries of the Romanian and East German parties. During that meeting, Ulbricht requested the Romanians to push their agricultural specialization and to increase per hectare output in order to provide the industrial Communist states with better food supplies. He naturally included his own country in that category. Simultaneously, Ulbricht criticized the Romanian preference for the products of "capitalist" industry, even in cases where there were corresponding items of Communist origin. Gheorghiu-Dej answered that Romania took into consideration first the quality of the goods and requested, in his turn, that the industrial Communist states raise the quality of their products to the level of world market requirements.

We must not forget that, shortly before, Romania had complained because of the poor quality and late delivery of industrial equipment manufactured in Czechoslovakia. Thus, we can only reach the conclusion that the conflict of interests between Romania and the industrial Communist states of Comecon was deeply rooted. A communiqué of the Romanian Central Committee, of March 8, 1963, mentioned the existence of serious economic controversies between the Khrushchev Project for economic integration and the multilateral industrial development policy of the Bucharest regime.

On the one side, the Romanian Communists were no longer willing to accept exploitation by the industrial Communist states and sought new economic relations with the Western industrial countries, while on the other the industrial Communist states insisted that Romania should accept the suggested plan for economic integration. Gheorghiu-Dej went even further: on visiting, in November 1963, the industrial sites of the Argeş district and Oltenia (Little Wallachia) he praised – to the surprise of all – the valuable contribution of the big Western enterprises to the industrialization of Romania, thus underlining that he intended to develop his economic relationship with the free world even more. Simultaneously, numerous Western experts appeared in Romanian factories and the renewal of the traditional economic and cultural relations with the West gained visible impetus.

Polemics Among Eastern Economists

Meanwhile the polemics between the Soviet Camp and Romania about Romania's industrialization also gained ground among economic experts.

The economist Huber, for instance, did not hesitate to advise small countries with a flourishing agriculture – that is, Romania – to concentrate on agriculture and to renounce any idea of developing a heavy industry. Another Communist area economist Willi Knutz, criticized the people who opposed economic integration within Comecon, and his criticism was, once more, addressed to Romania.

An irate answer came from the Romanian economist C. Murgescu (in *Viaţa Economică,* June 5, 1964) based on the famous Statement of April 22–26, 1964, which underlined the arguments supporting economic independence. This Statement of the Central Committee of the Romanian Workers' Party asserted for the first time, with the required clarity, Romania's right, as a sovereign state in all fields – economic, social, political, etc. – to make its own decisions.

Based on the same Statement and according to the principle of national sovereignty, Romania turned down the proposed economic integration of Eastern Europe, the establishment of a Common Planning Authority, and also participation in founding mixed international organizations, which reminded Romanians, quite rightly, of the Sovroms. This meant that Romania, in a fairly late endeavor toward independence, prepared to elude Moscow's tyrannical tutelage, keeping in its own hand the reins of the country's economy.

Romania's Resistance in the Service of Western Europe

Romania's economic resistance to Soviet exploitation thereby led to a frustration of the Eastern Europe Integration Plan and to the postponement, into the distant future, of Moscow's political and economic aims in Europe.

In this way – perhaps involuntarily – Romania rendered Western Europe a great service, in the sense that no monolithic block of Communist states, integrated within Comecon, confronted the West, but instead only the traditional national states of Central and Eastern Europe, with whom negotiations and understandings are simpler to achieve. Meanwhile, Western Europe gained a welcome respite, in order to consolidate its own economic, political, and social integration, burdened though it was by many problems.

The Romanian Communists were probably afraid that the "Council for Mutual Economic Assistance" was just another device for economic exploitation and political domination by Moscow, a new body to subordinate Romania's interests to the exclusive benefit of the Soviet Union. The Romanian Communists' method of resistance against integration was to plead national sovereignty and to express preference for bilateral negotiations, instead of the multilateral ones suggested, thus avoiding a head-on clash with the common front of the Comecon states and seeking out a single partner – or adversary – as the case might be.

In fact, Romania turned down the invitation to join the internal price system of the Communist Bloc, since this was just one more disguised attempt to return to the economic exploitation of Romania. The new price system, scheduled to go into effect on January 1964, forecast an approach to the world market prices of 1957–1961. But during that period, the prices for agricultural products were low, those for industrial goods high, so that Romania – whose foreign trade had remained, to a great extent, dependent on exports of agricultural and oil products – would have been at a disadvantage by applying the new price system.

Because of the Romanian protests, Comecon delayed the introduction of the new price system until the beginning of 1965 and accepted a new, and for

Romania a more favourable, basis for calculating prices, by no longer basing them on the world market prices of 1957-1961, and replacing that basis with the prices of the years 1960–1964. Romania's opposition to the Soviet attempts at exploitation thereby started to bear fruit.

The Soviet-Romanian Economic Polemic

Romania's efforts to achieve economic independence brought a Soviet reply, which was not long delayed.

It started with a polemic in a radio-program on the controversial subject of East European economic integration. On May 30, 1964 Radio Moscow criticized people who intend to pursue their economic development in isolation, without mentioning the Romanians. Radio Bucharest nevertheless answered on June 5, 1964 – in very similar terms to the first esoteric Sino-Soviet attacks – by explaining that those who intend to initiate a new polemic, that is the Soviets, have no sense of responsibility and create a harmful atmosphere. Given this prompt reaction, Moscow reversed its attitude and recognized that each country is entitled to retain and defend its national characteristics and interests.

Nevertheless, the Soviet-Romanian controversy reached its highpoint in June 1964, when *Viaţa Economică*, in indignant and forceful terms, answered Walew. Professor L.B. Walew – from Moscow University – had published a plan suggesting the creation of a complex economic zone in the region of the Lower Danube.

The Economic Zone suggested by Professor Walew included an area of 150,000 sq.km., with about 12,000,000 inhabitants, composed of 6 of the 16 "regions" of Romania (Oltenia, Argeş, Bucharest, Ploeşti, Galaţi and Dobrogea), of the northern part of Bulgaria and the Soviet district along the Danube Delta (South Bessarabia) which had been Romanian territory before the war.

Simultaneously with turning down Walew's project, the Romanians criticized, in strong terms, the entire Soviet plan for the creation of economic complexes among neighboring states, as put forward by G. Sorokin, G. Karhin, P. M. Alampiev, I. M. Maergois, A. E. Probst, N. D. Stolpov, and N. F. Ianitki. And last but not least, Khrushchev's own idea – of economic cooperation on a broader scale – as presented in the September 1962 issue of *Problems of Peace and Socialism*.

Criticism Addressed to the Soviet Leadership

The Romanians, very susceptible to any kind of economic exploitation after their own experiences, quite rightly saw a new attempt in all this type of projects by the Soviet Union to impose its own system of neocolonial exploitation.

The Romanians turned down the association suggested by Professor L.B. Walew, to which Romania was supposed to contribute 2/3 of its territory, 3/4 of its population, 70% of its power stations, with rich gas, salt, and other deposits, in contrast to a ludicrously low Bulgarian-Soviet contribution. But what the Romanians resented most was the fact that such plans and projects, presented under the modest label of "Economic Complexes," were a threat to the territorial integrity of the country and were designed to counteract the ideas of nation and state.

To all appearances, this was a first and serious blackmail attempt against Romania which was confronted with the choice of accepting economic integration within Comecon, or risking dismembration. Romania's refusal to take advantage of Moscow's latest form of "international socialist specialization" and the adoption of a common planning body aroused unleashed hysterical rage in Khrushchev and induced him to threaten the Romanians with the partition of their state.

Bucharest's Communist rulers seem to have taken this threat very seriously. They mobilized public opinion, they discussed Moscow's attempts at extortion in public meetings, they criticized Khrushchev by name and – it appears – had the courage to reply to the threat of partition by raising the problem of Bessarabia, a Romanian province annexed by the Soviet Union after the Second World War.

With all the means at their disposal, the Romanians defended the idea of a Romanian national state and refused the latest and most dangerous Soviet demand, made in barely disguised terms, to detach Romanian territory by simple administrative measures, and all that in the name of Marxist-Leninist principles.

Support from Red China

Moscow, as a result of Bucharest's unequivocal answer, was forced once more to retract. *Izvestia* published a severe criticism of Walew's plan, shining proof that Romania's opposition to Moscow's pressure and blackmail were finally rewarded.

It should be recognized that the historic moment was propitious for conducting such a half-independent economic and national policy. Soviet troops had left the country and could not return without causing serious international complications. The Soviet Union had engaged its force and prestige in its controversies with Peking and could not afford to provoke a new schism within the Communist camp.

Red China supported Romania in its resistance and in its economic policy, aiming at a national industry, on the basis of its own forces first and only secondly on the help from Communist Economic Cooperation. It also appears that the United States, followed by other industrial states of the free world, had decided to help Romania economically, in order to enable it to retain its independence.

We can conclude that the Soviet exploitation of Romania had aroused the suspicion of all its citizens against their powerful neighbor and had also stimulated the wish to achieve economic and political independence and to refuse any kind of cooperation that might, once more, expose the country to extortion. Should Romania succeed in resisting energetically, in the future, too, the attempt to integrate Eastern Europe economically, we can assume that the price which the Soviet Union would have to pay could be significant.

That price could amount to giving up the pan-Russian dreams in Eastern Europe, or simply in the whole of Europe.

Der Europäische Osten, No. 118, Munich, January 1965, pp. 23-32.

XVI

A POLITICAL SHIFTING OF ONE'S GROUND

From the Soviet point of view, the word Bessarabia and the problem it raises ceased to exist on June 28, 1940, when the Romanian province was annexed by the Soviet Union, following Moscow's ultimatum to the Romanian government. Bessarabia, it is said, was nothing more than the name given to a colonial appendage of a capitalist state, Romania, and thus as a historical injustice eliminated now and forever from the political map of the world. Solving a territorial conflict by the stroke of a pen and by renaming the contested region is an easy solution, the more so since the new name chosen reminds one more than the old of the ties of this province with Romania. For, if Bessarabia derives its name from the Bassarab dynasty, the founders of Wallachia, the present name of Socialist Moldavia, adopted by the Soviets, demonstrates this province's ethnic and historic ties to Romanian Moldavia, of which it was an integral part until 1812. Erased from the political map of the world, Bessarabia proved, nevertheless, to be a living reality, creating serious difficulties for the very ones who tried to bury it. One can even say that the roughly 20,000 square miles of Romanian soil occupied by the Russians after the Second World War (some 17,350 for Bessarabia and 2,460 for Bucovina and the Herța Region) causes more problems for the Soviet Union than all the other 245,000 square miles of territory annexed by that country after the same war. When the Treaty of Paris was signed in 1947, surrendering Bessarabia to the Soviet Union, nobody would have guessed that this territory would soon become an object of international preoccupation. It is true that, before the Paris Conference, the Romanian opposition had tabled a memorandum on the problem, protesting the annexation; but for the realists it was clear that since Romania was a small and defeated state, which had substantially less military force than the Soviet Union, and since none of the Great Powers was interested in supporting its claims against the Soviet superpower, Bessarabia was lost forever.

It so happened, however, that, in spite of these considerations and forecasts, the Bessarabian problem (we understand by this Bessarabia and Northern Bucovina) remains current and is even becoming more so. To begin with, we must underline that the Romanian government has not formally demanded the restitution of the territory annexed by the USSR, nor has it raised the problem in diplomatic channels. It did not ask for more autonomy for Socialist Moldavia or for more rights for the "Moldavian" people. The Bessarabian problem is present in a more subtle way, in a way characteristic of communist regimes: in a form, disguised and allusive, which means much for the analyst, while realists remain skeptical.

At the end of two years of latent evolution, the Bessarabian problem, which surfaced unexpectedly in 1964, was such as to affect the Russian-Romanian relations. For the first time, the Soviet press, usually cautious when it comes to touching upon subjects sensitive to the allied communist countries, warned Bucharest of the consequences of its vindictive policy.

The Internationalist Thesis

Yet, at the beginning, the Romanian Communist Party whole-heartedly embraced the Soviet thesis which maintains that Bessarabia wants to remain part of the USSR in order to enjoy the blessings of the communist system, rather than suffer under the yoke of the Romanian bourgeoisie. The union of Bessarabia with Romania is explained as an act of force, being presented as follows: "Exploiting a moment of bitter struggle between the Romanian workers and peasants and the «White Guards», the Romanian oligarchy tore from the body of the Federation of Soviet Republics the Moldavian Soviet Republic of Bessarabia." The resolution of the Third Congress of the Romanian Communist Party in 1924 seemed to assume that the supreme aspiration of the Bessarabian population was to be returned to the Soviet Union. It declared: "The workers and peasants of Bessarabia, who witnessed the first period of the liberating Russian Revolution and who are now being crushed under the boot of the Romanian military dictatorship, daily display their national-revolutionary aspiration of being reunited with the USSR." The above-mentioned resolution considered it necessary to aid the "persecuted nationalities" and to grant them the right of self-determination "to the point of complete change from their existing status." In order to facilitate the break with Romania and the union with Soviet Russia, a plebiscite was advocated "to give the Bessarabian population the opportunity to decide its own fate." The thesis of the Romanian Communist Party had, therefore, been clearly formulated and repeatedly restated: Bessarabia had been forcefully occupied by the Romanian Army and had been subjected to forced Romanization by the closing down of Russian schools and the banning of the use of the Russian language in the army and in public institutions. It was added that, in spite of this, the Bessarabian population did not harbor resentment against the Romanian workers and peasants, that it wished to help "destroy the power of the oligarchy" and to "create a Soviet Romania." We see, therefore, that, at that time, the Romanian Communist Party had thoroughly espoused the internationalist thesis which placed Soviet interests above the national interests of Romania. The Romanian national state was to be destroyed, because it was a bourgeois state, and to be divided in order to facilitate the installation of a communist regime and the creation of a Soviet Romania.

Without any reservation, without the slightest hesitation, the Romanian Communist Party adopted the Soviet thesis. The resolution adopted by the Fourth Congress of the Romanian Communist Party in 1928 subscribes to the Soviet line, according to which the Bessarabians are not Romanian, but constitute a distinct, Moldavian nationality. "It is the duty of our party to sustain, by all means, the struggle of the Bessarabian workers for their unity with Socialist Moldavia." Socialist Moldavia, at the time, only stretched to the east of the Dniester. The same policy was adopted by the Fifth congress, in a resolution published in 1932, according to which Romania had occupied foreign territories and colonized them at the expense of the oppressed and exploited Moldavian, Ukrainian, Russian, Bulgarian, Hungarian, German, Serbian, Turkish, and Jewish nationalities. The partition of these nationalities from the Romanian state was again proposed as the only reasonable solution to the nationalities problem in Romania.

With the arrival of Soviet troops in Romania, Bessarabia was virtually cut off from the rest of the country and incorporated *de facto* by the Soviet Union. All the books, articles, and studies on Bessarabia were withdrawn and all reference to the province was and is banned, even from private conversations. Even more, the word "Bessarabia" has been purged from all publications existing in public libraries. At the moment of the cession of Bessarabia, the Romanian Communist Party did not make the slightest gesture of protest. Considering the resolutions of the Communist Party as validation, and the annexation of Bessarabia by the Soviets justified, the authorities would no longer have any reason to speak on the subject, except tangentially, in school books and in encyclopaedias, where it could not be avoided. But the space allotted to Bessarabia is reduced to a minimum and the explanations begin to look embarrassingly terse. The Stalinist historian Mihail Roller ventures to mention in his work the Bucharest Peace Treaty of 1812, which surrendered Bessarabia to the Russians and holds that Bessarabia was thus liberated from the Turkish yoke and from local feudalism. The formulation becomes more equivocal in the Encyclopaedic Dictionary published in 1962 where it is simply stated that, after the Treaty of Bucharest (1812), Bessarabia "became part of Russia". The *History of Romania,* printed in 1964, takes another step toward objectivity and dares to announce that the Russians, who had occupied the Danubian Principalities from the beginning of hostilities, evacuated that territory, with the exception of the region between the Dniester and the Pruth, the latter territory being incorpo..ted into the Russian Empire. The assignment to Romania of the three southern districts of Bessarabia, decided upon by the Congress of Paris in 1856, is qualified, however, as an act of constraint imposed upon Russia in order to deprive her of the right of being a Danubian power. On this point, too, we witness a change of attitude.

Under the pretext of the discovery of new documents in the Vienna archives, the historian C. C. Giurescu announced at the beginning of 1964 that the chapter concerning the Congress of Paris will be revised, apparently in a sense more favorable to the Romanians. More recent events are treated by Roller in the same pro-Soviet spirit, the union of Bessarabia with Romania in 1918 being regarded as an act of seizure following military occupation organized with the complicity of the Allies, while the 1940 Soviet annexation is viewed as "liberation". The encyclopaedia speaks of occupation in 1918 and of restitution in 1940. One must await the publication of Volume V of the *History of Romania* in order fully to appreciate the length of the way covered from the Stalinist interpretation of the Bessarabian problem to the nationalist one. Until then, in order to evade personal responsibility, Romanian historians approach the delicate subject of Bessarabia by not only adopting the interpretation of the Soviet historians, but also by even translating certain Russian expressions unknown in the Romanian language. To say that Bessarabia entered the composition of Russia is to translate incorrectly the Russian word *"obrazovavsit,"* used in the Soviet encyclopaedia to explain the first annexation of Bessarabia.

Declaration of Independence

The word "Bessarabia," which one could not put on paper or pronounce without incurring grave risk, was to re-enter the every day vocabulary and public discussions in the summer of 1964. At that time, the diplomats stationed in Bucharest said that the whole country was discussing, at the level of the basic organizations of the Communist Party, the economic depredations perpetrated by the Soviets in Romania. At that time, the seizure of Bessarabia and Northern Bucovina was denounced as the most painful instance of Soviet looting and the worst injustice committed against Romania. How can one explain this sudden political turnabout? What generated the courage to raise a problem considered the tabu of all tabus? Political chronology suggests an explanation: in March 1964, Romanian Prime Minister Ion Gheorghe Maurer, while visiting Beijing, became conscious of the insoluble conflict between the USSR and China, and seized the opportunity offered Bucharest to rely on Beijing to counter the suffocating embrace of Moscow, which was trying economically to integrate all the countries of Eastern Europe. Relying on Chinese support, Bucharest dared publish, in April 1964, its "Declaration of Independence" by means of which it no longer recognized Moscow's tutelage, and organized, the following month, a veritable anti-Soviet campaign, resuscitating the Bessarabian problem. If this did not happen at Beijing's instigation, it happened at least with its tacit approval. Bucharest considered that thanks to the aggravation of the Sino-Soviet conflict, which was shaping up fast as a territorial issue in Asia, Romania could remind the world of the seizure of Bessarabia and of Northern Bucovina without running the fatal risk of Soviet economic and military sanctions. In fact, the Soviets, faced with the unexpected claim by the Chinese to some 600,000 square miles of territory in Asia, adopted a prudent wait-and-see attitude vis-à-vis the Romanian irredentist allusions. In other words, Romania had found in China a great power ready to endorse its territorial claims. This became very evident on July 10, 1964, when Mao Tse-tung, interviewed by Japanese Socialists, attacked the Soviet imperialist policy of annexing foreign territory in Europe and Asia, and mentioned expressly the annexation of Romanian territory. Of all European countries which had been territorially amputated by Russia after the Second World War, Romania was the only one ready to lend an ear to the words of the Chinese leader. The Baltic countries, incorporated by the Soviet Union, had no chance of establishing contact with Beijing; Poland, interested in obtaining recognition for its western border on the Oder-Neisse line, refused to succumb to the temptation of hypothetical territorial compensation eastward; Czechoslovakia was more interested in keeping the Sudetenland than recovering the sub-Carpathian Ruthenia with the fictitious help of a distant ally. Finally, East Germany could not be tempted by the Chinese bait either, knowing that it existed as a state only by the grace of the Soviet Union. Romania, however, with its independent inclinations, could play Beijing's game and undermine the USSR in Eastern Europe, where Mao now posed as the only defender of the right to self-determination of the European peoples. The reaction to Mao's incendiary declarations was prompt. *Pravda* spoke of an attempt to instigate territorial disputes between socialist countries by discussing international agreements of the Second World War. *Prace* of Bratislava said indignantly that Mao's statements could only be applauded by West Germany. The Romanian press did not publish the Mao interview. It appeared, however, that the Romanians, assured of Chinese support, began to implement their own plan of escalating the Bessarabian problem. In September 1964, Ion Gheorghe Maurer went again to Beijing, allegedly in an attempt to mediate in the Sino-Soviet conflict, which Romania did not want to see disappear. At the time, the Bucharest government, realizing that the Bessarabian problem was being debated merely within the confines of the socialist camp, sought to obtain, in addition to Mao's support, that of the fathers of communism. And what support could be more prestigious for Bucharest than to call Marx himself to the witness stand! Such a thing did not look impossible, since Marx and Engels had expressed their views on Bessarabia in several of their works. Among these are *The Foreign Policy of Russian Tzarism* in which Engels, one of the founding fathers of communism, simply admitted that "Bessarabia is Romanian and Poland, Polish. One cannot speak in these cases of the reunion of ethnic groups which were scattered, but related, and could be called Russian; we are faced here with a flagrant, forceful conquest of foreign territories; simply, with stealing." But one did even better than that, for, digging into the archives of the Amsterdam Institute for International Social History, historian Andrei Oțetea came upon notes made by Marx from a book by French historian Elias Regnault on the Moldavian-Wallachian problem and Russian-Romanian relations. This unpublished manuscript of Marx's served Romanian interests excellently, because it makes Marx appear a convinced defender of the Romanian cause, condemning the economic exploitation of the Moldavians and Wallachians by the Russians, as well as the seizure of Bessarabia. It appears that Marx's notes on the Romanians were already printed in Bucharest in May 1964, but that the distribution of the book was postponed – for causes unknown – until November the same year. By a strange coincidence, the same sort of delay was the fate of the interview with Mao, dated July 12, 1964, but published only on September 2, 1964, by *Pravda,* which also commented on it. The fact is that the notes of Marx, printed in 20,500 copies, were sold out in a few days, showing how eager the readers were to learn that criticizing the Russians was again permitted in Romania. It is said that the Soviet Embassy in Bucharest hurriedly bought up a great many copies, in order to prevent their distribution. The reprinting of the book had been promised in advance, but Bucharest did not consider it productive to provoke new Soviet protests by insisting on going ahead. Instead of re-editing Marx, the Romanians chose to produce the Engels article, who came to his friend's help, supporting the rights of the Romanians over Bessarabia. The Romanian zealots pulled a letter out of Engels's works which he had addressed to the Romanian socialists in 1888 deploring "the abduction, twice in a row, of Bessarabia," as well as the Russian invasions of Romania. One could have gone further to cite, in support of the Romanian cause, the right of all peoples to self-determination, recognized by Lenin and at a certain moment by Stalin himself. No doubt, Stalin is no longer a reference, even in the communist bibliography, but appealing to Lenin would have been possible. As a matter of fact, Miron Constantinescu reproaches the Moscow Institute of Marxism-Leninism in an article that it did not reproduce, in the works of Lenin, a message that the latter had addressed to the workers and peoples of Austro-Hungary, on behalf of the People's Commissaries, underlining the necessity for the respect of the peoples' right to self-determination to the point of their separation from the state.

The Soviets found themselves in a most uncomfortable position, for they could not remain silent in the face of the Romanian allusions that Bessarabia was Romanian and could not, on the other hand, openly criticize the views of their ideological masters, Marx and Engels. Finally, they chose to reply indirectly, not criticizing the Romanian publishing of Marx's notes, but a Swiss daily which had reported on the book. It was Ivan Ivanovici Bodyul (Bodiul in the Romanian spelling), the secretary of the Communist Party of Moldavia, who found a pretext to criticize the *Journal de Genève's* affirmation that Bessarabia had been annexed for the first time by Russia in 1812. Against all evidence, Bodyul wanted to convince his readers that the Moldavians of Bessarabia had in 1711 expressed their desire to unite with Russia. Bodyul was particularly irritated – without admitting it – not by the historical truth of the abduction of Bessarabia, but by the more current problem of the publishing of Marx's notes by the Romanians to which the Swiss paper had drawn attention. Another historian of the Moldavian Socialist Republic, A. Grekul, raised the subject more directly, trying to prove, by citing quotations from Marx's work, that, during the 19th century, the Balkan peoples regarded Russia as their ally and deliverer.

One would have thought that this was an academic dispute, without political implications, had it not been for additional signs which created a general atmosphere of fervent nationalism and invited interpretations ambiguous, to say the least, as regards the Bucharest government's position on Bessarabia. Thus, the 107th anniversary of Moldavia's union with Wallachia was celebrated in January 1966 under the banner of all-Romanian unity, but with no allusion whatsoever to the fact that the provinces had been annexed by the USSR. Likewise, the 500th anniversary of the Monastery of Putna, erected by Stephen the Great, who reigned over Greater Moldavia, occasioned vibrant patriotic manifestations only few miles from the new Soviet border. The occasion saw the reprinting of a book by Nicolae Iorga on Stephen the Great *(Ştefan cel Mare)* which first appeared before the First World War and abounded in Bessarabian allusions.

It should be noted, however, that the introduction to the new edition made no secret of the fact that Iorga's work had "obvious political aims in the ideological preparation for *complete* national unification." Even more significant was the appearance, for the first time in Romania, of maps featuring Bessarabia. There had been some information that some such maps had been distributed by the Chinese Embassy earlier, but this time they were exhibited at the Bucharest Museum of the History of the Romanian Communist Party, as well as at the National Unity Museum of Iaşi, in the guise of ethnographical and economic maps. According to some information, the Bucharest government's publishing house printed a map of Bessarabia with the Russian names of towns, villages, and rivers replaced by their true Romanian names. Finally, while a Soviet monograph considered writer Bogdan Petriceicu Haşdeu to be a Russian writer, the Romanians promptly replied that Hașdeu could only be considered a Romanian writer. Born in Bessarabia, he had studied in Kharkov and was included in a Soviet monograph on *"Russian-Romanian Literary Relations in the First Half of the 19th Century"* as a Russian author, due to his Moldavian origin, although he emigrated to, settled in, and wrote in Romania. This small controversy regarding literary history augmented the number of Soviet-Romanian encounters, but is devoid of any particular significance. A position was more clearly taken only on May 7, 1966, when Nicolae Ceaușescu, Secretary-General of the Romanian Communist Party, rejected, in a resounding speech, the resolutions of the Third, Fourth, and Fifth congresses of his party. Ceaușescu stated that those resolutions were prejudicial to Romanian national unity and had been forced upon the Romanian Communist Party by the Comintern. This had been possible – added the Romanian secretary-general – because the Comintern was in the habit, between the two world wars, of imposing foreigners upon the leadership of the Romanian Communist Party who docilely carried out Moscow's orders. This speech, which was aimed at tracing the main political lines for the editing by the Romanian historians of a RCP history, resulted in the fact that Bucharest formally renounced the Soviet thesis that the Moldavians of Bessarabia are a different nationality from the Romanians and that Bessarabia is an integral part of the Soviet Union. The escalation of the Bessarabian problem had reached a critical point, not yet the breaking point. Marx had protested posthumously against the annexation of Bessarabia, the responsibility was his, and perhaps also that of the Romanian Academy, which had published his notes. This time, the situation was different, because it was the Secretary-General of the Romanian Communist Party who had unequivocally denounced the resolutions which gave Moscow the right to annex certain portions of Romanian territory. The fateful name of Bessarabia had not been spoken, but the allusion arising from the context could not have been clearer. The praise Soviet historians gave to their Romanian colleagues for having adopted Leninist positions on Bessarabia and having renounced the political ideal of a Greater Romania had proved premature.

The Support of China

Again, Moscow's reaction was silence. A silence that could be explained by the fact that the Soviet Union did not want, on the eve of the conference of the Warsaw Pact member countries, which was to meet in Bucharest, to give Romania one more reason for insisting of its demand that all military blocs be dissolved, or to push Romania into the arms of Peking, which was just then preparing to send Chou En-lai to Bucharest. Moreover, the USSR was too involved in its serious border conflict along the Amur River to provoke another one along the Pruth River. And the Asian problem was far from being amiably solved, particularly after the breaking off of the 1964 negotiations. The Chinese Communist leaders reiterated Mao's position (Chou En-lai, August 1965 and Chen Yi on January 18, 1965 and May 24, 1966), while the Soviet leaders stated that their country was ready to face any military situation (Adzhubey, August 3, 1964 and Podgorny on July 1, 1966). The Soviet Union was even going to weaken its forces stationed in Eastern Europe, in order to strengthen its Asian defenses. Under these circumstances, Chou En-lai, arriving in Bucharest in the middle of June 1966, decided to convince the Romanians to enter the neutrals' camp and cross over into the realm of orthodox Communism, which the Chinese professed to represent. It was probably with an eye on Bucharest that the Chinese urged, shortly before Chou's visit to Romania, the other Communists to choose once and for all between Soviet revisionism and Maoist orthodoxy.

Peking may have believed that, after the speech of Ceauşescu, who had pleaded for the dissolution of the Warsaw Pact and revised the position of the Romanian Communist Party on Bessarabia, the Romanians were ready to line up with the Chinese. The speech delivered by Chou En-lai at the airport in Bucharest was promising: China approved of and encouraged Romania's policy of independence.

Wishing to please their Romanian hosts, the Peking Chinese folklore group, which was in Bucharest at the same time as the Chinese delegation, presented a gala evening performance during which the artist Chin Lien-fin sang in Romanian a song with the evocative title: "This Is My Moldavia." The bomb exploded, however, at the final session, which had been postponed for three hours because Chou En-lai and Ceauşescu could not agree upon certain passages of the speech which the Chinese guest was to deliver. Surely, the object of disagreement must have been very important to have interfered to such an extent with protocol. Did the Chinese offer the Romanians the sort of bait which would have shaken them out of their neutrality, such as political support for the formal campaign to reclaim Bessarabia? In that case, it is possible that the Romanians judged such provocation and the risks it carried too great. The fact remains that Ceauşescu and Chou En-lai could not agree and that the Sino-Romanian meeting and Chou's visit ended in failure. The Romanians continued to practise neutrality and the Soviets refrained from poisoning the atmosphere by commenting on the incendiary speech which had been delivered by Ceauşescu on May 7, 1966.

One might have thought that the climax of the Bessarabian crisis had passed. In reality, the Soviets were going to be confronted with disquieting national manifestations in Socialist Moldavia itself. The Moldavian Romanians had learned, no doubt, of Bucharest's new foreign policy, which was parting ways with Moscow's. They had also learned, from Podgorny, from his Chişinău, October 1964 speech, of Mao's opinion regarding the Romanian rights over

Bessarabia. Such a political climate was likely to awaken Moldavian nationalism. It appears from articles published in the daily *Moldova Socialistă* that the Moldavians were beginning to have thoughts about national claims, particularly in the cultural, economic, and political fields. To begin with they demanded that they be permitted to use Romanian (or Moldavian, as it was called there) as their first language; that their books and newspapers replace the Cyrillic alphabet with the Latin one; that the leading cadres in the economy and the party be recruited to a greater extent from among Moldavians. Official propaganda, worried by this state of affairs, endeavored to convince the Moldavians of the correctness of the party policy, of the interest of the population in learning Russian – the tongue of proletarian unity – and that the Cyrilic alphabet would aid the Moldavians in learning Russian. Aleksandr Filipovich Gheorghiţă, the prime minister of Socialist Moldavia, explained that the large proportion of Russian, Ukrainian, Byelorussian, and other cadres in Moldavia was due to the lack of Moldavian specialists. In the framework of a vast ideological campaign against national prejudice, the Moscow regime denounced the "calumnies" spread for the purpose of belittling Soviet achievements and glorifying the Romanian past. It was mainly the young, victims of bourgeois propaganda broadcast by radio stations, who had become skeptical, passive, and disinclined to understand the policy of the party. The Moldavian historians were invited to study more closely the period of the "occupation" of Bessarabia by the Romanians and to point out their misdeeds; the authorities were to exercise, in a neo-Zhdanovite spirit, their publishing rights; finally, the ideologists and activists were to propagate the internationalist idea and that of Russian Moldavian brotherhood. In February 1967, Bodyul resumed the offensive, before the Central Committee of the Moldavian Communist Party he vehemently denounced the Moldavian nationalistic tendencies which, instead of decreasing, were acquiring more importance and substance. A scapegoat was found in the person of the propaganda chief, V. K. Barbulat, who was fired. The alarm of the authorities and the mobilization of cadres in the fight against Moldavian nationalism are in themselves proof of the seriousness of the situation. It is possible that the Soviets consented to certain concessions, promoting more Moldavians to positions of greater responsibility in the economy, but it is doubtful that the ethnic structure of political and administrative bodies will be altered in favor of the Moldavians. According to Soviet statistics, the Moldavians represent 65% of the population of Socialist Moldavia, (75% in the rural areas), but they are represented in a proportion of only 35% in the Central Committee elected in March 1966.

In the present circumstances, Moscow does not seem ready to grant the Moldavians proportional representation, for the simple reason that it does not trust them. Moldavian nationalism is much more dangerous than that of other minorities in the Soviet Union, because Moldavians are separated from their natural center of attraction, Romania, by an easily accessible border. An agreement signed in Bucharest in March 1966 authorizes mutual visits between the Soviet Union and Romania, no visa being required, but only a simple invitation from relatives living on the other bank of the Pruth. If these visits become frequent, the regime historians will have a lot of difficulty showing that there is no relationship between Moldavians and Romanians, for, after crossing the border, that argument will no longer persuade even the young Moldavians who have never lived in Romania. Even though it may seem unrealistic, the idea of correcting the unjust fate imposed upon Bessarabia after the Second World War, through its annexation by the USSR without popular consent, has surfaced in the minds of Moldavians. The First Secretary of the Moldavian Communist Party makes us aware of it while denouncing the bourgeois apologists who belittle Soviet achievements, trying to sow hostility between socialist countries (specifically between the USSR and Romania) with their requests for the revision of the results of the Second World War. It seems that apologists exist outside (in Romania) as well as inside, in Socialist Moldavia, where they are labeled "antisocial elements." In the new, more liberal political climate following Stalin's death, Moscow has to consider Romania's national feelings and satisfy certain claims of the Moldavian minority. The major conflict which Russia had in Asia and the complications which have arisen in Eastern Europe, where the integration – economic, political, and military – is not advancing to any great extent because of Romanian obstruction, have forced Moscow to follow a policy of prudence and conciliation and to encourage Bucharest to "escalate" the Bessarabian problem slowly. A recent example proves this. June 28, the date of the acceptance by Romania of the 1940 Soviet ultimatum on Bessarabia, is celebrated in the Soviet Union as reunification day for Socialist Moldavia. This day was observed in 1966 in both Moscow and Chişinău, as discreetly as possible, in order to provoke neither the Moldavians, nor the Romanians. The Moscow *Pravda* barely mentioned the event on the fourth page, giving it only a few lines. In Chişinău, where there were no meetings and no public speeches, the local press simply listed the local economic achievements under the Soviet regime. On the same occasion, the Romanian Communist Party published, very apropos, in its theoretical magazine, an article containing the following meaningful sentence: "On June 28, 1940, following an ultimatum of the Soviet government, accepted by the Romanian government, Bessarabia and Northern Bucovina became a part of the USSR". This was the first time that the party had ever used the word "ultimatum", which means coercion. It was also the first time that the Romanian Communists had spoken of the acceptance of this ultimatum by the government, leaving it up to the exegetes to conclude that the people had not been consulted and had not accepted the ultimatum and the annexation of Bessarabia. One could have also noted that, in the Romanian government's answer to the 1940 ultimatum, one spoke of the mere evacuation of Bessarabia, avoiding the use of the word cession and underlining that the government was *forced* to accept the conditions imposed upon it. The armistice convention of September 12, 1944, as well as the Peace Treaty of Paris signed in 1947, cite as the legal foundation for the new annexation of Bessarabia the so-called Accord of June 28, 1940 which cannot be anything but void under international law, since it was accepted only under pressure. It is very difficult to understand how the treaty of Paris, signed by the conquerors of Germany, could be based on the 1940 annexation, which only existed because of the pact between Hitler and Stalin.

In conclusion, it can be said that the Bessarabian problem was raised as much more of a historical than a political problem. The regime only decided once to make use of direct and clear language – when it inscribed in the almanach of Romanian National Holidays published under the aegis of the Bucharest Patriarchate, March 27, 1918 as the date of the proclamation of Bessarabia's union with Romania. This almanach, a publication of low circulation, printed for Romanians living in North America, has, however, neither the weight, nor the political meaning of an official stance.

The hesitation of the Bucharest government can be explained by the fact that the Soviet Union is in a position to exert considerable pressure upon Romania in the economic field, let alone militarily. However one should not overlook the trump cards which Romania itself holds in other areas and which are now anything but negligible quantities. First, the determination of the Moldavian population of Northern Bucovina and Bessarabia to remain Romanian; secondly, the communist doctrine as formulated by Marx, Engels, and Lenin; thirdly, the growing power of China, and finally, world public opinion – that considerable element whose influence led to the emancipation of Asia and Africa and which could one day play a determining role in favor of the Romanian claims. At a time when Stalin's errors in internal policy are being castigated, it seems that the moment has also come to denounce his mistakes in the field of foreign policy, of which the annexation of Bessarabia and Bucovina constitutes a flagrant example.

Aspects des Relations Russo-Roumaines.
Rétrospectives et orientations.
(Paris: Minard, 1967), pp. 227-239.

BIBLIOGRAPHY:

"Appeal to All Members and Activists of Romanian Union of Communist Youth", *Tineretul Leninist,* 1 May 1925.

I.I. Bodyul, "On the Preparations for the Semi-Centennial of the Great Socialist October Revolution and the Tasks of the Party Organization of the Republic", *Moldova Socialistă,* 16 February 1967.

I.I. Bodyul, *Molodezi Moldavii,* 28 November 1966.

I.I. Bodyul, "Report to the Twelfth Congress of the Moldavian Communist Party", Radio Chişinău, 2 March 1966.

I.I. Bodyul, "Sobranie Respublikanskogo Partiinogo Aktiva", *Sovietskaya Moldavya,* 23-24 December 1965.

I.I. Bodyul, "V Sostoianii i Merak Vluchsheniia Marksiskogo Leniniskogo Vospitaniia Trudiashchikhsia Respubliki, *Sovietskaya Moldavya,* 5 January 1966.

Bolshaya Sovietskaya Entsiklopedia /Big Soviet Encyclopaedia/ (Moskva: 1950, vol. V), p. 82.

Calendarul Credinţa /Faith Calendar 1967/, Detroit (Michigan: Ed. Episcopia Misionară Ortodoxă Română din America, 1967), p. 12.

"The Capital Heartily Greeted Comrade Chu-En Lai", *Scînteia,* 17 June 1966.

N. Ceauşescu, "The Romanian Communist Party, Continuer of the Revolutionary and Democratic Struggle of the Romanian People, of the Traditions of the Workers' and Socialist Movement in Romania", *Scînteia,* 8 May 1966.

G. Cioranesco, "Ein Sowjetischer Teilungsplan", *Der Europäische Osten,* January 1965, pp. 23-32.

G. Cioranesco, "L'Exploitation Soviétique des Richesses Économiques Roumaines", *La Nation Roumaine,* August-September 1964.

"Talks between the Delegations of the CC of the Romanian Workers' Party and the Chinese Communist Party", *Scînteia,* 4 March 1964.

M. Constantinescu, "V. I. Lenin's Message to the Workers and Peoples of Austria-Hungary, 2-3 November 1918", *Studii, Revista de Istorie,* January 1966.

"Declaration on the Stand of the Romanian Workers' Party in the Problems of the International Communist and Workers' Party Adopted by the Broad Plenum of the CC of the Romanian Workers' Party of April 1964", *Scînteia,* 26 April 1964.

Dicţionarul Enciclopedic român /Romanian Encyclopaedic Dictionary/, (Bucharest: Editura Politică, 1962, vol. 1), p. 308.

A Diordiţa, Gheorghiţă, "V Edinnoi Bratskoi Zemlie Narodov SSSR", *Sovietskaya Moldavya,* 28 December 1965.

Fr. Engels, "The Foreign Policy of Russian Czarism (1890)", p. 39, in *The Russian Menace to Europe* (Glencoe, Illinois: P.W. Blackstock and B.F. Hoselitz, 1952), p. 288.
M. Frenkel, "Romania Borrows from Soviet Line to Further Her Independence", *New York Times,* 19 December 1964 (International Edition, 21 December 1964).
A. Grekul, "IstokiVelikogo Bratstva", *Sovietskaya Moldavya,* 22 June 1966.
H. Heinrich, "Bukarest und die Bessarabien Frage", *Frankfurter Rundschau,* 6 July 1966.
A. Hoffman, "The Show of Chinese Artists", *România Liberă,* 21 June 1966.
N. Iorga, *Istoria lui Ştefan cel Mare* /History of Stephen the Great/, (Bucharest: Editura pentru Literatură, 1966), p. 2.
Istoria României /History of Romania/, (Bucharest: Editura Academiei RPR, vol III and IV, 1964).
D.S. Kornovan, "Vyshe Urobenii Internationalnogo Vospitaniia Trudiashchikhsia", *Sovietskaya Moldavya,* 19 December 1966.
Mao Ce-Tungove Vyroky, *Praca,* 4 September 1964.
K. Marx, *Însemnări despre Români* /Notes on the Romanians/ (Bucureşti: Editura Academiei RPR, 1964).
T. Nicolescu, "Romanian Echoes", *Secolul XX,* April 1966.
Observations Concerning the Draft Peace Treaty with Romania (Paris: Blanchard, 1946).
R. Payot, "Le Sort des Roumains de Bessarabie", *Journal de Genève,* 7 May 1965.
"Departure to Peking of the Romanian Party and State Delegation", *Scînteia,* 28 September 1964.
N. Popescu-Bogdăneşti, "Unpublished Documents on the History of Romania, Interview with Professor C.C. Giurescu", *Contemporanul,* 27 January 1967.
"Po Povodu Besedy Mao Tse Duna s Gruppoi Yaponskikh Sotsialistov", *Pravda,* 2 September 1964.
Presa Muncitorească şi Socialistă din România /Workers' and Socialist Press of Romania/, (Bucharest: Editura politică, 1964, vol. I), p. 190.
"The Communists' Trial", *Tineretul Leninist,* 22 June 1966.
"The Trial of the Revolutionary Peasantry and of the Union of Communist Youth", *Bolşevismul,* 1925.
R. Ravdin, "Plamia nad Dnestrom", *Sovietskaya Moldavya,* 26 March 1961.
E. Regnault, *Histoire Politique et Sociale des Principautés Danubiennes* (Paris: Paulin et Le Chevalier, 1855).
Resolution on the National Issue in Romania, in *Documente din Istoria Partidului Comunist din România 1923-1928* /Documents from the History of the Romanian Communist Party/, (Bucharest: Editura pentru Literatură Politică, 1953, vol. 2).

M. Roller, *Istoria RPR* /The History of Romania/, (Bucharest: Editura de Stat, 1956).

"L'U.R.S.S. Rejette les Prétentions Roumaines sur la Bessarabie", *Le Monde,* 16 March 1967.

Voicu Ştefan, "Pages from the Struggle of the Romanian Communist Party against Fascism for Independence and National Sovereignty (1934-1940)", *Lupta de Clasă,* June 1966.

N. Berezniakov, I. Kopanskii and I. Platon, *Pod Krasnim Znamenem Revoliutsii* /Under the Red Flag of the Revolution/ (Chişinău: Cartea Moldovenească, 1965).

GENERAL BIBLIOGRAPHY

1. Abrudan, Paul, "The Monetary and Material Aid Given by the Transylvanians to Support the War for Romania's State Independence", I and II, *Revista de Istorie* Nos. 1 and 2, 1977.
2. Adăniloaie, Nichita, "The Achievement of National Independence – Crowning the Romanian People's Century – Old Aspirations toward Freedom", *Revista de Istorie* No. 4, 1977.
3. Adăniloaie, Nichita, "Economic Implications of Turkish Domination in the Romanian Principalities (1750-1859)" *Revista de Istorie* No. 3, 1981.
4. Alexandrescu, Vasile and Căzănişteanu, Constantin, "Foreign Opinions on the Romanian Army in the Independence War of 1877-1878", *Revista de Istorie* No. 4, 1977.
5. Almăşan, Dumitru, "Our 1848 Revolution Within the European Context", *România Liberă*, 9 June 1978.
6. Amalrik, Andrei, *L'Union Soviétique Survivra-t-elle en 1984?* (Paris: Fayard, 1970).
7. Andrei, Ştefan, "The Foreign Policy of Socialist Romania, Continuity, Innovative Spirit, and Responsibility", *Lumea* No. 12, 18 March 1982.
8. Anghel, Gheorghe, "The Mobilization of the Entire Country in a Just, Popular, and National War", I and II, *Revista Economică* Nos. 6 and 7, 11 and 18 February 1977.
9. Antip, Constantin (Major-General), "A Première in Romanian Historiography", *Viaţa Militară* No. 3, 1977.
10. Antonescu, Mihai, *Im Dienste des Vaterlandes* (Bucharest: 1942).
11. Ardeleanu, Ion and Muşat, Mircea, "1918: The Romanian Socialists and the head of the Struggle of the Masses for the Completion of the Process of Forming the National State", *Anale de Istorie*, XXI, 1975.
12. Avon, Earle of, *The Eden Memoirs*, Vol. III, *The Reckoning* (London: Cassel and Co., 1965).

13. Bălan, Ion Dodu, Preface in *Octavian Goga, Opere,* Vol. I /Octavian Goga's Work/ (Bucharest: Editura pentru Literatură, 1967).
14. Bălan, Ion Dodu, "Goga Centennial", *Flacăra* No. 14, 2 April 1981.
15. Bantea, Eugen (Major-General), "The Experience of the Independence War and the Development of the Armed Forces of Romania Before World War I", *Revista de Istorie* No. 3, 1977.
16. Baraschi, Silvia, "Written Sources on Dobrogean Settlements on the Banks of the Danube in the 11th to 14th Centuries", *Revista de Istorie* No. 2, 1981.
17. Barbul, Gheorghe, *Mémorial Antonescu, le Troisième Homme de l'Axe* (Paris: Editions de la Couronne, 1950).
18. Bărbulescu, Petre, "A Great Romanian Diplomat", *Lumea* No. 10, 4 March 1982.
19. Barghorn, Frederick C., *The Soviet Nationalism* (New York: Oxford Univ., 1956).
20. Basdevant, Denise, *Against Tide and Tempest: The Story of Romania* (New York: Robert Speller and Son, 1965).
21. Bazin, M., "Sotsialno-Ekonomicheskie Preobrazovania Moldavskogo Sela", *Kommunist Moldavii* No. 11, 1970.
22. Berezniakov, N., Kopanskii, I., and Platon, I., *Pod Krasnim Znamenem Revoliutsii* /Under the Red Flag of the Revolution/, (Chişinău: Cartea Moldovenească, 1965).
23. Berindei, Dan, "From the 1848 Revolution to Union and Independence", *România Liberă,* 27 May 1978.
24. Betea, Vasile, "A Romanian Diplomatic Mission to the Crimea", *Magazin Istoric* No. 4, 1977.
25. Bindreiter, Uta, *Die Diplomatischen Beziehungen Zwischen Oesterreich-Ungarn und Rumänien in den Jahren 1875-1888,* /Diplomatic and Economic Relations Between the Austro-Hungarian Empire and Romania in 1875-1888/, (Vienna, Köln: Bohlan, 1976).
26. Black, Cyril E., "Russia and the Modernization of the Balkans", in Charles and Barbara Jelavich, eds., *The Balkans in Transition* (Berkeley and Los Angeles: University of California Press, 1963).
27. Bodyul, Ivan Ivanovich, "Sobranie Respublikanskogo Partiinogo Aktiva", *Sovietskaya Moldavya,* 23-24 December 1965.
28. Bodyul, Ivan Ivanovich, "V Sostoianii i Merak Vluchsheniia Marksiskogo Leniniskogo Vospitaniia Respubliki, *Sovietskaya Moldavya,* 5 January 1966.
29. Bodyul, Ivan Ivanovich, "Condition of Marxist-Leninist Education of Working People in the Republic and Measures for Its Improvement", *Cultura,* No. 2, 1966.
30. Bodyul, Ivan Ivanovich, "Report to the Twelfth Congress of the Moldavian Communist Party", Radio Chişinău, 2 March 1966.

31. Bodyul, Ivan Ivanovich, *Molodezi Moldavii,* 28 November 1966.
32. Bodyul, Ivan Ivanovich, "Speech at the Moldavian CP CC on 13 February 1967", *Moldova Socialistă,* 16 February 1967.
33. Bodyul, Ivan Ivanovich, "On the Preparations for the Semi-Centennial of the Great Socialist October Revolution and the Tasks of the Party Organization of the Republic", *Moldova Socialistă,* 16 February 1967.
34. Boicu, Leonid, "The Conquest of State Independence – An Expression of the Assertion of the Will to Freedom of the Romanian People", *Era Socialistă* No. 1, 1977.
35. Bolintineanu, Alexandru, "The Concept of National Independence in the Foreign Policy of Socialist Romania", *Revista de Istorie* No. 4.
36. Bova Scoppa, Renato, *Colloqui con Due Dittatori* (Rome: Ruffolo, 1949).
37. Bova Scoppa, Renato, *La Pace Impossibile,* (Turin: Rosenberg and Sellier, 1961).
38. Brezinski, Zbigniew, *Between Two Ages. America's Role in the Technotronic Era,* (New York: The Viking Press, 1970).
39. Buescu, Victor, "Les Roumains d'Asie", *Stindardul* Nos. 8-9, March-April 1954 and Nos. 102-103, April-August 1968.
40. Buzatu, Gheorghe, "The History of the Romanians in Some Recent Foreign Works", *Cronica* No. 8, 23 February 1979.
41. Călăfăteanu, Ion, "Gafencu's Biography", *Magazin Istoric* No. 8, 1979.
42. Campbell, John, "The European Territorial Settlement", *Foreign Affairs* Vol. XXVI, Nos. 1-4, October 1947–July 1948.
43. Cândea, Virgil, "Romania's Concept of Independence", *Magazin Istoric* No. 4, 1977.
44. Carlyle, Margaret, *Documents on International Affairs,* 1939-1946, Vol. II, *Hitler's Europe,* (London, New York, Toronto: Oxford University Press, 1954).
45. Căzănişteanu Constantin and Ionescu Mihail, "1876 – A Romanian Diplomatic Mission to Constantinople», *Magazin Istoric* No. 2, 1977.
46. Căzănişteanu Constantin and Ionescu Mihail, "The Historical Victory of Independence War Gained Through the Heroic Struggle of the Romanian People", *Scînteia,* 23 April 1977.
47. Căzănişteanu Constantin and Ionescu Mihail, "Romania's Comprehensive and Substantial Contribution to the Final Victory over Fascism", *Scînteia,* 6 July 1979.
48. Căzănişteanu, Constantin, "Consequences of the Russian-Austrian-Turkish Wars in the 18th Century on the Romanian Principalities", *Revista de Istorie* No. 2, 1981.
49. Ceauşescu, Ilie, "Pages from the Chronicle of the Romanian People's Struggle for Independence", *Anale de Istorie* No. 1, 1977.

50. Ceauşescu, Nicolae, "The Romanian Communist Party, Continuer of the Revolutionary and Democratic Struggle of the Romanian People, of the Traditions of the Workers' and Socialist Movement in Romania", *Scînteia,* 8 May 1966.
51. Ceauşescu, Nicolae, Interview with the Mexican daily *El Nacional,* reprinted in *Scînteia,* 10 May 1978.
52. Ceauşescu, Nicolae, "Speech at the Popular Meeting in Bucharest", *Scînteia,* 11 June 1978.
53. Cernatoni, Alexandru, "National and Universal Concepts in a Political Destiny", *Contemporanul* No. 11, 12 March 1982.
54. Certan, E., "Russia's Progressive Role in the Liberation of the Southeast European Peoples from Under the Turkish Yoke", *Comunistul Moldovei* No. 12, 1978.
55. Chiriţă, Grigore, "The Attitude of the European Powers to the Proclamation of Romania's Independence", *Revista de Istorie* No. 4, 1977.
56. Chiuzbăian, Gabriel Iosif, "The Creative Ideal of Nicolae Titulescu", *Săptămîna* No 589, 26 March 1982.
57. Churchill, Winston Leonard Spencer, *The Second World War,* Vol. I, *The Gathering Storm* (London: Cassel and Co., 4th edition, 1955).
58. Churchill, Winston Leonard Spencer, *The Second World War,* Vol. III, *The Grand Alliance* (London: Cassel and Co., 1950).
59. Churchill, Winston Leonard Spencer, *The Second World War,* Vol. IV, *The Hinge of Fate* (London: Cassel and Co., 1951).
60. Churchill, Winston Leonard Spencer, *The Second World War,* Vol. V, *Closing the Ring* (New York: Bantam, 1977).
61. Churchill, Winston Leonard Spencer, *The Second World War,* Vol. VI, *Triumph and Tragedy* (New York: Bantam, 1977).
62. Ciachir, Nicolae, *România în Sud-Estul Europei, 1848-1886 /Romania in Southeastern Europe, 1848-1886/* (Bucharest: Ed. Politică, 1968).
63. Ciachir Nicolae, "Romanian Diplomacy an Active Factor on the European Arena on the Eve of the Independence War", Part. II, *Lumea* No. 8, 17 February 1977.
64. Ciano, Galeazzo, *Diario,* 1937-1943 (Milan: Rizzoli, 1980).
65. Cioară I., "Griviţa, Pleven, Smîrdan, Rahova – An Itinerary of Heroic Struggle", *Lumea* No. 18, 28 April 1977.
66. Ciobanu, Ştefan, *La Bessarabie, Sa Population, Son Passé, Sa Culture* (Bucharest: Académie Roumaine, 1941).
67. Cioculescu, Şerban, "90 Years Since Octavian Goga's Birth", *România Literară* No. 17, 1971.
68. Ciopraga, Constantin, "We", *Tribuna* No. 14, 1981.

69. Ciorănescu, George, "L'Exploitation Soviétique des Richesses Economiques Roumaines", *La Nation Roumaine,* August-September 1964.
70. Ciorănescu, George, "Ein Sowjetischer Teilungsplan", *Der Europäische Osten,* January 1965.
71. Ciorănesco Georges, Filiti Grigore, Florescu Radu, Ghermani Dionisie, Gorju A., Korne Michel, Neculce Nicoară, *Aspects des Relations Russo-Roumaines. Rétrospectives et Orientations* (Paris: Minard, 1967).
72. Ciorănesco Georges, Filiti Grigore, Korne Michel, Missirliu A., Neculce Nicoara and Suga A., *Aspects des Relations Soviéto-Roumaines 1967-1971. Sécurité Européenne* (Paris: Minard, 1971).
73. Ciorănescu, George, "Michael the Brave – Evaluations and Revaluations of the Wallachian Prince", RAD Background Report/191 (Romania), *Radio Free Europe Research,* 1 September 1976.
74. Ciorănescu, George, "Vlad the Impaler – Current Parallels with a Medieval Romanian Prince", RAD BR/23 (Romania), *RFER,* 31 January 1977.
75. Ciurea, Emil, *Traité de Paix avec la Roumanie, 10 Février 1947,* (Paris: Pedone, 1954).
76. Collitt, Leslie, "Romania and Russia Argue over the Past", *Financial Times,* 10 August 1979.
77. Coman, Ion, "The Command of the Romanian Army in the Independence War of 1877-1878", *Anale de Istorie* No. 1, 1977.
78. Constantinescu, Miron, "V. I. Lenin's Message to the Workers and Peoples of Austria-Hungary, 2-3 November 1918", *Studii, Revista de Istorie,* January 1966.
79. Constantinescu, Miron, Daicoviciu Constantin and Pascu Ştefan, *Istoria României /History of Romania/,* (Bucharest: Editura Didactică şi Pedagogică, 1971), Compendiu, Plate No. 13.
80. Constantiniu, Florin, "Aspects of the Crisis of the Antonescu Regime on the Eve of the National Anti-fascist and Anti-imperialist Armed Insurrection", *Revista de Istorie* No. 7, 1979.
81. Corbu, Constantin, "The Operations of the Romanian Army in the First Stage of the Independence War (April-August 1877)", *Revista de Istorie* No. 4, 1977.
82. Cretzianu, Alexandre, *La politique de Paix de la Roumanie à l'Egard de l'Union Soviétique* (Paris: Institut Universitaire Roumain Charles Ier, 1954).
83. Cretzianu Alexandre, *The Lost Opportunity* (London: Jonathan Cape, 1957).
84. Crihan, Anton, "Le Dernier Crime des Soviets. La Déportation Planifiée de la Population Roumaine de Bessarabie", *La Nation Roumaine,* May 1955.
85. Csucsuja, Ştefan, "The Independence War as Seen by the Hungarian Progressive Public Opinion of the Time", *Revista de Istorie* No. 4, 1977.

86. Cuculescu, Victor, "Independence and Sovereignty – Requirements of the New World Economic and Political order", *Revista Economică* No. 19, 13 May 1977.
87. Curticăpeanu, Vasile, "Octavian Goga's Struggle for the Implementation of the Romanian Unified State", *Studii. Revista de Istorie* No. 5, 1969.
88. Dallin, David Julievich, *"Soviet Russia's Foreign Policy 1939-1942"* (New Haven: Yale University Press, 1943).
89. Dascălu, Nicolae, "Romania and the Versailles Peace Treaties", *Revista de Istorie* No. 2, 1977, p. 335 (on Eliza Campus, "The Problem of Noninterference in Domestic Affairs at the Paris Peace Conference", report presented to the Cuza University of Iași on 26 November 1976).
90. Deakin, F.W., *The Brutal Friendship: Mussolini, Hitler, and the Fall of Italian Fascism* (New York: Harper and Row, 1962).
91. Degras, Jane, *Soviet Documents on Foreign Policy* (London, New York, Toronto: Oxford University Press, 1953, Vol. III, 1933-1941).
92. Dilks, David, *The Diaries of Sir Alexander Cadogan O.M. 1938-1945* (London: Cassel and Co., 1971).
93. Diordița (Gheorghiță), Aleksander Filipovich, "V Edinoi Bratskoi Zemlie Narodov USSR", *Sovietskaya Moldavya,* 28 March 1965.
94. Diordița (Gheorghiță), Aleksander Filipovich, "V Edinoi Bratskoi Zemlie Narodov SSSR", *Sovietskaya Moldavya,* 28 December 1965.
95. Djilas, Milovan, *Une Société Imparfaite. Le Communisme désintégré,* (Paris: Kalmann-Levy, 1969).
96. Driault, Edouard, *Napoléon et l'Europe,* 5 vol. (Paris: 1910-1927).
97. Dumitru, Ion, *Forme de etnocid în URSS /* Forms of Ethnocide in the Soviet Union /, (Munich: Avdella-Cenad, 1969).
98. Dzyuba, Ivan, *Internationalism or Russification,* (London: Weidenfeld and Nicolson, 1968).
99. East, Gordon W., "The New Frontiers of the Soviet Union", *Foreign Affairs,* July 1951.
100. Emerit, Marcel, "L'Enquête de Napoléon Ier sur les Principautés Roumaines, *Revue Historique du Sud-Est Européen,* Nos. 4-6, 1936.
101. Enescu, Ion, *Politica Externă a României în Perioada 1944-1947 /Romania's Foreign Policy During the 1944-1947 Period /,* (Bucharest: Editura Științifică și Enciclopedică, 1979).
102. Engels, Friedrich, "The Foreign Policy of Russian Czarism (1890)", p. 39, in *The Russian Menace to Europe* (Glencoe, Illinois: P.W. Blackstock and B.F. Hoselitz, 1952).
103. Ermarth, Fritz, "Anti-Soviet Nationalism in Moldavia", *Radio Free Europe Research, USSR,* 18 April 1960.

104. Ermarth, Fritz, "The View from Moscow", *Radio Free Europe Research, USSR,* 6 July 1965.
105. Ermarth, Fritz, "A Note on Personnel Changes in Moldavia", *Radio Free Europe Research, USSR,* 17 March 1967.
106. Fântânaru, Ion, "The Foreign Policy of Socialist Romania, an Expression of the Enduring Aspirations of the People for Freedom and National Independence, Peace, and Progress throughout the World", *Scînteia,* 16 March 1982.
107. Feis, Herbert, *Churchill, Roosevelt, and Stalin: the War They Waged and the Peace They Sought* (New Jersey: Princeton Univ. Press, 1957).
108. Fischer-Galati, Stephen, "The Moldavian Soviet Republic in Soviet Domestic and Foreign Policy" in Roman Szporluk ed., *The Influence of East Europe and the Soviet West on the USSR,* (New York: Praeger, 1976).
109. Franck, Nicolette, *La Roumanie dans l'Engrenage,* (Paris, Brussels: Elsévier Séquoia, 1977).
110. Frankel, Max, "Romania out for Herself Now", *New York Times,* 19 December 1964.
111. Frankel, Max, "Romania Borrows from Soviet Line to Further Her Independence", *New York Times,* 19 December 1961 (International Edition, 21 December 1964).
112. Frunză, Ion, *Bessarabien. Rumänische Rechte und Leistungen* (Bucharest: Dacia, 1941).
113. Gafenco, Grégoire, *Préliminaires de la Guerre à l'Est. De l'Accord de Moscou (21 Août 1939) aux Hostilités en Russie* (22 Juin 1941) (Fribourg, Switzerland: Egloff, 1944).
114. Gafenco, Grégoire, Gafencu's Letter to Iuliu Maniu, Geneva, 8 September 1946, Hoover Foundation Archives.
115. Gafenco, Grégoire, "Romania's Exploit – an Act of Justice", *Magazin Istoric* No. 8, 1979.
116. Garosci, Aldo, "Alla Ricerca della Verità", *Gli Ebrei nell'URSS,* (Milano: Garzanti, 1966).
117. Georgescu, Titus and Gheorghe, Matei, "The Assistance Granted to Romania by the Soviet Union at the Paris Peace Conference", *Studii. Revista de Istorie şi Filosofie* No. 1, 1954.
118. Gheorghiu I. and Nuţu C., *Adunarea Naţională de la Alba Iulia, 1 Decembrie 1918* /National Assembly from Alba Iulia, 1 December 1918/, (Bucharest: Editura Politică, 1968).
119. Ghermani, Dionisie, *Die Bevölkerungsfrage Bessarabiens in Geschichtlicher Perspektive,* (Munich: 1961), Manuscript.
120. Ghibu, Onisifor, *Amintiri despre Octavian Goga*/Recollections on Octavian Goga/ (Cluj: Dacia Publishing House, 1974).

121. Ghibu, Onisifor, "Two Lives", *Viaţa Românească* Nos. 4-5, April-May 1981.
122. Ghica, Ion (General), "Note to N. Ionescu; Constantinople, 25 November – 7 December 1876", and "Constantinople, 6/18 December 1876", in Macovescu, "All the Prerogatives of a Sovereign State", *Magazin Istoric* No. 2, 1977.
123. Gîrbea, Titus, "Meetings with General Sănătescu", *Magazin Istoric* No. 8, 1979.
124. Giurescu, Constantin C., *Amintiri I* /Recollections I/, (Bucharest: Editura Sport-Turism, 1976).
125. Graham, Malbone W., "The Legal Status of Bucovina and Bessarabia", *The American Journal of International Law* Vol. XXXVIII, 1944.
126. Greceanu, Ion, "The Last Wish of Nicolae Titulescu", *Magazin Istoric* No. 3, 1981.
127. Grekul, A., "Istoki Velikogo Bratstva", *Sovietskaya Moldavya,* 22 June 1966.
128. Grigorenko, Piotr, "Pour le 72-e Anniversaire d'Alexis Kosterine", *Samizdat* No. 1, (Paris: Seuil, 1969).
129. Grigorenko, Piotr, "La Déportation des Tartares de Crimée et ses Conséquences", *Michel Slavinsky, La Presse Clandestine en URSS, 1960-1970,* (Paris: 1970).
130. Grondijs, Lodewik Hermen, *Bessarabia,* (Bucharest: 1940).
131. Grosul, E.S., "The Dark Years of Romanian Landlords' Occupation. The Socio-Economic and Political Condition of Working People on the Territory of Occupied Bessarabia, Reflected in a New Work of Moldavian Historians", *Moldova Socialistă,* 3 December 1970 and *Sovietskaya Moldavya,* 18 December 1970.
132. Halifax, Earl of (Edward Frederick Lindley Wood), *Fullnes of Days* (London: Collins, 1957).
133. Heinrich, H., "Bukarest und die Bessarabien Frage", *Frankfurter Rundschau,* 6 July 1966.
134. Heitmann, Klaus, "Rumänische Sprache und Literatur in Bessarabien und Transnistrien", *Zeitschrift für Romanische Philologie,* Vol. 81.
135. Hillgruber, Andreas, *Hitler, König Carol und Marschall Antonescu: die Deutsch-Rumänischen Beziehungen 1938-1944* (Wiesbaden: Franz Steiner Verlag, 1954).
136. Hillgruber, Andreas, *Staatsmänner und Diplomaten bei Hitler* (Frankfurt am Main: Bernard und Graefe Verlag, 2 Vol., 1967 and 1970).
137. Hoffman, A., "The Show of Chinese Artists", *România Liberă,* 21 June 1966.
138. Hull, Cordell, *The Memoirs of...,* Vol. II (London: Hodder and Stoughton, 1948).

139. Ionescu, Toader, "The Contribution of Transylvanian Romanians to the Independence War", *Revista Economică* No. 16, 22 April 1977.
140. Iorga, Nicolae, *Istoria lui Ştefan cel Mare* /History of Stephen the Great/, (Bucharest: Editura pentru Literatură, 1966).
141. Iosipescu, Vasile (Lieutenant Colonel), "Romania, Unflinching Promoter of the Principles of Independence and National Sovereignty", *Viaţa Militară* No. 4, 1977.
142. Ismay, Lord (General), *Memoirs of General Lord Ismay* (Lionel Hastings), (London: Heinemann, 1960).
143. Jelavich, Barbara, *Russia and the Romanian National Cause, 1858-1859* (Bloomington: Indiana University Publications, 1959).
144. Kalustian, L., "Constantin Stere – The Man of Storm", *Flacăra* No. 18, 30 April 1981.
145. Kandyba, Ivan, "Le Programme de l'Union Ouvrière et Paysanne d'Ukraine", *Samizdat* No. 1 (Paris: Seuil, 1969).
146. Khrouchtchev, Nikita Sergeyevich, "Extrait du Rapport au XXe Congrès du PC US", Roy Medvedev, *Faut-il Réhabiliter Staline?* (Paris: 1969).
147. Kofos, Evanghelos, *Greece and the Easter Crisis 1875-1878*, (Salonica: 1975).
148. Kolarz, Walter, *Russia and her Colonies*, (London: Philip, 1952).
149. Kornovan, Dimitry, "Vyshe Urobenii Internationalnogo Vospitaniia Trudiashchikhsia", *Sovietskaya Moldavya*, 19 December 1966.
150. Kornovan Dimitry, "The Friendship of the Peoples of the Soviet Union, Source of Strength in the Struggle for Communism", *Comunistul Moldovei*, January 1967.
151. Lache, Ştefan and Ţuţui, Gheorghe, *România şi Conferinţa de Pace de la Paris* /Romania and the 1946 Paris Peace Conference/ (Cluj-Napoca: Dacia, 1978).
152. Launay, Jacques de, "Nicolae Titulescu, the Man", *Magazin Istoric* No. 1, 1982.
153. Lazarev, Artem Marcovich, *Moldovskaya Sovetskaya Gosudarstvennost i Bessarabskiy Vopros* /The Organization of the Soviet Moldavian State and the Bessarabian Problem/, (Chişinău: Cartea Moldovenească, 1974).
154. Lebedev, N.I., *Rumyniia v Gody Vtoroi Mirovoi Voiny, Vneshnepoliticheskaia i Vnutrepoliticheskaia Istoriia Rumynii v 1938-1945 gg.* (Moskow: Izdatelstvo Imo, 1961).
155. Lebel, Germaine, *La France et les Principautés Danubiennes (du XVI-e Siècle à la Chute de Napoléon)* (Paris: Presses Universitaires de France, 1955).

156. Lenin, Vladimir Ilich Ulyanov, *Despre Problema Națională și Național-Colonială, /On the National and National-Colonial Issue/* (Bucharest: Publishing House for Political Literature, 1958).
157. Lenin, Vladimir Ilich Ulyanov, *Opere Complete /Complete Works/,* Vol. 30 (Bucharest: Political Publishing House, 1965).
158. Lenin, Vladimir Ilich Ulyanov, "Trois Lettres au Congrès. La Question des Nationalités ou 'l'Autonomie' ", *Samizdat* No. 1, (Paris: Seuil,1969).
159. Lozovan, Eugène, "La Romania Extrême-Orientale", *Festschrift Walter von Wartburg zum 80. Geburtstag,* (Tübingen: 1968).
160. McNeil, William Hardy, *America, Britain, and Russia: Their Cooperation and Conflict, 1941-1946* (London: Oxford University Press, 1953).
161. Macovescu, George, "The Diplomatic Efforts of Nicolae Titulescu", in *Nicolae Titulescu, Documente Diplomatice /Diplomatic Documents/* (Bucharest: Editura Politică, 1967).
162. Macovescu, George, "The Feeling of National Dignity", *Magazin Istoric* No. 1, 1977.
163. Macovescu, George, "All the Prerogatives of a Sovereign State", *Magazin Istoric* No. 2, 1977.
164. Macovescu, George, "Strong Through our Right and the Justice of Our Cause", *Magazin Istoric* No. 4, 1977.
165. Macovescu, George, "The Governments", *Magazin Istoric* No. 5, 1977.
166. Macovescu, George, "I Want Romania To Live", *Contemporanul* No. 8, 19 February 1982.
167. Macovescu, George, "Romania Has Paid Too Heavy a Price for Its Right to Life Ever to Renounce It", *Contemporanul* No. 10, 5 March 1982.
168. Macovescu, George, "Peace Is One of the Best Means of Preserving Our National Unity", *ibid.,* No. 11, 12 March 1982.
169. Maisky, Ivan, *Memoirs of a Soviet Ambassador; the War 1939-1943* (New York: Charles Scribner's Sons, 1968).
170. Makarov, "Die Eingliederung Bessarabiens und der Nord Bukovina in die Sowjet-Union", *Zeitschrift für ausländisches offentliches Recht und Völkerrecht* Nos. 1-2.
171. Manuilă, Sabin and Filderman, W., "Jewish Population in Romania 1940-1957", *România* No. 18, 1957.
172. Mao, Tse-tung, "Mao's Statement to the Japanese Socialist Delegation", Dannis J. Doolin, *Territorial Claims in the Sino-Soviet Conflict, Documents and Analysis,* (Stanford University: 1965).
173. Marcea, Pompiliu, "Octavian Goga Today", *Transilvania* No. 3, 1981.
174. Marinescu, Beatrice and Rădulescu-Zoner, Șerban, "We Shall Rely on the Patriotism af All Romanians", *Magazin Istoric* No. 4, 1977.

175. Marx, Karl, *Însemnări despre Români /Notes on the Romanians/* (Bucureşti: Editura Academiei RPR, 1964); *Însemnări despre Români. Texte manuscrite Inedite cu un Comentariu /Notes on Romanians. Unpublished Manuscripts with a Commentary/* (Madrid: Carpaţii, 1965).
176. Mastny, Vojtech, "The Benes-Stalin-Molotov Conversations in December 1943", New Documents in *The American Historical Review* Vol. XVII, No. 5, December 1972.
177. Mastny, Vojtech, *Russia's Road to the Cold War* (New York: Columbia University Press, 1979).
178. Mehedinţi, Simion, *La Roumanie à la Frontière Orientale de l'Europe,* (Bucharest: Dacia, 1942).
179. Mendec, V., "Rural Constructions", *Cultura* No. 8, 1965.
180. Michaelis, Herbert and Schraepler, Ernst, *Ursachen und Folgen vom Deutschen Zusammenbruch 1918 and 1945 bis zur Staatlichen Neuordnung Deutschlands in der Gegenwart* (Berlin: Documenten-Verlag Dr. Norbert Wendler).
181. Moarcaş, Mircea, "Independence and National Sovereignty– Basic Ideas of the Foreign Policy of Socialist Romania", *România Liberă,* 9 May 1977.
182. Mocanu, Vasile, "New Data on the Anti-Hitlerite Attitude of the Romanian Army: Essential Prerequisite of the Victory of the August 1944 Insurrection", *Anale de Istorie* No. 4, 1976.
183. Moisiuc, Viorica, "From Romania's Historical Archives" (X), *Anale de Istorie* No. 2, 1978.
184. Mokhov, N., and Muntyan, "In the Interest of Truth" (in Russian), *Sovietskaya Moldavya,* Chişinău, March 5, 1975.
185. Mosse, W.E., *The Rise and Fall of the Crimean System 1857-1871,* (London: Macmillan, 1963).
186. Murgoci, Gheorghe, *La population de la Bessarabie. Etude Démographique avec Cartes et Tableaux Statistiques. Préface par Em. de Martone* (Paris: 1920).
187. Muşat, Mircea and Irimia, Vasile, "German Documents on August 23: A Well-Defined Day in the History of the War", *Magazin Istoric* No. 8, 1979.
188. Muşat, Mircea, "Considerations Concerning the Consequences of the Domination and Foreign Interferences on Romanian People's Historical Evolution", *Anale de Istorie* No. 2, 1981.
189. Muşat, Mircea, "A Brilliant Romanian Diplomat, a Great Man of His Time", *Scînteia,* 16 March 1982.
190. Muşat, Mircea and Irimia, Vasile, "Nicolae Titulescu, Defender of Unity, Independence, and National Sovereignty", *Anale de Istorie* No. 1, 1982.
191. Nagy, David, "Soviet Census Shows Birth Rate Still Falling", UPI, 17 April 1971.

192. Nanu, Frederic, "The First Soviet Double-Cross", *Journal of Central European Affairs,* Vol. XII, No. 3, October 1952.
193. Netea, Vasile, "Century-Old Testimonies to the National Solidarity of the Romanians", *Lumea* No. 16, 14 April 1977.
194. Netea, Vasile, "In the Service of the Fatherland", *Rumänische Rundschau* No. 1, 1982.
195. Niciu, Martin, "Nicolae Titulescu and World Peace", *Tribuna* No. 11, 18 March 1982.
196. Nicolae, Alexandru, "Der Angriff auf die Menschliche Substanz Rumäniens", *Zeitschrift für Geopolitik,* Band XXII, 1951.
197. Nicolescu, T., "Romanian Echoes", *Secolul XX,* April 1966.
198. Nimigeanu, Dumitru, *Însemnările unui Ţăran Deportat din Bucovina* /Notes of a Peasant Deported from Bucovina / (Paris: Fundaţia Regală Universitară Carol I, 1958), p. 246 ; English Issue, *Hell Moved Its Borders* (London: Blandford Press, 1960).
199. Nove, Alec, "La Populazione Ebraica nell'URSS; Consistenza, Struttura Professionale ed Istruzione". *Gli Ebrei nell'URSS,* (Milano: Garzanti, 1966).
200. Oddud, Afanasij Lukic, *Sowjet Moldawien* (Berlin: SWA-Verlag, 1949).
201. Olteanu, Constantin, "Romania's Military Contribution to the Defeat of Nazi Germany", *Era Socialistă* No. 16, 20 August 1979.
202. Opreanu, Mircea, "Russifizierungsaktion in Bessarabien stärker denn je", *Stindardul* No. 93, 1966.
203. Oţetea, Andrei, *Istoria Poporului Român* /History of the Romanian People/, (Bucharest: Editura Stiinţifică, 1970), Plate No. 24, between pages 128 and 129.
204. Papuc, Ion, "Constantin Stere Today (II)", *Luceafărul* No. 27, July 1979.
205. Pascu, Ştefan, "Moments in the Struggle of the Romanian People for the Formation of the National State", *Magazin Istoric,* Vol. X, No. 2, Febr. 1976.
206. Pavelescu, Ion, "The Centenary of the Achievement of Independence", Interview with Professor Dumitru Almaş, *România Liberă,* 21 February 1977.
207. Payot, R., "Le Sort des Roumains de Bessarabie", *Journal de Genève,* 7 May 1965.
208. Pelivan, Ion G., *La Bessarabie sous le Régime Russe* (1812-1918), (Paris: Lahure, 1919).
209. Pelivan, Ion G., *Les Droits des Roumains sur la Bessarabie* (Paris: Imprimerie des Arts et des Sports, 1920).
210. Petric, Aron, "The Consolidation of National Independence: A Basic Factor in Romania's Development", *Revista de Istorie* No. 4, 1977.

211. Petric, Aron, "The Romanian Communist Party: Leader of the Revolutionary Struggle for National and Social Liberation", *Era Socialistă* No. 16, August 1979.
212. Plyusch, Leonid, *Le Monde,* 4 February 1976.
213. Popescu-Bogdăneşti, N., "Unpublished Documents on the History of Romania, Interview with Professor C.C. Giurescu", *Contemporanul,* 27 January 1967.
214. Popescu, Dan, "National Independence – The Fiery Goal of the Thinking of Our Predecessors, the Promoters of the Country's Industrialization" I and II, *Revista Economică* Nos. 12 and 13, 1977, p. 24 and 12, respectively.
215. Popescu, Dumitru Radu, "Looking at Himself", *Viaţa Românească* No. 1, 1979.
216. Popescu, Dumitru Radu, "The Porphyrogenite", *Transilvania* No. 4, 1979.
217. Popescu-Puţuri, Ion, "The RCP Program on Romania's National Independence, *Anale de Istorie* No. 1, 1977.
218. Popescu-Puţuri, Ion, "For a Just Cause. Romania's Joining World War I in August 1916", *Anale de Istorie* No. 6, 1977.
219. Popescu-Puţuri, Ion, "For a Just Cause. Romania's Joining the World War I in August 1916", *Anale de Istorie* No. 2, 1978.
220. Popescu, Teodor, "On a Volume of Documents Devoted to Romania's Foreign Policy", *Anale de Istorie* No. 5, 1981.
221. Porţeanu, Alexandru, "1877-1977 – State Independence – The Cause of the Entire Romanian Nation", *Lumea* No. 17, 21 April 1977.
222. Porţeanu, Alexandru, "The Socialist Movement and the Problems of Independence, Sovereignty, and National Unity", I, *Revista de Istorie* No. 4, 1977, pp. 634-635; Georgeta Tudoran, "The Centenary of Independence", *România Liberă*, 25 April 1977.
223. Porţeanu, Alexandru, "1877-1977: Significance of the Achievement of Romania's Independence in the Testimonies of the Time", *Lumea* No. 18, 28 April 1977.
224. Potra, George, "The Vital Strength of the Principles of International Law", *Era Socialistă* No. 5, 1982.
225. Prevost, Michel, *Românii şi Ruşii /Romanians and Russians/* (Bucharest: 1925).
226. Prokot, Gerd, "The Decisive Front: from the Balkans to Vienna", *Neues Deutschland,* 9 August 1979.
227. Quinlan, Paul D., *Clash over Romania: British and American Policies Toward Romania: 1938-1947* (Los Angeles: American-Romanian Academy of Arts and Sciences, 1977).
228. Rădulescu, Savel, *Nicolae Titulescu, 1882-1941* (Bucharest: Casa Scînteii, no date).

229. Rădulescu-Zoner, Şerban, "Romania and the Struggle for Liberation of the Balkan Peoples (1875-1877)", *Era Socialistă* No. 4, 1977.
230. Ravdin, R., "Plamia nad Dnestrom", *Sovietskaya Moldavya,* 26 March 1961.
231. Regnault, Elias, *Histoire Politique et Sociale des Principautés Danubiennes* (Paris: Paulin et Le Chevalier, 1855).
232. Roller, Mihai, *Istoria RPR /The History of Romanian Republic/* (Bucharest: Editura de Stat, 1956).
233. Roman, Valter, "Notes on Nicolae Titulescu, *România Literară* No. 12, 18 March 1982.
234. Savor, George and Heiman Léo, "Moldavia: a Russian Satellite", *The Ukrainian Quarterly* No. 2, 1956.
235. Schechtmann, Joseph B., "The Option Clause in the Reich's Treaties on the Transfer of Population", in *American Journal of International Law* Vol. XXXVIII, 1944.
236. Serafim, George, "Independence and National Sovereignty – An Objective Law of Social Development, a Basic Imperative of History", *Lumea* No. 20, 12 May 1977.
237. Seton-Watson, Hugh, *History of the Romanians* (Cambridge, England: Cambridge University Press, 1934).
238. Seton-Watson, Hugh, *The Decline of Imperial Russia 1855-1914* (New York: Frederick A. Praeger, 1952).
239. Seton-Watson, Hugh, *The Russian Empire 1801-1917* (Oxford: Clarendon Press, 1967).
240. Shabad, Theodor, "Soviet 1970 Census", *New York Times,* 17 April 1971.
241. Shapiro, Henry, "Russian Orthodox Church to Elect new Patriarch and end Schism", *UPI,* 2 June 1971; "Russian Prelate Urges Removal of the Curses on the Old Believers", *New York Times,* 2 June 1971.
242. Simion, Aurică, "Pînă la Orice Sacrificiu în Interesul Poporului Român" /Down to the Last Sacrifice in Interest of the Romanian People/, *Magazin Istoric* Vol. X, No. 7, July 1976.
243. Simion, Aurică, *Preliminariile Politico-Diplomatice ale Insurecţiei Române din August 1944 /Political-Diplomatic Preliminaries of the August 1944 Romanian Insurrection/* (Cluj-Napoca: Dacia, 1979).
244. Smal-Stocki, Roman, *The Captive Nations. The Nationalism of the Non-Russian Nations in the Soviet Union* (New York: Bookman Assoc., 1960).
245. Smith, Gaddis, *American Diplomacy During the Second World War, 1941-1945* (New York, London, Sydney: John Wiley and Sons, 1965).
246. Solzhennitsyn, Alexander, *Sunday Times,* 3 March 1974.
247. Stalin, Joseph Vissarionovich, "Report at the Fourth Conference of the CC with Nationalities Officials, 10 June 1933, on the Practical Measures for Applying the Resolution on the National Question of the Twelfth Party

Congress". *Changing Attitude in the Soviet Russia. The Nationalities Problem and the Soviet Administration. Selected Reading on the Development of the Soviet Nationalities Policies. Selected, Edited and Introduced by Rudolf Schlesinger* (London: Routledge and Kegan Paul, 1956).
248. Stalin, Joseph Vissarionovich, "Marxism and the National Question", *Works II* (Moscow: Foreign Languages Publ. House, 1960).
249. Stănescu, N.S., "Observing States' Sovereign Rights – A prerequisite for the Construction of a New International Order", *Lumea* No. 20, 12 May 1977.
250. Stavrianos, Leften Stavros, *The Balkans Since 1453* (New York: Holt, Rinehart, and Winston, 1958).
251. Ştefan, Marian, and Mocanu, Vasile, "Plevna", *Magazin Istoric* No. 5, 1977.
252. Şteflea, Ilie (General), "The Head of the General Staff Resisted the Pressure of the Wehrmacht", *Magazin Istoric* No. 8, 1979.
253. Steinon, Charles, *Le Mystère roumain et la défection russe* (Paris: Plon, 1918).
254. Suciu, Dumitru I., "The Banat Romanians' Solid Support for the Independence War", *Revista de Istorie* No. 3, 1977.
255. Tătărescu, Gheorghe, "Statements of Gheorghe Tătărescu, Royal Adviser and Prime Minister" *Universul,* June 1940.
256. Teodor, Dan, "The Roman World in the Second Half of the First Millennium", *Era Socialistă* No. 11, 5 June 1981.
257. Trohani, George and Nemoianu, Larisa, "The Political History of Getae-Dacians in the Sixth-Seventh Centuries B.C.", *Revista de Istorie* No . 2, 1981.
258. Trotsky, Léon, "La Question Ukrainienne, pour une Ukraine Soviétique, Ouvrière et Paysanne, Unique, Libre et Indépendente", *Samizdat* No. 1 (Paris: Seuil, 1969).
259. Turcu, Constantin, "A Champion for the Extension of Romania's Foreign Relations", *Rumänische Rundschau* No. 1, 1982.
260. Udler, Rubin and Komarnitki V., "Moldavian Linguistic Atlas", *Cultura* No. 16, June 1965.
261. Udres, Traian, "The Policy of Alliance of the Romanian Communist Party: the Setting up of the National Democratic Bloc in June 1944", *Revista de Istorie* No. 6, 1979.
262. Uhling, Carl, *Die Bessarabische Frage, eine Geopolitische Betrachtung* (Breslau: Ferdinand Hirt, 1926).
263. Ungheanu, Mihai, "Goga's Literary and Political Destiny", *Luceafărul* No. 14, 1981.
264. Ushakov, V.B., *Hitlerite Germany's Foreign Policy* (Moscow: Publishing House of the Institute of International Relations, 1961).
265. Ushakov, V.B. and Niri, A., "Hitlerite Germany's Foreign Policy", *Analele Institutului de Istorie a Partidului de pe lîngă CC al PMR* No. 5, 1962.

266. Valeriu, Stan, "Report on Alexandru Cernat, Memoirs. The 1877-1878 Period", Bucharest: Ed. Militară, 1976 in *Revista de Istorie* No. 4, 1977.
267. Vasile, Radu, "Strengthening the Country's Defense Capacity in the 1866-1877 Period with a View to Independence", *Revista de Istorie* No. 2, 1977.
268. Voicu, Ştefan, "Pages from the Struggle of the Romanian Communist Party against Fascism for Independence and National Sovereignty (1934-1940)", *Lupta de Clasă,* June 1966.
269. Wagener, Hans-Jurgen, "Commentary", *Radio Liberty,* 17 october 1969.
270. Woodward, Llewellyn, *British Foreign Policy in the Second World War,* Vol. II (London: Her Majesty's Stationery Office, 1971).
271. Zaharia, Gheorghe, "The Making of the Unified National State – the Century-old Dream of the Romanian People", *Magazin Istoric* Nos. 4, 5 and 6, 1978.
272. Zaharia, Gheorghe, "The Entire Contry Called to Arms", *Magazin Istoric* No. 7, 1979.
273. Zaharia, Gheorghe, "The Unanimous Will of the People" *Magazin Istoric* No. 8, 1979.
274. Zincă, Haralamb, "Through the Archives of Hour ‚H' ", *România Literară,* 9 August 1979; Marcel Olteanu, "Bucharest, Ineradicable City", *Contemporanul* No. 34, August 1979.
275. Agerpres, 25 June 1979.
276. Agerpres, 12 June 1981.
277. Agerpres, 17 March 1982.
278. *Anale de Istorie* No. 2, 1977.
279. "Anti-communist Resistance in Bessarabia. A Soviet Colonel about the Bessarabian Recruits", *Stindardul* Nos. 78-79, 31 January 1964.
280. AP, 8 April 1982.
281. "Appeal to All Members and Activists of Romanian Union of Communist Youth", *Tineretul Leninist,* 1 May 1925.
282. Archives Nationales, AF IV, 1967 Russie 1807-1808, Correspondances de Savary et de Caulaincourt; 1699 Rapports de Caulaincourt.
283. (The) Atlantic Charter, 14 August 1941, in Walter Consuelo Langsam, *Documents and Reading in the History of Europe Since 1918* (Chicago: Lippincott, 1951).
284. "Bessarabia under the Soviet Regime", *Cronica Românească* No. 12, 1952.
285. *Bolshaya Sovietskaya Entsiklopedia /Big Soviet Encyclopaedia /* (Moskva: 1950, Vol. V).
286. *Calendarul Credinţa /*Faith Calendar/, 1967, Detroit (Michigan: Ed. Episcopia Misionară Ortodoxă Română din America, 1967), p. 12.
287. "The Capital Heartily Greeted Comrade Chu-En Lai", *Scînteia,* 17 June 1966.

288. "Centennial of Nicolae Titulescu's Birth, Commemorative Gathering, *Scînteia*, 17 March 1982.
289. Communiqué No. 4, From the Royal Palace, *Universul*, Bucharest, 28 June 1940.
290. Communiqué of the General Directorate for the Permutation and Organized Hiring of Workers, Attached to the Council of Ministers of Moldavian SSR", *Moldova Socialistă*, 24 January 1965.
291. "The Communists' Trial", *Tineretul Leninist*, 22 June 1966.
292. "Congress of Writers of Moldavian SSR", *Cronica Românească* No. 10, October 1954, p. 23.
293. "Decade of Moldavian SSR", *Cronica Românească* Nos. 5-6, May-June 1953, p. 18.
294. "Declaration on the Stand of the Romanian Workers' Party in the Problems of the International Communist and Workers' Party Adopted by the Broad Plenum of the CC of the Romanian Workers' Party of April 1964", *Scînteia*, 26 April 1964.
295. *Délégation Bessarabienne. Les Roumains devant le Congrès de la Paix. La Question de la Bessarabie* (Paris: 1919).
296. Departure to Peking of the Romanian Party and State Delegation", *Scînteia*, 28 September 1964.
297. *Dicţionarul Enciclopedic român* /Romanian Encyclopaedic Dictionary/, (Bucharest: Editura Politică, 1962, vol. 1).
298. *Documents on German Foreign Policy, 1918-1945,* Vol. IX-XII, (London: Her Majesty's Stationery Office, 1956-1962).
299. (L')Explication des Difficultés entre Moscou et Bucarest. L'URSS Rejette les Prétentions Roumaines sur la Bessarabie", *Le Monde*, 16 March 1967.
300. *Facts and Comments Concerning Bessarabia, 1812-1940* (London: 1941).
301. "Facts from the Shadow. Romania in the 1876-1877 Period", *Lumea* Nos. 5 and 7, 3 and 10 February 1977.
302. *Flacăra* No. 6, 12 February 1982.
303. *Foreign Relations of the United States, Diplomatic Papers 1941* Vol. I-IV (Washington: United States Printing Office, 1958-1966).
304. "The Formation and Consolidation of the Capitalist Order (1848-1878)", *Istoria României /The History of Romania/*, Vol. IV, (Bucharest: The Academy Publishing House, 1964).
305. "From Romania's Historical Archives", I, *Anale de Istorie* No. 1, 1976.
306. *Geopolitica şi Geoistoria* Nos. IX-X, 1941, p. 31, *apud* What Do Bessarabia and Northern Bucovina Signify to Us", *Cronica Românească* No. 6, 1951.
307. "Glavnoie Upravlenie po Preseleniiu Organizovannomu Naboru Rabochih pri Soviete Ministrov Moldavskoi SSR", *Sovietskaia Moldavia*, 31 March 1955 (French Translation in *La Nation Roumaine*, 15 May 1955).

308. *History of the Communist Party of the Soviet Union* (Moscow: Foreign Languages Publ. House, 1960).
309. *Istoria României* /History of Romania/ (Bucharest: Editura Academiei RPR, vol. III and IV, 1964).
310. *Journal Officiel,* 10 November 1920.
311. "(The) Leaders of the Moldavian Soviet Socialist Republic", *Cronica Românească* Nos. 4-5, 1954.
312. Mao Ce-Tungove Vyroky, *Praca,* 4 September 1964.
313. *Mémoire Concernant la Bessarabie et la Bucovine du Nord (avec Une Carte Ethnographique)* (Bucharest: 1940).
314. *Moldova Socialistă,* 17 April 1959.
315. *Moldova Socialistă,* 27 April 1969.
316. "Nationalism and Party Squabbles in Moldavia", *Radio Free Europe Research, URSS,* 6 February 1970.
317. "Nationalities Policy: Burning Problem, Publicistic Panacea", *Radio Free Europe Research, URSS,* 8 March 1971.
318. "New Deportations of Population into Bessarabia", *România* No. 13, 15 March 1957.
319. *New York Times,* 22 May 1951.
320. *Observations Concerning the Draft Peace Treaty with Romania* (Paris: Blanchard, 1946).
321. "Opposition in the Ukraine", *Radio Free Europe Research, URSS,* 3 March 1971.
322. "The Permanence of Romanian Foreign Policy: Nicolae Titulescu's Centennial Exhibition", *ibid.,* 19 March 1982.
323. "Po Povodu Besedy Mao Tse Duna s Gruppoi Yaponskikh Sotsialistov", *Pravda,* 2 September 1964.
324. *Presa Muncitorească şi Socialistă din Romania* /Workers' and Socialist Press of Romania / (Bucharest: Editura Politică, 1964, vol. I).
325. *Pro Bessarabia and Bucovina* (London: 1958).
326. *Programul Partidului Comunist Român de Făurire a Societăţii Socialiste Multilateral Dezvoltate şi Înaintarea României spre Comunism* /The RCP Program for the Creation of a Multilaterally Developed Socialist Society and Romania's Advance Toward Communism / (Bucharest: 1975).
327. *Radio Chişinău,* 22 March 1954.
328. Radio Moscow in Romanian, 4 May 1977.
329. Radio Moscow in Romanian, 24 January 1979.
330. Radio Moscow in Romanian, 26 August 1979.
331. Radio Peking in Romanian, February 4 and 20, and March 21, 1976.
332. RCP CC Archives, Collection No. 50, File 477.

333. *Recensămîntul General al Populatiei României din 29 Decembrie 1930,* Vol. II, Ist Part /General Census of Romania's Population of 29 December 1930/, (Bucharest: 1939).
334. Resolution on the National Issue in Romania, in *Documente din Istoria Partidului Comunist din România 1923-1928* /Documents from the History of the Romanian Communist Party/ (Bucharest: Editura pentru Literatură Politică, 1953, vol. 2).
335. *România* No. 72, 1963.
336. *România în Războiul Antihitlerist* /Romania in Anti-Hitlerite War/ (Bucharest: Editura Militară, 1966.
337. *România Liberă,* 12 August 1979; *Scînteia,* 28 July and 19 August 1979; Radio Bucharest, 18 August 1979.
338. *(The) Romanian Encyclopaedia* (Bucharest: Imprimeria Naţională, 1943), Vol. IV.
339. Romanian Situation Report / 37, *RFER,* 22 October 1976, Item 4.
340. Romanian SR / 16, *RFER,* 12 May 1977, Item 1.
341. The Royal Decree for the Union of Bessarabia with Romania is dated 9 April 1918 in Iaşi, where the government resided during the German occupation of Bucharest.
342. *Scînteia* 10 May, 1977.
343. "Session of Supreme Soviet of Moldavian Socialist Republic", *Cronica Românească* No. 7, 1954.
344. "The Solemn Ceremony at which the Soviet Union Handed Over Historical Treasures of Romanian Art", *Scînteia,* 7 August 1956.
345. "Soviet Polemics with Romanian Historians", *Radio Free Europe Research, USSR,* 18 January 1971.
346. *Sovietskaya Moldavya,* 18 February 1970.
347. Strana Sovetov, "Biografiia Rosta", *Izvestia,* 17 April 1971.
348. "Talks between the Delegations of the CC of the Romanian Workers' Party and the Chinese Communist Party", *Scînteia,* 4 March 1964.
319. Tanjug, Sofia, 20 February 1978.
350. Tanjug, 18 March 1978.
351. Tass, 30 September 1981.
352. "(The) Trial of Revolutionary Peasantry and of the Union of Communist Youth", *Bolşevismul,* 1925.
353. "L'U.R.S.S. Rejette les Prétentions Roumaines sur la Bessarabie", *Le Monde,* 16 March 1967.
354. *(La) Vérité sur les Rapports Germano-Soviétiques de 1939 à 1941* (Paris: The US Department of State, Editions France-Empire, 1948).
355. "What Do Bessarabia and Northern Bucovina Signify to Us?", *Cronica Românească* No. 6, 1951.

INDEX[1]

Abjarsk, new Asian settlement founded by recently deported Moldavians, 214.
Abkhaz, Autonomous Soviet Socialist Republic, an administrative division of the Georgian SSR. Russian protectorate in 1810; annexed in 1864; proclaimed autonomous region in 1919 and raised to the status of republic in 1921, 213.
Academy of Science and Arts of the Yugoslav Republic Macedonia, founded in 1967; headquarters in Skoplje, 46.
Academy of Science of the USSR, founded by Peter the Great in 1725; headquarters in Moscow, 14, 43, 224.
Academy of the Socialist Republic Romania, founded in 1879; reorganized in 1948; headquarters in Bucharest, 73, 262.
Acquarone, Pietro, duke of (1890-1948), Italian general and statesman; first count and since 1942 duke, 152.
Adaniloaiei, Nichita (1927), Rom. historian, 38.
Adrian, George (1820-1889), Rom. general; war minister (May 24, 1867-Aug. 12, 1868); author of the bill on army organization (July 29, 1868), 55.
Adrianopole, today Edirne, city in European Turkey, near the borders of Greece and Bulgaria. The treaty of Adrianopole concluding the Russo-Ottoman war of 1828-1829 was signed on Sept. 14, 1829 recognizing: Greece's autonomy as a tributary state; Serbia's autonomy; Russia's title to Georgia and other Caucasian principalities; free navigation of Russian shipping through the Straits of Dardanelles and Bosporus and the suppresion of the Ottoman trade monopoly in Moldavia and Wallachia, 42, 62.
Adzhubey, Aleksei (1959), Khrushchev's son-in-law. Journalist; chief-editor of Izvestia newspaper, 263.
Aegean Sea, 46.
Africa 197, 231, 266.
Akkerman, see Cetatea Albă.

---

1 This Index offers two kinds of explanation: those directly connected to the facts mentioned by the studies contained in the present book; others which recall some general historical data and circumstances (diplomatic history of various countries, the main stipulations of international treaties, etc..., thus helping the reader to easily place events in their historical context.

Akmolinsk, city in Kazakh SSR, 120 miles NW of Karaganda, 214.

Alampiev, Piotr Martinovich (1901), Soviet economist, author of the study "USSR Districtual Economic Division", Moscow, 1963, 252.

Alba Iulia, historical town in Transylvania where the union of Transylvania with Romania was proclaimed on Dec. 1, 1918, 82, 91, 92.

Albania, under Turkish rule from 15th century until Nov. 28, 1912 when it proclaimed its independence; became a kingdom under the king Zogu I (1928), and was proclaimed a Popular Republic on Jan. 11, 1946, 26, 27.

Alecsandri, Vasile (1821-1890), Rom. poet and dramatist; minister of foreign affairs (1859-1860) and Romanian minister in Paris (1885), 225.

Alekseyev, Mikhail Vasilyevich (1857-1918), chief of staff of the Imperial Russian Armies in 1915-1916, 87, 88.

Alexander I of Russia, Aleksandr Pavlovich (1777-1825), emperor of Russia (1801-1825), 10, 23, 25, 26, 28-30, 32, 36, 41, 42, 83.

Alexander II of Russia, Aleksandr Nikolayevich (1818-1881), emperor of Russia (1855-1881), 44, 53, 57-60, 62.

Alexei, Aleksey Mikhailovich (1629-1676), tzar of Russia (1645-1676), 35.

Alexeievca, Alekseyevka, town in Kazakh SSR, Akmolinsk *oblast,* 60 miles NW of Akmolinsk, 214.

Alexianu, George (+1946), professor of public law at Bucharest University (1941-1946); Royal Resident of Suceava region (Aug. 13, 1938–Feb. 1, 1939); Royal Resident of Bucegi region (1939); governor of Transdnistria, 141.

Allied Control Commission, agency created by art. 18 of the Romanian-Soviet armistice convention of Sept. 12, 1944, 66, 170.

Allied Powers, or *Allies in World War I,* term used to indicate the states allied against the Central Powers during WW I or against Axis Powers during WW II. The chief Allied Powers during WW I were the British Empire, France and Russia linked by the Treaty of London (Sept. 5, 1914), 87, 101, 132, 258.

Allied Powers in World War II, in a restrictive meaning were: France, Great Britain, USSR, USA and China; in an extensive meaning the term is applied to all the war time members of the United Nations, 10, 55, 137, 148, 150-157, 160-163, 165-167, 169, 170, 183-190, 192.

Almaş, Dumitru, (1908), Rom. historian; researche on Rom. modern history, 226.

Altai, Altay Mountains, major mountain system of Central Asia, at the junction of USSR, China and Mongolia, 214.

Amalric, Andrei (1938-1980), Soviet dissident writer, author of the *Involuntary Journey to Siberia* and *Will the Soviet Union Survive Until 1984?* Arrested in 1970; convicted of "anti-soviet fabrications" and sentenced to three years in labor camp. He emigrated in summer 1976 to USA, 13, 231.

America, North, 266.

American, 158, 187, 247.

Amsterdam, nominal capital of the Netherland, 260.

Amur River, river in eastern Asia, forming part of the frontier between Soviet Union and China, 196, 209, 211, 214, 262.

Anale de Istorie, Rom. historical magazine issued in 1955 in Bucharest by the *Institute for Historical, Social and Political Studies* of RCP CC, 73, 84, 86.

Andrassy, Gyula, count (1823-1890), first Hungarian prime minister and Austria-Hungary foreign minister (1871-1879), 45, 46, 49, 77, 79, 81.

Andrei, Ştefan (1931), Rom. communist statesman. Engineer; started his political career in the *Union of Students'Associations* and *Union of the Working Youth* (1960-1963). Deputy chief of CC's section for relations with the socialist countries (1965); alternate member of CC (1969) and full member (1972); alternate member of Political Executive Committee (1976); foreign affairs minister (1978), 100.

Andreossi, Antoine-François, Count (1761-1828), French general and diplomat, 32.

Andrews, Christopher Columbus (1829-1922), American lawyer; minister to Sweden and Norway (1869); consul general to Brasil (1882-1885); secretary of state of forestry board (1911-1922), 89.

Anenii-Noi, village in Bessarabia, Tighina district, today in the Moldavian SSR, 239.

Anglo-American, 186-188.

Anglo-Saxon, 162, 165, 167, 170.

Anglo-Soviet Alliance, a 20-year Anglo-Soviet alliance treaty was signed on May 26, 1942, 147-150, 154.

Ankara, capital of Turkey since 1923, 102, 153, 156, 160, 184, 186, 187.

Antonescu, Ion (1882-1946), Rom. general; marshal (23. 08. 1941); chief of the state, "Conducător" (6. 09. 1940-23. 08. 1944), 10, 128-131, 134, 135, 137, 139-144, 151, 152, 154-156, 161-168, 181-193.

Antonescu, Mihai (1904-1946), Rom. foreign minister and vice-premier (June 1941-August 23, 1944), 131, 137, 139, 141, 142, 151-153, 156, 166, 167, 183, 184, 188, 189.

Apostolski, Mihajlo (1906), Macedonian historian; director of the Macedonian Institute for National History (1942); Macedonian CP organizer; Chairman of the Academy of Science and Arts of Yugoslav Republic Macedonia, 46.

Apoziţia, Rom. literary and historical magazine, Munich (1973–), 20.

Arabic alphabet, 223.

Arbure or *Arbore, Zamfir* (1848-1933), Rom. writer and publicist, historiographer of Bessarabia, 198.

Archangel, see Arkhangelsk.

Arcis-sur-Aube, village in France, 17 miles north of Troyes, scene of a bloody battle between Napoleon and the Allies (March 1, 1814), 216.

Arciz, village in Bessarabia, Cetatea-Albă district, now in Ukrainian SSR, 216.

Argeş, district in Romania, south of the Carpathian Mountains, 250, 252.

Argetoianu, Constantin (1871-1952), Rom. political leader; president of the Agrarian Union (1932); prime minister (28. 09.-22. 11. 1939) and foreign minister (27.06.-4. 07. 1940), 115, 136.

Arion, Eraclie (1838-1903), Rom. general. During Rom. War of independence he took part, as colonel, in the armistice negotiations with the Turks, 62.

Arkhangelsk, important Soviet fluvial and maritime port on the northern Dvina River, 31 miles from the Withe Sea, 84, 214.

Armenia, Soviet Socialist Republic, situated on the southern flanks of the Caucasus Mountains, 12, 240.

Armenian, 229.

Armistice, convention signed on Sept. 12, 1944, in Moscow, by Romania and the United Nations, puting an end to the hostilities between the signatories, 168, 183-189, 266.

Asia, 11, 13, 196, 197, 199, 200, 202, 211, 214, 215, 218, 221, 222, 228, 231, 259, 265, 266.

Asian or *Asiatic,* 210, 263.

Aspects des Relations Russo-Roumaines: Rétrospectives et Orientations, title of a collective study issued in 1967, in Paris. See *General Bibliography,* Cioranesco, Filiti, etc..., 19, 266.

Assembly of the Captive Nations, political organization of exiled people representing Central and Eastern European countries now under communist rule, 210.

Astrakhan, city and *oblast* in European Russian SFSR along the lower Volga River, 209.

Atachi, Ataki, Otaci, village in Bessarabia, Hotin district, today in Moldavian SSR, on Dniester River, opposite Mogilyov-Podolsky, 210, 239.

Atamenko, Moldavian minister of local industry (1955-1957), 201.

Atherton, Ray (1883), USA's minister to Bulgaria (1937); acting chief of the European Division in the State Department (1940-1943), 147.

Atlantic Charter, joint declaration issued on Aug. 14, 1941 by British prime minister Winston Churchill and USA president Franklin D. Roosevelt, 145-148, 154.

Aubert, French captain belonging to Napoleon's Grande Armée, 27.

August 23, 1944, Rom. coup d'état organized by king Michael, the political parties and the army, which reversed marshal Antonescu's regime, suspended the hostilities against USSR and declared war against Germany, 168, 209.

Aur, new settlement of recently deported Moldavians in Kharabovsk Territory, 214.

Austerlitz, Battle of, called also the *Battle of the Three Emperors* i. e.: Napoleon, Alexander I of Russia and Francis I of Austria (Dec. 2, 1805). Napoleon's victory forced Austria to sign the treaty of Pressburg, 23.

Australia, 134.

Austria-Hungary Empire (1867-1919), a dual state created in 1867 with the approval of the parliament of the *Ausgleich* (compromise) between the Hungarian nation and the Habsburg dynasty. This empire was divided after World War I among the independent states of Austria, Hungary and Czechoslovakia, while a part of its territory united with Italy, Poland, Romania and Yugoslavia, 36, 44-47, 53, 55, 66, 75, 77, 84, 86, 89, 95, 96, 121, 214, 260.

Austrian, 17, 23, 36.

Austrian Empire (1804-1867), proclaimed by emperor Francis on Aug. 14, 1804 to maintain Austria's position when Napoleon proclaimed himself emperor. Its place was taken in 1867 by the Austria-Hungary Empire, 23, 28-31, 38, 41, 42.

Averescu, Alexandru (1859-1938), Rom. marshal and political leader three times prime minister (March-May 1918; March 1920-December 1921 and March 1926-June 1927). He was born in Izmail, Bessarabia, today in Ukrainian SSR, 226.

Powers, Axis coalition led by Germany, Italy and Japan during World War II. The Proclamation of Axis Rome and Berlin (oct. 25, 1936) was followed by the German-Japanese Anti-Comintern Pact (Nov. 25, 1936), the German-Italian political and military alliance (May 22, 1939) and the Tripartite Pact linking Germany, Italy and Japan (Sept. 27, 1940), 143, 151, 152, 159, 185-187.

Azerbaijan, Soviet Socialist Republic located on the western shore of the Caspian Sea. Capital: Baku, 12, 223, 240.

Azov, Sea of, 196, 213.

Babadag, tableland and town in northern Dobrogea, 76, 81.

Badoglio, Pietro (1871-1956), Italian field marshal (1926); chief of staff of the Italian armed forces (1919, 1925, 1937-1940); prime minister (July 1943-June 1944). He successfully extricated Italy from World War II in arranging an armistice with the Allies in Sept. 1943, 193.

Băiceni, village in Romania, Iași district, center of neolithic culture of Cucuteni type, 35.

Baker, British general, 60.

Bălăceanu, Ion (Iancu) (1828-1914), Rom. statesman and diplomat; minister of foreign affairs (Jan. 30-Apr. 4, 1876); plenipotentiary minister to Paris, Constantinople, Vienna, Rome and London, 77.

Bălcinești, settlement of Moldavians deported in Soviet Far East, Russian SFSR, 214.

Balkan Entente, mutual defense agreement between Greece, Romania, Turkey and Yugoslavia, signed on Feb. 9, 1934, 102, 103.

Balkan Federation, political plan conceived during World War II as a barrier against communist expansion, 153, 167.

Balkan Peninsula, 23, 29, 40-45, 47, 49, 54, 55, 57-60, 65-67, 86-88, 102, 103, 110, 122, 129, 132, 136, 153, 154, 156, 158, 160, 162, 166, 167, 187, 188, 261.

Balta, city in Ukrainian SSR, Odessa *oblast.* Capital of Moldavian Autonomous SSR (1924-1928), 17.

Bălți, Beltsy, city in Bessarabia, Bălți district, today in north-central Moldavian SSR, on the right bank of Răut River, 210, 239.

Baltic States, 110, 132, 137, 146-148, 198, 200, 202, 206, 228, 229, 259.

Balts, 210, 222.

Banat, historical province of Eastern Europe, divided by the Treaty of Trianon (June 4, 1920) between Romania, Yugoslavia and Hungary, 32, 82, 88, 91, 113, 162, 191.

Baranovsky, Afanasyi Grigorievich (1909), Moldavian specialist in phitophisiology; minister of public education (1953-1954), 201.

Barbarossa Plan, Hitler's directive no. 21, signed on Dec. 18, 1940, whose subtitle was "Operation Barbarossa"; it laid down the plan for the campaign against the Soviet Union, 130, 182.

Barbul, Gheorghe (1915), marshal Antonescu's secretary for foreign affairs. He related the Antonescu-Hitler meetings in his book *"Memorial Antonescu",* see *General Bibliography,* 139.

Barbulat, V.K., Moldavian communist leader, chief of propaganda (1964-1967), 203, 264.

Barnaul, city in Altai Territory, in Russian SFSR, SW Siberia, on the left bank of Ob River, 211.

Basarab I, Prince of Wallachia (cca 1310-1350). He secured Wallachia's independence by defeating the Hungarians in the battle of Possada (1330), 35.

Basarabi, Rom. dinasty founded by Basarab I which ruled Wallachia from the 14th to the 16th century, 255.

Basarabia Nouă, settlement of Moldavians deported to the Soviet Far East, Russian SFSR, 214.
Basdevant, Denise, French contemporary historian; author of the book *Terres Roumaines Contre Vents et Marées,* Paris, Editions de l'Epargne, 1961. English issue: *Tide and Tempest: The Story of Romania,* New York, 1965, 40, 44, 48.
Bashkirs, Turkish people from USSR, settled between the Volga and the Urals, and numbering over 1,000,000 men, 11, 215, 217.
Basilescu, Nicolae (1860-1938), professor of economics at Iaşi University (1892); transfered to Bucharest, Faculty of Law (1896), 89.
Bastianini, Giuseppe (1899-1961), Italian diplomat, statesman and journalist; undersecretary of state to the foreign ministry (1936-1939), 152.
Bavaria, 216.
Bayazid I, Yldîrîm (1347-1403), Ottoman sultan (1389-1402), 56.
Baylen, Spanish city in Andalusia, where general Duponty signed a French capitulation in 1808, 27.
Beaverbrook, William Maxwell Aitken, 1st baron (1879-1964), member of Winston Churchill's war cabinet as minister of aircraft production (1940-1941) and minister of supply (1941-1942); British lend-lease administration in USA (1942) and lord privy seal (1943-1945), 145.
Beijing, see Peking.
Belgian, 248.
Belgium, Belgique, proclaimed its independence in 1830 and its perpetual neutrality in 1831, 53, 54, 149, 191.
Belgorod-Dnestrovsky, town in USSR, Ukrainian SSR, Odessa *oblast,* whose Romanian name is Cetatea-Albă, 199.
Belgrade, capital city of Yugoslavia, located at the confluence of the Danube and Sava Rivers. Belgrade came under Serbian rule in 1284 and became Serbia's capital in 1807-1813, and again in 1867. In Belgrade the Helsinki follow-up Conference on European Cooperation and Security took place (1977-1978), 244.
Beliaev, P.A., minister of commerce of the Moldavian SSR (1954); member of the Moldavian CP CC (1956), 201.
Beltsy, Beltzi, see Bălţi.
Belzhaev, Isaac Moiseyevich (1908), Soviet contemporary historian, 61.
Bender, Bendery, see Tighina.
Benes, Edvard (1884-1948), Czechoslovak statesman; foreign minister (1918-1935); prime minister (1921-1922); president of the republic (1935-1938; 1938-1945 and 1945-1948). He was one of the founders of the Little Entente, 165, 188.
Bengel, Jonat Albrecht (1687-1752), Pietist theologian, professor and preacher of a speculative-apocalyptic inspiration, 216.
Benton, James Webb (1892), American diplomat; first secretary to USA legation in Bucharest (1939-1941), 138, 139.
Berdan, American gun of 10.7 mm and 4.300 k., used by the Russian infantry. Its breach loading was manipulated with some difficulty, 56.
Berdyansk, settlement of Moldavians deported in the Soviet Far East, named after the Ukrainian city from Zaporozhe *oblast* (today Osipenko), 214.

Berezina, River in the Belorussian SSR, tributary of the Dnepr where a fiercely fought battle took place between the Russian army and the French Grande Armée, during Napoleon's retreat from Moscow, 216.

Berg, Lev Semionovich (1876-1950), Sov. geographer and ichtyologist born at Tighina; doctor of zoology (1934); he published about 700 studies, 226.

Beria, Lavrenty Pavlovich (1899-1953), Soviet party and state leader, in charge of the USSR Commissariat for Internal Affairs – NKVD – (1938); deputy prime minister (1941); marshal of USSR (1945) and one of the four deputy prime ministers and minister for internal affairs after Stalin's death, 197.

Berlin, capital of Germany (1871-1945), 22, 77-78, 108-110, 112, 113, 122, 129, 136, 158.

Berlin, Congress of (June 13-July 13, 1878), international meeting of major European powers convened to solve the crisis caused by the San Stefano treaty, which was signed by Russia and Turkey at the conclusion of Russo-Turkish war of 1877, 15, 49, 62, 63, 67, 73, 74, 77-81.

Berlin, Treaty July 13, (1878), recognized the independence of Serbia, Montenegro and Romania; created the principality of Bulgaria under ottoman suzerainty; transformed southern Bulgaria, i.e. Rumelia, into an autonomous region within the framework of the Ottoman empire; recognized the Austro-Hungarian occupation of Bosnia and Hercegovina, etc..., 11, 45-49, 82.

Bern, capital of Switzerland since 1848, 167.

Berry Burton Yost (1901), American diplomat; temporary consul in Cairo and secretary of legation in Egypt (1938); charged with special mission to occupied Greece (1941); consul to Istanbul (1942); consul general to Turkey (1943); USA representative in Romania, appointed in Oct. 1944, 168, 169.

Bessarabia, passim.

Bessarabian parliament, see Sfatul Țării.

Bessarabka, village in Bessarabia, Cetatea-Albă district, today in Moldavian SSR, on Kogîlnic River, 239.

Bindreiter, Uta, Austrian contemporary historian, 40, 46-49.

Bismarck, Otto von (1815-1898), founder and first chancellor of the German empire; principal architect and president of the Congress of Berlin (1878), 48, 53, 63, 67, 77-80.

Black Sea, 22, 23, 32, 33, 35, 66, 76, 81, 85, 92, 128, 147, 198, 213, 218, 247.

Blaga, Lucian (1895-1961), Rom. poet and philosopher, 101.

Block of Democratic Parties, see National-Democratic Block.

Bodnăraş, Emil (1904-1976), Rom. communist leader; member of RCP (1934); sentenced to eight years detention which he spent in Doftana, Aiud, Galaţi and Braşov prisons (1934-1942); member of the RCP operative leading group charged with organizing the Romanian August 1944 national insurrection,

Bodyul, Bodiul, Ivan Ivanovich (1918), Moldavian Communist leader; secretary of Volintirov local committee (1955); candidate member of Moldavian CC (1965); second secretary of the MCP CC (1959-1961); first secretary of the MCP CC (May 29, 1961); deputy of USSR supreme Soviet (1960), 203, 205, 224, 227, 229, 261, 264.

Bogatânga, settlement of Moldavians deported to the Soviet Far East, Russian SFSR, 214.

Bohlen, Charles Eusthis (1904-1974), chief of the State Department's Division of East European Affairs, 163.
Boldur, Alexandru (1886-1982), Rom. historian specialist in Moldavia's medieval history and Bessarabia's history, 15, 20.
Bolgrad, city in Ukrainian SSR, Izmail *oblast,* 25.
Bolshevik Revolution, armed insurrection begun on the morning of November 7 (oct. 25, 1917 old style) when the Bolsheviks proclaimed the overthrow of the Russian Provisional Government, 96.
Bolsheviks, members of the left wing of the Russian social-democratic party who, led by Lenin, seized the control of the government in October 1917, 97.
Boris III (1894-1943), tzar of Bulgaria (1918-1943), 113, 153.
Borisov, chairman of the council of people's commissars of Moldavian CP, 202.
Borodino, Battle of (Sept. 7, 1812), also named the Battle for Moscow, took place during Napoleon's invasion of Russia. Napoleon's victory allowed French troops to occupy Moscow, 216.
Bosnia, Turkish province assigned to Austro-Hungarian occupation at the Congress of Berlin (1878) and annexed to the Austro-Hungarian empire (Oct. 7, 1908) and finally to Serbia (Oct. 26, 1918), 45, 46.
Bosporus, strait uniting the Black Sea and the Sea of Marmara, of strategic importance for Istanbul's defence, 55.
Botev, Khristo (1848-1876), Bulgarian poet and national hero who led the revolutionary movement against Turkish rule, 66.
Botoşani, town in Romania, located in north Moldavia, 15, 37, 160.
Bova-Scópa, Renato (1892), Italian diplomat; plenipotentiary minister to Bucharest (1941-1944), 151, 152.
Brâncuşi, Constantin (1876-1957), Rom. sculptor, pioneer of the modern, abstract sculpture, 101.
Braşov, town in Romania, situated in the center of the country, south east Transylvania, 106 miles north of Bucharest, 101.
Brătianu, Constantin (Dinu) (1866-1948?), Rom. political leader, president of the National Liberal Party (1934-1947), 143, 144, 184, 186, 187.
Brătianu, Gheorghe (1898-1953), Rom. historian and statesman; president of the National Liberal "Georgist" Party (1933-1938); vice-president of the National Liberal Party (1938-1947), 73, 104, 143.
Brătianu, Ion Constantin (1821-1891), Rom. statesman and one of the principal architects of modern Romania. Together with his brother Dumitru he founded the Liberal Party (1866) and served as premier from 1876 to 1888 – except for a brief interval in 1881–48, 56, 57, 67, 74, 75, 77, 80, 81.
Brătianu, Ionel (1864-1927), Rom. statesman; president of the National Liberal Party (1909-1927) and five times premier (1908-1910, 1914-1918, 1918-1919, 1922-1926 and June-Nov. 1927). He played an important role in the achievement of Great Romania, 68, 95, 97.
Bratislava, Pressburg or *Pozzony,* capital of Slovakia, situated on the Danube, 259.
Brătuşeni, village in Bessarabia, Bălţi district, today in Moldavian SSR, near Bălţi, 239.

Brauchitsch, Heinrich Alfred Walter von (1881-1948), German field-marshal and army commander in chief, during the first part of World War II (Sept. 1939-Dec. 1941), 140.

Bravicea, Bravichy, village in Bessarabia, Orhei district, today in central Moldavian SSR, 210.

Brest-Litovsk, Russian town on the right bank of Bug River where the negotiations and the signature of peace treaties concluding World War I took place between the Central Powers and the Ukrainian Republic and Soviet Russia (March 3, 1918), 89, 90.

Brezhnev, Leonid Ilich (1906-1982), Soviet political leader and statesman; first secretary of the Moldavian CP CC (1950-1952); first secretary of Kazakhstan CP CC (1955); first secretary of Soviet Union CP CC (1964-1966) and general secretary (1966-1982) and president of the Supreme Soviet Presidium (1960-1964 and 1977-1982), 52, 197, 202, 209, 214, 227, 243, 244.

Briand, Aristide (1862-1932), French statesman, 11 times premier between 1906-1932. Briand's war cabinet (Oct. 1915-March 1917) was forced to resign because of the unsuccessful Balkan campaign, 84, 85.

Briceni, Brichany, Britchansk, town in Bessarabia, Hotin district, today in N. Moldavian SSR, 55 miles E of Cernăuţi, 210, 211, 239.

Brieni, village in Bessarabia, Cetatea-Albă district, today in Ukrainian SSR, 216.

Brienne-le-Château, village in France, on the Aube River, where French troops reported a victory against the Allied troops fighting against Napoleon (Jan. 29, 1814), 216.

Britchansk, see Briceni.

British, meaning all the peoples of the British Commonwealth of Nations, 231.

Brizon, Pierre (1878-1924), French statesman; socialist deputy (1910-1919), 84.

Brusilov, Aleksey Alekseyevich (1853-1926), Russian general during World War I who achieved "Brusilov's break-through" against Austria-Hungary's front (June-August 1916), overrunning Bucovina and Galicia, 85, 87.

Brzezinski, Zbigniew (1928), American statesman and publicist; professor of public law and government at Columbia University (1960); assistant to president of the USA for national security affairs (1977), 198.

Bucharest, Bucureşti, permanent capital of Wallachia (1659-1862); capital of Romania (1862-1918);capital of Great Romania since 1918, 17, 27, 32, 44, 64, 67, 75, 77, 78, 81, 84, 88, 103-105, 109-111, 113, 117, 123, 130, 139, 142, 151, 156, 170, 183, 187, 190, 191, 224, 228, 229, 249, 250, 252, 256, 258-261, 263, 265, 266.

Bucharest Treaty of (May 28, 1812), ended the Russo-Turkish war of 1806-1812; it allowed Russia to annex Bessarabia, 9, 11, 17, 22, 32, 36, 41, 56-58, 82, 84, 257, 261.

Buchman, local Moldavian CP secretary, 202.

Bucov, Bukov, Emilian Nestorovich (1909), Moldavian writer; editor-in-chief of the magazine *Nistru* since 1966, 224, 225.

Bucovina, Bukovina, historical region, integral part of Moldavia since its foundation (14th century); ceded by the Ottoman empire to Austria (convention of May 7, 1775); united with Romania (decision of the General Congress of Bucovina, Nov. 28, 1918); union internationally recognized (Treaty of Saint- Germain, Sept. 10, 1919). Northern Bucovina was occupied by USSR (ultimatum of June 26, 1940) and annexed by

the Soviet Union by Paris Peace Treaty (Feb. 10, 1947), 15, 19, 34, 36, 38, 84, 88, 91, 96, 97, 109, 120-122, 130, 131, 137, 142, 158-160, 163, 166, 211, 255, 259, 266.
Bucovina, Northern, 10-12, 16, 18, 33, 38, 108, 112, 115-117, 119, 120-122, 127-131, 136-138, 140, 142, 146, 147, 150, 151, 154-170, 199, 207, 208, 212, 213, 219, 228, 246, 256, 258, 265, 266.
Bucovina, Southern, 121.
Budapest, Buda became the seat of the national government in 1790; united with Pest (1872) and increased its importance after the Compromise with Austria (1867), 45, 46, 168.
Bulboca, village in Bessarabia, Tighina district, southwest of Chişinău, today in Moldavian SSR, 239.
Bülow, Bernhard Ernst von (1815-1879), German secretary of foreign affairs (1873) and Bismark's counsellor, 77, 80.
Bülow, Bernhard Heinrich Martin Karl, Fürst von (1849-1929), German ambassador to Romania (1888-1893); foreign minister (1897-1900) and imperial chancellor (1900-1909), 47.
Buescu, Victor (1909-1970), Rom. classicist; editor of some Latin texts; translator from Portuguese into Rom., 214.
Bug, River, in USSR, Ukrainian SSR, 806 km long, springing in the Volhynia-Podolia Hills and flowing into the Black Sea, 16, 35, 138-141, 219.
Bugeac, Steppe of, Tartarian name given to southern Bessarabia, 22, 33, 35, 217.
Bujor, Mihai Gheorghiu (1881-1964), Rom. communist; fled to Russia (1917); participated in the defense of Soviet Russia, 17.
Bulgaria, under Turkish rule from 14th century until 1908; its fight for national liberation climaxed in the 1876 revolt; autonomous principality under Turkish suzerainty (1878); independent kingdom (1908), 41, 45, 46, 60, 64, 66, 76, 81, 84, 87, 89, 113, 128, 139, 153, 166, 167, 170, 183, 217, 218, 252, 253.
Bulgarian, 63, 87, 136, 204, 205, 216, 218, 221, 257.
Burks, Richard Voyles (1924), American historian; policy director of Radio Free Europe (1961-1965); professor at Wayne State University (1967); specialist in East European history, communist parties from satellite countries and ideological problems, 16, 226.
Busche-Haddenhausen Hilmar, count von (1867-1939), German plenipotentiary minister to Bucharest (1914-1916), 89.
Buttovich, Soviet contemporary writer, 222.
Buzatu, Gheorghe (1939), Rom. historian; contribution on Romania's contemporary history, 68.
Buzdugan, Ion (1880-1967), Bessarabian poet, 96.
Byelo Russia, Belorussia, White Russia, Soviet European republic founded in 1919; capital: Minsk, 12, 205.
Byelorussians, descendants of east Slavic tribes; they came under Russian suzerainty in the late 18th century, 12, 197, 229, 264.
Byzantine, 35.
Byzantium, 29.

Cadogan, Sir Alexander George Montagu (1884-1968), British diplomat; Foreign Office vice undersecretary (Jan. 1938-Feb. 1946), 150.
Cahul, south Bessarabia district, located on the left bank of the Pruth River, part of which was integrated in Ukrainian SSR and part in Moldavian SSR, 35, 205, 239.
Cainargea-Mică, see Kuchuk Kainarji.
Cairo, English consular residence (1883-1914); royal residence (1914-1953) and since 1953 capital of the republic, 156, 160, 165, 169, 184, 187-190.
Cairo Conference (Nov. 22-26, 1943), Anglo-Americano-Chinese conference which adopted a declaration concerning the war's aims against Japan, 153, 156.
Călăraşi; Calarash, city in Bessarabia, Lăpuşna district, today in central Moldavian SSR, on Bîc (Byk) River, 30 miles NW of Chişinău, 210.
Camencea, see Kamenka.
Camenet, see Kamenec.
Campbell, Ronald Hugh (1838-1953), British diplomat; ambassador to Belgrade (1935-1939), to Paris (1939-1940) and to Lisbon (1940-1945), 138.
Cannes, 101.
Cantacuzino, Constantin (cca. 1650-1716), Rom. diplomat, historian and geographer; supporter of an antiottoman policy, 65.
Cantemir 1 and Cantemir 2, villages in Bessarabia, Cetatea-Albă district, today in the Ukrainian SSR, 239.
Cantemir or *Kantemir, Antioh* (1708-1744), Russian poet and statesman; ambassador to England (1723-1736); minister plenipotentiary to Paris (1736-1744), 226.
Cantemir, Dimitrie (1673-1723), prince of Moldavia (1710-1711), and later prince of the Russian empire. Member of the Berlin Academy (1714) he wrote a documented study on Moldavia's geography, *Descriptio Moldaviae,* printed in 1771, 35, 65.
Capitulations, privileges granted by the Ottoman empire to Moldavia and Wallachia during the 14th century whose existence was contested by some historians, but supported by historical tradition. The treaties of Kuchuk Kainarji (1774) and Paris (1856) recognized their existence, 36.
Carol I, Hohenzollern-Sigmaringen (1839-1914), first prince (1866-1881) and later king of Romania (1881-1914). During his reign Romania won its national independence from the Ottoman empire (May 9, 1877). He concluded a political-military alliance with Germany and Austria-Hungary (1883) and supported Romania's participation during the World War I on the side of the Central Powers, 57-59, 61-64, 75, 78.
Carol II, Hohenzollern-Sigmaringen (1893-1953), king of Romania (1930-1940). On the domestic scene he undermined the basis of parlamentary democracy and introduced a corporatist dictatorship; on the international scene he promoted a policy based on the alliance with Great Britain and France. After the Axis Powers compelled him to give up Northern Transylvania and Southern Dobrogea, he was forced to abdicate (Sept. 6, 1940), 94, 108, 112, 114, 117, 133, 137, 170, 188.
Carpathian Mountains, 30, 34, 78, 85, 86, 92, 143, 168, 183, 190, 213, 223, 225.
Cărpineni, village in Bessarabia, Lăpuşna district, today in Moldavian SSR, 200, 210, 239.
Casablanca Conference (Jan. 14-23, 1943), Anglo-American conference which decided the common military policy for the year 1943, such as the military operations in Africa and the opening of a second front in Italy, 160.

Caspian Sea, 213.
Caucasus Mountains, 206, 209, 213, 214.
Caucasian, 200, 210.
Caulaincourt, Armand-Augustin-Louis, Marquis de (1773-1827), French general and diplomat; ambassador to Russia (Nov. 1807-Feb. 1811) where he worked for establishment of peace between France and Russia, against Napoleon's policy, 26-30.
Cazacu, Petre (1871), Rom. physician and historian; deputy in "Sfatul Ţării", his main book *Moldova dintre Prut, şi Nistru* /Moldavia between Pruth and Dniester/ (Iaşi: Viaţa Românească, 1923) is a judicious account of Bessarabia's history, 15.
Căzănişteanu, Constantin (1931), Rom. historian, specialist in modern and military history, 36, 37.
Ceauşescu, Ilie (1926), Rom. communist historian; contributions concerning RCP and Communist Youth Union's history, 63.
Ceauşescu, Nicolae (1918), first secretary of RCP CC (1965-1969); secretary general of the RCP CC since 1969; member of the Political Executive Committee since 1974; president of the Socialist Republic Romania since 1974, 34, 39, 42, 52, 68, 82, 100-102, 262, 263.
Central Powers, coalition of states during the World War I including Germany, Austria-Hungary, Ottoman Empire and Bulgaria, 49, 86-89.
Ceremhovo, town in USSR, Russian SFSR, in southern part of central Siberia, the region of Baykal Lake, 214.
Cernat, Alexandru (1828-1893), Rom. general; minister of war (Apr.-Aug. 1877 and March-Nov. 1878); commander in chief of Rom. army during the Independence War (1877-1878), 59, 60.
Cernăuţi, Chernovtsy, city in Ukrainian SSR, capital of Cernovtsy *oblast*, in North Bucovina, on the right bank of Pruth River. Important economic center which rapidly developed under Austrian rule (1775-1918), and under Romanian sovereignty (1918-1940 and 1941-1944), 91, 115, 120, 131, 211-213.
Certan, Evgeny Evgenevich, Moldavian contemporary historian, 40-46, 47, 49, 50.
Cetatea-Albă, Belgorod Dnestrovski (Russ.), *Akkerman* (Turk.), important Moldavian medieval commercial center and military fortified town. Stormed by the Turks in 1484; ceded to Russia in 1812; returned to Romania in 1918; today included in Ukrainian SSR, Odessa *oblast*, 35, 115, 128, 131, 199, 209, 211, 216, 219.
Chamberlain, Arthur Neville (1869-1940), British prime minister (1937-1940); supporter of the appeasement policyi towards Hitler, to gain time for his country's rearmament, 132.
Champagny, Jean-Baptiste de Nompère, conte de (1756-1834), French diplomat and statesman; ambassador to Vienna (1801); minister of interior (1804); foreign affairs minister (1807-1811). He was responsible for the Franco-Russian negotiations at the Erfurt Congress (1808), 25, 27-31.
Chelmno Klum, defile where Napoleon's general Vandamme was taken prisoner by the Russians, in 1813, 216.
Chen, Yi (+ 1972), Chinese communist statesman; foreign affairs minister (1958-1972), 263.

Chernyshevski, Nikolai Gavrilovich (1828-1889), Russian writer and utopian socialist who promoted the materialist aesthetics, 44.

Chilia, Kilija, important Moldavian medieval commercial center and fortified town located on the left bank of Chilia (a Danube branch). Chilia was under Moldavian, Turkish (1484-1812), Russian (1812-1918) and Romanian (1918-1940 and 1941-1944) rules. Today it is included in the Ukrainian SSR, 35, 75, 76, 81.

Chin Lien-fin, contemporary Chinese professional singer, 263.

China, the largest Asian state. The Chinese republic was proclaimed ba Sun Yat-sen at Nanking (1911). After a period of anarchy Chiang Kai-shek, commander of the National Revolutionary Army, imposed his authority (1928), but he was defeated by Mao tse-tung, leader of the Chinese communists (1948-1949). The People's Republic was proclaimed in 1949, 13, 16, 20, 213, 220, 224, 231, 252, 253, 258, 259, 263, 266.

Chinese, 231, 259, 261, 263.

Chișinău, Kishinev, city in the Moldavian SSR, on the right bank of the Bîc (Byk) River, first mentioned in 1436; became the capital of Bessarabia (1818) after its annexation by the Russians (1812); returned to Romania (1918-1940); back to USSR (1940); again back to Romania (1941-1944) and assigned to USSR by Paris peace treaty (1947), 12, 14, 15, 22, 49, 95, 97, 115, 131, 191, 193, 201, 206, 209, 216, 224, 229, 238, 239, 263, 265.

Chișinovka, settlement of Moldavians deported to the Soviet Far East, Russian SFSR, 214.

Chu En-lai (1898-1976), Chinese communist statesman; prime minister of the State Council of the Central Popular Government (1949-1954); chairman of the State Council (1954-1976) and chairman of the Popular Political Consultative Council for the whole of China (1934-1976), 262, 263.

Christian, 41, 43, 196, 230.

Church, Romanian Orthodox, dominant Christian church in Romania, autocephalous since 1885, 94.

Church, Romanian Uniate, Greco-Catholic church, created in 1698, when some Romanian orthodox priests from Transylvania accepted the union with Rome, 94.

Churchill, Winston Leonard Spencer (1874-1965), British statesman, leader of the conservative party (1940-1955); war minister (1919-1921); leader of a coalition government (1940-1945) and of a conservative government (1951-1955). He led Great Britain to the victory in World War II, 132, 134, 145, 146, 148, 150, 153, 158, 160, 166.

Chuvak, Chuvash, ethnic minority in USSR living in the Chuvash Autonomous SSR of Russian SFSR, 11, 215, 217, 218.

Chvertko, P.V., candidate member of the Kirgiz CP Bureau (1955-1967) and chairman of the Kirgiz KGB (1961-1967); chairman of Moldavian KGB (1967); candidate member of the Moldavian CP Bureau (1971), 200.

Ciano, Galeazzo, conte di Cortelazzo (1903-1944), Italian diplomat and statesman, son-in-law of Benito Mussolini; minister of foreign affairs (1936-1943), 113, 132, 152, 153.

Cîmpulung, town in Romania, Argeș district, first mentioned in 1300. Cîmpulung was the first capital of Wallachia, 78.

Ciobanu, Ştefan (1883-1950), Rom. literary historian who studied ancient Romanian cultural relations with cultures of neighbouring peoples, 15.

Ciorănescu, George (1918), Rom. historian living in France, 19.

Ciucea, village in Romania, Cluj district, with a memorial house devoted to the Rom. poet Octavian Goga, 97.

Ciupercă, Nicolae (1882), Rom. general; minister of the national defense (1938-1939); commander-in-chief of Romanian IVth army on the Soviet front (1941), 144.

Clark-Kerr, Sir Archibald John (1882-1951), British diplomat; ambassador to Moscow (1942-1946), 162, 163.

Clarke, Henri-Jacques-Guillaume (1765-1818), French Marshal and minister of war under Napoleon, 23, 24.

Clio, 20.

Clodius, Carl August (1897-1946), German diplomat; director of the trade policy department, 185.

Collit, Leslie, British contemporary journalist, 191.

Coman, Ion (1926), Rom. general; chief of the general staff (1979); deputy minister of national defense (1974-1976); minister of national defense (June 15, 1976-March 29, 1980), 60.

Comecon, Council for Mutual Economic Assistance, socialist international organization for economic cooperation among communist states, founded in Jan. 1949 by Bulgaria, Czechoslovakia, Hungary, Poland, Romania and USSR. Later members: Albania (from 1949 to 1962), German D.R. (1951), Mongolia (1962) and Cuba (1972), 249-251, 253.

Comintern, see International, Third.

Comunistul Moldovei, theoretical and political monthly magazine of the Moldavian CP CC, issued since 1956 in Chişinău, in Rom. language but with Cyrillic characters, 40.

Constant, Jean-Louis (named also *Emile*) (1861-1950), French lawyer and statesman; deputy (1893-1919) affiliated to the democratic left; under secretary of state to the interior ministry (1911-1912), 85.

Constanţa, Romania's main seaport, located at about 200 km east of Bucharest. Conquered by the Turks in the 15th century, Constanţa developed as a modern, industrial and commercial center after 1878 when it was returned to Romania, by the Berlin Congress (1878), 76, 81, 140.

Constantinescu, Alexandru (1859-1926), Rom. statesman; member of the National Liberal Party (1882); minister of the interior (1916-1918), 97.

Constantinescu-Iaşi, Petre (1892-1977), Rom. historian, specialist in history of arts, 17.

Constantinescu, Miron (1917-1974), Rom. historian and sociologist; communist activist entrusted after August 23 with various important functions on party and state line, 18, 260.

Constantinople, see Istanbul.

Constantinople, Ambassadors' Conference (1876-1877), conference of European Guarantor Powers convoked by England after the signing of the Turkish-Serbish armistice (Oct.-Nov. 1876). From this conference Romania hoped to obtain its independence through the formula of the absolute neutrality, 54, 55, 74.

Constitution of Moldavian Soviet Socialist Republic, (April 15, 1978), see its analysis in present book, pp. 238-245.
Constitution of the Soviet Union (Oct. 1977), 238, 240, 242, 244.
Corabia, town and harbour in Romania, Olt district, on the left bank of the Danube, 59.
Cornovan, Dimitri Semionovich (1928), Moldavian party activist and statesman; member of the USSR CP (1951); member of the Moldavian CP CC Presidium (1962-1966), 227.
Coroban, Vasile Pavlovich (1910), Moldavian literary critic and historian, 226.
Corti, Luigi (Lodovico), conte (1823-1888), Italian diplomat; plenipotentiary minister to Stockholm (1864), Madrid (1867), Washington (1870) and Constantinople (1875). As Italy's foreign affairs minister he represented his country to the Berlin Conference (1878), together with the count Launy, Italian ambassador to Berlin, 79, 81.
Coşeni, village in Bessarabia, Bălţi district, today in Moldavian SSR, 210.
Cossaks, term referring to the semi-independent Tatar groups inhabiting the Dnieper region, living in autonomous military communities. Under the Soviet rule their communities were suppressed, 32.
Coste, Brutus (1910-1984), Rom. diplomat; chargé d'affaires to Washington (1939-1941), 138.
Costin, Miron (1633-1691), Rom. humanist and historiographer, author of a history of Moldavia from 1595 to 1661, 225.
Covurlui, small district in Romania, confined by Siret, Pruth and Danube; today renamed Galaţi district, 37.
Craiova, city in southwestern Romania, on Jiu River, 115 miles west of Bucharest, first documentary mention in 1475, 78, 101.
Craiova Treaty (Sept. 7, 1940), Romanian-Bulgarian negotiations which started in Craiova, on Aug. 19, 1940 on Hitler's advice, ended with a treaty rectifiyng the Romanian-Bulgarian frontier in the Dobrogea's sector. Romania gave up to Bulgaria the Southern Dobrogea – or Cadrilater – composed of two districts: Durostor and Caliacra, 128, 218.
Creangă, Ion (1837-1889), Rom. writer, author of the *Childhood Recollections* and charming fairy-tales, 225.
Cretzianu, Alexandru (1895-1979), Rom. diplomat, member of the delegation to the Paris Peace Conference (1919); secretary of the legation in London (1920-1922), Rome (1923-1926) and Bern (1926-1932); secretary general of the foreign ministry; plenipotentiary minister to Ankara (1943-1944), 111, 153, 156, 160, 165, 187.
Crihan, Anton (1893), Rom. statesman; deputy in "Sfatul Ţării" (1917-1918); state secretary for agriculture (1918); deputy in Rom. Parliament (1919-1932); professor of agronomics at Chişinău (1933), 210.
Crimea, during the 15th century the Tatars founded in Crimea a khanate under Turkish sovereignty; Crimea was annexed by Russia in 1783 and was the theater of the Crimean war (1853-1856) and also of fiercely fought battles during World War II, 25, 41, 52, 83, 140, 213, 219.
Crimea Autonomous Republic, was founded in 1921 and was populated primarily by Tatars. During World War II the Tatars were dispersed (1945), accused of collabor-

ation with the Germans, and Crimea passed to the Russian SFSR and later to Ukrainian SSR, (1954), 217.

Crimean War (Oct. 1853-Feb. 1856), between Russia on one side and England, France, Turkey and Sardinia–Piedmont on the other side, ended with the Congress and peace treaty of Paris, 42, 47.

Cripps, Sir Richard Stafford (1889-1952), British statesman, member of the Labour Party; ambassador to Moscow (May 1940-Jan. 1942), 145, 148.

Crişana, historical province in Romania, between Transylvania and Hungary, united with Romania in 1918 at the same time as Transylvania, 82, 91, 113.

Criuleni, village in Bessarabia, Orhei district, on the left bank of Dniester, today in Moldavian SSR, 207.

Crown Council, Romanian, (June 27, 1940), took place under king Carol II chairmanship with the participation of: Gheorghe Tătărescu, prime minister; Nicolae Iorga, Constantin Argetoianu, general E. Ballif, Victor Iamandi, Victor Antonescu, Victor Slăvescu, Mircea Cancicov, Ion Gigurtu, Ernest Urdăreanu, Silviu Dragomir, Mihail Ghelmegeanu, Miţiţă Constantinescu, Mihail Ralea, Petre Andrei, Traian Pop, general Ion Ilcuşu, Constantin C. Giurescu, N. Hortolomei, Radu Portocală, Ion Christu, Aurelian Bentoiu, Ştefan Ciobanu, I. Macovei and general Florea Ţenescu, chief of the General Staff, 114.

Crutzescu, Radu (1892-1953), Rom. diplomat; plenipotentiary minister to Warsaw (1921-1924), Bruxelles, Prague (1924-1930) and Berlin (1938-1940), 112, 113.

Cucuteni-Băiceni, village in Romania, Iaşi district, center of a neolithic culture (4-3. mill b.C.), 35.

Cumans, Turanian nomadic people who emigrated (11th century) from the Black Sea and Azov Sea shores towards central Europe and clashed with Hungarian forces (13th century), 217.

Curticăpeanu, Vasile (1923), Rom. historian; contributions to Transylvania cultural history, 94-96, 98.

Curzon Line, a demarcation line between Poland and USSR, first proposed as an armistice line during Russo-Polish war (1919-1920) wich became later with the Soviet-Polish treaty (Aug. 16, 1945) almost the official frontier between Poland and USSR, 219.

Cuza, Alexandru Ion (1820-1873), first prince of the Romanian United Principalities (1859-1862) and of Romanian national state (1862-1866), 15, 43, 44.

Cyrillic alphabet, 223, 240, 264.

Czartoryski, Adam Jerzy (1770-1861), Polish statesman who worked for the restoration of his country and its union with Russia. Close adviser of tzar Alexander I; deputy minister of foreign affairs (1802) and later minister (1804-1806), 23.

Czechoslovakia, the Czechs' Lands and Slovakia came under the Habsburg's rule in the 16th and 17th centuries; when the Austria-Hungary empire was founded, the Czechs' Lands remained under Austrian rule and Slovakia under Hungarian rule. After the Austria-Hungary's collapse (1918), Czechoslovakia was created by the merging of Bohemia, Slovakia and Ruthenia, 165, 188, 228, 250, 259.

Dacia, name given in ancient times to the territory inhabited by the Dacian people, roughly corresponding to the present-day Romanian territory, 92.

Dacia, Ó ès új Dacia – old and New Dacia – title of an historical study by Hust András (1742), 35, 81, 86.

Dacia Viitoare, Rom. magazine printed in Paris, Brusselles, (1883), 92.

Dacians, 34, 35, 82.

Daco-Romanians, name given by the philologists to the Romanian population living north of the Danube to differentiate them from the Romanian population living south of the Danube, 16, 34.

Daicoviciu, Constantin (1898-1973), Rom. historian and archeologist who specialized in Dacian studies, 18.

Dalbiez, Victor (1876-1954), French statesman, author of a bill (1915) on the better utilization of civil and military personnel during World War I. Minister of French Liberated Provinces (1924), 85.

Danube River, 11, 16, 23, 25, 27-32, 34, 35, 47-49, 59, 60, 64-66, 76, 79-81, 85, 110, 128, 131, 136, 152, 153, 158, 170, 183, 186, 190, 198, 218, 247, 252, 258.

Danube, European Commission of the Danube, with the headquarter at Galați, was established in 1856 as an authority of 8 powers over the mouths of the River charged with clearing obstructions and deepening the channels. After the Treaty of Versailles the Danube was internationalized (1921) under the *International Commission of the Danube* with jurisdiction over the navigable course of the river, from Ulm to Brăila. Romania attained the control over the lower Danube by Sinaia agreement (1938). In 1940 Germany forced the *International Commission* with the headquarter at Vienna, to dissolve. Paris peace treaty (1947) provided for the Danube's complete internationalization. A new Danube authority set up in 1948 at the Soviet Union instigation is composed only by the rivarian powers except West Germany, 48, 81, 122, 137.

Danubian Federation, various plans for a closer political-economic cooperation among Central European countries, such as André Tardieu's Plan (1932) and other similar projects discussed during World War II, 153.

Danubian Principalities, see Romanian Principalities.

Dardanelles, 158.

Darienko, Petru Stepanovich (1923), Moldavian poet and communist activist; chief of section of Moldavian CP CC in charge of literature and arts (1952); chief editor of *Moldova Socialistă* (1953-1963); minister of culture (1963-1967), 203, 225.

Davidescu, Gheorghe, Rom. plenipotentiary minister to Kremlin (1941-1944); secretary general of foreign affairs ministry, 18, 111, 115, 117, 138, 139.

Dealul Mare, a hill located in the west part of the Moldavian plain, on the left bank of the Siret, south of the source of the river Bahlui, 183.

Declaration of Independence, Romanian (April 1964), a declaration of RCP whitch stated that the management of the economy should be left to the Romanian state, because "it is one of the fundamental, essential attribute of the sovereignty of a socialist state". This nationalist stand on economics developed into a Romanian autonomous politic stand within the communist block, 259.

Declaration of the Rights of the Peoples of Russia, declaration published by the Soviet government shortly after its victorious establishment (1917), 90, 91.

Dekanosov, Vladimir Georgievich (1898-1953), deputy people's commissar for foreign affairs (1939) and simultaneously USSR ambassador to Germany (1940-1941), 121.

Delirium, The, title of a novel by Marin Preda, presenting a courageous description of marshal Antonescu's regime */Delirul,/* (Bucharest: Cartea Românească, 1975), 185.
Denmark, 191.
Derzhavin, Derjavin, Nikolai Sebastianovich (1877-1953), Soviet historian and philologist; author of a *History of Bulgaria* (Leningrad: USSR Academy, 1945), 35.
Diortitsa, A.F., see Gheorghiță.
Disraeli, Benjamin, Earl of Beaconsfield (1804-1881), British statesman, twice prime minister (1868 and 1874-1880), 48, 63, 79, 80.
Djilas, Milovan (1911), Yugoslav political writer and communist leader, vice president of the state and president of the General People's Assembly (1953); imprisoned for defiance against the regime (1956); released (1961) and imprisoned again for the publication in the west of his *Conversations with Stalin,* 230.
Dnepr, Dnieper, River, 140, 141, 219.
Dnepropetrovsk, city in Ukrainian SSR, on the right bank of Dnieper River, 212, 213.
Dniester, Dnestr, Rom. Nistru, River, the main water artery of Moldavian SSR, 10, 16-18, 22-24, 29, 32, 33, 35-38, 86, 91, 92, 110, 117, 128, 129, 131, 135, 138-144, 150, 151, 154, 155, 161, 162, 181-183, 186, 190, 196, 201, 212, 213, 218, 219, 223, 225, 257, 258.
Dobrogea, Dobruja, historical province located in SE Romania, between the Danube and the Black Sea. Independent under the leadership of Balica, Dobrotich and Ivanco (14th century), Dobrogea passed under Wallachian rule during Mircea cel Bătrân (1386-1418) and later Turkish rule (1417-1878). The Congress of Berlin gave north Dobrogea to Romania (1878), and the Bucharest peace treaty added to it the south Dobrogea (Cadrilater) in 1913. The Cadrilater was ceded to Bulgaria by the Craiova treaty (1940), 15, 48, 49, 73, 81, 84, 88, 136, 170, 213, 218, 252.
Dobrogea, Southern, Cadrilater, Silistra, names given to the ancient Durostorum, occupied by the Turks in the 15th century; the Congress of Berlin attributed this region to Bulgaria (1878); the Bucharest peace treaty to Romania (1913) and the Craiova treaty again to Bulgaria (1940), 113, 122, 128, 218.
Dobrogeanu-Gherea, see Gherea.
Dobrolyubov, Nikolai Alexandrovich (1836-1861), influential Russian critic who rejected traditionalist and romantic literature, 44.
Docul, local Moldavian CP secretay, 202.
Don, River, 150.
Dondușăni, Dondușeni, village in Bessarabia, Soroca district, today in Moldavian SSR, 239.
Donets, Basin, one of the main coal-producing and industrial areas of USSR, 212.
Donetsk, administrative region in the eastern part of Ukrainian SSR, 213.
Donici, Alexandru (1806-1866), Rom. fabulist and translator from Russian poets, 198.
Dorohoi, town in NE Romania, Moldavia, 75 miles NW of Iași, 117.
Draganov, Parvan (1890-1945), Bulgarian diplomat; plenipotentiary minister to Berlin (1938-1942); minister of foreign affairs (June-Sept. 1944); executed by the communist regime (Feb. 1th, 1945), 113.
Dragomir, Ilie, one of the characters of D.R. Popescu's novel *The Porphyrogenite,* 185.

Drokien, Rom. *Nădușița,* village in Bessarabia, Soroca district, today in N Moldavian SSR, 19 miles of Soroca, 210.
Druță, Ion (1928), Moldavian writer, author of various books describing the life in the Moldavian village under Soviet rule and the peasants' reactions to this new life, 227.
Dubăsari, Dubossary, district and town on the left bank of Dniester, in Moldavian SSR, 199.
Duce, Il, see Mussolini.
Dunai, Rom. *Dunărea,* settlement of Moldavians deported in Soviet Far East, Russian SFSR, 214.
Dungans, Chinese *T'ung-Kan* or *Hiu,* or *Hui-Hui,* Chinese Muslims of northwest China. Some of the Dungans have settled in USSR, in Uzbek SSR and Kazakh SSR, 228.
Dunn, James Clement (1890), American diplomat; senior official in the State Department (1935-1937); counsellor at San Francisco and Potsdam Conferences (1945); counsellor at London and Paris Conferences (1945-1946), 147.
Dutch, 248.
Dzyuba, Ivan Mikhailovich (1931), prominent Ukrainian literary critic, detained in Kiev for having sent to the west a diary of a deceased young poet (1965). He is the author of the study *Internationalism or Russification* (Dec. 1965), criticizing Soviet policy of Russification and supporting the Ukrainian cultural renaissance, 226.
East Germany, see German Democratic Republic.
Eastern Campaign or *Russian Campaign,* offensive launched on June 22, 1941, by the Third Reich against USSR, 140, 142, 144, 182.
Eastern Question, diplomatic problem of eventual distribution of Ottoman empire territories the great European powers were preoccupied with, during the 19th and 20th centuries, 42, 45.
Eden, Robert Anthony, 1st earl of Avon (1897-1977), British statesman; foreign affairs secretary (1935-1938); secretary of state for war (1940); again foreign secretary (1940-1945) and prime minister (1955-1957), 145-150, 153, 155, 156, 158, 159, 166.
Edinița, Edineți, Yedintsy, town in Bessarabia, Hotin district, today in N Moldavian SSR SW of Mogilyov-Podolsky, 206, 210.
Egypt, an independent state in 9th-10th century; it passed under the Mameluks (1250-1517) and Turks (1517-1798) dominations; under French (1798-1805) and British (1882-1922) occupations; became a constitutional monarchy (1922-1952) and finally a republic (1953), 56, 156.
Ekaterinoslav, see Dnepropetrovsk.
Eminescu, Mihail (1850-1889), one of the most famous Romanian poets, 50, 225.
Encyclopaedic Dictionary, Romanian, Dicționarul Enciclopedic Român, Vol. I (Bucharest: Editura Politică, 1962), 257, 258.
Encyclopaedia, Soviet, Bolshaya Entsiklopediya, first edition in 65 volumes, 1926-1947, 258.
Enescu, George (1881-1955), Rom. violonist, conductor and composer, 101.
Engels, Friedrich (1820-1895), one of the founders of scientific communism, friend and the closest collaborator of Marx, 16, 17, 42, 60, 83, 214, 260, 261, 266.
England, 26, 28, 30, 74, 75, 78, 79, 87, 123.

Entente Cordiale (April 8, 1904), political and military agreement between Great Britain and France to settle their litigious problems and to cooperate against the German menace, 83, 84, 87, 88.

Erfurt, city located in the German Democratic Republic. Erfurt was the scene of the Congress attended by Napoleon, Alexander I and several German kings (Sept.-Oct. 1808), 10, 28, 29, 32, 36, 41.

Estonia, the smallest of the three Baltic states. Estonia was incorporated into Russia after Peter the Great's victory over Sweden (1700-1721); it proclaimed its independence after World War I (Feb. 24, 1918); and was again incorporated into USSR during World War II (Aug. 1940), 118.

Estonian, 229.

Europe:

Europe, 11-13, 23, 26, 27, 31, 41, 42, 48-50, 54, 56, 61, 62, 65, 73, 75, 77, 78, 100, 108, 115, 118, 122, 123, 128, 129, 134, 137, 145, 147, 148, 151-153, 158, 159, 167, 169, 186, 196, 197, 221, 222, 231, 251, 254, 259.

Central Europe, 155, 224, 251.

Eastern Europe, 23, 28, 30, 108, 122, 157, 219, 231, 251, 252, 254, 259, 263, 265.

South Eastern E., 9, 13, 40, 44, 45, 47, 65, 102, 118, 159, 191.

Western E., 11, 13, 23, 24, 28, 33, 40, 46, 47, 63, 102, 118, 159, 191.

Europäische Osten, Der, West German magazine founded in Munich (1954), 254.

European Federation, political project for a voluntary association of European states which would conserve their sovereignty, 13, 153, 159, 167.

Evian-les-Bains, town in France, Haute Savoie, near Lausanne, 104.

Evren, Kenan, Turkish general; head of state (1980); head of the National Security Council and chief of the General Staff of the Army (1980-1983), 102.

Eylau, today Bagrationovsk, city in Soviet Union, Russian SFSR, scene of an undecided battle between French troops under Napoleon command and Russian and Prussian troops, 25.

Fabricius, Wilhelm August Julius (1882-1964), German diplomat; plenipotentiary minister to Bucharest (April 1936-Jan. 1941), 110, 112, 117, 120.

Fălciu, region in Romania, SE Moldavia, on the lower Pruth River. Before Bessarabia's annexation by the tzarist Russia (1812), Fălciu district extended on both banks of Pruth River, 37.

Far East, 211, 213, 231.

Federal Republic of Germany, see Germany.

Fère-Champenoise, village in France, in Marne department. Site of the battle between French Napoleonic troops and the anti-napoleonic allied troops (March 25, 1814), 216.

Ferşampenuaz-Mare, village in Bessarabia, Cetatea-Albă district, today in Ukrainian SSR, 216.

Ferşampenuaz-Mic, village in Bessarabia, Cetatea Albă district, today in Moldavian SSR, 216.

Filiti, Grigore (1923), Rom. engineer and historian, living in France, 19.

Filonski, V., Soviet colonel, chief of the political section of Moldavian SSR military commissariat, 207.

Financial Times. World Business, weekly issued in London, 191.

Finland, was part of Sweden (12th century – 1809); annexed by Russia (1809); proclaimed its independence (1917); participated in the military intervention against Soviet Union (1919-1920); opposed by arms the Soviet invasion (1939-1940); fought on German side in the war against USSR (1941-1944), 28, 29, 31, 97, 114, 118, 130, 132, 134, 137, 138, 145-150, 167, 183, 229, 230.

Flondor, Iancu (1865-1924), Rom. statesman; president of the Bucovina National Council which voted Bucovina's union with Romania (1918), 91.

Florescu, Radu, Rom. historian living in the USA, 19.

Floreşti, Floreshty, city in Bessarabia, Bălţi district, today in northern Moldavian SSR, near Bălţi city, 206.

Focşani, city in Romania, SW Moldavia, on Milcov River, near the border between Moldavia and Wallachia. Focşani region was during World War I the site of violent fights opposing Romanian and Russian troops to the German ones, on the battles fields of Mărăşti, Mărăşeşti and Nămoloasa, 27, 88, 190.

Focşani-Galaţi Line, Rom. military defensive line of World War I linking the Carpathian Mountains with the Danube on a shorter front which made possible the defense of Moldavia, 168.

Focşani-Nămoloasa, a sector of Focşani-Galaţi military front during World War I, 190.

Foreign office, department in charge with foreign affairs in Great Britain, 154.

Foreign Policy of Russian Tzarism (The), an essay by Fr. Engels representing the final views of Marx and Engels on Russian foreign policy (1890), 260.

France, 10, 23-31, 32, 38, 43, 44, 47, 53, 55, 60, 84, 85, 87, 92, 104, 108, 112, 118, 128, 132, 133, 158, 169.

Francis I (1708-1765), Holy Roman emperor (1745-1765); he founded the dinasty of the Habsburg-Lotharingia and married Maria Theresa, 30.

Franz (Francis), Joseph I (1830-1916), emperor of Austria since 1848 and king of Hungary since 1867, 44, 47.

French, 15, 197, 216, 231, 248.

Friedensfeld, village in Bessarabia, Cetatea-Albă district, today in Ukrainian SSR, 216.

Friedenstahl, village in Bessarabia, Cetatea-Albă district, today in Ukrainian SSR, 216.

Friessner, Johannes (1892-1971), German general, commander of the south Ukrainian German Armies (1943), 189.

Frunze, city in USSR, capital of the Kirgiz SSR, located in the Chu River Valley, 125 miles of Alma-Ata, 213.

Frunze de Dor, title of one of Moldavian writer Ion Druţă's books describing life in a Moldavian village under Soviet rule, 227.

Führer, see Hitler.

Gafencu, Grigore (1892-1957), Rom. diplomat, journalist and statesman; minister of foreign affairs (1938-1940); pleni-potentiary minister to USSR (1940-1941), 130, 131, 135, 143, 155, 170, 181, 189, 192.

Gagautzs, Găgăuz, people of Turkish origin but of Christian faith, living in the Moldavian SSR, Dobrogea and Bulgaria, 204, 216, 217.

Galaţi, Galatz, city and port in Romania, located on the left bank of the Danube, greatly devastated during World War II, 168, 190, 252.

Galib effendi, Turkish plenipotentiary to Bucharest peace conference (1812). Shortly after the signature of Bucharest Peace Treaty, he was decapitated by the Sultan's order, together with his colleague, Dimitri Morouzi, who had also represented the Ottoman empire at Bucharest negotiations, 32.

Galicia, eastern European province, incorporated into the Kievan Russia (981); independent (1087); annexed to Volhynia (1200); annexed to Poland (1349); attached to Austria (1772) and finally to the Ukrainian SSR (1939), 29-30, 34, 131.

Geneva, 161, 189.

Geneva, Convention on Definition of Aggression, an abortive protocol of 1925 making an attempt at the definition of aggression. It specified two forms of aggression, namely the resort to war in violation of the undertakings contained in the Covenant of the League of Nations, and the refusal to accept summons of a competent court or tribunal or to abide by the decision of the League Council, 161.

Genoese, in the middle ages Genoa established an active trade exchange with some Black Sea ports such as Caffa, Sudak, Chilia, Vicina, 35.

Georgescu-Buzău, Gheorghe (1909), Rom. historian; research on Rom. 18th and 19th centuries history, 226.

Georgia, Gruziya, historical region of Transcaucazia. Russia granted Georgia independence in return of its suzerainty (Treaty of Georgiev, 1783). After World War I Georgia proclaimed its independence (Jan. 1921); since 1936 it is one of Soviet Union republics, 12, 240.

Georgians, 229.

Germans, 15, 119, 120, 127, 152-154, 162, 185, 186, 190-192, 197, 207, 208, 216, 220, 246, 248, 257.

German Army High Command, in German: *Oberkommando des Heeres* (OKH), at the beginning of German attack on Soviet Union (June 22, 1941) the heads of the OKH were Werner von Brauchitsch and Franz Halder, 183, 189.

German Democratic Republic, after World War II Germany was divided into two states: the Federal Republic Germany or West Germany (Sept. 1949) and the German Democratic Republic (oct. 7, 1949), 199, 249, 259.

Germany, the First Reich or the Holy Roman Empire was founded in the 10th century (962-1806); the Second Reich was created by Bismark (1871-1933) and the Third Reich was established by Hitler (1933-1945), 10, 13, 19, 23, 28, 30, 31, 45, 47, 77, 84, 89, 104, 108-114, 117, 118, 120-123, 127, 129, 130, 132, 133, 135-139, 141, 142, 148, 150, 151, 153, 158, 159, 167, 183, 184, 186, 206, 229, 246, 259, 266.

Gerstemberg, Alfred von (1893-1959), German general; commander of the *Luftwaffe* in Romania (1942-1944), 191.

Getae-Dacians, see Dacians.

Gheorghe, Ştefan, prince of Moldavia (1653-1658); he signed an alliance treaty with the Russian tzar Alexei Mikhailovich (May, 1656), 35.

Gheorghiţă, Aleksandr Filipovich (1911), born in Gandrabudy, now Odessa *oblast;* graduate of Leningrad Finance Academy (1938) and of the Higher Party School of CPSU CC (1957); member of the Moldavian CP (1938); minister of finance (1933-1936, 1938-1940 and 1946-1955); deputy chairman of Moldavian council of ministers (1955-1958); chairman of the council of ministers and minister of foreign affairs

(1959-1970); deputy of USSR Supreme Soviet (1950, 1954 and 1958), 201, 203-205, 264.
Gheorghiu-Dej, Gheorghe (1901-1965), Rom. communist statesman; secretary general of RCP CC (1945-1954); first secretary of RCP CC (1955-1965); prime minister (1952-1955); president of the state council (1961-1965), 250.
Gherea, Dobrogeanu (1855-1920), Rom. sociologist and literary critic, leader and ideologist of Rom. social-democracy, 66.
Ghermani, Dionisie (1922), Rom. historian living in West Germany, 19.
Ghibu, Onisifor (1883-1976), Rom. educator. Wrote various studies on the history of Rom. education and culture, 15, 20, 94-98.
Ghica, Emil (1848-1911), Rom. diplomat; secretary of Rom. diplomatic agency in St. Petersburg (1874); volunteer to the Rom. independence war (1877-1878); plenipotentiary minister to Belgrade (1885), Athens (1888), St Petersburg (1889) and Vienna (1891), 53, 75, 76.
Ghica, Grigore III, prince of Wallachia (1768-1769) and of Moldavia (1764-1767 and 1774-1777). He protested in 1777 against Bucovina's transfer to Austria and was decapitated by the sultan, 36.
Ghica, Ion (1829-1891), Rom. diplomat and statesman; diplomatic agent to Constantinople (1872-1877) and after the outbreak of Romanian-Russian-Turkish war (1877-1878) Rom. attaché to tzar Alexander II and later plenipotentiary minister to St Petersburg, 53.
Giers, Nikolay Karlovich (1820-1895), Russian statesman during the reign of Alexander III; acting foreign affairs minister (1878) and foreign affairs minister (1882), 76.
Gigurtu, Ion (1886), Rom. statesman; deputy (1926); minister of trade and industry (1938); minister of foreign affairs (May 31 –June 27, 1940) and prime minister (July 4–Sept. 4, 1940), 110-112, 136, 193.
Gîrbea, Titus, Rom. general; during World War II he represented Rom. general staff to the German Army High Command, 183, 189.
Giurescu, Constantin C. (1901-1977), Rom. historian, author of a synthetis concerning the history of Rom. people and of various historical studies, 258.
Gladky, Dimitri Spiridonovich, second secretary of Moldavian CP CC (1952); first secretary of the MCP CC (1952-1954); deputy of the USSR Supreme Soviet (1954, 1958 conventions); member of the economic commision of USSR Supreme Soviet of nationalities (1957-1958), 202, 203.
Globe, The, English newspaper, 78.
Glodeni, village in Bessarabia, Bălți district, today in the Moldavian SSR, 206, 210.
Gnadesfeld, village in Bessarabia, Cetatea-Albă district, today in Ukrainian SSR, 216.
Göring, Hermann (1893-1946), Nazi Party leader and Hitler loyal supporter; marshal; commander of *Luftwaffe* since 1935, 112, 140, 141.
Goga, Octavian (1881-1938), Rom. poet and publicist who played an important role in the achievement of Romanian national unity. Prime minister of a rightist government (1937-1938), 94-98.
Goga, Veturia, wife of Octavian Goga, 95, 97.
Golumb, local Moldavian CP secretary, 202.
Gorban, B.A., one of the Moldavian CP secretaries (1952), 203.

Gorchakov, Alexandr Michailovich, prince (1798-1883), Russian statesman; minister of foreign affairs during Paris and Berlin conferences (1856-1882), 45, 47, 48, 57, 64, 74-77, 79, 80.

Gorj, Alexandru, pseudonym of a Rom. historian living in France, 19.

Gorni-Dubnic, Dubniak, fortified point southwest of Pleven conquered on oct. 12/24, 1877 by the Russian troops commanded by general Gurko, with the help of Romanian units, 59.

Grand Trianon, see Trianon.

Grand vizier, sultan's prime minister in the Ottoman empire, 25.

Grande Armée, Napoleon's army composed of about 453.000 men when it started the Russian campaign, numbering only 10.000 men after the crossing of Berezina River, 32.

Grandi di Mordano, Dino (1895), Italian diplomat; foreign affairs minister (1929-1931) and ambassador to London; justice minister and chairman of the Fascist Chamber and Senate (1939-1943), 152.

Great Britain, 10, 43, 46, 47, 53, 55, 61, 87, 92, 104, 108, 119, 128, 129, 132-136, 139, 143, 145-152, 154-159, 161-164, 166-170, 182, 184-187, 192.

Great Powers, name given to the most important European – and more recently world powers – whose number is changing in function of their political, economic and military influence. During the 19th century the European Great Powers were: Austria-Hungary, England, France, Prussia (Germany), Russia and Turkey. Italy acceded recently to this status, while Austria disappeared. Among non-European Great Powers are: China, Japan and USA, 53, 55, 61, 63, 73-76, 88, 89, 92, 255, 259.

Great Russians, east branch of Slavs, settled in the Upper Volga region. They formed and organized a state continuously expanding its frontiers towards Asia and Europe under the banner of the Great Russians' supremacy, 12, 14, 33, 196, 201, 215, 219, 220, 240.

Great Soviet Encyclopaedia, see Encyclopaedia, Soviet.

Greece, was conquered by the Turks (14-15th centuries); proclaimed its independence (1821); became a kingdom (1832) and later a republic (1974). During World Wars I and II Greece fought on the side of the Entente and Allies, against the Central Powers and Axis Powers, 45, 47, 103, 156, 158, 166.

Greeks, 41, 47, 59, 79, 80.

Grekul, Filip Alexandrovich (1916), Moldavian historian; member of USSR CP (1940); specialist in Moldavian middle age history, 261.

Grigorenko, Petro (1907), former Soviet army general; major general with the Red army in World War II; head of the cybernetics department at the Frunze Military Academy in Moscow (1959); he began to criticize Khrushchev for creating a new personality cult and took the defense of the national rights of the Crimean Tatars. Arrested in 1964 and placed in the Leningrad Psychiatric Institute after he protested the Soviet invasion of Czechoslovakia (1968). He was demoted, expelled from the CP and again incarcerated in a psychiatric hospital until 1974. He now resides in the USA, 207, 229, 244.

Grigoriopol, town in Moldavian SSR, on the left bank of Dniester, 23 miles ENE of Chişinău, 239.

Grivitsa, name of two redoubts of the Pleven's defensive system during the 1877 war; one of them was conquered by the Romanian troops (Aug. 30–Sept. 11, 1877), 66.

Grodiansk, see Glodeni.

Guinnes, Walter Edward first baron Moyne (1880-1944), British statesman and diplomat; appointed in August 1942 deputy minister of state in Cairo. In Jan. 1944 he was appointed minister resident in the Middle East and was assassinated by terrorists, in Cairo, 160, 161.

Gunther, Franklin Mott (1885-1941), American diplomat; USA plenipotentiary minister to Bucharest (1937-1940), 133, 135-137, 139, 142, 143.

Halder, Franz (1884-1972), German general; chief of the general staff (1938); he opposed Hitler's war project, 140.

Halifax, Edward Frederick Lindley Wood, 1st earl of (1881-1959), British statesman and diplomat; viceroy of India (1925-1931); foreign secretary (1938-1940) and ambassador to USA (1941-1946), 132, 148, 149.

Hâncești, Kotovskoye, village in Bessarabia, Bălți district, today in central Moldavian SSR, 18 miles SW of Chișinău. Hâncești was renamed in 1944 Kotovskoye, after the Bolshevik military leader Kotovski who was born there, 210.

Hapsburg, Habsburg, one of the principal European dynasties which reigned in the Holy Roman Empire (1273-1806), Austria (1282-1918), Hungary (1526-1918), part of Italy, Spain, Netherland, etc., 23, 83, 102.

Hapsburg Empire, see Austrian Empire.

Harriman, William Averell (1891), American statesman and diplomat; ambassador to Moscow (1942-1946); to London (1946); trade minister (1946-1948), 164, 168.

Harrison, Leland (1883), American diplomat; envoy extraordinary and minister plenipotentiary to Romania (1935-1937) and since 1937 to Switzerland, 167.

Hașdeu, Bogdan Petriceicu (1838-1907), pioneer in Romanian language and historical studies introducing the method of critical investigation of Romanian history, 198, 226, 262.

Hauterive, Alexandre-Maurice, Blanc de Lanautte, comte de (1754-1830), French diplomat of the First Empire, 24.

Heath, Donald R. (1894), American diplomat; vice consul in Bucharest (1921-1923); first secretary to Berlin embassy (1938-1941), 136.

Heitmann, Klaus (1930), German professor of Romance Philology at Heidelberg University, 16, 227.

Helsinki, city in Finland founded in 1550; it became capital of the duchy (1812) and later of the republic (1919); it was also the seat of the Conference on Security and Cooperation in Europe, which edited a *Final Act* on respect of human rights and fundamental freedoms (1975), 244.

Hercegovina, region in the middle of present Yugoslavia; invaded by the Turks (1386) and transformed into Turkish province (1463); it passed under Austria-Hungary's occupation (1878); was annexed to the Austria-Hungarian Empire (1908) and finally to Serbia (Oct. 26, 1918), 46.

Herescu, Mihai, Russ. Heraskov, Mihail Mateevich (1733-1807), Russian author who could be considered as the last pseudo-classical Russian writer of the 18th century, 226.

Herriot, Edouard (1872-1957), French historian and statesman; president of the radical party (1919-1957); prime minister (1924-1925; July 1926; June-Dec. 1932), 100.

Herța, a small strip of land and a village at 17 miles SE of Cernăuți, 10, 33, 117, 118, 120, 212, 255.

Herzen, Alexandr, Ivanovich (1812-1870), Russian journalist and philosopher who originated the theory of Russian unique path to socialism or peasant populism, 44.

Himmler, Heinrich (1900-1945), German national-socialist politician, one of the principal exponents of Nazi terror, 154.

Hîrșova, town in Romania, Constanța district, on the right bank of the Danube, 76, 81.

Historians, French, 260; Hungarian, 35; Marxist, 17-19, 42, 65, 68; Moldavian, 14, 19, 45, 225, 226, 264; Romanian, 11, 18, 19, 34, 36, 42, 52, 53, 56, 58, 60, 64, 65, 82, 181, 182, 191, 225, 258, 262; Stalinist, 257; Western, 16, 40, 42, 43, 47, 49, 225.

History of Moldavia (The), a book by A.M. Lazarev, see *General Bibliography,* 16.

History of Romania, The, a book by Miron Constantinescu, Constantin Daicoviciu and Ștefan Pascu, see *General Bibliography,* 18.

History of Romania, a book edited by Romanian Academy, see *General Bibliography,* 257, 258.

History of the Romanian People, a book by Andrei Oțetea, see *General Bibliography,* 18.

Hitler, Adolf (real name Schicklgruber) (1889-1945), chief of the Nazi party (1920); chancellor (1933); dictator by cumulating and merging the offices of chancellor and president (1934); he caused the outbreak of World War II, 12, 112, 113, 117-119, 121-123, 128-130, 134, 139-142, 145, 148, 151-153, 158, 167, 182, 185, 190, 192, 193, 230, 246, 266.

Hitlerism, 246.

Hoffmann, Max (1869-1927), German general of the World War I; chief of staff of the eastern front (Aug. 1916); together with Richard von Kühlmann, then foreign minister, he negotiated at Brest-Litovsk German treaties with Ukraine and Russia, 90.

Hohenzollern, Albrecht, prince von, German major in reserve; he worked with the general staff of the German Military Mission in Bucharest (1942-1944), 192.

Horthy de Nagybánya, Miklós (1868-1957), Hungarian admiral and statesman; regent and dictator of Hungary (1920-1944), 151.

Hotin, Khotin, town in Bessarabia, today in Moldavian SSR, on the right bank of the Dniester, at 175 miles north of Chișinău. Its fortress was built by the Moldavian prince Alexandru cel Bun (1400-1432). Hotin became a Turkish raya in 1723, 33, 128, 199, 210, 211, 214, 219, 221.

Huber, East German economist, 250.

Hull, Cordell (1871-1955), American secretary of state (1933-1944). Influenced by W. Wilson's philosophy he worked for the organization of United Nations and was awarded the Nobel prize for peace (1945), 133, 135, 136, 138, 139, 148-150, 159, 163, 164, 168.

Hungarian, 35, 102, 192, 257.

Hungary, the Hungarian kingdom was founded in the 10th century and became a powerful medieval state extending its control over Transylvania and Croatia. South H. became a pashalik (1541); by the Karlowitz peace treaty Hungarian lands came under

Habsburg rule (1699); Hungary obtained the domestic autonomy (1867); proclaimed its independence as a communist republic (March-Aug. 1919); formed a constitutional monarchy (1920) and proclaimed a popular republic (1946), 92, 101, 102, 113, 114, 121, 122, 128, 133, 134, 138, 139, 141-143, 145, 151, 153, 159, 167, 183, 220.

Huszti, András (end of 17th or beginning of 18th century – 1755), Hungarian historian, 35.

Iacobici Iosif (1884), Rom. general; minister of war (1941); chief of the general staff (1941-1942), 144, 182.

Ianitki, N.F., communist economist, 252.

Iaşi, principal city of Moldavia, located on the Bahlui River; residence of Moldavian princes (since the 15th century); capital of Moldavia Principality (1565-1862); capital of Romania during World War I (1916-1918) when Bucharest was occupied by the German army; scene of a fierce battle during World War II. A peace treaty between Russia and Turkey was signed at Iaşi (Jan. 9, 1792) giving to Russia the territory between Bug and Dniester, 11, 32, 34, 36, 37, 89, 95, 96, 160, 183, 191, 193, 229.

Iedinetz, see Ediniţa.

Ignatiev, Nikolay Pavlovich, count (1832-1908), Russian diplomat and statesman who played an important role in his country's foreign policy during the reign of Alexander II. Ambassador to Constantinople (1864); he negotiated the treaty of San Stefano (1878), 61, 75.

Ilieni, village in Romania, SW Transylvania, near Făgăraş, 191.

Iliescu, Dumitru (Dimitrie) (1865), Rom. general; second in command of the Rom. general staff when Romania entered World War I on the side of the Allied Powers (Aug. 14, 1916); he resigned when the Central Powers occupied Bucharest (Nov., 1917), 88.

Il'in, Vladimir, Soviet political commentator of APN *(Novosti* Press Agency), 43.

Illyria, territory along the Dalmatian coast which was incorporated by Napoleon in his empire, 25, 29.

Ilyasenko, Kiril Fedorovich (1915-1980), member of the Moldavian CP CC (1954); deputy to the Moldavian Supreme Soviet (1955 and 1959 conventions); head of the department of Science and Culture (1955-1962); chairman of the State Scientific-Technical Commission of the Council of Ministers in charge with the culture (1963); Chairman of the Presidium of the Moldavian Supreme Soviet, 203.

Institute for Historical and Social-Political Studies, Rom. *Institutul de Studii Istorice şi Social-Politice de pe lîngă CC al PCR,* Rom. institute founded on March 26, 1951, with the aim of studying the history of Rom. Workers' Movement, the history of RCP and that of workers' mass organizations, 73, 82.

Institute for International Social History, Amsterdam, International Instituut voor Sociale Geschiedenis, located in Amsterdam; owns a vast library with 500,000 volumes and archives especially on the labour movement, 260.

Institute of Marxism-Leninism, Moscow, founded in 1920 in Moscow, under the name *Marx-Engels-Institut;* changed its name into *Marx-Engels-Lenin-Stalin-Institut,* to become since 1953 the *Institute of Marxism-Leninism.* It is subordinated to the CP CC, 260.

International Diplomatic Academy, Paris, founded in 1926 as a non-governmental organization, 100.

International Revolution, ideology promoting world revolution. This was the aim of the Comintern, 223.

International, Third, or Comintern (1919-1943), international revolutionary organization founded by Lenin with the stated purpose to unite the communist parties, but serving practically the Kremlin's aim of controling the other communist movements, 186, 262.

Inul, settlement of Moldavians deported in Soviet Far East, Russian SFSR, 214.

Ioffe, Adolf Abramovich (1883-1927), Soviet diplomat; took part at the peace negotiations in Brest-Litovsk (1917-1918); Russian SFSR plenipotentiary to Germany (1918); to China (1922-1923); to Great Britain (1924) and to Austria (1924-1925), 89.

Ion, Petre, member of RCP, 161.

Ionescu, Nicolae (1820), Rom. statesman; foreign minister (July 24, 1876 – Apr. 3, 1877). He supported the idea of Romanian neutrality in the eventuality of a Russo-Turkish war and tried to obtain from the European powers a guarantee of this neutrality, 54.

Iorga, Nicolae (1871-1940), Rom. historian, publicist and statesman; prime minister (1931-1932); author of a vast work, more than 16,000 titles. He played an important role in Romania's cultural life, 15, 20, 73, 114, 185, 261.

Iran or Persia, 158.

Irkutsk, capital city of the Irkutsk *oblast,* in the Russian SFSR, at the mouth of Irkut River, 214.

Iron Guard, Rom. political organization founded in 1927 by Corneliu Zelea Codreanu, of Christian and Fascist inspiration, which played an important role in Romania between 1930-1941, 185.

Isaccea, town in Romania, Dobrogea region, Tulcea district, on the right bank of the Danube, 76, 81.

Ismail, Izmail, town in Bessarabia, now in the Ukrainian SSR, Odessa *oblast,* on the north bank of the main Danube branch, 35, 128, 199, 209, 211.

Ismay, Hastings Lionel, 1st baron (1887-1963), British general, secretary of the Committee of Imperial Defense (1938-1940); chief of staff to Churchill (May 1940) in his capacity as minister of defense, 132.

Israel, republic in Middle East, founded on May 14, 1948 on the basis of an UN decision (Nov. 29, 1947), 33.

Istanbul, capital of the Byzantine Empire (324-1453) under the name of Constantinople; capital of the Ottoman Empire (1453-1923), 23-25, 28, 32, 33, 36, 41, 47, 53, 61, 88, 118, 156.

Istru, Bogdan, by his real name *Ion Bădărău* (1914). He printed a collection of poems in Romania, in Chișinău, when Bessarabia still belonged to Romania (1937), and continued his literary activity in Moldavian SSR where he became secretary (1946-1947) and later vice president (1958-1965) of the Moldavian Writers' Union, 225.

Italian, 248.

Italinsky, Andrei Yakovlevich (1743-1827), Russian ambassador to Constantinople (1802-1806), 24.

Italy, the unification of Italy was achieved in 1859 and 1861 under the scepter of the Savoy dynasty; the kingdom proclaimed in Turin (March 17, 1861); B. Mussolini became dictator (1922) and entered World War II on the side of Germany; the republic was proclaimed on June 2, 1946, 15, 23, 30, 44, 53, 55, 79, 87, 92, 104, 112, 113, 129, 132, 152, 153, 193.

Ivan IV the Terrible, Ivan Vasilyevich (1530-1584), first tzar of Russia (1547-1584). He extended Russian territory conquering the Tatars khanates of Kazan (1552) and Astrakhan (1556) and began the conquest of Siberia, 224.

Izvestia, USSR Supreme Presidium newspaper, founded in Petrograd (today Leningrad) in March 1917, and printed since March 1918 in Moscow, 169, 253.

Japan, signed the Anticomintern pact with Germany (Nov. 1936), and the Tripartite Pact (Sept. 1940) which recognized Japanese supremacy in Asia. Japan attacked US navy at Pearl Harbor (Dec. 7, 1941) and signed the surrender (Sept. 2, 1945) and the peace treaty with US (Sept. 1951), which was not undersigned by USSR, 13, 92, 139.

Japan's Socialist Party, see Party.

Japanese, 259.

Jelavich, Barbara (1923), American historian; professor of East European history at Indiana University, Bloominton (1967), 40, 42.

Jena, city on Saale River, where Napoleon defeated the Prussian army (oct. 14, 1806); today in East Germany, 24.

Jewish, 257.

Jews, people of Mosaic religion, 110, 127, 185, 198, 207, 208, 216, 217, 221, 229.

Jiu River, in southwestern Romania, rising in Carpathian Mountains and flowing into the Danube, 59.

Jodl, Alfred (1890-1946), German general, chief of the armed forces operations staff (Aug. 23, 1939 – 1945); Hitler's adviser on strategic and operational problems; directed all Germany's campaigns, except the invasion of Russia, and signed the act of capitulation (May 7, 1945), 130.

Joint Chiefs of Staff, US military body created in 1941 to study and advise on all aspects of World War II, 157, 163.

Journal de Genève, French language newspaper of liberal and protestant inspiration, published since 1826 in Geneva, 26.

Kainardzha, see Kuchuk Kainarji.

Kalavach, see Călăraşi.

Kamenec-Podolsky, town in today USSR, on the left bank of Smotric, 35.

Kamenka, village in Moldavian SSR, on the left bank of Dniester, south of Soroca, 206.

Kamiensc, town in NW Poland, 25.

Karavansky, Svyatoslav (1920), Ukrainian poet and journalist, sentenced in 1945 to 25 years imprisonment on charges of participation in the Ukrainian nationalist movement; amnistied in 1960 he was re-arrested in 1965 and made to serve without trial the remaining nine years of his original sentence because of his protest against the Russification of the Ukrainian schools. In 1970 he was put on trial in prison, and given an additional sentence for the petitions he wrote from the labor camp, criticizing the violation of civil rights. While in a Mordovian labor camp he joined a Helsinki group formed by the political prisoners of many nationalities (1979). In Nov. 1979 he emigrated to USA, 205.

Karhin, G., Soviet contemporary economist, 252.

Karlowitz, Carlowitz, today *Sremski Karlovaci,* town in Serbia, autonomous region Vojvodina, site of the congress which settled the war between the Holy Leagues (Russia, Austria, Venice and Poland) and the Ottoman empire (1683-1699). The Treaty of Carlowitz (Jan. 26, 1699) provided that: Transylvania, central Hungary and Slavonia be transfered from Turkish control to Austria; Venice received the Peloponnesus and most of Dalmatia; Poland lost its conquests in Moldavia but regained Podolia and part of the Ukraine; Turkey and Russia concluded a two-year armistice, 17, 36.

Karnikov, F.I., one of the Moldavian CP secretaries (1951), 202.

Karpinyani, see Cărpineni.

Kasso, Lev Aristidovich (1856-1914), Russian historian of Romanian stock, born in Bessarabia; professor at Moscow University; minister of education (1910-1914); author of the book *Rossia na Dunae i obrazovanie Bessarabskoi oblasti/* Russia at the Danube and creation of the Bessarabia *oblast/,* Moscow: 1913, 185.

Kazakhs, Kazaks, people inhabiting mainly the Kazakh SSR, 210, 211, 213, 219, 222, 229.

Kazakhstan, Kazakh Soviet Socialist Republic, is located in Central Asia, inhabited by the Muslim people of the Kazakhs, speaking a Turkic language, 12, 206, 209, 211, 213, 219.

Kazan, capital of the Tartar Autonomous S S R since 1920, 226.

Keitel, Wilhelm (1882-1946), German field-marshal; chief of staff of the armed forces bureau (1935); head of the armed force high command during World War II, and chief of Hitler's personal military staff, 130.

Kelet, Hungarian daily, issued in Budapest (1874-1880), 58, 62.

Khabarovsk, city located in the Russian SFSR, on the right bank of the Amur River, 214.

Kharkov, city in the Ukrainian SSR, founded in 1656, capital of the Ukrainian SSR (1917-1934), 262.

Kherson, city in the Ukrainian SSR, on the right bank of Dnieper River, 212.

Khotin, Chotin, see Hotin.

Khristov, Khristo (1915), Bulgarian historian, specialist in modern and contemporary Bulgarian history, 46.

Khrushchev, Nikita Sergeyevich (1894-1971), first secretary of USSR CP CC (1953-1964); prime minister (1958-1964). He opened up more than 70,000,000 acres of virgin land in Siberia, where he sent thousands of young labourers from European Russia to work the soil, 197, 214, 220, 250, 252, 253.

Kiev, capital of the Ukrainian SSR, on Dnieper River, is the third city of the USSR, 96, 219.

Killinger, Manfred von (1886-1944), plenipotentiary minister to Bratislava (1940); ambassador to Bucharest (1941-1944). He commited suicide when the Soviet troops entered Bucharest, 144, 185.

Kirgizia, Soviet Socialist Republic of central Asia, inhabited by the Turkic people of Kirgiz (44% of the republic's population). It was an autonomous SSR (1926) and became a SSR (1936), 12, 213.

Kirgiz, Turkic people former nomads of central Asia, 213.

Kirovograd, city in Ukrainian SSR, on Ingul River, 212, 213.

Kiselev, (Kiselyov), Pavel Dmitriyevich, count (1788-1872), Russian general and statesman; administrator of Romanian Principalities (Moldavia and Wallachia), during a Russian occupation (1829-1834), 42.
Kishinev, see Chişinău.
Klees, A., philologist, 16.
Klessheim, Austrian resort near Salzburg, 152.
Klimanov, V.I., chief of section of the Moldavian CP CC, in charge with transportation (1952); minister of motor transport and highways (1955-1961), 203.
Kniatiasa Mountains in Ruthenia, 120.
Knutz, Willi, East German economist, 250.
Kofos, Evangelos, professor at Georgetown University, USA (1964); author of the study *Nationalism and Communism in Macedonia* (Tessaloniki: Institute for Balkan Studies, 1964), 253 p., 40, 45.
Kogălniceanu, Mihail (1817-1891), Rom. historian and statesman, he played an important role in the Romanian Principalities' Union (1859); minister and later prime minister (1863-1865); foreign affairs minister (1876, 1877-1878), he was one of the fathers of Romania's independence, 15, 48, 58, 61, 62, 64, 75, 78, 80, 81.
Kolarz, Walter, British journalist; editor with BBC, 215, 226.
Kollontay, Aleksandra Mikhailovna, (1872-1952), Soviet diplomat; plenipotentiary minister to Oslo (1927-1930); ambassador to Stockholm (1930-1945), 165, 184.
Konstantinov, Anton Sidorovich, first secretary of the Moldavian Komsomol CC (1955-1957); secretary of Moldavian TU Council (1960); member of the Moldavian CP CC (1956-1960 and 1963-1966); deputy to the Moldavian Supreme Soviet (1955-1959 and 1967 conventions); Presidium member of Moldavian Supreme Soviet (1963); head of propaganda department (1967), 203.
Korne, Mihai (1930), Rom. exile politician living in France, 19.
Korolkov, Mitrofan Vlasovich, chief of section of the Moldavian CP CC in charge with controlling Moldavian administrative bodies (1949); candidate member of the Moldavian CP CC (1956), 203.
Korotnyan, Vasilij Spiridonovich, chief of section of the Moldavian CP CC; vice minister of Moldavian SSR in charge with the finance (1949-1952), 20.
Korpensk, see Cărpineni.
Kosovo, region in Siberia inhabited mainly by Albanians, 47.
Kotienpansk, see Coşeni.
Kotovski, Grigore Ivanovich (1881-1925), one of the organizers of Moldavian Autonomous Republic; member of the USSR CP (1920); he took part in the civil war and in the liberation of south Ukraine, 225.
Koval, Fedor Stefanovich, Moldavian minister of agriculture, (1949-1958), 201.
Koval (Kovalj), Nikolay Grigorevich, first secretary of Moldavian CP CC (1948-1950); chairman of State Planning Commission (1960); deputy to the USSR Supreme Soviet (1946 and 1950 conventions), 202.
Kozacov, Ivan Dimitrievich, one of the Moldavian CP secretaries (1954), 203.
Krasnodar, city in Russian SFSR, port on the right bank of the lower Kuban River, 213.

Kremlin, The Moscow, medieval fortress built on the central Moscow's hill, center of Russia's governments (1620-1712), and also of the Soviet government, 13, 111, 115, 117, 121, 154, 165, 197, 203, 205, 206, 210, 216, 248.

Kriworulov, local Moldavian CP secretary, 202.

Kruka, Prussian guns, 56.

Kuchuk Kainarji, (Kücük Kaynarka), village in NE Bulgaria where was signed the peace treaty between Russia and the Ottoman empire (July 21, 1774), concluding the Russo-Turkish war (1768-1774). By this treaty Russia extended its frontiers to the southern Bug River; annexed the port of Azov, the fortress of Kerch and Yenikale and part of the Kuban province. The treaty also recognized Russia's right to protect the Christians living in the Ottoman empire, and proclaimed the right of free commercial navigation on Black Sea and through the Straits, 24, 40, 41, 43.

Kuril Islands, chain of islands in Russian SFSR, Sakhalin *oblast,* ceded by Japan to USSR in 1954, 13.

Kursk, city in Russian SFSR, on the Seym River, where German tanks were defeated during World War II (July-August 1943), 150.

Küstendge, see Constanța.

Kutuzov, village in Moldavian SSR, 239.

Lache, Ștefan, Rom. historian; has contributions on Romania's contemporary foreign policy, 183-188, 190, 192.

Lăpușna, Lapushna, village in Bessarabia, Lăpușna district, today in W Moldavian SSR, 22 miles of Chișinău, 210.

La Rochefoucauld, Alexandre, comte de (1767-1841), French statesman; minister to Saxe (1802); ambassador to Vienna (1805) and to the Hague (1808), 24.

Latin Alphabet, 223, 264.

Latin culture, 227.

Latin language, 222.

Latour-Maubourg, Just-Pons Florimond de Fay, marquis de Latour-Maubourg (1781-1837), French diplomat; second secretary and later chargé d'affaires to Constantinople (1806-1812), where he assisted ambassador Sebastiani, 32.

Latvia, Sovietic Socialist Republic, located on the eastern shores of the Baltic Sea, which was an independent republic (1920-1940) and was proclaimed a SSR on Aug. 5, 1940, 12, 118, 202, 206.

Latvians, 229.

Lauriston, Jacques-Alexandre-Bernard Law, marquis de (1768-1828), French marshal (1823), diplomat and minister, 31.

Lavrentiev, Anatolii Iosifovich, Soviet plenipotentiary minister to Sofia (1939-1940) and to Bucharest (June 13, 1940 – 1941); ambassador to Bucharest (1952-1953), 110.

Lazarev, Artem Markovich (1914), member of the Moldavian CP CC; minister of education (1949-1952); third secretary of the CC (1952-1954); minister of culture (1954); deputy to the Moldavian Supreme Soviet (1955, 1959 conventions), 9, 11, 14-20, 22, 33, 84, 203, 238.

League of Nations, international organization established at the end of the World War I with the purpose of preventing aggression and preserving the *status quo* created by World War I peace treaties, 100, 104.

Leahy, William Daniel (1875-1959), USA fleet admiral (Dec. 1944); personal chief of staff to president Roosevelt (1933-1945), 162.
Lebanon, Arab republic on the eastern shore of Mediteranean Sea, which was under Ottoman rule (1517-1918), French mandate (1920), republic under French control (1926) and independent republic (1943), 33.
Lebedev, Nikolai Ivanovich (1925), Soviet historian, specialist in contemporary history, 144.
Lebey, André, French member of the Parliament during World War I, 84.
Leipzig, Battle of the Nations (Oct. 16-19, 1813), decisive defeat of Napoleon by the allied troops (Austrian, Prussian, Russian and Swedish), marking the end of the French empire east of Rhine, in Germany and Poland, 216.
Lenin, Vladimir Ilich Ulyanov (1870-1924), founder of the Russian communist party; leader of the bolshevik revolution (1917); president of Soviet government (1917-1924); author of the official communist ideology known under the name of leninism, 13, 38, 84, 86, 89, 90, 91, 97, 197, 214, 226, 230, 260, 266.
Leningrad, city in USSR; Baltic port at the mouth of the Neva River; founded by Peter the Great and named St Petersburg it was renamed Petrograd (1914), and finally Leningrad (1924), 134.
Leninism, principles of history and revolution formulated by Lenin who has assigned to the communist élite the role to infuse the workers with the consciousness of the need for revolution, 230, 231, 262.
Leygues, Jean-Claude-Georges (1857-1933), French statesman, supporter of Clémenceau's policy during World War I, 85.
Lipcani, Lipkany, town in Bessarabia, Orhei district, today in N Moldavian SSR, on Pruth River, 40 miles E of Cernăuți, on Romanian-Ukrainian border, 239.
Lipovan, population of Russian stock, belonging to the Old Believers religious dissenters, established in Danube delta, 216, 221.
Lithuanian, 229.
Lithuanian Soviet Socialist Republic, Lithuania, state located on the shores of Baltic Sea, united with Poland by the union of Lublin (1569) till the end of the 18th century when it was annexed by the Russian empire; became independent after the Russian Revolution of 1917, was incorporated into the USSR after World War II, and proclaimed a SSR in Aug. 1940, 12, 118, 158, 159, 203.
Little Entente, regional security organization formed between World War I and World War II by Czechoslovakia, Romania and Yugoslavia, with the aim of defending their territorial integrity and political independence, 102.
Litvinov, Maksim Maksimovich (1876-1951), Soviet diplomat and commissar for foreign affairs (1930-1939). He urged the League of Nations to make plans for resisting Germany, 104.
Livadia, town in Crimea, north of Yalta, site of the Romanian-Russian negotiations concerning the crossing by Russian troops of Romanian territory in the event of a Russo-Turkish war (Sept. 29–Oct. 11, 1876), 56, 57.
Liveanu, Vasile (1928), Rom. historian; contribution to Romania's social and political situation during the 20th century, 17.

Lloyd George, David (1863-1945), British statesman; leader of the liberal party; prime minister during World War I (1916-1922). He played an important role at the Paris Peace Conference (1919) and during the negociations for the Versailles treaties, 85, 132.

Loftus, Lord Augustus William Frederick Spencer (1817-1904), English diplomat; ambassador to Vienna (1858), Berlin (1860), Munich (1862), St Petersburg (1871), 75.

Logănești, settlement of Moldavians deported to Soviet Far East, in Russian SFSR, 214.

London, England's official capital since the end of the 11th century, (1914), 26, 30, 78, 103, 134, 145, 147-150, 153, 158, 159, 166.

Longuet, Jean, (1876-1938), French socialist deputy during World War I, belonging to the socialist party's minority opposed to the war; author of a motion in favour of a peace based on Russian revolution, 85.

Lost Opportunity, The, title of a book written by Rom. diplomat Alexandru Cretzianu, telling of his diplomatic mission during World War II, which was to negotiate with the Allies representatives the terms under which Romania would have to leave the Axis Powers, 187.

Lugansk, see Voroshilovgrad.

Lupan, Andrei Pavlovich (1912), Moldavian writer and communist party activist; member of USSR CP (1956); president of the Moldavian Supreme Soviet (1963-1967); president of the leading committee of Moldavian Writers' Union (1946-1962) and secretary of USSR Writers' Union (1954-1971), 225.

Luxembourg, the duchy was ceded to France by the treaty of Campo Formio (1797); in 1814 the city was confined by the Prussians and later by Hessa's soldiers, 216.

Lvov, Lwow, Lemberg, main center of Galicia, controlling east-west routes across the Carpathian Mountains; attributed to Austria (1772); returned to Poland (1919); was seized by USSR (1939); ceded to Poland (1945), 120.

Lvov, Georgy Yevgenyevich, prince (1861-1925), Russian social reformer and statesman; president of the Russian provisional government established during the February revolution (1917), 95.

Macedonia, region of SE Europe in S Balkan Peninsula, politically divided among Bulgaria, Greece and Yugoslavia. Macedonia passed to the Bulgarians (9th century), to the Serbs (14th century), to the Turks (15th century to 1912). The treaty of Bucharest divided Macedonia among Bulgaria, Greece and Serbia (1913); the treaty of Neuilly (1919) and the peace treaty of 1947 perpetrated minor adjustments to the Balkan frontiers and Macedonia's division, 23, 47.

Măcin, town in SE Romania, Dobrogea, on the *Dunărea Veche* arm, 9 km of Brăila, 76, 81.

Maciu, Vasile (1904), Rom. historian; has contributions concerning Romania's modern history, especially the 1821-1918 period, 73.

Mackensen, August von (1849-1945), German field-marshal during World War I; commanded German-Austrian 11th army in western Galicia where he obtained a series of victories leading to the defeat of the Russians at Brest-Litovsk and Pinsk (Aug.-Sept. 1915), the overruning of Serbia (Oct.-Nov. 1915) and the occupation of Romania (1916-1917), 87.

Mackensen, Georg (1883-1947), German diplomat; minister to Budapest (1933-1937); state secretary with the foreign affairs ministry (1937-1938); ambassador to Rome (1938-1943), 113.
McVeagh, Lincoln (1890), American publisher and diplomat; extraordinary envoy and minister plenipotentiary to Greece (1933-1941); ambassador to Greek and Yugoslav governments in exile in Egypt (1943); ambassador to Greece (1944). He served as 1st lieut., later captain and major in the American Expeditionary Forces during World War I, 156, 160, 163, 164, 166.
Macovescu, George (1913), Rom. diplomat; member of Rom. CP since 1936; minister of foreign affairs (1972-1978), 53-56, 63, 102-105.
Madan, L.A., Soviet author of the Moldavian Grammar of 1930, 223.
Maergois, Maergojz, Isaak Moiseevich, Soviet contemporary economist, author of the book: *Voprosy ekonomiceskoj i politiceskoj geografii zarubznych stran,* Moskva: Akad Nauk SSSR, 1971, 252.
Magazin Istoric, Rom. monthly historical magazine, issued in Bucharest (1967) in more than 100,000 copies, 189.
Magheru, Mihai, RCP member, 161.
Magyar Polgar, Hungarian language periodical issued in Cluj (1867-1886 and 1898-1904), 62.
Mahmudia, village in Romania, Dobrogea, on the Danube's Sfântul Gheorghe arm, 76, 81.
Mahmut, Mahmud II (1785-1839), Ottoman sultan (1808-1839), who contributed to the modernization of his empire. During his reign he fought Russia twice (1806-1812 and 1828-1829), and his defeats weakened the position of the Ottoman empire in Balkans, 32, 41.
Maisky, Ivan Mikhailovich (1884), Soviet ambassador to London (1932-1943); USSR deputy people's commissar for foreign affairs (1943-1946), 148-150, 153, 166.
Manchuria, historic region of northeast China, 214.
Mangalia, town in SE Romania, Dobrogea region, on the Black Sea, 27 miles S of Constanta, 48, 49, 81.
Maniu, Iuliu (1873-1953), Rom. statesman; president of the Transylvanian *"Consiliul Dirigent",* Leading Council, which proclaimed Transylvania's union with Romania (Dec. 1, 1918); president of the National-Peasant Party (1926); prime minister (1928-1930 and 1932-1933). DuringWorld War II he supported Romania's drive against USSR for the reconquests of Bessarabia and Northern Bucovina, but opposed the campaign of Romanian troops beyond Romania's ethnical frontiers. He was the main organizer of the August 1944 coup d'état. Condemned by the communist regime to life imprisonment (Nov. 1947) he died in prison, 10, 142-144, 151, 154-175, 160-166, 168-170, 181, 183, 184, 186-189, 190.
Mao Tse-tung, Mao Tse-dun (1893-1976), Chinese statesman, soldier and ideologist; chairman of the Chinese CP (1949-1976) and president of the republic (1949-1959), 20, 259, 260, 263, 264.
Maoist, 263.
Maramureş, province in NW Romania, 82, 91, 113.
Maret, Hugues-Bernard, duc de Bassano (1763-1839), French statesman and diplomat of Napoleon; minister of foreign affairs (April 1811-Nov. 1813), charged to conclude

treaties of alliance with Prussia and Austria before Napoleon's campaign in Russia, 31.

Marmont, Auguste-Frédéric-Louis, Viesse de, duc de Raguse (1774-1852), governor of Dalmatia (1806). He forced the Russians to raise the siege of Ragusa and secured control over the Adriatic. He introduced a modern administration in the Illyrian provinces and was made duc of Raguse (1808), 25.

Marr, Nikolai Yakoblevich (1865-1934), Soviet philologist, orientalist and archaeologist, 223, 224.

Marx, Karl Heinrich (1818-1883), economist, sociologist, philosopher and revolutionist, the founder of the Marxist movement, author of the "Bible of the Communism", *Das Kapital* (3 volumes, 1867, 1885 and 1894), and of the *Manifest der kommunistischen Partei* (1848), the latter in collaboration with Friedrich Engels, 11, 16, 17, 36, 37, 42, 83, 97, 214, 228, 229, 260-262, 266.

Marxism-Leninism, adaptation by Lenin of Marxism to Russian conditions of life, placing more emphasis on the leading role of the communist party, 68, 253.

Masséna, André, duc de Rivoli and prince d'Essling (1758-1817), French general of the Revolutionary and Napoleonic wars; made marshal (1804), duc de Rivoli (1808) and prince d'Essling (1810), 24.

Masterson, Ted, British lieutenant, 156.

Mateevici, Alexandru (1888-1917), Rom. poet of Bessarabian descent, author of an ode devoted to the Romanian language, 222.

Maurer, Ion Gheorghe (1902), Rom. communist statesman; member of the RCP CC (1945-1974); member of the Polit Bureau (1960-1965), of Political Executive Committee (1965-1974) and of Permanent Presidium (1965-1974). Minister of foreign affairs (1957-1958); president of Presidium of the Grand National Assembly (1958-1961) and prime minister (1961-1974), 258, 259.

Mecca, sacred city of the Islam, situated in today's Saudi Arabia, 197.

Medgidia, town in SE Romania, Dobrogea region, on the Danube-Black Sea Canal, 18 miles of Constant, a, 76, 81.

Mediterranian Sea, 23, 29, 33, 47, 231.

Mehmet Ali Pasha (1769-1849), vice-roy of Egypt (1805); founder of the dynasty that ruled Egypt until the middle of the 20th century, 56.

Melkov, Yuri Dmitrievich (1921), member of the Moldavian CP Bureau, and second secretary of the Moldavian CP CC (1967-1973); candidate member of the CPSU CC (1952-1982); deputy Chairman of RSFS committee for people's control, 202.

Melnik, Aleksander Antonovich, one of the Moldavian CP secretaries (1952); vice-chairman of the Moldavian Council of Ministers (1953), 201.

Melnikov, Nikolai Afanasevich, (1918-1973), head of USSR CP CC Section (1949-1961); candidate member CC USSR CP (1961-1966); second secretary CC Moldavian CP (1961-1965); deputy USSR Supreme Soviet (1963 convention); deputy Moldavian Supreme Soviet (1963), chief of local industry, cultural-personal goods and domestic service department of USSR State Planning Committee (1965-1973), 203.

Manemencioglu, Numan (1892), Turkish diplomat and politician; secretary of embassy in Vienna, Bern, Paris, Bucharest and Athens; chargé d'affaires to Budapest; secretary general of the ministry of foreign affairs; minister of foreign affairs (1942-1944); ambassador to France (1944), 153, 156.

Merlin, F., French deputy during World War I, 85.

Metternich, Klemens Fürst von (1773-1859), Austrian statesman and diplomat; minister of foreign affairs (1809). He applied the policy of balance of powers; led the final Allied coalition against Napoleon and played an important role at the Vienna Congress (1814-1815) which established a new European order, 30, 31.

Michael de Hohenzollern, Rom. *Mihai I* (1921), king of Romania under regency (1927-1930), and after abdication of his father, Carol II (1940-1947). He led the coup d'état of Aug. 23, 1944 and opposed the establishment of a communist dictatorship in Romania until he was forced to abdicate (Dec. 30, 1947), 156, 168, 181, 189, 190, 192, 193.

Michelson (Mikhelson), Ivan Ivanovich (1740-1807), Russian general (1797); during the early stages of the Russo-Turkish war of 1806-1812 he commanded the army of Dniester and occupied without resistance Moldavia and Wallachia (1806), 23, 24.

Middle East, 9, 33, 156, 158, 160.

Midhat, Pasha (1822-1883), twice grand vizir of the Ottoman empire. In 1876 led the coalition which deposed sultan Abdül-aziz, 56.

Mihalache, Ion (1882-1964), Rom. statesman; founder of the Peasant Party (1918) which merged with the Transylvanian National Party, forming the National-Peasant Party (1926). President of the N.-P. Party (1933-1937); minister of agriculture (1919-1920 and 1928-1931) and minister of the interior (1930-1931). He opposed communist dictatorship, was arrested and died in prison, 142, 182.

Milev, local secretary of the Moldavian CP, 202.

Milyukov, Pavel Nikolaevich (1859-1943), Russian statesman and historian; foreign minister of the provisional government (1917), 95.

Minard, publishing house in Paris, 231, 266.

Mircea the Old, Mircea cel Bătrân, prince of Wallachia (1386-1418). He opposed the Ottoman thrust into the Balkan region; obtained a big victory against Bayazid I at Rovine (1394); extended his rule over Dobrogea (1388-1389) and fortified Danubian fortresses, but eventually agreed to pay tribute to the Turks in exchange of Ottoman noninterference in Wallachian domestic affairs, 50.

Moldavia, Rom. principality founded in the 14th century on the upper Siret, by Bogdan I (1359-1365). During the reign of Alexandru cel Bun it extended its frontiers until the Dniester, the Danube and Black Sea. Moldavia opposed the expansion of Ottoman empire but finally was compelled to pay a tribute to the sultan against the recognition of its autonomy. During the 18th century Russia increased its ascendency over Moldavia which passed under Moscow protection by the treaty of Kuchuk Kainarji (1774). The Ottoman empire surrendered a part of Moldavian territory, namely Bucovina, to Austria (1775) and Bessarabia, to Russia (1812). In 1859 Moldavia united with Wallachia under prince Alexandru Ioan Cuza, to form the new state of Romania, which acquired its independence in 1878, 10, 14-16, 18, 19, 22-32, 34-37, 40-44, 47, 48, 57, 65, 74, 75, 80, 85, 86, 88-90, 111, 116-118, 131, 136, 137, 148, 163, 164, 166, 183, 190, 197, 204, 209, 214, 221, 225, 255, 261, 263.

Moldavian Autonomous Democratic Republic, was proclaimed on Dec. 2, 1917 by *Sfatul Ţării* (Bessarabia's Parliament) within the framework of the Russian Democratic Federative Republic, 91, 96-98.

Moldavian Autonomous Socialist Soviet Republic, was established in 1924 on the left bank of Dniester, with Tiraspol as its capital. It has an area of 3,200 square km, and a population estimated in 1938 at 600,000. Following Soviet annexation of Bessarabia (1940), Moldavian ASR – with the exception of some predominantly Ukrainian districts – joined central Bessarabia to form the Moldavian SSR (Aug. 2, 1940), 128, 199-201, 204, 212, 222, 224, 225, 239.

Moldavian Grammar, printed in 1930, in Tiraspol, by L.A. Madan, 223.

Moldavian Soviet Socialist Republic, consisted of the central part of Bessarabia and Moldavian Autonomous SSR which were joined after Soviet annexation of Bessarabia (Aug. 2, 1940). Capital: Chişinău, 10, 12, 16, 19, 40, 86, 91, 96, 97, 128, 197-202, 204-221, 224, 225, 227-229, 231, 238-245, 255-257, 261, 263-265.

Moldavian-Wallachian Principalities, see Romanian Principalities.

Moldavians, 11-17, 41, 86, 110, 198-200, 202, 204-206, 208-214, 219-230, 238-242, 256, 257, 260-266.

Moldova Socialistă, Moldavian periodical, first issued on May 1924 in Odessa, under the name of *The Red Ploughman. M.S.* is an organ of the Moldavian CP CC and is printed now in Chişinău, 210, 241, 264.

Moldo-Wallachian Principalities, see Romanian Principalities.

Molotov (Skryabin), Viacheslav Mikhailovich (1890), Soviet statesman and diplomat; minister of foreign affairs (1939-1949; 1953-1956), 18, 108-111, 113, 115, 117, 119-122, 129, 130, 149, 150, 161, 162, 164, 165, 168.

Monde (Le), French daily founded in 1944, succeeding *Le Temps* 13.

Mongols, Asian people, creators of a vast empire which in the 13th century, under Genghis Khan's leadership, extended from Pacific to the Dnieper River, 196.

Montenegro, was incorporated into the Serbian empire (12th century); became independent (1389) and increased its teritory under the decision of Berlin Congress (1878). Today it is one of the six Yugoslavian republics, 56.

Montreux, health resort in Switzerland, on the shore of Geneva lake, where the Montreux Convention of the Straits was signed (1936), 104.

Mordovet, Josif Lavrentevich, Moldavian minister of internal affairs (1949-1953); member of the MCP CC (1954); deputy to USSR Supreme Soviet (1954); chairman of the state security commitee (1954), 201.

Morouzi, Alexandru, prince of Wallachia (1793-1796; 1799-1801) and of Moldavia (1792, 1802-1806, 1806-1807), 24.

Morouzi, Dimitrie, Turkish plenipotentiary to Bucharest peace Conference (1812). See note on Galib effendi, 32.

Moroz, Valentin Yakovych (1936), Ukrainian historian; he protested the destruction of the Ukrainian cultural values. Arrested in Aug. 1966; incarcerated in Lutsk camp prison for six months. Rearrested in June 1970 and sentenced to 6 years' prison, 3 years' camp and 5 years' exile, 226.

Moscow, capital of USSR on Moskva River, 9, 13, 26, 30, 31, 33, 53, 67, 97, 103-105, 109, 111, 118-120, 122, 130, 134-137, 145-151, 153, 159-166, 168, 169, 187, 188,

196-204, 217, 221, 222, 225-227, 229, 240, 247-249, 251-253, 255, 259, 260, 262-265.

Moscow Battle, see Borodino.

Moscow Conference (Nov. 5-6, 1943), of USA, USSR and Great Britain foreign affairs ministers, which adopted a Declaration on general security, 156, 160.

Moselm, 228.

Moose, W.E., British contemporary historian; author of the studies: "Britain, Russia and the Question of Serpents Island and Bolgrad. Two incidents in the Execution of the Treaty of Paris, 1856", in: *The Slavonic and East European Review,* XXIX, 72, 1950, pp. 86-131, and of "England, Russia and the Rumanian Revolution of 1866", *Ibid.,* XXXIX, 92, pp. 73-94, 40.

Moyne, First baron, see Guinness, Walter Edward.

Munich, München, city in West Germany, capital of Bavaria, 20, 39, 50, 68, 81, 92, 105, 123, 171, 193, 245, 254.

Münnich, Burchardt Cristopher (1683-1767), Russian general (1721); field-marshal and prime minister. Under his command the Russian army occupied without resistance Crimea (1736) and Moldavia (1739) where Constantin Cantemir – son of the Moldavian prince Antioch — was received at Iaşi with princely honours. For a short time Moldavia proclaimed its independence under Russian protection, 37.

Murgescu, Costin (1919), Rom. economist; has contributions concerning the international economic relations and the history of Romanian economy, 250.

Muşat, Mircea (1930), Rom. historian, specialist in Romanian modern and contemporary history, 73.

Muscovite Empire, see Russian empire.

Mussolini; Benito (1883-1945), Italian statesman; founder of fascist regime (1922); he ruled Italy for more than 20 years, and joined Hitler during World War II, 113, 119, 152, 155, 184, 193.

Muzeul de Istorie al Partidului Comunist, al Mişcării Revoluţionare şi Democratice din România, Museum of History of Romanian Communist Party and of Romanian Revolutionary and Democratic Mouvement, was founded in Bucharest between 1948-1951, 100, 261.

Mystère Roumain et la Défection Russe, book by Charles Steinon, published in 1918. It furnished details on Russia's opposition to the unity of Romanian people, 89.

Nădejde, Ion (1854-1928), Rom. publicist, sociologist and statesman who joined the socialist movement, 83.

Nămoloasa, village on Siret, Galaţi district, 88, 190.

Nanu, Frederic C., Rom. diplomat; plenipotentiary minister to Stockholm (1944), 165, 166, 184, 187.

Napoleon I, Bonaparte (1769-1821), emperor of France (1804-1814 and 1815). Military campaigns: Italy (1796-1797); Egypt (1798-1799); Prussia (1806); Austria (1809); Russia (1812). Famous battles: Arcole (1796); Marengo (1800); Austerlitz (1805); Jena (1806); Wagram (1809); Leipzig (1813); Waterloo (1815), 10, 12, 23-33, 36, 41, 216.

Napoleon III, Bonaparte, Charles-Louis (1808-1873), emperor of France (1852-1870). Wars and military interventions against: Russia (Crimean war, 1853-1856); China

(1857-1860); Austria (1859); Indochina (1859-1862); Mexico (1862-1867); Prussia (1870-1871), 44.

Nartov, Naum Arianovich (1894), Soviet historian; member of USSR CP since 1918. One of the first Moldavians from USSR who studied Moldavian historical problems, 226.

National Bank of Romania, see Romanian National Bank.

National-Democratic Block, anti-Hitlerite political coalition constituted in June 1944 by the communist, social-democratic, national-peasant and national-liberal parties, with the aim of overthrowing Antonescu's regime. The Block was dissolved in Oct. 1944, 193.

National United Front of All Patriots, Rom. *Frontul Patriotic Antihitlerist,* was founded in Oct. 1944 on the basis of a program worked out Sept. 24, 1944, with participation of RCP, Ploughmen's Front, Patriots' Union, Madosz (Union of the Hungarian Workers), Socialist Peasant party and some local organizations of the Social-Democratic Party. The historical parties — the National-Peasant and National-Liberal parties – did not join this Front, preferring to oppose Antonescu's regime from independent positions, 161.

National Unity Museum of Iaşi, Rom. *Muzeul Unirii-Iaşi,* was founded in 1955 and located in the old palace of prince Alexandru Ioan Cuza, 261.

Nazi Party, German contracted name of the *Nationalsozialistische Deutsche Arbeiterpartei,* party founded in 1919, which seized control of Germany in 1933 under Hitler's leadership, 17, 182, 193, 208.

Neculce, Ion (1672-1745), Rom. chronicler, author of a Moldavian chronicle covering the 1661-1743 period, 225.

Neculce, Nicoară, pseudonym of a Rom. historian living in France, 19.

Negruzzi, Costache (1808-1868), Rom writer. Among the first to discover the importance of folklore inspiration in the cultured literature, 225.

Nelidov, Aleksandr Ivanovich (1835-1910), prominent Russian diplomat. He was appointed first counsellor to Constantinople (1877) where he devotedly backed N.P. Ignatev. On the eve of the Russo-Turkish war (1877-1878) he was on a secret mission to Bucharest where he obtained Romanian approval for the transit of the Russian army heading for Turkey. During the war he served as chief of the diplomatic chancellor's office of Grand Duke Nikolai Nikolaevich, commander-in-chief of the Russian army, 75.

Nesselrode, Karl Robert Vassilievich, count (1780-1862), Russian diplomat; foreign affairs minister (1822-1856); he strove to promote Russian preponderance in the Balkan Peninsula and cut down the French influence over the Ottoman empire, 42.

Netherland, (The), 149, 191.

New York, city and port in USA on the Atlantic Ocean at the mouth of Hudson River, 170.

Nicholai, or Nikolai Nikolaevich (1831-1891). The third son of emperor Nicolas Ist; adjutant-general in the Russian armed forces since 1856; general field-marshal since 1878. During the Russo-Turkish war of 1877-1878 he was the commander-in-chief of the Russian army on the Danube River. The Grand Duke was right from the beginning in favor of a military cooperation with the Romanian army, but tzar Alexander II and foreign affairs minister Gorchakov conditioned such cooperation on the acceptance by the Romanians of a Russian supreme commander. The agreement on Romanian-Russian military cooperation was achieved in Aug. 28, 1877, at a meeting of king Carol I, the tzar and the Grand Duke, 53, 58-60, 62.

Nicolae, Alexandru, pseudonym of a Rom. contemporary writer living in W. Germany; author of the study "Der Angriff auf die Menschliche Substanz Rumänien" in *Zeitschrift fur Geopolitic,* Band XII, 1951, 207, 208, 211, 212.

Niemen, Neman River, river in USSR which springs in Belorussia, 25.

Nikolaev, Nikolayev, city in USSR, Ukrainian SSR, 213.

Nikon, in secular life named *Nikita Minov* (1605-1681), patriarch of Moscow and All Russia. He introduced some changes into the church ritual which provoked the schism with the *Raskolniki* (old Believers), 221.

Nikopol, town in northern Bulgaria, on the Danube River, opposite the Romanian town of Turnu Măgurele, 59.

Nimigeanu, Dumitru (1906), Rom. peasant from Tereblecea village, in northern Bucovina, who in 1941 was deported to Kazakhstan. He described his six years of Siberian captivity in the book *Hell moved its borders* (London: Blanford Press, 1960), 207.

Nisporeni, Nisporiensk, village in W Moldavian SSR, 30 miles of Chişinău, 210.

Nistor, Ion (1876-1962), Rom. historian and statesman, specialist in Bucovina's political, cultural and religious history and also in Moldavia's relations with the neighboring-nations, 15, 20, 96.

NKVD, Russ. *Narodny Komissariat Vnutrennikh Del,* People's Commisariat of Internal Affairs, Soviet political agency in charge of domestic security (1934-1946). It was dissolved in 1946 and replaced by the MVD, Soviet Police Organization, 200.

Notovsk, see Hânceşti.

Novaia i Noveishaya Istoriia, Modern and Contemporary History, an official publication of the Institute of History of the Academy of Sciences of the Soviet Union, published in Moscow since 1957, and devoted to the study of the socio-economic, political and intellectual history of European and American countries, in modern and contemporary times, 55.

Novikov, Nikolai Vassilievich, (1903), Soviet ambassador to Cairo (1943-1944); to US and simultaneously to Cuba (1946-1947), 160, 163, 164, 169.

Ocniţa, Oknitsa, town in N Moldavian SSR, 16 miles WSW of Mogilyov-Podolsky, 210.

October Revolution (Oct. 24 / Nov. 6, 1917), uprising of the Bolshevik party led by Lenin to seize the political power in Russia, 94-97, 240.

Oder River, river which springs in Czechoslovakia and crosses Central Europe, 31.

Oder-Neisse Line, border line established between Poland and Germany by the Allied Powers, at the end of World War II. Frontier recognized by the German Democratic Republic through a treaty signed with Poland at Zgorzelec (July 6, 1950), and by the West Germany through treaties with the USSR (Dec. 7, 1970) and Poland (Aug. 12, 1970), 259.

Odessa, city in USSR, Ukrainian SSR. During World War II fell to German and Romanian troops, following a two-month siege (Oct. 1941), and was placed under Romanian administration until 1943, 96, 115, 138, 140, 141, 212, 213.

Odorhei, town in central Romania, Transylvania, 100 miles of Bucharest, 191.

O.K.H., Ober Kommando des Heeres, see German Army High Command.

O.K.W., Ober Kommando der Wehrmacht, see German Army High Command.

Olăneşti, village in Bessarabia, Cetatea-Albă district, on the right bank of Dniester, today in Moldavian SSR, 239.

Old Believers, Russ. *Starovery,* Russian religious dissenters who refused to accept the liturgical reforms imposed by Patriarch Nikon (1652-1658), 221.

Olteanu, Constantin (1928), Rom. colonel-general (1980) and minister of the national defense since 1982, 191.

Olteanu, Marcel, Rom. colonel-general retired in 1979, 191.

Oltenia, Lesser Wallachia, historical region, the W part of Wallachia (Romania), 36, 64, 78, 88, 162, 250, 252.

Omsk, city in USSR, Russian SFSR, 1,400 miles E of Moscow, 213, 214.

Oprescu, Gheorghe, false identity taken by Rom. poet Octavian Goga in 1918, when he crossed Russia en route from Romania to France, 97.

Optants' Question (March 15, 1923–June 4, 1930), international difference between Romania and Hungary, resulting from Romanian landlords' expropriation, also applied to the Hungarian landlords from Transylvania who had chosen to emigrate to Hungary, 101.

Orăşeanu, Alexandru, Rom. general, 144.

Orenburg, city in USSR, Russian SFSR, on the right bank of Ural River, which in 1938 was renamed Chkalov, after the Russian flyer Valeri Chkalov, 214.

Orhei, Orghyev, city in central Moldavian SSR, 25 miles of Chişinău, 37, 210, 239.

Orient, 23, 26, 28, 33.

Orkheievka, settlement of Moldavians deported to Soviet Far East, 214.

Orthodoxes, see Christians.

Osman Nuri paşa (1832-1900), Ottoman paşa and muşir (field-marshal); commander of Turkish army defending Pleven against Russo-Romanian attacks (1877), 59.

Oţetea, Andrei (1894-1977), Rom. historian; contributions on Guicciardini (1927), Tudor Vladimirescu (1945) and Marx's notes on the Romanians (1964), 226, 229, 260.

Otto, Louis-Guillaume, comte de Mosloy (1754-1817), French diplomat of German stock; plenipotentiary minister to Great Britain (1800-1802); ambassador to Austria (1810--1813), 31.

Ottoman Empire, see Turkey.

Ottomans, see Turks.

Oubril, Petr Jakovlevich, baron d', Russian diplomat and statesman; chargé d'affaires to France (1803-1804); Russian negotiator of the peace treaty between Russia and France, signed on July 8/20, 1806, and known as "the Oubril Treaty". Although the treaty was not ratified by the Russian government it retained its importance because of the insight it gave concerning the purposes of Russian diplomacy during the Napoleonic era. Oubril was banished by the tzar to his estates, because he had exceeded the tzar's instructions during the peace treaty negotiations between Russia and France, 23.

Pacific Ocean, 214.

Pacific War, the military battles which occurred between US and Japan during World War II (1941-1945), 158.

Palmuta, Act of (1775), surrending Bucovina to Austria, 36.

Papen, von Franz (1879-1969), German diplomat and statesman; chancellor (June-Dec. 1932); ambassador to Austria (1934-1938) and Turkey (1939-1944), 153.
Papuc, Ion, Rom. contemporary writer, 50.
Paraclia, village in Moldavian SSR, 239.
Paris, 28, 89, 97, 100, 170, 216, 231, 266.
Paris Conference (May 22-August 19, 1858), reuniting the signer-states of Paris Treaty (March 30, 1856), has approved of a Convention on future political, social and administrative status of the Romanian Principalities, 74.
Paris Congress (Feb. 25-March 30, 1856), put an end to the Crimean war and discussed the stipulations of the Paris treaty (March 30, 1856), 49, 258.
Paris Peace Conference (Jan. 18, 1919-Jan. 21, 1920), convoked by the 27 victorious states in World War I, for the signing of peace treaties with the defeated states: Germany (Versailles, 1919), Austria (Saint Germain en Laye, 1919), Bulgaria (Neuilly-sur-Seine, 1919), Turkey (Sèvres, 1920), and Hungary (Trianon, 1920), 67, 101.
Paris Peace Conference (July 29-oct. 15, 1946), reunion summoned after World War II by the Allied Powers to discuss the terms of peace treaties with some defeated European states, 64, 67, 169, 170, 189, 247, 255.
Paris Treaties (Feb. 10, 1947), imposed after World War II by the victorious Allies on Bulgaria, Finland, Hungary, Italy and Romania, 11, 23, 66, 170, 255, 266.
Paris Treaty (March 30, 1856), ended the Crimean war and stipulated, among other regulations, the abolition of Russian protectorate on the Rom. Principalities, which remained under Ottoman suzerainty, with the collective guarantee of the Great European Powers (France, England, Austria, Russia, Turkey, Prussia and Sardinia). Russia was obliged to surrender southern Bessarabia and the mouths of the Danube to Turkey (Moldavia); the Danube River was open to shipping for all nations and an European Danube Commission was established, 11, 43, 47, 48, 79.
Party:
Communist Party, Moldavian, the only political power allowed to function in Moldavian SSR. It has about 125.000 members (1970), and is part of the USSR Communist Party, 200-204, 224, 225, 241, 261, 264, 265.
Communist Party, Romanian, founded by the decision of the General Congress of the Socialist Party (Bucharest, May 8-12, 1921), was affiliated to the Third International, with Gheorghe Cristescu as secretary general. Congresses: 1921 (May, Bucharest), 1922 (Oct., Ploieşti), 1924 (Aug., Vienna), 1928 (July, Kharkov), 1931 (Dec., Moscow). The National Conference (Oct., 1945) elected Gheorghe Gheorghiu-Dej as its secretary general; and the 10th Congress elected Nicolae Ceauşescu as its secretary general (Aug. 1969), 68, 100, 161, 168, 181, 182, 186, 192, 193, 256-258, 262, 263, 265.
Communist Party of USSR, has its origin in the Second Congress of the Russian Social-Democratic Workers' Party (Oct., 1903), when Lenin's group won a temporary majority in the party's CC, called *Bolsheviki* i.e. those of the majority. In 1912 Lenin created a distinct Bolshevik organization which changed its name into *"The Russian Communist Party"* (1918), and later into *"The Communist Party of Soviet Union"*

(1952), the leading political force in USSR, numbering over 14,000,000 members (1970), 20, 201-203.

Conservative Party, Romanian, active since 1862 on parliamentary scene, but oficially founded in Feb. 1880. It represented the interest of the big landlords opposing social domestic reforms and supporting in foreign policy an alliance with the Central Powers. Its most prominent leaders were: A. Lahovary, P.P. Carp, T. Maiorescu, N. Filipescu, Al. Marghiloman, etc. The conservative party ended its activity in 1922, largely because it has discredited itself following its collaboration during World War I with the German occupation troops, 101.

National-Christian Party, Romanian, or *Cuzist,* founded in 1935 by the merging of the *National-Christian Defense League,* led by A.C. Cuza, and the *National-Agrarian Party,* led by Octavian Goga. This new party obtained in the 1937 general elections 9.15 per cent of the votes, and O. Goga became Romania's prime minister, 94.

National-Liberal Party, Romanian, appeared as an united political body in 1875, and became the most important Romanian party, ruling the country for more than 40 years. It represented, in Romania's bipartite system, the interests of the bourgeois class. In its 1911 and 1921 programs the party maintained the idea of Romania's modernization through a policy of industrialization. The most prominent liberal leaders were: the brothers Ion and Dumitru Brătianu, C.A. Rosetti, D.A. Sturza and Ion Brătianu's sons Ionel, Vintilă and Dinu, to whom Gheorghe Brătianu, the son of Ionel, I.G. Duca and Gheorghe Tătărescu should be added. The NLP ended its legal activity in 1947, 143, 170, 186, 188-190.

National-Peasant Party, Romanian, founded in 1926 through the union of the Romanian *National Party,* led by Iuliu Maniu, and the *Peasant Party* led by Ion Mihalache. This party represented the interests of the peasantry and lower bourgeois class. In 1938 it ceased its activities, maintaining only a leading group, to oppose Antonescu's military dictatorship. After World War II the NPP was prohibited and its leaders, Maniu and Mihalache, condemned to life imprisonment (July, 19, 1947), 142, 151, 155, 161, 170, 186-190.

Socialist Party, French, founded in 1905 as a section of the Workers' International – *Section Française de l'Internationale Ouvrière* (SFIO). Its left wing founded in 1920 the French Communist Party, 85.

Socialist Party, Japanese, founded in Nov. 1946; it was in power from May 1947 to March 1948 as part of a post-war coalition government. In 1951 it was divided into a right-wing and a left-wing, which reunited in 1955 with a joint socialist program, 259.

Socialist Party, Romanian, whose full name was the *Social-Democratic Party of the Workers of Romania,* was founded in Apr. 1893. Conventions: 1894, 1895, 1898 and 1899, when some intellectuals left the Socialist Party and joined the Liberal one. The remainder of the Socialist Party continued its activity under the name of *Social-Democratic Party of Romania,* and held conventions in 1912, 1914 and 1915. The party changed again its name in 1918, when it became the *Socialist Party of Romania,* which united with the Communist Party in Feb. 1948, 94, 260.

Pascu, Ştefan (1914), Rom. historian; carried research on Transylvania's social and economic relations of production in the middle ages period, 18.

Pătrăşcanu, Lucreţiu (1900-1954), Rom. communist leader and sociologist; member of the RCP CC (1945-1948) and of the Political Bureau (1946-1948); minister without portofolio (Sept.-Nov. 1944); minister of justice (1944-1948). He was executed (1954) and rehabilitated post-mortem (1968), 168, 188, 192.

Pavlodar, city in USSR, Kazakh SSR, 209, 211.

Pavlov, Wladimir, Sov. diplomat, first secretary and chief translator to Berlin embassy (1940-1941), 121.

Peabody, guns produced in US, in the Peabody works, Massachussetts, 55, 56.

Peking, Pekin, Beijing, capital of the People's Republic of China; since the 13th century it has been – on and off – the capital of the whole Chinese state, 16, 253, 258, 259, 262, 263.

Pella, Vespasian (1897-1960), Rom. jurist and diplomat; professor of penal law at University of Bucharest; president of the Rom. group participating in the Balkan conferences; Rom. delegate to the disarmament conference; Rom. minister to Bern, 167.

Penal Code, Romanian, the first unified Rom. penal code for all Rom. provinces, was promulgated after World War I (March 17, 1936). Revised by the communist regime in 1948, 1953 and 1955, 242.

Peter the Great, Alekseevich (1672-1725), tzar (1682-1721), and emperor of Russia (1721-1725). He contributed to securing his country's access to the Baltic and Black Seas; entered an antiottoman alliance with the Moldavian prince D. Cantemir, but was defeated by the Turks at Stănileşti (1711), 35, 83.

Petric, Aron (1915), Rom. historian; researcher on Rom. contemporary period and on RCP history, 226.

Petrograd, see Saint Petersburg.

Philippide, Alexandru (1859-1933), Rom. philologist and linguist; author of the theory of the process of re-Romanization ot the north of the Danubian territories after the 7th century, 20.

Piedmond, Piemonte, historical region located in NW Italy, in the Po Valley. Victor Emmanuel II, originally king of Piedmont and Sardinia, became Italy's first king, 1861, 15.

Piedmontese, 15.

Pietist, adept of the Protestant sect of Pietism, which was founded in 1671 by the German theologian Philipp Jakob Spener. Pietism lays emphasis on the personal faith, rigour and asceticism, 216.

Pimen, secular name *Sergey Izvekov* (1910), Soviet Union Patriarch (1971), 221.

Pisarenko, Natalja Filipovna, Moldavian CP CC chief of section in charge with the indoctrination of women (1949); member of CC (1954, 1956), 203.

Piteşti, city in Romania, on Argeş River, 70 miles W of Bucharest, 78.

Pleven, Plevna, town situated in N Bulgaria, key-fortress of the Ottoman empire, where under Osman paşa's command the Turkish army resisted the combined Russian-Romanian attacks, from Aug. 22 until Dec. 10, 1877, 59, 60.

Ploieşti, city in Romania, between the Prahova and Teleajen Rivers, 35 miles N of Bucharest, 58, 101, 191, 252.

Plyushch, Leonid, Ivanovich (1939), Ukrainian mathematician and dissident; placed in a psychiatric hospital in Dnepropetrovsk (1974) from where he was released in 1976 and sent to Vienna. Now living in France, 13.

Podgorny, Nikola Viktorovich (1903), Soviet statesman; president of the Presidium of the Supreme Soviet (1965-1977), 263.

Poklevsky-Koziel, Stanislav Alfonsovich (1868-1937), Russian diplomat; plenipotentiary minister to Bucharest (1913). He continued to represent unofficially Russian interests in Romania after the communist revolution and till 1934, 119.

Poland, was divided theree times in modern times between Prussia, Austria and Russia (1772, 1793 and 1795). Napoleon created a Great Warsaw Duchy (1807), which was again divided by the three old partners at the Vienna Congress (1814-1815). After World War I Poland was reestablished as an independent republic (Nov. 1918), and was again divided between Germany and USSR (Aug. 23, 1939), 24, 35, 68, 103, 118, 132, 146, 149, 150, 157-159, 183, 206, 219, 220, 228, 230, 259, 260.

Pole, 83.

Polianov, Aleksey Andreyevich, Russian diplomat, 88.

Polish, 260.

Popescu, Dumitru Radu (1935), Rom. novelist and playwright who dealt with an abnormal, unusual world, 188.

Popescu-Puțuri, Ion (1906), Rom. historian and communist militant; research on Rom. workers' movement and RCP history, 53, 63, 82, 83, 85, 86.

Popovici, Andrei, Rom. contemporary historian; author of the book *The Political Status of Bessarabia. With an Introduction by James Brown Scott,* Georgetown University, Washington: Ransdell, 1931, 16.

Portugal, 183.

Potsdam, town on the southwest border of Berlin, royal residence under Frederick the Great, seat of Allied leaders' conference (July 17-Aug. 2, 1945), namely of Harry Truman, Clement Attlee and Joseph Stalin, 248.

Prace, Czechoslovak trade unions' newspaper issued in Prague since 1946, 259.

Pravda, official newspaper of USSR CP, published in Moscow. Founded in 1912, 259, 260, 265.

Preda, Marin (1922-1980), Rom. novelist, who in short stories and novels expressed his opinions on various problems of contemporary life, 185.

Pressburg, Treaty of (Dec. 26, 1805), signed by Austria, after Napoleon's victories at Ulm and Austerlitz. By its stipulations the Holy Roman Empire was dislocated, the kingdoms of Bavaria and Würtemburg were created, and Austria had to give up some of its territories, 23, 30.

Primorsk, city in USSR, Russian SFSR on north coast of Vistula Lagoon, called Koivisto, while belonging to Finland (until 1940), 213.

Problems of Peace and Socialism, theoretical magazine of communist and workers' parties, issued in Prague since 1958, 252.

Probst, Abram Efimovich, Soviet contemporary economist, 252.

Procope, Hjalmar (1889), Finnish lawyer and economist; joined the Foreign office (1918); minister of foreign affairs (1924-1925 and 1927-1931); minister to Poland (1926-1927) and USA (1939-1944), 138.

Promised Land, Canaan, Biblical name of Palestine, 216.

Prost, Henri, (1918-1954), French contemporary historian; author of the book *Le Destin de la Roumanie* (Paris: Berger-Levrault, 1954), 16.

Prussia, state founded in 1618, became kingdom under the Hohenzollern dynasty (1701); participated in the three divisions of Poland increasing its territories (1772, 1793 and 1795); participated in coalitions against Napoleon, losing some of its territories after the Jena defeat (1806); recuperated some of these territories at the Vienna Congress (1814-1815); achieved German unity defeating Austria (1866) and France (1870-1871). Its king, Wilhelm I, became emperor (1871); after World War I Prussia was a state member of the German republic, and after World War II it was divided between USSR and Poland. In 1947 the Allied Control Commission dissolved the Prussian state, 26-28, 53.

Prussian, 15, 24.

Pruth River, river forming the frontier between today's Romania and the USSR, 10, 22, 23, 32, 35, 37, 38, 81, 86, 88, 90-92, 117, 120, 132, 135, 136, 156, 160, 162, 168, 198, 199, 221, 225, 228, 258, 263, 265.

Putna, monastery in Romania, founded by the Moldavian prince Ştefan cel Mare, between 1466-1469, 261.

Quinlan, Paul, American contemporary historian, author of the book *Clash over Romania.* See General Bibliography, 185.

Quadruple Alliance, see Central Powers.

Râbniţa, Rîbniţa, Rybnitza, district and town in Moldavian SSR, on the left bank of Dniester, 50 miles of Chişinău, 199, 239.

Raczinski, Edward, count (1891), Polish diplomat; ambassador to Great Britain (1934-1945); acting minister of foreign affairs (1941-1943); living in London since 1945, 159.

Rada of Kiev, an Ukrainian Parliament established in Kiev after the abolishment of tzarism. The Ucrainian government intended to subordinate the right of selfdetermination of the Bessarabians to the Central Ukrainian Rada, 219.

Rădăuţi, town in Romania, Bucovina, which has a 14th century church containing the tombs of the first Moldavian voivodes, 211.

Rădescu, Nicolae (1874-1953), Rom. general; prime minister (Dec. 1944-Feb. 1945); demoted under Soviet pressure and condemned to detention. He emigrated to US (1947), 144.

Radio, Bucharest, 252.

Radio, Free Europe, 39, 50, 68, 81, 92, 105, 123, 171, 193, 245.

Radio, Moscow, 43, 252.

Radio, Peking, 16.

Radul, M.M., one of the Moldavian CP secretaries (1951), 202.

Rasova, village in Romania, Dobrogea, on the Danube arm of Ialomiţa lake, south of Cernavodă, 81.

Red Army, the new army gradually created in Russia – in the late winter of 1917 and the early spring of 1918 – heavily relied on recruits from the working class and on Red Guard units transformed by decree into the Red Army, 187.

Regnault, Elias (1801-1868), French historian who had contacts with 1848 Romanian exiled revolutionaries living in Paris. He wrote a book on the social and political history of the Danubian Principalities, which was used by K. Marx as a documentary source, 260.

Reichstadt, today *Zakupy,* a castle in Bohemia. On July 8, 1876 the tzar Alexander II and emperor Franz-Joseph, assisted by Gorchakov and Andrássy, concluded a verbal agreement for the event of a collapse of the Ottoman empire consequent to the Russian-Turkish war Moscow was preparing. Austria agreed to an expansion of the Russian frontiers corresponding to those existing before 1856; in exchange for the Austrian neutrality Russia agreed that Vienna annex Bosnia and Hercegovina. By the same agreement Austria consented that South Bessarabia be annexed by Russia, 45, 46, 77.

Resnic, see Rezine.

Reuters, Ltd., British news agency, located in London; it was founded by Paul Julius Reuter, in 1851, 241.

Revisionism, a movement initiated by Eduard Bernstein (1850-1932) aiming at the revision of the marxist doctrine, and, in a more recent acception, an accusation brought by the Chinese communists against N. Khrushchev and L. Brezhnev, alleged to have deviated from the classical marxism-leninism, 263.

Revolutionary Petrograd, article due to Rom. poet Octavian Goga on Russian revolutionary events occured in the winter of 1917, published in that year, 96.

Rezine, Rezina-Tîrg, city in E Moldavian SSR, on the right bank of the Dniester River, opposite to Rîbnița, 210.

Ribbentrop, Joachim von (1893-1946), German diplomat and statesman under the Nazi regime; foreign affairs minister (1938-1945). He negotiated the Anticomintern Pact (1936), the Pact of Steel with Italy (1939), the German-Soviet Nonaggression Treaty (1939), and the Tripartite Pact with Japan and Italy (1940). He represented Nazi Germany at the Vienna Award by which Northern Transylvania was ceded to Hungary (Aug. 30, 1940), 108-110, 112, 118, 121-123, 153.

Ribbentrop-Molotov Pact, see Soviet-German Nonaggression Pact.

Rîbnița, town in Moldavian SSR, on the left bank of Dniester, 199.

Rocca delle Camminate, Mussolini's summer residence, 152.

Roller, Mihail (1908-1958), Rom. historian, one of the fervent pioneers of marxist-leninist theory, applied to Romanian history, 257, 258.

Romania, in the middle ages there appeared two Romanian independent states: Wallachia – also called *Țara Românească* – and Moldavia. They united in 1859 and won their independence in 1878. After World War I Transylvania, Bessarabia and Bucovina – Romanian territories incorporated by Austria-Hungary and tzarist Russia – united with Romania (1918), but Bessarabia and Northern Bucovina were again incorporated rated by USSR, 9-11, 13, 15-18, 20, 22, 33, 34, 38, 42-49, 52-58, 60, 62-68, 73-89, 92, 96, 100-103, 108-123, 127-193, 198, 199, 204, 207-210, 212, 215, 219-221, 223, 228, 229, 231, 246-266.

România, Rom. newspaper which appeared under M. Sadoveanu's direction during World War I (Feb. 2, 1917-March 23, 1918), for the Rom. soldiers fighting on the front, 96.

România Nouă, Rom. newspaper published in Chișinău (1917-1918), 97.

Românești, Romanovka, town in Moldavian SSR, on Kogîlnic River, 45 miles of Chișinău, 200.

Romanians, name given to the population living in Romania, Moldavian SSR, northern and southern Ukrainian SSr, and in some parts of the Balkans (Vlachs), 9-12, 14-16, 18, 34, 35, 43, 44, 46, 48-50, 54, 63-65, 67, 86-93, 97, 101, 102, 104, 105, 110, 119, 127, 133, 134, 138, 141, 150-155, 160, 163, 165, 166, 170, 182, 184, 204, 205, 207, 210, 212-214, 216, 218, 220-229, 239- 241, 244-266.

Romanian Encyclopaedic Dictionary, Dicționar Enciclopedic Român, 4 vol. (București: Editura Politică, 1962, 1964, 1965, 1966), 86.

Romanian National Bank, banking agency founded in 1880, with an initial capital of 30 millions gold lei; nationalized in 1946, converted into a state bank in 1948, 119, 121, 247.

Romanian National Central Council, Consiliul Național Român Central, political organization founded on Oct. 18/31, 1918 in Transylvania to represent the Romanian population and express its national claims at the conclusion of the World War I, 91.

Romanian Navy, the Paris Peace Treaty with Romania (Febr. 10, 1947), stipulated that Romania was allowed to have a fleet of a maximum total of 15,000 tons, 247.

Romanian Principalities, name used before the Berlin Treaty (1878), to designate the Danubian Principalities, 10, 17, 24-30, 32, 36, 37, 41-44, 48, 55, 65, 80, 83, 258, 260.

Romanian-Russian Military Convention (April 4/16, 1877), see Russo-Romanian Convention.

Romanian-Russian Military Convention (Aug. 4/17, 1916), Romania signed with the Entente Powers two agreements: an alliance treaty and a military convention (Aug. 4/17, 1916). Under the military agreement Russia agreed to send to the Dobrogea front one cavalry and two infantry divisions. At the same time, Russia undertook to support Romania's war effort by an offensive on the Galician front, and France and England by another offensive on the Salonica front, 84.

Romanian-Russian-Turkish War (1878), Russia declared war to Turkey in April 1877; Romania entered the war on the Russian side (April 30, 1877) and proclaimed its independence (May 10, 1877). The Romanian and Russian armies, commanded by king Carol I, stormed Pleven. The Congress of Berlin (1878) recognized Romania's independence, 9, 49, 52-72, 82.

Romanian Socialist Party, see Socialist Party.

Romanian Workers' Party, Partidul Muncitoresc Român, name given to the RCP between 1948-1965, 250.

Romanist, specialist in the study of Romance languages or Roman law, 223.

Romanization, 256.

Romanovka, see Românești.

Românul, Rom. political, commercial and literary daily, issued in Bucharest (1857-1864, 1865, 1866-1905, 1914-1915), 56.

Rome, capital of Italy since Jan. 26, 1871, 196, 197, 222.

Roosevelt, Franklin Delano (1882-1945), 32nd president of USA (1933-1945), during the depression and World War II. At his request, the Congress voted the war resolutions against Japan (Dec. 8, 1941), and against Germany and Italy (Dec. 11, 1941). He met with the Allied leaders Churchill and Stalin at Teheran (1943) and Yalta (1945), 135, 147-150, 157, 158, 160.

Roques, Pierre-Auguste (1857-1920), French minister of war during World War I (Aug.-Dec. 1916); charged with an inspection mission of the Salonica front, 85.

Rosenberg, Alfred (1893-1946), chief ideologist of Nazism; since July 1941 he was *Reichsminister* of the occupied eastern territories, 141.

Rosso, Augusto (1885-1964), Italian diplomat; plenipotentiary minister (1927-1932); ambassador to Moscow (1936-1941), 120.

Rostov, city in USSR, Russian SFSR, on the right bank of Don River, 25 miles of Azov Sea, 209.

Royal Palace in Bucharest, on Calea Victoriei, built by architect Nenciulescu (1935-1937), on the site of the old house belonging to Golescu family, 190.

Rud, Gherasim Yakovlevich (1907), partisans' commissar during World War II; deputy of USSR Supreme Soviet (1941-1958); Moldavian SSR foreign affairs minister (1944-1958); chairman of Moldavian SSR Council of Ministers (1946-1958), 201.

Rumyantsev, Nikolay Petrovich, count (1754-1826), Russian statesman and diplomat; president of the state council (1810); in his capacity as foreign minister (1808) he promoted closer relations with France, 26-28.

Russia, Kievan Russia, led by prince Oleg, was founded in the second half of the 9th century; at the end of the 15th century Ivan III annexed all east Slavic lands — Great Russian, Belorussian and Ukrainian territories — as well as Novgorod (1478); Ivan the Terrible, who took the title of tzar, annexed the khanate of Kazan, Astrakhan and the Lower Volga, and began expanding toward Siberia which was annexed in the 17th century. Ukraine united with Russia in 1654; Peter the Great (1682-1725) annexed Lithuania, Latvia and Estonia, and some regions of Finland. During the 18th century Russia participated in the three divisions of Poland (1772, 1793, 1795). After the wars against Turkey (1768-1774, 1787-1791), Russia annexed Crimea and the N Black Sea steppe, reaching the Dniester. In 1812 she annexed Bessarabia and expanded its empire in Asia, with Kazakhstan and western Georgia. In the second half of the 19th century it extended its rule over the Caucasus, Central Asia and the Far East. See also Russian empire, and Soviet Union, 9-11, 13, 18, 22-33, 35-38, 40-50, 52-55, 57, 58, 61, 62, 64, 66, 67, 73-81, 83-90, 94-97, 108, 111, 118-122, 129, 130, 132, 133, 136-140, 144, 148, 149, 153, 158, 160-163, 166, 168, 196, 197, 206, 213, 215, 216, 218-221, 225, 226, 229-231, 257-259, 265.

Russians, 9, 11, 12, 17, 22, 24-27, 29, 31, 33-35, 56, 59, 60, 64, 81, 89, 109, 110, 113, 117, 118, 120, 137, 140, 147, 149, 150, 154, 155, 158, 163, 166, 168, 186-189, 196, 197, 201-206, 208, 209, 211, 214-218, 220-231, 241, 242, 254-258, 260-262, 264.

Russian-Austrian-Turkish War (1735-1739). The dispute arose in 1735 when the Russians attempted to modify the frontier between the Ukraine and the Ottoman empire. In 1737 Austria entered the war as Russia's ally, and concluded a separate peace (Belgrade, Sept. 1739), ceding Northern Serbia and Little Wallachia to Turkey. Russia signed a peace settlement the same month (Sept. 1739) agreeing to demilitarize the sea of Azov and renouncing the right to have warships on the Azov and Black Seas, 36.

Russian-Austrian-Turkish War (July 26, 1787-Jan. 9, 1792), the war broke out because sultan Abdul Hamid called in an ultimatum for the removal of Russian consuls from Bucharest and Iaşi and the evacuation of Georgia. Turkey was defeated and had to accept the armistice of Galaţi (Aug. 11, 1791) and the peace of Iaşi (Jan. 9, 1792). See Iaşi Peace Traty, 36.

Russian Empire, the expansion of the Russian empire was prepared during the reign of Peter I. Russia incorporated the Ukraine (1654), Crimea (1783), Poland (1772, 1793 and 1795), Galicia and western Volhynia (1939), Estonia, Lithuania, Bessarabia and Northern Bucovina and some Finnish territories (1940). The expansion into Asian territories included Georgia (1801), Northern Azerbaijan (1813), the Armenian province of Yerevan (1828), the Chechens (1859), Turkestan (1860), the Circassians' territories (1864), a long strip of the Pacific coast (Treaty of Peking, 1860), and the control over the Sakhalin and Kuril islands (Treaty of St Petersburg, 1875). After World War II the expansion of the Russian empire continued in both European and Asian directions, subordinating the East European countries and entering Afghanistan, 23, 28, 29, 36, 38, 42, 215, 220, 223, 229-231, 258.

Russian-German Agreement (Sept. 5, 1940), offered to the German living in Bessarabia and in Northern Bucovina the possibility to emigrate to Germany. On the basis of this agreement 93,548 Germans from Bessarabia and 52,000 from Northern Bucovina were resettled in West Germany, 208.

Russian Republic, Russia, or *Russian,* an abbreviation of Russian Soviet Federative Socialist Republic, one of the most important among the 15 republics of the USSR, 213, 219, 221, 240.

Russian Revolution of 1917, the bourgeois-democratic revolution of Feb. 1917 which led to the overthrow of the tzarist regime, and ended in the Oct. 1917 revolution with the establishment of the communist regime. On 2/15 March power was assumed by an all-Liberal Provisional Government with the exception of Aleksandr Kerenski who was a socialist. This government was reorganized four times until Oct. 1917, when it was overthrown by the October Revolution. See October Revolution, 94-97, 256.

Russian-Turkish War (1711), in 1710 Turkey declared war to Russia. Peter the Great and his ally, the Moldavian prince Dimitrie Cantemir, were defeated at Stănileşti (1711), 36, 261.

Russian-Turkish War (1768-1774), the pretext for war was provided by a Cossacks' incursion on Balta. In 1769 the Russian general Galitzin occupied Moldavia and Wallachia; in 1770 Russia obtained a great naval victory at Çeşme. The peace treaty was signed at Küçük Kaynarka. See Küçük Kaynarka, 36.

Russian-Turkish War (1806-1812), was declared by Russia in support of the Serbian insurrection, and ended with Moscow's victory and the conclusion of the Bucharest Peace Treaty. See *Bucharest Treaty of,* 32, 41.

Russification, see chapter XIII, 191-231, 241, 242.

Russo, Alecu (1819-1859), Rom. writer; one of the pionneers of Rom. literary criticism, 227.

Russo-Romanian Military Convention (Apr. 16, 1877), allowed Russian troops to cross Romanian territory during the war of 1877 which Moscow intended to declare to the Ottoman empire. The Convention was negotiated at Livadia by prime minister Ion

Brătianu and war minister Gh. Slăniceanu representing Romania, chancellor Gorceakov representing Russia (Oct. 1876). The Convention was signed in Bucharest by Rom. foreign minister M. Kogălniceanu and the Russian diplomatic agent to Bucharest, Dimitrie Stuart (Apr. 16, 1877), 45, 47, 58, 76.

Ruthenians, 204, 216, 219.

Ruttner, M., contemporary historian, 40.

Saint-Aulaire, Charles, comte de, (1866-1954), French diplomat; plenipotentiary minister to Romania (1916); author of *Confession d'un Vieux Diplomate,* (Paris: Flammarion, 1953), 197.

Saint-Julien, Josef, count, Austrian diplomat, general and field-marshal; plenipotentiary entrusted with a special mission in France (July 1800), in Russia (Oct. 1809); extraordinary envoy and plenipotentiary minister to Saint Petersburg (1810-1812), 30.

Saint Petersburg, city in Russia, founded in 1703 at the mouth of Neva River by Peter the Great; served as national capital (1712-1918); was renamed Petrograd (1914-1924) and Leningrad in 1924, 10, 26, 27, 31, 44, 45, 61, 62, 64, 75, 88, 90, 94-97, 158.

Sakhalin Island, Jap. *Karafuto,* island of the far eastern Russian SFSR, contested between Russia and Japan since mid-19th century; completely under Soviet control since 1945, 211.

Sakharov, Andrey Dmitriyvich (1921), Soviet scientist who carried research on the hydrogen bomb. He founded a Committee for Human Rights (1970); won the Nobel Prize for Peace (1975) and was exiled by the Soviet regime to Gorky (1980), 13.

Salisbury, Robert Arthur Talbot Gascoyne Cecil, 3d marques of (1830-1903), English statesman; leader of the conservative paraty; prime minister (1885-1886, 1886-1892, 1895-1902). In his capacity as adviser to Disraeli and an foreign secretary (April 1878), he contributed to the peaceful solution of the Balkan crisis, convincing Russia to take part in the Congress of Berlin, 54, 78, 79, 81.

Salonika, Thessaloniki, capital of Northern Greece. During World War I the Allies opened a second front in the Balkans (Oct. 1915) by landing troops in Salonika, 84, 87.

Salzburg, 44.

Samarkand, city in USSR, Uzbek SSR, 170 miles of Tashkent, 214.

Sănătescu, Constantin (1884-1947), Rom. cavalry general; commander of the garrison of Bucharest (1944); he was active in Marshal Antonescu's arrest (Aug. 23, 1944); prime minister (Sept.-Dec. 1944), 183, 189, 192.

Sângerei, Synzhereya, village in central Moldavian SSR, 14 miles of Bălți, 200.

San Stefano, Treaty of (March 3, 1878), peace settlement ending the Russian-Romanian-Turkish War (1877-1878). The treaty established: the autonomy of the Bulgarian principality; the recognition of Montenegro, Romania's and Serbia's independence; autonomy for Bosnia-Hercegovina, thus putting an end to Ottoman control over the Balkans. The terms of the San Stefano Treaty were modified by the Congress of Berlin (June 13-July 13, 1878), 45-47, 62, 64, 74, 76, 77, 79, 80.

Saratov, oblast in USSR, W Russian SFSR, in the basin of the middle Volga River, 215.

Sardinia, Sardegna, In the 19th century the kingdom of Sardinia was the center of political activity for Italian unity, 15, 43.

Sarrail, Maurice-Paul-Emmanuel (1856-1929), French general; commander-in-chief of Allied army on the Oriental front during World War I, 87.

Savary, Anne-Jean-Marie-René, duc de Rovigo (1774-1833), French general in the Napoleonic wars; after the signing of the Tilsit treaty (1807) he was Napoleon's envoy to St Petersburg, 26.

Savchenko, Ivan Tikhonovich (1908), chairman of State Security Committee of Moldavian Council of Ministers (1959-1967); member of Moldavian SSR CC (1960); member of Presidium of MCP CC (1960-1962); deputy of Moldavian Supreme Soviet (1963), 200.

Savfet, Mahomed, paşa, (1815-1883), Turkish diplomat and statesman; commissary to Romanian Principalities (1854); ambassador to Paris (1865-1866); minister of public instruction; grand vizier (1878); ambassador to Paris (1878); inspector of the imperial administration (1879), 53.

Savor, George, contemporary publicist, author of the study "Moldavia a Russian Satelite", *The Ukrainian Quarterly,* No. 2, 1956, 198, 205, 208.

Saxons, Rom. *Sas,* people belonging to the German population native from Flanders, Luxemburg, Meuse and Rhine valleys and Saxony, colonized by the Hungarian kings during the 12th and 13th centuries in some areas of Transylvania, 92.

Scalekos, N.A., vice-chairman of Moldavian Council of Ministers (1954), 201.

Schtchusev, Viktorovich (1873-1949), Soviet architect, 226.

Schulenburg, Friederich Werner, von (1875-1944), German ambassador to Moscow (1934-1941), 109, 110, 113, 119-122.

Schuyler, Cortlandt van Rensselaer (1900), US army officer; brigadier general (1943); chief of staff, antiaircraft command (1943); Legion of Merit (1945); US representative on the Allied Control Commission in Romania (1945), 170.

Scînteia, Rom. daily; organ of the RCP CC. First issued by the Romanian revolutionists in Odessa (1919); printed illegally (1931-1940); legally issued since Sept. 21, 1944, 191.

Scurtul, Skurtul, Maxim Vasilevich, secretary of Moldavian CP CC, in charge with the agriculture (1945-1961); member of CC Bureau (1954-1963); minister of State Purchasing Commission (1961-1962); deputy of Moldavian Supreme Soviet (1955 and 1963 conventions); deputy of USSR Supreme Soviet (1954 and 1958), 203.

Sébastiani, Horace-François-Bastien, comte (1772-1851), marshal of France; ambassador to Constantinople (1806); he reestablished good relations between Napoleon and Selim III and defended Constantinople against the English fleet, 24, 25.

Selim III (1761-1808), Ottoman sultan (1789-1807). He ascended the throne during the Austro-Russian war (1787-1792) and concluded the treaty of Sistova with Austria (1791) and the treaty of Iaşi with Russia (1792). Under the influence of Sébastiani, (Napoleon's ambassador to Constantinople), Selim III declared war on Russia and Grat Britain (1806), 24, 25.

Semionov, (Semenov), Vladimir Semionovich (Semenovich), (1911), Soviet diplomat; counsellor (1939-1940); diplomatic mission in Lithuania and Germany (1940-1941); in Sweden (1942-1945); ambassador to West Germany, political adviser to the chairman of the Soviet Control Commission in East Germany (1949-1953); USSR deputy minister of foreign affairs (1955-1978), 165, 184.

Serbia, became an autonomous principality under Turkish suzerainty and Russian protection after the Russo-Turkish war of 1828-1829. The Treaty of Berlin (July 1878) granted independence to Serbia, 30, 42, 47, 56.
Serbians, 257.
Serdyuk, Zinoviy Timofeevich (1903), Major general in reserve; graduate of the Moscow Higher School of the Trade Unions (1931); held Komsomol and Trade Unions positions in Moscow (1931-1934); party positions in Moscow and Kiev (1937-1941); second and later first secretary of Kiev *oblast* (1943-1949); first secretary of Moldavian CP CC (1955-1961); first deputy chairman of USSR CP Control Committee (1961-1962), 203.
Serpents' Island, a tiny island of some 3,000 square meters, located 23 miles east of the Danube Delta. Russia annexed *S.I.* under the Treaty of Adrianople (1829); the island was restored to Moldavia by the Paris Peace Treaty (1856); the Berlin Peace Treaty confirmed its restoration to Romania (1878). USSR did not claim it in 1940 and 1944, but the Soviet atlases show it as belonging to the Soviet Union, 48, 76, 79, 81.
Seton-Watson, George Hugh Nicholas (1916), professor of Russian history at London University of science (1951), 16, 40, 42, 43, 45, 49, 84.
Seton-Watson, Robert William (1879-1951), British historian, specialist in central and southeastern European history, 73.
Sevastopol, city and seaport in USSR, Ukrainian SSR, in the southwestern Crimean Peninsula. During World War II it underwent a Germanian-Romanian siege, 140
Sfatul Țării, Council of Bessarabia, composed of soldiers, workers and peasants, representing all the cohabiting Bessarabian nationalities, which on Dec. 2, 1917 proclaimed Bessarabia an autonomous republic and on March 27, 1918 voted its union with Romania, 17, 22, 86, 91, 210.
Sfîntu Gheorghe, town in Romania, Transylvania, Covasna district, on Olt River, 191.
Shakespeare, William (1564-1616), English poet and playwright, 94.
Shelest, Petr Yefimovich (1908), Ukrainian communist leader; member of CP since 1928; first secretary of Ukrainian CP CC since 1963, 220.
Shevchenko, Taras Hryhorovych (1814-1861), Ukrainian poet, champion of Ukrainian revival, 220.
Shiroky, commissar for internal affairs in Moldavian SSR, 200.
Shuvalov, Pyotr Andreyevich, count (1827-1889), Russian diplomat and political adviser to tzar Alexander II; member of Russian delegation to Paris Peace Conference (1856); ambassador to London (1874-1879), recalled because of his involvement in Russia's diplomatic troubles after the Russian-Turkish war of 1877-1878, 78-81.
Siberia, 15, 198, 206-211, 213-215, 219.
Sicilians, 15.
Sicily, island in the Mediteranean Sea. During World War II the Allied troops landed in Sicily on July 9, 1943, 153.
Sikorski, Wladislaw Eugeniusz (1881-1943), Polish general and statesman; chief of the general staff (1921), prime minister (1922-1923); prime minister of the Polish exile government (1939), 158, 159.
Silesia, historical region of central and eastern Europe, in the middle and upper Odra River basin, 26, 31.

Silistra, region and town on the right bank of the Danube River which was assigned to Bulgaria at the Berlin Congress (1878); became part of Romania after second Balkan war (1913) and returned to Bulgaria in 1940, 48, 49, 81.

Siret River, major Rom. river, separating north Romania from the Ukraine, and flowing into the Danube W of Galați, 30, 88, 89, 136.

Sistova, Svishtov, Peace of (Aug. 4, 1791), between Austrian empire and Turkey, by which Belgrade was returned to Turkey, 36.

Slavs, 34, 41, 45, 55, 129, 137, 152, 196, 197, 215, 218, 224.

Slobozia, town in Romania, Ialomița district, on the left bank of Ialomița River, 25, 26.

Slobozia, Slobodzeya, village in SE Moldavian SSR, on the left bank of Dniester River, 7 miles of Tiraspol, 199, 239.

Slovakia, proclaimed autonomous (Oct. 6, 1938) and later independent state under German protection (March 18, 1939), 158.

Smolensk, oblast in USSR, Russian SFSR, in the upper Dnieper River basin, 215.

Snagov, village in S Romania, 20 miles of Bucharest, 190.

Socialist Moldavia, see Moldova Socialistă.

Socialist Unity Front, Rom. *Frontul Unității Socialiste,* political permanent body founded by RCP on Nov. 19, 1968 in the interest of communist domestic and foreign policy, 73.

Solzhenitsyn, Alexandr Isayevich (1918), soviet writer and winner of Nobel Prize for literature. Arrested for writing a letter criticizing Stalin (1945); he spent eight years in prison and three in a detention camp; rehabilitated (1956); exiled from Soviet Union (1974) he was awarded the Nobel Prize the same year, 13.

Soroca, Soroki, city in N Moldavian SSR, on the right bank of the Dniester, 85 miles of Chișinău, preserving the ruins of a 15th century Genoese-Moldavian citadel, 18, 206, 210, 214, 239.

Sorokin, Gennadiy Mikhaylovich (1910), Soviet economist; member of the CP of the Soviet Union since 1939; director of the Institute of Economics of the World Socialist System attached to the Soviet Academy of Sciences since 1961; author of the book *Building Communism in the USSR and Cooperation of the Socialist Countries,* 252.

Souslensk, see Susleni.

Sovetskaya Etnografiia, Soviet magazine, founded in 1930, in Moscow, 241.

Sovetskaya Moldaviia, Moldavian newspaper; organ of the Moldavain CP CC published in Chișinău six times a week. Founded in 1925 under the name *Chervonii Orach* – The Red Ploughman; in 1930 it changed its name into its present one, 241.

Soviet, 12, 13, 16, 17, 150, 151, 155, 161, 163, 165-168, 170, 184, 187, 188, 190, 191, 199, 201, 204, 207-209, 214, 215, 221, 222, 224-230, 238-244, 247-249, 251-253, 255-259, 261-265.

Soviet Army, regular USSR army whose higher officers are members of the CP, military training including communist indoctrination, 246.

Soviet Empire, see Russian Empire.

Soviet-German Nonaggression Pact, or *Molotov-Ribbentrop Pact,* (Aug. 23, 1939), concluded in Moscow; it divided Eastern Europe into zones of influence, affecting

Finland, Estonia, Latvia, Lithuania, Poland and Romania, 10, 114, 118, 119, 122, 158.

Soviet Ultimatum to Romania (June 26, 1940), by which USSR called upon Romania to surrender Bessarabia and Northern Bucovina within 24 hours, whitout any other alternative but war, 10, 17, 169, 265.

Soviet Union, Union of Soviet Socialist Republics, federative state set up by the first Soviet Congress (Dec. 30, 1922) and composed of 15 socialist republics. Following signing of the German-Soviet Nonaggression Pact (Aug. 1939) USSR annexed the western part of Poland (Sept. 28, 1939), Estonia, Latvia and Lithuania (Aug. 1940), Bessarabia and Northern Bucovina (June, 1940). After World War II all these territorial conquests were internationally recognized as Soviet territories, 9-13, 16-20, 34, 38, 49, 103-105, 108-112, 114-116, 118-122, 127-138, 145-150, 152-163, 165-170, 181, 182-184, 187, 189, 192, 196-208, 211-213, 215-217, 219, 220, 222-224, 227-231, 238, 239, 241, 243, 244, 246-249, 251, 253-259, 261-266.

Sovrom, Soviet-Romanian mixed enterprises, set up after World War II by USSR to control Romania's main economic production such as: oil, coal, gas, timber, metals, uranium, constructions and chemical industries, means of transportation, insurances and films, 248, 249, 251.

Spain, was occupied by Napoleon's troops between 1808-1814, 27, 28, 183, 187.

Sremski Karlovici, see Karlowitz.

Springer, Anton, Austrian colonel, 60.

Stalin, Joseph Vissarionovich Dzhugashvili (1879-1953), general secretary of SU CP CC (1922-1953); president of Council of Ministers (1941-1953); president of Defense State Committee and Supreme Commander-in-chief of the USSR armed forces (1941-1945). He concluded a Nonaggression Pact with Hitler (1939); directed the Soviet army during World War II; repelled German armies and occupied East European lands, 121, 134, 145-150, 153, 159, 165, 166, 197, 200, 201, 204, 206, 214, 220, 223, 224, 230, 231, 239, 260, 265, 266.

Stalingrad, name given between 1925-1961 to the city of Volgograd. *St.* was the scene of a major battle in World War II (July 17, 1942-Feb. 2, 1943), marking a turning point in the German campaign in Russia, when 22 German divisions (cca 300,000 soldiers) were distroyed or surrendered, 150, 225.

Stalinist, 257, 258.

Stara Stambul, name of one Danube mouths, 76, 81.

State Council, Rom. *Consiliul de Stat,* supreme body of Socialist Republic Romania, elected by the Grand National Assembly for the term of a legislature, 53, 82.

State Department, 147, 148, 156, 157, 159-164, 166, 210.

Stavrianos, Leften Stavros, contemporary historian; specialist on Balkan problems; author of various books on Balkan history such as: *Balkan Federation. A History of the Movement Toward Balkan Unity in Modern Times* (1944); *The Balkan Since 1453* (1958); *The Ottoman Empire: Was It the Sick Man of Europe?* (1958), 40, 41.

Straits Question, The, the political and military problem concerning the passage of warships through the Bosporus and the Dardanelles. Under the Treaty of Hunkiar Iskelesi Russia obtained the right to request Turkey to close the Straits to warships of non Black Sea powers. This stipulation was cancelled by the London Straits Convention (July 15, 1841), 9, 33, 118, 136, 231.

Ştefănescu, Ştefan (1929), Rom. historian; researcher on Rom. feudal institutions, 18.

Şteflea, Ilie (1886-1946), Rom. general of the army (March 1942-Aug. 1944); chief of general staff (Jan. 20, 1942-Aug. 23, 1944); commander of the 4th Rom. army; arrested by the communist regime (1945), 183, 192.

Steinon, Charles, French publicist; author of the book *Mystère Roumain et la Défection Russe*, printed in 1918, whose subject is Russia's political interest to oppose Romania's unity, 89.

Stephen the Great, Rom. *Ştefan cel Mare*, prince of Moldavia (1457-1504). He defended Moldavia's independence against Hungary (Baia, 1467), Turkey (Vaslui, 1475 and Podul Înalt 1476), and Poland (Codrul Cosminului, 1497), 50, 261.

Stere, Constantin (1865-1936), Rom. statesman and writer, born in Cerăpcău, Bessarabia. Ideologist of Rom. populism, he fought against tzarist Russia and for Bessarabia's union with Romania, 15, 38, 50, 198, 226.

Stettinius, Edward Reilly Jr. (1900-1949), American industrialist and statesman; undersecretary of state (1943-1944); secretary of state (1944-1945); president Roosevelt's adviser at Yalta Conference and USA first permanent representative to the United Nations, 159.

Ştirbey, Barbu, prince (1873-1946), Rom. statesman; prime minister and foreign affairs minister (June 1927). He was the Rom. democratic opposition's representative negotiating in Cairo the terms of a Romanian armistice (1944), 160-162, 164, 184, 187.

Stockholm, 165-167, 184.

Stolpov, N.D., Soviet economist, 252.

Storojineţ, Storozhinets, city in Northern Bucovina, today in Ukrainian SSR, on the Siret River, 211.

Strachensk, see Străşeni.

Strasbourg, was confined by the allied armies during the Napoleonic wars, in 1814 and 1815, but without tangible results, 23, 216.

Străşeni, Strachensk, village in Bessarabia, today in central Moldavian SSR, on the Bîc River, 13 miles from Chişinău, 210.

Stürmer, Boris Vladimirovich (1848-1917), Russian statesman; prime minister (Jan. 20-Nov. 10, 1916), at the same time minister of the interior (March 3-July 7, 1916) and minister of foreign affairs (July 7-Nov. 10, 1916), 85, 88, 89.

Sub-Carpathian Ruthenia, Carpatho-Ukraine, Central European region; belonged to Hungary until 1920 when under the Treaty of Trianon it was incorporated into Czechoslovakia; its southern districts were ceded to Hungary (Nov. 2, 1938); proclaimed its independence (March, 1939) and was annexed by Hungary; at the end of World War II was ceded to USSR which turned it into a Transcarpathian *oblast*, 259.

Sublime Porte, see Ottoman empire.

Suceava, town in Romania, in Southern Bucovina; ancient capital of Moldavia (1388-1564) preserving to this day churches from 14, 16 and 17th centuries, 15, 160.

Suceava River, Moldavian river, tributary of Siret, 120.

Sudetenland, historical region comprising part of northern Bohemia and Moravia which became a major source of dispute between Germany and Czechoslovakia until 1938 when it was transferred to Germany by the Munich Conference, 259.

Şuga, Alexandru, (1914), Rom. historian, living in W.Germany, author of the book: *Die völkerrechtliche Lage Bessarabien in der geschlichtlichen Entwicklung des Landes* (Köln: Luthe-Druck, 1958), 16.

Suleiman I the Magnificent, Soliman I (1494-1566), Ottoman sultan (1520-1566), 217.

Sulina, town and port on Black Sea at the mouths of the Danube, located in Romania; seat of the International Danube Commission, 76, 81, 170.

Sunday Times, British weekly, founded in 1822, 13.

Super Powers, new diplomatic notion introduced after World War II to designate the present world powers, such as US and USSR, 255.

Supreme Soviet, supreme state body in unional and autonomous Soviet republics, 108, 109, 200, 201, 238, 239, 243.

Susleni, village in Bessarabia, today in the Moldavian SSR, 8 miles from Orhei, 210.

Suvorov, Moldavian administrative-territorial unit, set up in Dec. 23, 1964; located in SE of Moldavian SSR, 239.

Svistov, see Sistova.

Swabian, native or inhabitant of Swabia, a former duchy of Germany, now a district of Bavaria, 92.

Sweden, 165.

Swiss, 53, 261.

Switzerland, Confederation Suisse, 54, 155, 183, 191, 216.

Tadzhikistan, Tadzhik Soviet Socialist Republic, in USSR, Central Asia; originally constituted as an autonomous republic within Uzbek SSR (1924); became a separate republic within USSR (1929), 12.

Tagliavini, Carlo (1903), professor of glotology at University of Padua (1935); member of many Italian and foreign linguistic and cultural associations, 16.

Talleyrand, Charles-Maurice de Talleyrand-Périgord (1754-1838), French diplomat and statesman; foreign minister (1797-1799) under the Directory, Consulate, Empire and Restauration; he was France's representative at the Congress of Vienna (1814-1815), 23-25, 28.

Talmaz, village in Bessarabia, Tighina district, today in the Moldavian SSR; first documentary mention 1595, 15.

Tambov, oblast, in USSR, W Russian SFSR on the plain of Oka and Don Rivers, 215.

Tannriöer, Suphi, Turkish plenipotentiary minister to Bucharest (1931-1944), 154.

Târnova, Tyrnovo, village in Bessarabia, today in N. Moldavian SSR, 30 miles of Bălți, 239.

Tartar, Tatar, 196, 207, 210, 213, 215, 217, 219, 222, 229.

Tashkent, capital of the Uzbek SSR, and fourth largest Soviet city, 226.

Task of the Proletariat in Our Revolution (The), pamphlet written by Lenin in Sept. 1917, where he recognized the right to self-determination for all peoples and nations living in tzarist Russia, 39, 90.

Tass, Telegrafnoe Aghenstvo Sovetskovo Soiuza, Soviet Central Agency founded in 1925, in Moscow, 12, 155.

Tătărescu, Gheorghe (1886-1957), Rom. statesman; president of the national-liberal party; prime minister (1934-1937 and 1939-1940); ambassador to France (1938-1939); vice president and minister of foreign affairs (1945); president of Rom. delegation to Paris Peace Conference (1946), 110-112, 116-118, 133, 135, 169, 187, 188.

Tatars, see Tartars.

Taurida, ancient name of Crimea, 212.

Tavda, city in USSR, Russian SFSR, harbour on Tavda River, 211.

Teheran, Tehran, capital city of Iran; seat of the Teheran Conference (Nov. 28-Dec. 1, 1943) between W. Churchill, F.D. Roosevelt and J. Stalin. There it was decided that the West allied invasion in France will be supported by a Soviet offensive on the eastern front, 153, 160, 162, 187.

Teiul, settlement of Moldavians deported to Soviet Far East, Russian SFSR, 214.

Teresenco, P.F., one of the Moldavian SSR CP secretaries (1952), 203.

Third Reich (1933-1945), name given to the Nazi regime in Germany during Hitler's rule; see Germany, 108-110, 112, 113, 123, 127, 128, 135, 189, 191.

Third Rome, name given to Moscow, after the fall of Constantinople (1453), 196.

Thracians, ancient Indo-European tribe which had spread from the Aegean Sea to the North Carpathian Mountains and from the Dniester River and the Black Sea to Morava and the Tisza River. First mentioned by Homer, 82.

Thugut, Jean-Amédée-François de Paule, baron de (1736-1818), Austrian diplomat and statesman who began his career as translator in Constantinople; he served in Paris as a channel of communication between Marie-Antoinette et Mirabeau (1791); minister of foreign affairs (1794); supporter of the Austrian alliance with England against France, 41.

Thurson, Walter (1895), counsellor of USA embassy to Moscow (1939), ambassador to El Salvador (1944), 136.

Teodor, Dan (1933), Rom. archaeologist and historian; researcher on 6-13 centuries in Romania, 34.

Tighina, Bendery, city in Bessarabia, today in SE Moldavian SSR, on the right bank of the Dniester, 32 miles from Chișinău; a 15th century Moldavian fortress is preserved there; under Turkish rule (1538-1812) renamed Bender, 15, 35, 141, 214, 239.

Tilea, Viorel (1896-1972), Rom. diplomat; plenipotentiary minister to London (1932-1940); lost his Rom. citizenship during general Antonescu's regime (1940); he tried to organize a Rom. exile opposition to the communist regime (1944) and had his Rom. citizenship withdrawn for a second time (1947), 132, 133.

Tilsit, today *Sovetsk,* city in Russia, today Russian SFSR, 30 miles from Kaliningrad, seat of the signature of the Treaties of Tilsit between France and Russia (July 7, 1807), and France and Prussia (July 9, 1807), after France's victory over the 4th coalition, 25-27, 31, 36.

Timofeievca, settlement of Moldavians deported to Soviet Far East, Russian SFSR, 214.

Timosenko, Semyon Konstantinovich (1895-1970), Soviet marshal; people's commissar of defense (1940-1941); commander-in-chief of large Soviet military units during World War II, 226.

Timpul, Rom. newspaper published in Bucharest (1876-1884, 1889-1900 and 1919-1922) as official organ of the conservative party, 225.

Tiraspol, city in SE Moldavian SSR, on the left bank of the Dniester, 40 miles from Chişinău; founded in 1793; capital of the Moldavian Autonomous SSR (1930-1940), 199, 223, 239.

Tîrgovişte, town in S-Central Romania; Wallachian capital (1383-1698); preserves the ruins of a 14th century pallace and of several churches of the 16 and 17th centuries, 78.

Tîrgu Neamţ, town in Romania, in Moldavia, 183.

Tîrnova, Tyrnovo, village in Moldavian SSR, 30 miles from Bălţi, 210.

Tisza, Istvan (1861-1918), Hungarian statesman; prime minister (1903-1905 and 1913-1917). He opposed domestic reforms and defended the Austro-Hungarian dualism, 83.

Titulescu, Nicolae (1883-1941), Rom. diplomat and statesman; minister of finance (1917 and 1920); Romania's permanent delegate to League of Nations (1920-1936); plenipotentiary minister to London (1922-1926 and 1928-1932); minister of foreign affairs (1927-1928 and 1932-1936); president of the League of Nations (1930 and 1931). He was one of the champions of European collective security and a supporter of the Little Entente and of the Balkan Entente, 100-105, 119.

Tkack, Dimitri Grigorevich, secretary of the Moldavian CP CC (1949); deputy of USSR Supreme Soviet (1954), 203.

Togliatti, Tolyatti, city in USSR, Russian SFSR, on the Volga River, named until 1964 Stavropol, 211.

Tolstoy, Piotr, count (1761-1844), Russian general; ambassador to Paris (1807-1808), 25-27.

Tomsk, city in USSR, Russian SFSR, 125 miles NE from Novosibirsk, 214.

Touraine, historical province in central France, traversed by Loire River, 15.

Trafalgar, Battle of (Oct. 21, 1805), naval battle between a Franco-Spanish fleet under Adm. Pierre de Villeneuve and the British fleet under Adm. Horatio Nelson, which established the British naval supremacy, 23.

Transcaucasia, Transcaucasian, region of USSR, south of the Caucasus Mountains, 240.

Transdnistria, Transnistria, former administrative division between Dniester and southern Bug, organized during the Romanian military occupation of this region (1941-1943), 130, 140, 141, 143, 151, 182, 201, 208, 220.

Transylvania, historic province in central Romania; in ancient times part of the kingdom of Dacia; later Roman province (106-271), conquered by the Magyars (1003); autonomous principality subjected to Turkish suzerainty (1541); under Mihai Viteazul's Wallachian rule (1599-1600); attached to the Habsburg empire (Treaty of Carlowitz, 1699); a Habsburg crown land (1848); integrated into Hungary (1867); united with Romania (Dec. 1, 1918); divided between Romania and Hungary (Vienna Award, Aug. 30, 1940); restored to Romania (Paris Peace Treaty, Feb. 10, 1947), 15, 35, 58, 62, 65, 82, 83, 86-88, 91, 94-97, 101, 102, 113, 121, 122, 128, 137, 138, 141-143, 153, 160, 161, 165, 168, 191.

Transylvania, Northern, part of Transylvania – 43,500 sq. km and 2,6 mil. inhabitants – separated from Romania by the Ribbentrop-Ciano arbitration (Vienna Award, Aug. 30, 1940) and ceded to Hungary, 128, 129, 133, 141, 144, 151, 182, 188, 191, 192.

Trianon, two small châteaux in the park of Versailles, 11 miles of Paris; the peace treaty between Entente Powers and Hungary was signed in the Grand Trianon (June 4, 1920), 92, 102.

Tripartite Pact, military alliance signed by Germany, Italy and Japan (Sept. 27, 1940), 10, 129, 138.

Tritiacova, settlement of Moldavians deported to Soviet Far East, Russian SFSR, 214.

Trotsky, Leon Davidovich Bronstein (1879-1940), one of the leaders of the Russian 1905-1907 revolution and of October 1917 revolution; commissar of foreign affairs (1917-1918) and of war (1918-1924); leader of antistalinist opposition, 89, 220.

Tulcea, town in Romania, Dobrogea, on the Sfîntu-Gheorghe arm of the Danube River, 40 miles from Galaţi, 76, 81.

Tulcea Sanjak, Ottoman administrative district on the Danube, 76, 81.

Turgai, town in USSR, Kazakh SSR, 70 miles NE from Akmolinsk, 214

Turkestan, vast region in Central Asia, inhabited by a Turkic-speaking population; source of tension between Soviet Union and China, 209, 213.

Turkey, held at one time the entire Balkan region and SE Europe as far as Vienna, the Middle East and North Africa. This empire declined after the 18th century and especially during the 19th and early 20th centuries, when many European countries under Ottoman rule became independent. The present Turkey's boundaries were established by the Treaty of Lausanne (1923), 17, 23-25, 27-32, 36, 38, 41, 43-47, 53-57, 65, 67, 74, 76, 77, 103, 119, 132, 153, 167, 183, 196, 218.

Turkish, 257.

Turkmenistan, Turkmen Soviet Socialist Republic, located in south-west Soviet Central Asia; conquered by Russia (1869-1885); became a SSR in 1924, 12.

Turkmens, Turkomans, Muslim population, branch of the Turkic linguistic group, many of whom are living as nomads, in Turkmen SSR, Iran, Afghanistan, Irak, Syria and Turkey, 11, 207, 215, 217, 218, 222, 223, 229.

Turks, 17, 25, 32, 35, 36, 50, 56, 59, 65.

Turtucaia, Tutrakan, city and port in NE Bulgaria, on the right bank of the Danube, 87.

Ţuţui, Gheorghe (1921), Rom. historian; researcher on Rom. contemporary history, 183-188, 190, 192.

Two Lives, title of an article written by Rom. educator Onisifor Ghibu, 95.

Tyrnow, see Tîrnova.

Tyumen, city in USSR, Russian SFSR, 180 miles E from Sverdlovsk, 211.

Udrea, Traian (1927), Rom. historian; researcher on Romania's domestic and foreign policy after World War II, 182.

Uighurs, people living in western China – Sinkiang – and in small numbers in USSR –Uzbek, Kazakh and Kirgiz SSR, 228.

Ukraine, Ukrainian Soviet Socialist Republic, second largest Soviet republic; Russia annexed the left-bank Ukraine (east of the Dnieper) and Kiev – in 1667; the right-bank section during the second and third partitions of Poland (1793 and 1795); *U.* proclaimed SSR in Dec. 1917; since 1939 *U.* enlarged its area by annexation of SE Poland (1939), Northern Bucovina, North and South Bessarabia (1940) and Transcarpathian *oblast* (1945), 12, 13, 16, 35, 96, 111, 120, 128, 140-142, 160, 183, 190, 199, 200, 205, 206, 211-213, 217-220, 239, 240.

Ukrainian, 110, 111, 136, 170, 197, 198, 200-206, 208, 215, 217-221, 226, 229, 230, 257, 264.

Ulbricht, Walter (1893-1973), East German communist leader; deputy prime minister (1949); general secretary of the SED (1950-1971); chairman of the State Council (1960), 249.

Ungheni, Moldavian administrative-territorial unit set up on Nov. 1, 1940 on the left bank of the Pruth by the Soviet authorities, 239.

Union of Soviet Socialist Republics, see Soviet Union.

United Nations, international organization, successor to the League of Nations; established by a charter on Oct. 24, 1945 to maintain world peace and promote international cooperation, 149, 154, 157-159, 210, 220, 243.

United States of America, USA, proclaimed its independence after the war of independence (1775-1783) by the *Declaration of Independence* (July 4, 1776). After World War I, USA became the world's most powerful country; during World War II it played an important role in defeating Nazi Germany, 10, 12, 55, 56, 133-139, 146-152, 154-157, 159-161, 163, 164, 167-170, 182, 184, 186, 187, 192, 198, 230, 247, 253.

University of Bucharest, founded in July 1864 with three Colleges: law, philology and science, to which the College of medicine was added, in 1878, 16, 75.

University of Moscow, founded in 1755, on the initiative of M.V. Lomonosov as the first University in Russia, 252.

Ural Mountains, 11, 211, 214, 215, 217.

Ureche, Grigore (cca 1590-1647), Moldavian chronicler; author of the oldest chronicle in Romanian language, *Letopiseţul Ţării Moldovei* (1359-1594), 15, 225.

Urechia, Vasile Alexandrescu (1834-1901), Rom. historian and member of the liberal party, 75.

Ushakov, V. B., contemporary Soviet historian, 191.

Usik, P. V., vice chairman of the Moldavian SSR Council of Ministers (1953); full member of the Moldavian CP CC (1956), 201.

USSR, see Soviet Union.

Ussuri River, Chinese *Wu Su-li,* forms over a long stretch the frontier between USSR and China. Scene of many Soviet-Chinese clashes which retained world attention in March 1969, 214.

Uzbekistan, old name of the *Uzbek Soviet Socialist Republic,* founded in 1924, in Central Asia, 12, 213, 217, 222.

Văcărescu, Elena (1866-1947), Rom. poet who wrote in French; honorary member of Rom. Academy (1925); member of Rom. delegation at Paris Peace Conference (1947), 101.

Vandamme, Dominique-René, comte d'Unebourg (1770-1830), French general; took part in the Battle of Austerlitz (Dec. 2, 1805); falling prisoner during the battle of Kulm he was sent by the Russians to Siberia, 216.

Vasile, Radu, Rom. contemporary historian, 56.

Vatican City, ecclesiastical state; seat of the Roman-Catholic Church, 184.

Venice, aristocratic republic since 697; ruled by the Habsburg (1797-1805 and 1815-1866) and France (1805-1814); incorporated into Italy (1866), 44.

Verdun, garrison town in NE France, scene of a long battle during World War I, 86.

Vernescu, Gheorghe (1830-1900), Rom. statesman; minister of justice under prince Alexandru Ioan Cuza, and many times minister of the interior, justice and finance under king Carol I, 76.

Viaţa Economică, Rom. economic weekly magazine, issued in Bucharest since 1963 by the Romania's Society of Economic Sciences, 250, 252.

Viaţa Românească, Rom. literary and scientific magazine issued in Iaşi (1906-1916 and 1929) and later in Bucharest (1930-1940). Suppressed in 1940, it reappeared in 1944 as a monthly magazine of the Romanian Writers' Union, 94-98.

Vicovul de Sus, village in Romania, Moldavia, Suceava district, 15.

Victor Emmanuel III (1869-1947), king of Italy (1900-1946); after the Allied troops' landing in Italy he arrested Mussolini and installed marshal Pietro Badoglio as prime minister (1943), 152.

Victoria, (1819-1901), queen of Great Britain (1837-1901); empress of India (1876-1901); during her reign Great Britain reached the climax of its political expansion, 79.

Vidin, city in NW Bulgaria, on the right bank of the River, liberated by Romanian army during the Russo-Romanian-Turkish war (1877-1878), 46.

Vienna, seat of the Holy Roman empire (1558-1806); capital of Austria-Hungarian Empire (1867-1918) and capital of Austria since 1918, 30, 34, 39, 46, 77, 91, 121, 158, 258.

Vienna Award (Aug. 30, 1940), decision of arbitration taken in Vienna by the Third Reich and Italy, surrendering to Hungary Northern Transylvania (43,500 sq. km and 2,600,000 inhabitants), 128-130, 185.

Vinogradov, Vladilen Nikolaevich, Soviet contemporary historian, 43.

Vişoianu, Constantin (1898), Rom. diplomat; plenipotentiary minister to the Hague and Warsaw; delegate to the League of Nations and to the disarmament conference; opposition emissary sent to Cairo for armistice negotiations with Allies' representatives (May, 1944); minister of foreign affairs (Dec. 1944-March, 1945); chairman of Romanian National Committee in Washington (1952-1975), 187.

Vladivostok, the main Pacific seaport of Russia which served during World War I to transit Western military supplies to the Russian troops, 84, 196, 213, 214.

Volga River, the largest river of Russia and Europe, 12, 122, 211, 217, 218.

Volintiri, Volontirovka, village in Bessarabia, today in SE Moldavian SSR, 29 miles from Tighina, 200.

Volkov, Moldavian CP CC chief of section in charge with science and higher education (1952), 203.

Vorobeyev, Pavel Fedorovich, head of industry and transportation sections of the Moldavian CP CC (1955-1963); member of the Moldavian CP CC (1958); deputy of the Moldavian Supreme Soviet (1959), 203.

Voronezh, oblast in USSR, Russian SFSR, in the basin of the Don River, 215.

Voroshilovgrad, Lugansk, city in USSR, Ukrainian SSR, on the Lugan River, which until 1935 had been called Lugansk, 213.

Vorovic, chairman of the Moldavian CP Central Executive Committee, 202.

Waddington, William-Henry (1826-1894), French diplomat and statesman; minister of foreign affairs (Dec. 1877); France's representative to Congress of Berlin (June-July 1878); prime minister (Feb. 1879-Dec. 1879) retaining also his possition as minister of foreign affairs and demonstrating active interest in Balkan problems, 48, 49, 78-81.

Walew, Lubomir Borisovich (1915-1981), Soviet economist and geographer; professor at Moscow University, 9, 246-254.

Wallach, ancient name given to the Thraco-Roman population living north and south of the Danube, 15, 16, 41.

Wallachia, Walachia, name given by the foreigners to the principality *Țara Românească* – The Romanian Land – founded in the 13th century between south Carpathian Mountains and lower Danube; secured independence from Hungary (1330); recognized Turkish suzerainty (1417); united with Moldovia (1859) and achieved independence from Turks (1878), 10, 15, 22-32, 35-37, 40-43, 57, 65, 77, 85, 88, 89, 214, 255, 261.

Wallachian, 260.

Warsaw, capital of Poland (1596); of the Great Duchy of Poland (1807-1813); of the kingdom of Poland included in the tzarist empire (1815-1918); capital of the republic of Poland since 1918, 250.

Warsaw, Duchy of (1807-1813), set up by Napoleon and placed under the rule of king Frederick Augustus (1807); ruled by Russian administration (1813), 27, 30, 31.

Warsaw Pact, Warsaw Treaty Organization (May 14, 1955), treaty of friendship, cooperation and mutual assistance between eight European, socialist countries (Albania – until 1968; Bulgaria, Czechoslovakia, German Democratic Republic, Hungary, Poland, Romania and USSR), with a total military strength of about 6,000,000 men, 262, 263.

Washington, 135-138, 145, 155-158, 231.

Wehrmacht High Command, see German Army High Command.

Weizsaecker, Ernst von (1882-1951), state secretary in the German foreign ministry (1938-1943), 109, 112, 113.

Wells, Sumner (1892-1961), American diplomat; president Roosevelt's personal adviser; undersecretary of state (1937-1943), 132, 148, 149.

Wesenmayr, Edmond, SS head in the German foreign ministry, 192.

Western Democracies, see Allied Powers in World War II.

Western Powers, see Allied Powers in World War II.

White Guards, various forces in Russia of the years 1917-1919, which opposed the Bolsheviks. The white resistance forces in the South-European Russia were placed under the command of the general A.I. Denikin (April, 1918); in the north the *W.G.* were organized from Arkhangeslsk up to the northern Dvina; in the east they were under Kolchak's orders, 256.

Wilhelm II (1859-1941), German emperor (1888-1918), considered responsible for the outbreak of World War I, 85, 89.

William, Friedrich Wilhelm Karl (1783-1851), prince of Prussia, went in 1808 to St Petersburg, 27.

Winant, John Gilbert (1889-1947), American diplomat; ambassador to London (1937-1939 and 1941); member of the European Council Committee (1943), 147, 149, 150, 159.

Woermann, Ernst (1888-1979), director of the political department of the German foreign ministry (1938); state undersecretary (1938-1943); ambassador to China (1943-1945), 113.

Wolfschanze, Hitler's general headquarters near Rastenburg. Scene of von Stauffenberg's attempt against Hitler (July 20, 1944), 151, 167.

World War I (July 28, 1914-Nov. 11, 1918), between the Central Powers on one side and the Allied and Associated Powers on the other side, 9, 15, 19, 82-84, 94, 101, 102, 108, 119, 123, 132, 135, 150, 155, 158, 214, 219, 226, 261.

World War II (Aug. 26, 1939-May 8, 1945 end of the war in Europe; Sept. 2 and 9, 1945 end of the war in Asia), opposed Axis Powers to the Allies, 9, 10, 61, 123, 127, 132, 137, 147, 154, 197, 209, 214, 219, 220, 229, 231, 253, 255, 259, 265.

Würtemberg, former German state in south Germany made into a kingdom by Napoleon, 216.

Xenopol, Alexandru D. (1847-1920), Rom. historian, economist and philosopher. He wrote the first modern synthesis of the history of the Romanian people *(Istoria Românilor din Dacia Traiană),* 5 vol., Iași, 1888-1893), and worked out a theory of history explaining historical events in a determinist way, 20.

Xenopol, A.D., Institute of History and Archaeology, Rom. *Institutul de Istorie și Arheologie "A.D. Xenopol",* founded in 1940 in Iași by professor Ilie Minea with the aim of carrying out archaeological research on Romanian soil and historical studies concerning Romanian people's past; prints its own magazine: *Anuarul Institutului de Istorie și Arheologie "A. D. Xenopol",* 34.

Yilmaz, T., Turkish contemporary historian, 60.

Ypsilanti, Ipsilanti, Constantin, prince of Moldavia (1799-1801) and of Wallachia (1802-1806, 1806-1807, July-Aug. 1807); opposed the Ottoman rule; backed Serbian riots against the Turks (1804); removed by the Porte (1806); returned to the Wallachian throne with Russian help (1806), but clashed with the boyars and retired to Russia, 24.

Yugoslavia, Socialist Federal Republic, modern Y. dates since the end of World War I (Dec. 1, 1918). The new state included the old territories of the Serbian kingdom – Serbia, Montenegro and part of Macedonia – to which were added some new territories inhabited by southern Slavs living before World War I in the Austria-Hungarian empire: Bosnia, Hercegovina, Croatia, Slovenia, Vojvodina, Dalmatia and Slavonia. During World War II Y. was attacked by Germany and Italy (1941) and occupied by their military forces until Oct. 1944; at the end of the war it was proclaimed Popular Federative Republic (Nov.1945), 103, 156, 162, 166, 199.

Zaharia, Gheorghe (1916), Rom. historian; researcher on Rom. military history, foreign affairs and international relations, 82, 84, 182.

Zaionchkovsky, Andrey Medarovich (1862-1926), Russian general of World War I, 87.

Zaliskin, Mikhail, Soviet historian, 55, 58.

Zâmbreni, settlement of Moldavians deported to the Soviet Far East, Russian SFSR, 214.

Zaporozhye, Zaporozhe, city in USSR, Ukrainian SSR, on the left bank of Dnieper River, 280 miles SE from Kiev, 213.

Zelinski, Nikolai Dimitrievich (1861-1953), Sov. chemist, born in Tiraspol; dealt with the chemistry of hydrocarbons and with organic catalysis, 226.

Zguriţa, Zguritz, village in Bessarabia, Soroca district, today in N. Moldavian SSR, 210.
Zhagov, 89.
Zhdanovite, adept of Zhdanov, Andrey Aleksandrovich (1896-1948), partisan of strenghthening government control over Soviet culture and of fighting western influence, 264.
Zincă, Haralamb (1923), Rom. communist novelist, author of the novel *Şi a fost ora "H",* (It was "H" Hour), devoted to the Rom. 23 Aug. insurrection, 191.
Zotov, Pavel Dmitrievich (1824-1879), Russian general; head of general staff during Russo-Turkish war (1877-1878), 59.

The author expresses his gratitude to the following persons who helped him to edit the present book:

Ann Anielewski, for the general editing;
Nicolae Cristea, for the translation from German into English of the chapter XV and for the final reading;
René de Flers, for Russian consultations;
Aurelia Leicand, for the translation from Romanian into English of the chapters III, IV, V, VI, VII, VIII, IX, X, XI, XII, and XIV and for the proof reading;
Romilo Lemonidi for the translation from French into English of the Preface and the chapters I, II, XIII and XVI.

Culegere și procesare computerizată
INFO-TEAM Ltd. București
Tel/Fax: 659.46.26